JOHN GOWER:

RECENT READINGS

JOHN GOWER:
RECENT READINGS

Papers presented

at the meetings of the John Gower Society

at the International Congress on Medieval Studies
Western Michigan University, 1983-1988

edited by R. F. Yeager

SMC XXVI

Medieval Institute Publications

WESTERN MICHIGAN UNIVERSITY

Kalamazoo, Michigan--1989

© Copyright 1989 by the Board of the Medieval Institute
Kalamazoo, Michigan 49008-3851

Library of Congress Cataloging-in-Publication Data

John Gower, recent readings : papers presented at the meetings of the
    John Gower Society at the International Congress on Medieval
    Studies, Western Michigan University, 1983-1988 / edited by R.F.
    Yeager.
        p.   cm. -- (SMC ; 26)
    Includes bibliographies.
    ISBN 0-918720-99-0. -- ISBN 0-918720-26-5 (pbk.)
    1. Gower, John, 1325?-1408--Criticism and interpretation-
-Congresses. 2. Gower, John, 1325?-1408. Confessio amantis-
-Congresses. I. Yeager, Robert F. II. John Gower Society.
III. International Congress on Medieval Studies. IV. Series:
Studies in medieval culture ; 26.
CB351.S83 vol. 26
[PR1987]
940.1'7 s--dc20
[821'.1]   89-12456
                                                                CIP

Cover design by Elizabeth King
Printed in the United States of America

IN MEMORIAM

Peter C. Braeger
1960-1988

scholar, colleague, friend

CONTENTS

ILLUSTRATIONS

"The Illustrations in New College MS. 266 for Gower's Conversion Tales"
Plates are from New College MS. 266, in the Bodleian Library, Oxford University and are reproduced with the kind permission of the curators of the Bodleian Library.

"Miniatures as Evidence of Reading in a Manuscript of the *Confessio Amantis*"
Plates are from Pierpont Morgan MS. M. 126 and are reproduced with the kind permission of the Pierpont Morgan Library.

INTRODUCTION

Writing in 1871, James Russell Lowell began an essay by asking his readers, "Will it *do* to say anything more about Chaucer?" Some sixty-two pages later, he had answered his question copiously. Along the way, Lowell found occasion to speak of Chaucer's friend John Gower--and used the opportunity to settle on that writer's shoulders a New England version of Flecknoe's mantle. As the "undertaker of the mediaeval legend" Gower, in Lowell's estimation, "has positively raised tediousness to the precision of science, he has made dulness an heirloom for the students of our literary history. . . . [You] learn to dread, almost to respect, the powers of this indefatigable man."[1]

Were Lowell with us today, he still would find among readers of English poetry a staunch number to agree with his assessment. Old ideas, as the proverb says, die hard. Over a century after Lowell's essay saw print John Gower yet labors under the dark and ill-fitting cloak tailored for him by Lowell and others of like opinion. Nevertheless, a resurrected Lowell would find surprises also. Especially in the last decade Gower's reputation has begun to change again, this time with some signs of permanence. Scholars and critics have opened his books once more, to discover there a talent worthier respect than dread. Recently it has seemed easier to understand Chaucer's good will toward the "moral" friend and fellow author into whose tutelary watchfulness he commended *Troilus and Criseyde*--and easier also to assess the positive value Chaucer's adjective must have borne. An increasing body of enlightening work is one result of this new interest, some of which it is the purpose of this volume to present.

The thirteen essays included here all have a common origin in the sessions sponsored by the John Gower Society at the International Congresses on Medieval Studies held at Western Michigan University during the last five years. Each represents a fresh approach, unpublished elsewhere and rewritten exclusively for this collection. That they are the effort of scholars from many lands--West Germany, Great Britain, Canada, and the United States--is testimony to the widening readership Gower's poetry is receiving. Their topics and concerns are equally diverse and, in that diversity, offer a representative sample of the many directions taken by Gower studies today.

In the first essay, entitled "Nature and the Good in Gower's *Confessio Amantis*," Hugh White seeks definition of Gower's two key terms. To do so, he places Gower's poem in the context of Alain de Lille and the *Roman de la Rose* before focusing on what Gower meant by "kinde." Ultimately, White finds that Gower creates a precarious balance "between love on the one hand and reason and virtue on the other" which is best maintained when the demands of "kinde" are put to rest at last.

On a lighter note, James Dean pursues Gower's neglected "comic" sensibility and voice, arguing in "Gather Ye Rosebuds: Gower's Comic Reply to Jean de Meun" that, while Amans and Genius have much in common with the Confessor and Lover of Jean de Meun's *Roman de la Rose*, "at the last, Gower swerves away from the *Roman* in a distinctive and . . . comic way. But this is *moral* comedy and not . . . 'opera bouffe'." A careful analysis of the endings of the *Confessio* and the *Roman* establishes Dean's view.

Writing in a similar vein, Linda Barney Burke takes "Genial Gower: Laughter in the *Confessio Amantis*" as her subject, pointing out the relevance of medieval ideas of natural laughter to Gower's narrative style. She thus stands foursquare in opposition to the common assessment (signally represented by Lowell) that Gower neither appreciated, nor created, humor.

In the course of her argument, Burke examines briefly the old theory of a "quarrel" between Chaucer and Gower, made manifest by Chaucer's supposed burlesque of his friend in the character of the Man of Law. This discussion is taken further by Winthrop Wetherbee in his essay, "Constance and the World in Chaucer and Gower." Wetherbee juxtaposes studies of the Constance story with analogues from Boccaccio and Gower's own tale, Apollonius, Prince of Tyre, which fills most of Book VIII of the *Confessio Amantis*. His conclusion--that Gower's tale has much to tell us of a unique kind--sheds new light on Chaucer also.

Gower's knowledge of, and uses for, the classics concern both Götz Schmitz and R. F. Yeager. Schmitz touches on Gower's relationship with Chaucer also, in a theoretical inquiry entitled "Gower, Chaucer, and the Classics: Back to the Textual Evidence." At the center of his study is the figure of Dido as she appears in Ovid, Chaucer, and Gower. Yeager's focus in "Did Gower Write *Cento?*" is style in the Latin *Vox Clamantis*; specifically, an argument is made that Gower experimented with *cento*, a late classical method of composition using lines and half-lines excerpted from primary authors such as Ovid.

Sources are also pursued by Robert M. Correale and Russell A. Peck. In "Gower's Source Manuscript of Nicholas Trevet's *Les Chronicles*," Correale takes up Gower's tale of Constance to see what can be learned about the text Gower used. In passing, he also discusses relations between the tale as it is told by Gower and by the Man of Law. His painstaking comparison provides us with a sound basis for assuming that both Gower and Chaucer were working with a source of the same manuscript group. In "John Gower and the Book of Daniel," Peck compares Gower's apocalypticism with what must have been his biblical inspiration. The key figure of his study is Nebuchadnezzar, who, with the statue of precious metals he sees in a dream, plays so prominent a role in the *Vox Clamantis*, the *Confessio Amantis*, and--quite clearly--in Gower's way of thinking about the world.

The next three essays, "Gower's Metaethics" by Michael P. Kuczynski, "God's Faithfulness and the Lover's Despair: The Theological Framework of the Iphis and Araxarathen Story" by David G. Allen, and "Aspects of *Gentilesse* in John Gower's *Confessio Amantis*, Books III-V" by Kurt Olsson, all share discussion of similar concerns from Book IV: the tale of Iphis and Araxarathen, distinctions of *otium* and proper and improper "besynesse," and Gower's use of sources--French, philosophical, and classical. But each brings a different emphasis to the material: for Allen, Gower's handling of Araxarathen reveals an awareness of the voluntarist thinking initiated by William of Ockham and his English followers, Thomas Bradwardine and others, including William Langland; for Kuczynski, who also invokes Langland as well as Abelard's influential treatise *Scito te ipsum*, the tale reveals Gower's deep concern for "meta-ethics . . . , that [medieval] branch of moral philosophy concerned with the nature of . . . language, the meaning of moral terms"; and for Olsson, whose complex argument ranges from Dante to Machaut, Ovid to Jean de Meun, Capellanus to Chaucer (with a bit of John of Salisbury thrown in for good measure), at issue is Genius's inability to grasp the imperatives of his double role as both venereal and moral voice, leaving it to Amans (and to us as readers, through him) to resolve the conflict in accord with true "reson" and "kinde."

Finally, Peter C. Braeger and Patricia Eberle examine the interaction of verse and visual representation in studies of the *Confessio Amantis* and its manuscript illuminations. Braeger discusses "The Illustrations in New College MS. 266 for Gower's Conversion Tales," concluding that the illuminations were intended as "visual analogues" to the text, and that they specifically capture moments of moral conversion and insight. Eberle's essay, "Miniatures as Evidence of Reading in a Manuscript of the *Confessio Amantis*," provides a seminal descriptive study of Pierpont Morgan MS. M. 126--one of the richest and least studied illuminated secular manuscripts we have from England--while demonstrating that the illustrators paid close attention to features of the text which were

> of importance to Gower himself: his interest in *ordinatio*, his view of the tales as playing an important role in conveying the "wisdom" of his poem, his interest in suggesting parallels and contrasts among the stories, and perhaps above all, his desire to be taken seriously as an *auctor*.

Lowell thought Gower left behind only "dulness" as his single "heirloom for the students of our literary history." But as the work of the thirteen "students" collected here demonstrates, he spoke to the agreement of an earlier time. About Gower (as Lowell himself found about Chaucer) it will indeed "*do* to say more," and Lowell's dank casting of Chaucer's friend as the attendant mortician at the interring of medieval literature is rapidly being revised. Truer to the recent critical interest in Gower is rather the judgment of Christopher Ricks, that "the poetry itself--six hundred years later--is still warm of flesh and bone and full of life."[2] In such a spirit of conviction was this book conceived; and in this spirit (we hope) it will be taken by its readers--at least upon their having turned the final page.

R. F. Yeager

NOTES

[1]James Russell Lowell, *My Study Windows* (Boston and New York, 1871), p. 259.

[2]Christopher Ricks, "Metamorphosis in Other Words," in *Gower's "Confessio Amantis": Responses and Reassessments*, ed. A. J. Minnis (Cambridge, 1983), p. 49.

NATURE AND THE GOOD
IN GOWER'S *CONFESSIO AMANTIS*

Hugh White

In *Studies in Words* C. S. Lewis remarked: "A medieval poet would have been surprised to find Great Mother Nature inspiring sins, for he would have supposed that her 'inspiration', so far as concerned man, lay in the *nature* (*animal rationale*) appointed by her for man."[1] There are passages in *Confessio Amantis* which might be offered as substantiation of Lewis's claim and the grounding he provides for it, but the weight of the evidence suggests that Gower's habitual understanding of the natural in that poem is not that of Lewis's medieval poet.[2] When Gower's discourse about Nature and the natural is at its most explicit, he does not suppose that the provision Nature makes for man includes his reason. This does not mean that in Gower's conception Nature's inspiration is always morally suspect--Nature's promptings may be in harmony with Reason's. But in the sphere of human love, central, of course, in the concerns of *Confessio Amantis*, an incompatibility between the drives of nature and the demands of morality makes itself troublingly apparent. That this should happen seems to me something of a saving grace for the poem. Recent criticism has done Gower much service, but there is, I think, a tendency to make *Confessio Amantis*, seen as competently encyclopedic and pleasurably didactic, appear a bland and rather complacent work.[3] But that is to sell Gower short: there is considerable astringency in Gower's

1

insistence on the intractability of the natural within man, in his awareness of the limited persuasiveness of the voice of reason, in his consciousness that the world is an environment normally fatal to our pursuit of moral perfection.[4]

The *Corpus Iuris Civilis* presents different definitions of the law of nature which testify to different understandings of that concept.[5] A basic dichotomy is apparent between understandings which relate the law of nature to man's ethical and rational capacities and the Ulpianic understanding according to which the law of nature is *quod natura omnia animalia docuit*.[6] Under *this* law of nature men and animals together are moved to such things as the *procreatio* and *educatio* of offspring. The law of nature can be seen, in fact, either as the law of (natural) reason, relating to man's nature as a rational being, or as the law of (non-rational) instinct, relating to the nature man shares with the animals.

Medieval writers on natural law handle the legacy of the *Corpus* in different ways.[7] Though it is possible to harmonize the law of nature as instinct with the law of nature as reason,[8] the two can also be seen as in opposition. In the following passage the natural as animal and the natural as rational are at odds over polygamy:

> In relation to man nature is regarded in two ways, that is as it refers to the nature of the genus or as it refers to the rational nature of the species . . . for man is at once an animal and a rational animal. According to the first understanding of nature, to have two females or several is not against nature. . . . According to the second understanding, it is against nature.

The passage goes on to explain this last remark by referring to what the *naturalis ratio* dictates.[9]

Peter of Tarentasia says that the answer to the question whether fornication is *contra ius naturale* depends on how one understands man's nature. He invokes the genus/species distinction to ascribe to man two kinds of *instinctus nature*: one he

2

shares with the animals (genus); the other is unique to him (species). Fornication is not against the natural law defined with reference to the genus, where reason is not involved, but it is against the law of nature defined with reference to the species, where reason *is* involved.[10]

It is clear, then, that there exists an understanding of the natural such that to act naturally may be to go against reason. And though in the instances just given reason is quite as natural as animal impulse, there are contexts in which the natural seems effectively to be the animal and, implicitly at least, *not* the rational. In Alexander of Hales man's rational capacity is implicitly contrasted with his *naturalis appetitus*, his *naturales motus*, and his *naturales actus*: reason has to discipline the natural if right moral action is to occur.[11]

Turning to literary texts in which a personified Nature figures importantly, we find that the relationship between Nature and man's reason is variable.[12] In Alain de Lille's *De Planctu Naturae* Nature has given man both reason and sensuality,[13] thereby establishing in him endemic moral warfare, in the hope (and man has disappointed this hope) that reason would triumph over sensuality.[14] For Nature is very much on the side of reason, being constructed with reference to the idea of the natural moral law over which, in fact, she presides.[15]

In certain other twelfth-century texts employing a personified Nature, that figure is a force for good.[16] Thus, in Bernardus Silvestris's *Cosmographia* Nature wishes order to be imposed on primordial chaos,[17] and operates as a faithful agent of the divine in the processes of creation, whilst in the *Anticlaudianus*, another work by Alain de Lille, Nature desires the creation of the perfect man, which she eventually accomplishes with the help of her sisters, the virtues (among whom is included Ratio).[18] In Jean de Hautville's *Architrenius* the goodness of Nature is triumphantly affirmed in the face of the hero's initial doubts, and her association with moderation (she marries Moderantia to Architrenius at the end of the poem) indicates

3

that she is at one with reason.[19]

However, in both the *Cosmographia* and the *Anticlaudianus* Nature is unable to produce the soul of man--her creativity takes place in the physical realm.[20] This means that in these works Nature does not provide man's reason, which is seated in the soul. Such is the case also in the *Roman de la Rose*. Jean de Meun's Nature explains what part of his endowment man owes to her:

> As for his physical person, he has nothing in body or limb worth as much as a ball of pomander except what I have given him--no quality of the soul either, except one thing. From me, his lady, he holds three capacities of body and soul, for I may well say without lying that I make him exist, live, and feel. . . . He has existence in common with the stones, life in common with the thick-growing plants, and feeling in common with the dumb animals: he is capable of much more still in that he understands in common with the angels.
>
> (lines 18999-19008; 19016-20)[21]

The capacity which man shares with the angels is not one Nature supplies:

> Without a doubt, I know well and truly that I did not give man his understanding. That does not fall under my jurisdiction. I am not wise or powerful enough to make anything so capable of knowledge. I never made anything which lasts: whatever I make is subject to decay.
>
> (lines 19025-32)[22]

The *antandement* is bound up with the immortal soul which is given by God alone. This Nature, associating herself with what man shares with the animals and distancing herself from his rational capacities, stands, as it were, on the Ulpianic side of the line dividing understandings of natural law.

In the earlier literary texts we have considered, Nature's inability to provide the immortal, rational soul did not mean that she was at odds with reason. In the *Roman de la Rose*, however, conflict does arise. The figure Reason condemns the kind of love practiced by the Lover,[23] but Nature, concerned that her corruptible creation should be continued through procreation, encourages the assault on the Castle of the Rose.[24] To this end an alliance is formed between Nature and Venus, the presiding deity of the Lover's kind of love, an alliance which Reason would no doubt consider unholy.[25] One should note further that fornication and adultery are not among the sins Nature condemns,[26] perhaps because she considers them legitimate means to her main end of procreation. This may remind us of how in certain passages cited above nature, understood generally and not as specific to man, permits, presumably indeed encourages, polygamy and fornication.

But Nature in the *Roman* is not completely amoral. In line with her desire for procreation, Nature is most concerned to condemn the failure to be sexually active and perverted sexual activity.[27] Nevertheless, she condemns many kinds of sin which have no connection with procreation, albeit she fails to condemn fornication and adultery. Her somewhat compromised position in the sphere of sex has not deprived her completely of morally normative status.

In *Confessio Amantis* nature and *kinde* terms are frequently used with moral force.[28] Thus, for instance, Nature condemns the vice of ingratitude--not surprisingly we may feel, since *unkinde* can mean ungrateful, as it does in this passage:

> The bokes speken of this vice,
> And telle hou god of his justice,
> Be weie of kinde and ek nature[29]
> And every lifissh creature,
> The lawe also, who that it kan,
> Thei dampnen an unkinde man.

> (V.4917-22)

The grounds for the claim that ingratitude is unnatural appear in what follows:

5

> It is al on to seie unkinde
> As thing which don is ayein kinde,
> For it with kinde nevere stod
> A man to yelden evel for good.
> For who that wolde taken hede,
> A beste is glad of a good dede,
> And loveth thilke creature
> After the lawe of his nature
> Which doth him ese.

(V.4923-31)

The unnaturalness of ingratitude is evidenced by the behavior of the animals. This is the case also with the unnaturalness of murder:

> For who that wolde ensample take,
> The lawe which is naturel
> Be weie of kinde scheweth wel
> That homicide in no degree,
> Which werreth ayein charite,
> Among the men ne scholde duelle.
> For after that the bokes telle,
> To seche in al this worldesriche,
> Men schal noght finde upon his liche
> A beste forto take his preie.

(III.2580-89)

The continuation of this passage is most significant. It shows that man possesses something that can be called *kinde*, which may be contrasted with his reason and which is, it seems, something he shares with the animals. The *kinde* within man, as well as the natural world outside him, indicates that murder is wrong:

> And sithen kinde hath such a weie,
> Thanne is it wonder of a man,
> Which kynde hath and resoun can,
> That he wol owther more or lasse
> His kinde and resoun overpasse,
> And sle that is to him semblable.
> So is the man noght resonable
> Ne kinde, and that is noght honeste,

Whan he is worse than a beste.

(III.2590-98)

Man is guided towards right moral action not only by a *kinde*
external to him, but also by an internal *kinde* which is explicitly
distinguished from human reason.

Though the passages I have quoted make it plain that the
non-human world and the non-rational within man can support
reason and morality, the fact remains that Gower is able to take
the *kinde* as something within man distinct from reason, and this
separateness opens up the possibility of conflict between reason
and the natural within man, a possibility in fact realized for
Gower in the sphere of human sexual love.[30] However, it is not
always realized. First, there are certain remarks in which *kinde*
and reason are at one. In these instances the *kinde* term may
make reference to man's nature in its entirety, including his
reason, and not exclusively to his instinctual side. This seems
likely to be the case when we are told:

> It sit a man be weie of kinde
> To love, bot it is noght kinde
> A man for love his wit to lese.

(VII.4297-99)[31]

In the following passage Genius moves from speaking about
love and *kinde* to speaking about love and reason in such a way
as to suggest that he is not associating *kinde* at this point with
the non-rational and animal side of man:

> Bot certes it is forto rewe
> To se love ayein kinde falle,
> For that makth sore a man to falle,
> As thou myht of tofore rede.
> Forthi, my Sone, I wolde rede
> To lete al other love aweie,
> Bot if it be thurgh such a weie
> As love and reson wolde acorde.
> For elles, if that thou descorde,
> And take lust as doth a beste,

7

Thi love mai noght ben honeste;
For be no skile that I finde
Such lust is noght of loves kinde.

(VIII.2016-28)[32]

Second, even where we seem to be dealing with a nature understood as the sponsor of sexual impulse and having nothing to do
with reason, that Nature can still be seen as having moral
authority:

For Nature is under the Mone
Maistresse of every lives kinde,
Bot if so be that sche mai finde
Som holy man that wol withdrawe
His kindly lust ayein hir lawe;
Bot sielde whanne it falleth so,
For fewe men ther ben of tho,
Bot of these othre ynowe be,
Whiche of here oghne nycete
Ayein Nature and hire office
Deliten hem in sondri vice,
Wherof that sche fulofte hath pleigned,
And ek my Court it hath desdeigned
And evere schal; for it receiveth
Non such that kinde so deceiveth.
For al onliche of gentil love
Mi court stant alle courtz above
And takth noght into retenue
Bot thing which is to kinde due,
For elles it schal be refused.

(VIII.2330-49)

When we inquire what kinds of sexual behavior fall under
Venus's condemnation as unnatural, we find indications that
they might include homosexuality and incest: perhaps Gower
supposes that there is an instinctive revulsion in man from these
sexual practices such that they may be understood to run counter
to the dictates of a Nature conceived as the sponsor of impulse.[33] But the indications are not absolutely clear. In the story
of Iphis and Iante, Iphis, really a girl, has been brought up as a

8

boy and betrothed to the girl Iante. The two children sleep in the same bed, and eventually Nature urges them to make love to one another. At this point Cupid intervenes and, overturning the (physical) law of nature, makes Iphis male in order that there shall be no violation of the natural order, which is taken as morally prescriptive (IV.481-505). But Nature appears to have inspired the whole problematic affair in the first place, so that one wonders what exactly her position is. Perhaps the fact that the lovers are not aware of the true facts of their case--they do "Thing which to hem was al unknowe" (IV.487)--does something to rescue Nature from a charge of self-contradiction. Perhaps the sexual attraction the lovers conceive for one another can be regarded as in some sense natural, Iphis's education as a boy having given her the natural male impulses. The issue is confused, but there are clearly special circumstances here which make it unsafe to claim on the strength of this episode that Nature may, as a general rule, urge people to homosexual behavior, and thus to sin.

Incest is a difficult matter too. On the one hand, the incest of Amon and his sister Thamar is *ayein kinde* (VIII.214-15), and the incestuous Antiochus loves *unkindely* (VIII.2004-08); on the other, there are instances in which Nature prompts to incestuous activity. After the Flood the sons of Noah marry incestuously "as nature hem hath excited," and this practice continues to be legitimate until the time of Abraham (VIII.94-98). In view of the special circumstances obtaining after the Flood, one might be able to reconcile these different views on the naturalness of incest,[34] but no such maneuvers are appropriate in the case of Canace and her brother Machaire. They fall in love:

> And so it fell hem ate laste,
> That this Machaire with Canace
> Whan thei were in a prive place,
> Cupide bad hem ferst to kesse,
> And after sche which is Maistresse
> In kinde and techeth every lif

9

Withoute lawe positif,
Of which sche takth nomaner charge,
Bot kepth hire lawes al at large,
Nature, tok hem into lore
And tawht hem so, that overmore
Sche hath hem in such wise daunted,
That thei were, as who seith, enchaunted.

(III.166-78)

In the light of these passages treating homosexuality and incest, Venus's assumption that there are certain kinds of sexual behavior which may be designated unnatural begins to look questionable. But, however that may be, the story of Canace and Machaire shows very clearly that Nature, for Gower, can operate against reason and conduce to vice. The implication of *enchaunted* at the end of the passage just quoted is that the lovers' reason is under a spell, their rational judgment has been suspended, and the opposition between Reason and Nature and Nature's capacity to prompt to vice are later explicitly acknowledged. Commenting on the story of Canace and Machaire, Genius tells how Tiresias was punished for being "to nature unkinde" (III.374) in separating two copulating snakes. He goes on:

So mihte it nevere ben honeste
A man to wraththen him to sore
Of that an other doth the lore
Of kinde, in which is no malice,
Bot only that it is a vice:
And thogh a man be resonable,
Yit after kinde he is menable
To love, wher he wole or non.

(III.384-91)

In an earlier comment on the story Genius had insisted that one must not be too harsh towards that which occurs under the compulsion of Love and Nature:

For it sit every man to have
Reward to love and to his miht,

10

> Ayein whos strengthe mai no wiht:
> And siththe an herte is so constreigned,
> The reddour oghte be restreigned
> To him that mai no bet aweie,
> Whan he mot to nature obeie.
> For it is said thus overal,
> That nedes mot that nede schal
> Of that a lif doth after kinde,
> Wherof he mai no bote finde.
> What nature hath set in hir lawe
> Ther mai no mannes miht withdrawe, ...
>
> (III.344-56)

It may be that these passages bear witness to a struggle to hold onto a conception of the natural as, in some sense, appropriate; but, however reluctantly, the acknowledgement has to be made that Reason and Nature do not always cooperate and that Nature can lead man into evil.[35]

Several passages in *Confessio Amantis* speak of the need to keep natural impulse under the control of reason, recognizing a latent antagonism in the two principles. The following lines draw out the moral of the story of Tobias and Sara, in which Tobias is, unlike Sara's previous seven husbands, saved from destruction by the fiend Asmod through achieving a balance between the demands of *lawe* and the instincts of *kinde* as he consummates his marriage:

> For god the lawes hath assissed
> Als wel to reson as to kinde,
> Bot he the bestes wolde binde
> Only to lawes of nature,
> Bot to the mannes creature
> God yaf him reson forth withal,
> Wherof that he nature schal
> Upon the causes modefie,
> That he schal do no lecherie,
> And yit he schal hise lustes have.
>
> (VII.5372-81)

Rational creature though he is, man is, like the animals, under

11

the influence of *kinde*, impinged upon by the laws of nature, here contrasted to the laws of reason, and unregulated submission to the natural could lead him into sin.[36] The natural sexual impulse has to be expressed in such a way that, in Genius's words, "love and reson . . . acorde" (VIII.2023). For this to be assured reason has to have a controlling say in sexual matters:

> And natheles thou schalt be lerned
> That will scholde evere be governed
> Of reson more than of kinde, . . .
>
> (III.1197-99)

But this brings us to the central difficulty. Is it always possible to make an accommodation between reason and nature in the sphere of sexual love so that reason is in control? The *natheles* of the passage just quoted follows this concession:

> Thou dost, my Sone, ayein the riht;
> Bot love is of so gret a miht,
> His lawe mai noman refuse,
> So miht thou thee the betre excuse.
>
> (III.1193-96)

Whatever may be desirable, whatever *scholde* be the case, and whatever Tobias manages, the power of *kinde* is here clearly affirmed to be superior to that of reason as they compete for the allegiance of sexual man. We recall the earlier comment that

> thogh a man be resonable,
> Yit after kinde he is menable
> To love, wher he wole or non.
>
> (III.389-91)[37]

A sense of the irreconcilability of the natural forces love and reason informs the ending of *Confessio Amantis*. Genius counsels Amans that the time has come to leave the life of love:

> For love, which that blind was evere,
> Makth alle his servantz blinde also.
> My Sone, and if thou have be so,
> Yit is it time to withdrawe,
> And set thin herte under that lawe,
> The which of reson is governed
> And noght of will.

(VIII.2130-36)

Amans should rather "Tak love where it mai noght faile" (VIII. 2086), directing his attention towards God. Later Venus suggests that holiness and susceptibility to the influence of Nature (she is speaking of Nature's influence in the sphere of love) are inimical to one another:

> For Nature is under the Mone
> Maistresse of every lives kinde,
> Bot if so be that sche mai finde
> Som holy man that wol withdrawe
> His kindly lust ayein hir law. . . .

(VIII.2330-34)

We have found Gower dallying with a vision of reason and nature reconciled, but here at the end of the poem he seems rather to insist that submission to the natural sexual impulse runs counter to the demands of morality and religion.[38] However, Gower recognizes that it is supremely difficult to evade the claims of nature: some holy men may manage the withdrawal of "kindly lust," but the majority of mankind remains subject to *kinde* as well as owing allegiance to reason. One might say that man is trapped between *kinde* and reason, a victim of the dual nature imposed upon him at his creation.

In the conception dominant in *Confessio Amantis* the natural for man stands distinct from reason. Sometimes, possibly even in the sphere of love, it functions as a moral guide, but it remains irrational, associated with the animal. Man's proper functioning as a rational creature, whose efforts should be directed towards heaven, may be compromised by the influence of the natural in the sphere of sexual love. A balance between love and reason may be achievable, but that cannot quiet Gower's uneasiness about the moral corrosiveness of sexuality: in the end, the only truly safe condition is one in which man is no longer subject to the influences of love and nature.

NOTES

A version of this essay was read to a John Gower Society session at the Twenty-First International Congress on Medieval Studies held at Western Michigan University, Kalamazoo, during May 1986. I should like to acknowledge with gratitude financial assistance received from the Medieval Institute of Western Michigan University, the University of the Witwatersrand, Johannesburg, and the Human Sciences Research Council of South Africa which enabled me to attend the Congress. My thanks are also due to Drs. J. Gorak, P. Hurst, C. B. White, and Prof. R. F. Yeager for various kinds of assistance with this essay.

[1]C. S. Lewis, *Studies in Words* (Cambridge, 1960), pp. 71-72.

[2]But see G. D. Economou, "The Character Genius in Alan de Lille, Jean de Meun, and John Gower," *Chaucer Review*, 4 (1970), 203-10, where it is argued that Gower re-aligns Nature and Reason after Jean de Meun had set them at cross-purposes, so that Nature in *Confessio Amantis* is a force for good. Contrastingly, in "Love, Nature and Law in the Poetry of Gower and Chaucer" in *Court and Poet*, ed. Glyn S. Burgess (Liverpool, 1981), pp. 113-28, Marie Collins sees love and Nature in Gower as antagonistic to reason. Denise Baker in "The Priesthood of Genius: A Study of the Medieval Tradition," *Speculum*, 51 (1976), 277-91, emphasizes the separation of reason and *kinde* in *Confessio Amantis*, and speaks of the *amoral* law of *kinde*. None of these studies seems to me quite to recognize the complexity of Gower's treatment of the natural. In "Natural Law and John Gower's *Confessio Amantis*," *Medievalia et Humanistica*, n.s., 11 (1982), 229-61, Kurt Olsson investigates illuminatingly the presence of various medieval understandings of natural law in *Confessio Amantis*. Olsson is well aware that the question whether the natural is good or evil cannot be simply answered, but his suggestion that Gower eventually proposes an unproblematically benign (if limited) kind of natural love, in which sensual impulse is not the only factor, is not, in my view, true to Gower's terminology. It is Olsson rather than Gower who conflates the various understandings of the law of nature: Gower prefers to think of the *kinde* as something distinct from reason. On Gower and Nature,

see also Henriette A. Klauser's "The Concept of *Kynde* in John Gower's *Confessio Amantis*" (Ph.D. diss., Fordham University, 1972).

[3]I am thinking in particular of some of the essays in *Gower's "Confessio Amantis": Responses and Reassessments*, ed. A. J. Minnis (Cambridge, 1983). This is, however, a very interesting and informative collection.

[4]Gower is understood to be more optimistic by A. J. Minnis in "'Moral Gower' and Medieval Literary Theory," in *Gower's "Confessio Amantis,"* pp. 50-78. See also, in the same volume, Elizabeth Porter's "Gower's Ethical Microcosm and Political Macrocosm," pp. 135-62, esp. p. 162. In "Gower's Characterization of Genius in the *Confessio Amantis*," *Modern Language Quarterly*, 33 (1972), 240-56, Donald G. Schueler suggests that natural love is "not, *per se*, in opposition to the divine will" (p. 254), though he thinks that love has to be controlled by reason. Baker says that "the law of *kinde* which Gower's Venus represents is morally ambiguous, for the sexual act which she incites can be subject to reason and therefore moral or subverted by lust and thus immoral" ("The Priesthood of Genius," p. 291). These views seem to me to fail to do justice to Gower's assertions (through Genius) that love makes all his servants blind and that therefore earthly love is to be abandoned in favor of charity (see VIII.2063-148). Though Genius wishes to see love governed by reason, if love is going to be pursued this solution to the problem for morality that love raises is not, in the end, radical enough. Ultimately, love is not to be controlled but abandoned, because virtue is always at risk from it, and man's attachment to his true end is always threatened by a force which is associated with that in him which is essentially of the earth.

[5]For a review of these definitions, see Brian Tierney, "*Natura, id est Deus*: A Case of Juristic Pantheism?" *Journal of the History of Ideas*, 24 (1963), 307-22. See also Olsson.

[6]For Ulpian's definition, see *Digest* I.1.1. In his *Summa Institutum* (I.2), Azo, commenting on various definitions of the law of nature found in the *Corpus* and in Gratian's *Decretum*, registers the dichotomy between the Ulpianic and other definitions: "Prima autem definitio [Ulpian's] data est secundum motum sensualitatis, aliae autem assignatae sunt secundum motum rationis" (The first definition is given with reference to the movements of the sensuality, the others with reference to the movement of the reason); cited in R. W. and A. J. Carlyle, *A History of Medieval Political Theory in the West*, 6 vols. (Edinburgh and London, 1928-36), 2:30 n. 1.

[7]On this, see O. Lottin, *Psychologie et Morale au XIIe et XIIIe siècles*, 6 vols. (Louvain, 1942-60), 2:71-100.

[8]See Aquinas, *Summa Theologica* I II q.94, a.2. Aquinas asserts that the natural law is derived from the reflection of reason on the impulses that are natural to man, impulses which are of three kinds resulting severally from man's nature as mere existent thing, as animal, and as rational being.

[9]"Natura in homine consideratur dupliciter, scilicet ut est natura generis, uel ut est natura speciei rationalis . . . homo enim est animal et est animal rationale. Primo modo habere duas uel plures non est contra naturam. . . . Secundo modo est contra naturam. . . ." This passage appears in a marginal note on an Avignon manuscript containing the *Commentary on the Sentences* of Peter of Tarentasia. The passage is quoted by Lottin, 2:92 n. 1. One might compare Aquinas's *Commentary on the Sentences* IV d.33, a.1, q.1.

[10]"Contra ius naturale illud dicitur esse quod est contra instinctum et dictamen nature. Instinctus uero nature duplex est: unus nature generalis qui est communis nobis et brutis; et hic est preter rationem et discretionem; alter uero specialis qui est proprius nobis, et hic est cum ratione et discretione. Primus instinctus generalis, quia sine ratione est, non distinguit sufficienter inter suam et non suam. Unde cognoscere non suam <non> est contra ius naturale generale. Secundus instinctus, quia cum ratione est, distinguit sufficienter inter suam et non suam; unde cognoscere non suam est contra ius naturale speciale." The passage, from Peter of Tarentasia's *Commentary on the Sentences*, is quoted by Lottin, 2:93 n. 1.

[11]"Praeterea, irrationabilia non habent vim per quam possint diiudicare naturales actus et probare probandos et reprobare reprobandos, immo appetitiva in eis est subiecta instinctui naturae; unde non est in eis potestas contradicendi naturali appetitui; homo vero habet potestatem diiudicandi naturales motus et probandi et reprobandi et etiam contradicendi naturali appetitui, et ideo est liber arbitrio" (*Summa Theologica* I II n 403; Besides, irrational things do not have the capacity to judge between natural acts and approve those that should be approved and disapprove those that should be disapproved; on the contrary, the appetitive faculty in them is subject to the instinct of nature. Man, on the other hand, has the ability to judge between natural motions, to approve them or to disapprove them, and further, he has the ability to go against the inclinations of the natural appetite and is therefore free in respect of his will).

[12]On this personified Nature see G. D. Economou, *The Goddess Natura in Medieval Literature* (Cambridge, MA, 1972).

[13]*De Planctu Naturae* VI.51-65. I use N. M. Häring's edition, *Studi Medievali*, 19 (1978), 797-879.

[14]"De rationis enim consilio tale contradictionis duellum inter hos pugiles ordinaui, ut, si in hac disputatione ad redargutionem sensualitatem poterit inclinare, antecedens victoria premii consequente non careat" (VI.66-68; For, on the advice of reason, I have set up a dispute of this kind between these combatants, with the result that, should reason be able to turn sensuality into an object of scorn in this debate, a victory, as antecedent, shall not lack its consequent in a reward). See also *De Planctu Naturae* II.232-34. Significantly, though Nature gives man both reason and sensuality, to succumb to sensuality is not regarded as in any way an expression of man's nature (as certain passages cited above in the text would allow), but as a derogation from human nature, a lapse into a bestiality sharply contrasted with *humanitas*. See *De Planctu Naturae* XVI.197-99.

[15]In his *Distinctiones* Alain gives *naturalis ratio* as a meaning of *natura*, citing in support a Pauline passage fundamental to Christian natural law theory: "Dicitur naturalis ratio, unde Apostolus ait quod *gentes, quae legem non habent, naturaliter quae legis sunt faciunt*, id est naturali instinctu rationis; et secundum hoc solet dici quod natura dictat homini ut non faciat aliis quod sibi non vult fieri, id est naturalis ratio" (*Distinctiones* under *natura, Patrologia latina* 210.871; italics as per *PL*: Nature means natural reason, and thus the Apostle says that *the gentiles who do not have the law do by nature the things of the law*, that is, by the natural instinct of reason; and accordingly one says that nature commands man not to do to others what he would not wish done to himself, nature here being natural reason).

[16]On these texts, besides Economou's *The Goddess Natura*, see Winthrop Wetherbee, *Platonism and Poetry in the Twelfth Century* (Princeton, 1972), and Brian Stock, *Myth and Science in the Twelfth Century* (Princeton, 1972).

[17]*Cosmographia* I.1, 1-66. The edition of the *Cosmographia* used here is that of C. S. Barach and J. Wrobel (Innsbruck, 1876), which bears the title *De Mundi Universitate*.

[18]*Anticlaudianus*, ed. R. Bossuat (Paris, 1955), I.214-42.

[19]*Architrenius*, ed. P. G. Schmidt (Munich, 1974), IX.291-96.

[20]*Cosmographia* II.3, 15-20; *Anticlaudianus* II.62-74.

[21]   n'il n'a pas, se je ne li done,
quant a la corporel persone,
ne de par cors ne de par mambre,
qui li vaille une pome d'ambre,

> ne quant a l'ame vraiement,
> fors une chose seulement:
> il tient de moi, qui sui sa dame,
> III. forces, que de cors que d'ame,
> car bien puis dire, san mantir,
> jou faz estre vivre et santir;
> . . . .
> il a son estre avec des pierres,
> et vit avec les herbes drues,
> et sent avec les bestes mues;
> oncor peut il trop plus an tant
> qu'il avec les anges antant.

The edition of the *Roman de la Rose* used here is that of Félix Lecoy, CFMA, 3 vols. (Paris, 1965-70). All translations from the Old French are my own.

[22]   San faille, de l'antandement
> connois je bien que vraiemant
> celui ne li donai je mie.
> La ne s'estant pas ma baillie,
> ne fui pas sage ne poissant
> de fere riens si connoissant.
> Onques ne fis riens pardurable;
> quan que je faz est corrumpable.

[23]*Roman de la Rose*, lines 4567-98.

[24]*Roman de la Rose*, lines 19305-375.

[25]Venus is interested only in pleasure, not in procreation, which Reason regards as that which legitimates sexual activity. It has been suggested (e.g., by Economou, *The Goddess Natura*, pp. 121-23) that Nature is tricked into lending her support to a cause which is fundamentally opposed to her own interests. But it might be argued that the alliance between Nature and Venus images the inextricability in the sexual act of the "good" motive of the desire to procreate and the "bad" one of the pursuit of pleasure. Nature, in Jean's scheme, is allowed to partake of the ambivalence of sex.

[26]For the sins condemned, see *Roman de la Rose*, lines 19181-245.

[27]See particularly *Roman de la Rose*, lines 19531-98, for the condemnation of the failure to be sexually active and 19599-656 for the condemnation of perverted sexual activity. The speaker here is Nature's priest, Genius.

[28]For the *Confessio Amantis* I use the text in the four-volume edition of Gower's *Works*, ed. G. C. Macaulay (Oxford, 1899-1902).

[29]The "Be weie of kinde" in this line should probably be taken after "and ek nature." This kind of distortion of natural word order is common in *Confessio Amantis*; see H. Iwasaki, "A Peculiar Feature in the Word-Order of Gower's *Confessio Amantis*," *Studies in English Literature*, 45 (1969), 205-20.

[30]For an opposing view, see Economou, "The Character Genius."

[31]Olsson suggests that the first *kinde* refers to man's animal nature, the second to his nature as a rational being ("Natural Law and John Gower's *Confessio Amantis*," p. 242). I doubt this separation between two sides of man's total nature is necessary. It would perhaps be possible to understand both *kinde*s as referring to man's animal nature, though this would involve a clear contradiction with other passages in which Gower has man's *kinde* in this sense making him precisely "his wit to lese."

Another possible instance of the use of *kinde* in a sexual context to refer to a nature which includes the rational side of man occurs at VII.4215-17:

> The Madle is mad for the femele,
> Bot where as on desireth fele,
> That nedeth noght be weie of kinde.

It is possible, however, that Gower means that there is no compelling natural impulse driving one towards sex with more than one person.

[32]The reference in line 2019 is to the story of Apollonius, which involves incest. The logical force of "Forthi" of line 2020 may be rather loose, allowing love against *kinde* to be a smaller category than love against reason, in which case *kinde*ness in love need not imply accord with reason.

[33]Aquinas considers homosexual practice to be contrary to the law of nature in the Ulpianic sense (*Summa Theologica* I II q.94, a.3 ad 2). Sodomy is condemned as unnatural at *Roman de la Rose* lines 19599-654.

[34]Klauser achieves a reconciliation (to my mind unconvincing) by understanding incest as *unkinde* only when one of the parties is unwilling ("The Concept of *Kynde*," p. 153). It is possible that when incest is denounced as against *kinde*, reference to reason is involved in the *kinde* terminology.

[35]Schueler remarks that "Gower finds the two young people [Canace and Machaire] innocent because they do not understand their crime" ("Gower's

Characterization of Genius in the *Confessio Amantis*," p. 253); see also Klauser, p. 149. I cannot see that Gower finds Canace and Machaire innocent. There is a *vice*, and though the *reddour* ought to be restrained, that is not because the pair is innocent, but because Nature has compelled them to their crime. It seems impossible, in spite of Schueler's contention (pp. 252-53), to suppose that in *Confessio Amantis* responsibility for sexual sin is deemed to be man's alone and not in any degree Nature's and Venus's, though it is true that certain sexual sins are against Nature and Venus (see, e.g., VIII. 2337-49).

[36]See also VII.4207-14; VII.4558-71; and the marginal comment at the beginning of VIII.

[37]Gower's final remarks on sexual love stress conflict between reason and the law of *kinde*; see VIII.3144-46.

[38]The refrain of *Cinkante Balades* 50 affirms that "Amour s'acorde a nature et resoun." But, whatever he might like to believe, Gower is usually more cautious than this. Even the *Traitié*, which celebrates married love, states that married love is a second best to celibacy, and the work is insistently aware of the problems that that love may encounter. The Latin verses printed by Macaulay at the end of the *Traitié* seem less than enthusiastic about love in general; it is, after all, an *iter carnale*.

GATHER YE ROSEBUDS: GOWER'S COMIC REPLY TO JEAN DE MEUN

James Dean

A quick unsystematic list of Gower stereotypes: he was a serious moral or ethical author; he was a satiric, topical, often digressive complaint poet who wrote one long narrative poem with three titles; he composed his poems around political themes, especially the Ricardian concerns with kingship and the common profit; he was a sometime poet of courtly love who took the *Roman de la Rose* as his model for the love story of *Confessio Amantis*.[1] These stereotypes, which have much truth in them, still dominate Gower studies.

Rarely is Gower accused of being a comic poet, although some recent studies might be said to offer evidence to the contrary.[2] In fact, I have no intention of arguing that Gower was an especially humorous poet or that when he managed comedy he rivaled Ovid, Boccaccio, or Chaucer. I do hope to show that in one moment from *Confessio Amantis*, at the end, Gower found something like a comic voice but in a limited or specialized way, in a way that depends for its force on the ending of Jean de Meun's *Roman de la Rose*. The joke is that whereas Amant of the *Roman* plucks his Rose in a passionate, idolatrous gesture, Amans of the *Confessio* discovers that he is too old to pluck, too old to plow. If C. S. Lewis is correct that Gower formulated his love story and his characters of Amans and the Confessor from Jean's French poem, it is also true that, at the last, Gower

21

swerves away from the *Roman* in a distinctive and I would say comic way. But this is *moral* comedy and not, as one misguided critic has termed it, "*opera bouffe*."[3] The comedy arises in that moral arena--the theater of love--that Derek Pearsall has termed "the area where [man's] moral being is most vulnerable."[4] Gower exploits this area to telling effect.

The respective endings of the *Roman* and the *Confessio* can be briefly summarized for purposes of comparison. In the *Roman*, Genius, invested with signs of Cupid's religion of Love, preaches to Love's barons in preparation for a final assault on the castle of Jalousie. Genius claims to speak on behalf of Nature, especially with regard to sexuality, urging the barons to wax and multiply: "Arez, por Dieu, baron, arez / et voz lignages reparez" (lines 19671-72; Plow, for God's sake, my barons, plow and restore your lineages).[5] He describes Deduit's garden and the Shepherd's Park, and invites the barons to choose between them. The barons rouse themselves to battle, and Venus herself leads the attack on Jalousie's castle, setting it afire and routing Dangier. When Bel Acueil gives the go-ahead, Amant, dressed as a pilgrim, sets off to find his Rose, his Pygmalion-like idol, and locates her behind a curtain concealing relics or objects of devotion. He is described as "jousting," "assaulting," or "plucking" the Rose--the metaphoric language shifts often:

> Formant m'i convint assaillir,
> souvant hurter, souvant faillir.
>   Se bohourder m'i veïssiez,
> por quoi bien garde i preïssiez,
> d'Herculés vos peüst mambrer
> quant il voust Cacus desmambrer. . . .

> (lines 21587-92)

(I had to assail it vigorously, throw myself against it often, often fail. If you had seen me jousting--and you would have had to take good care of yourself--you would have been reminded of Hercules when he wanted to dismember Cacus.)

He offers thanks to Venus and Cupid and curses to those who hindered his quest. He possesses his Rose--"par grant joliveté cueilli / la fleur du biau rosier fueilli" (lines 21747-48; I plucked, with great delight, the flower from the leaves of the rosebush)--and he wakes up.

At the close of *Confessio Amantis*, Gower's Amans, far away from his goal, writes a love complaint which the didactic Genius delivers to Venus. Venus appears to the narrator (who names himself as "John Gower" [VIII.2321][6] much as Jean de Meun spoke of himself in the *Roman* [see line 10535]); she tells him he is too old to love; and she advises him to withdraw from Love's enterprise. Gower faints but yet witnesses the dance of young lovers as well as a less vigorous dance of old lovers, including the hapless Aristotle. Some aged lovers crowd around the barely-conscious Gower and advise him to desist from loving. Then blind Cupid gropes for Love's arrow lodged in Gower's breast and extracts it. Genius, replacing Venus's lust with reason, understanding, and self-knowledge, confesses Gower; and Venus gives him beads inscribed *Por reposer* (VIII. 2907). Gower goes "Homward a softe pas" (line 2967)--a line and sentiment that Lewis thinks should have concluded the poem.[7] Nonetheless, 201 lines ensue on the world, reason, and will--lines that recall the Prologue of the *Confessio* and that help to set the poem in context of right conduct, proper loving, and the common profit.

*   *   *

Because he has been describing the "long disease" of his life throughout the *Confessio*, Gower never says he wakes up from his eight-book dialogue with Genius. This is a key point of difference between Jean's *Roman*, which is a dream-vision, and Gower's *Confessio*, which is not. But in other respects the ending of the *Confessio* answers, while not exactly refuting, the ending of the *Roman*. Read in this way, as I think it should be, the ending of the *Confessio Amantis* wittily repudiates the *carpe diem* conclusion of Jean's *Roman* and perhaps the implicit ethos of French *dits*. It also anticipates Ralegh's reply to Marlowe's *Passionate Shepherd*, especially the lines beginning "But could youth last and love still breed. . . ."[8] In the remainder of this essay I wish briefly to analyze two aspects of Gower's conclusion that indicate his dependence on the ending of Jean's *Roman*: the view of love and sexuality, and the language.

The issue of Jean's commitment to love and sexuality in the *Roman* is vexed, to say the least, and I cannot enter the full debate here. The original debate about sexuality and related issues in the *Roman* has been termed the "Querelle du Roman de la Rose." Jean was attacked in the early fifteenth century by those, such as Christine de Pisan and Jean Gerson, who professed shock or outrage at his alleged sexual frankness, although John Fleming has claimed that "by the end of the fifteenth century the poem was no longer clearly understood," as it once had been, as an ironic allegory.[9] Whatever Jean intended, a medieval reader could easily understand Jean to advocate sexuality as part of nature and to endorse Amant's plucking his Rose as service to refined love. I do not know whether Gower understood Jean to say this, but Gower's Amans receives a wholly contrary lesson, a lesson in the aging process rather than in youthful sexuality and its pratfalls. In the *Roman* Genius harangues the barons with the rallying cry "Plow, for God's sake, my barons, plow . . . "; and he proclaims this exercise of manly prerogative in a context of natural urges and compulsions. In the *Confessio*, by contrast, the will is there but not the means. Venus herself gives Gower the bad news about his age and abilities and in language that recalls the *Roman*:

> I wot and have it wel conceived,
> Hou that thi will is good ynowh;
> Bot mor behoveth to the plowh,
> Wherof the lacketh, as I trowe:
> So sitte it wel that thou beknowe

24

> Thi fieble astat, er thou beginne
> Thing wher thou miht non ende winne.

> (VIII.2424-30)

Gower seems not to recognize his "astat," since he is still submitting love-complaints to Venus like some youthful Troilus. In *rime riche* (doubling the insult), Venus proclaims: "Mi medicine is noght to sieke / For thee and for suche olde sieke" (VIII. 2367-68). Continuing the metaphor from nature, she says:

> The thing is torned into was;
> That which was whilom grene gras,
> Is welked hey at time now.

> (VIII.2435-37)

Venus concludes this discourse by admonishing Gower, in a version of *respice finem*, to "Remembre wel hou thou art old" (VIII.2439). Venus's speech to Gower is surprisingly tender and compassionate, as if she recognizes his long service to her and also realizes her responsibilities gradually to bring him to self-awareness. Jean's Amant is never seen to achieve such self-knowledge. At the end of the *Roman*, when the narrator wakes up, the plucking, in retrospect, better resembles an allegorical wet dream than an exercise in aging and morality, as it is in the *Confessio*.

There is something amusing, I suppose, about Gower's obtuseness and his failure to know himself. Measured against the *Roman*, it is ironic that Gower, far from actively consummating his love, lies prone and hapless as Cupid withdraws the arrow from his heart. Gower is not the plucker but the one who is plucked. Yet there is also something poignant in his retreat homeward, wiser and sadder, "a softe pas." The undercurrent of grief and reflection in this closing sequence seems to arise in reaction to Jean's sharply ironic *Roman* and yet is nothing at all like it.

If the actions and gestures of the principal characters are not especially comic--or, better, if the comedy is mingled with

25

pathos--there is considerable droll comedy and irony in the language of the *Confessio* at the end, especially so since French words and expressions insinuate themselves into the text at key moments. The words let us know that we should not view any of this as tragedy; we should not take it too seriously. The Frenchifying at the close goes beyond Gower's ordinary trilingual discourse--his Ricardian internationalism of Latin, French, and English writings. The French words have an echoic, anticlimactic, deflating quality that at once evokes and subverts an erotic atmosphere of *fin amors*. Each stage of Gower's conclusion--the love complaint, Venus's appearance, the narrator's disclosure of his name, the dance of lovers, and the consolation--has analogues in French romance, and the ambience is French and courtly.

The bill of complaint to Cupid and Venus--Gower terms it a "supplicacioun" (VIII.2184, 2301)--is a French convention, and the atmosphere is one of refined love. (Amans claims he enlisted the help of Genius in writing the letter by speaking "wordes debonaire" [VIII.2202].) The complaint section, in which we hear of "grace" (VIII.2253), "obeissance" (VIII.2281), and "mi lady" (VIII.2250), offers an exposition of Amans's disease of love--"The wofull peine of loves maladie" (VIII.2217)--which cannot be cured and which undermines his "resoun" (VIII.2222). There is no need to elaborate on this well-known erotic disease, which reached epidemic proportions in courtly medieval literature. From Andreas Capellanus's famous definition (*De arte* 1.1) to Guillaume de Lorris's explanation that Amor "c'est maladie mout cortoise" (line 2167), it is a very courtly illness.[10] Amans complains in conventional fashion that all other creatures, save he, have their "blisse" (VIII.2230)--a *topos* of love literature--and he reports that his will "debates" his reason. He describes how the world stands "evere upon eschange" and yet how Danger--the lady's aloofness--is always "in o place" such that he refuses "to do [him] grace" (VIII.2259; 2264; 2265). The figure of Dangier of course dominates important sections of the

Roman de la Rose, barring the way to the Rose (see, for example, lines 2811-3326 and 21237-39). Amans also finds the way to love blocked but for a very different reason than does Amant in the *Roman*.

Despite the language of French *gentilesse* in Amans's bill of complaint, English colloquialisms or informal, low-style expressions creep into his "supplicacioun." These sometimes amusing phrases undermine the otherwise sophisticated, courtly tone of the complaint, as when Amans describes his lovesick heart (the courtly disease) as "*bewhaped* with sotie" (VIII.2219)--"bewhaped" expressing befuddlement or hapless bewilderment[11]--or when he characterizes himself, Pandarus-like, as wrestling with love yet always "behinde" (VIII.2241). He explains that while he would like to sip from Jove's "swete tunne" of good fortune in love, so far he has drunk only from "the bitter cuppe" (VIII. 2256). The high-minded, courtly tone of the "supplicacioun" suggests idealism, but Amans's characterization of himself as hapless forces a reassessment. Reality intrudes; and although Amans tries to keep a sense of *amour propre* (in the bill of complaint and throughout the conclusion), we sense something like desperation. In this way the French words finally sabotage the courtly ambience so carefully established; Amans is a would-be gentle lover.

The form of this "letter" is itself significant and suggests French courtly poetry (or Chaucer's imitation of French courtly verse). The complaint is in Chaucer's *Troilus*-measure, rhyme royal, which Gower also used in *In Praise of Peace* (English) and in the *Cinkante Balades* and *Traitié pour essampler les amantz marietz* (French). The rest of the *Confessio*, except for the inserted Latin poems, is in octosyllabic couplets. Amans's complaint is modeled upon lyrics within narratives of Machaut or Froissart, some of which include lyric set pieces entitled *la complainte de l'amant*.[12] The *complainte* in Machaut's *Dit de la fonteinne amoureuse*, for example, begins, in *rime riche*,

Douce dame, vueilliez oïr la vois
De ma clamour, qu'en souspirant m'en vois,
Tristes, dolens, dolereus et destrois. . . .

(lines 235-37)

The language and rhyme scheme (aaab / aaab / bbba / bbba) are extravagant, though not at all unusual for a French *dit*, and I think it likely that Gower, with his complaint, hoped to imitate the French lyric-within-narrative form with a stanzaic pattern he felt was suitable both for love poetry and for philosophical reflection. A French gloss in the *Cinkante Balades* explains the rhyme-royal verse function: "Les balades d'ici jesqes au fin du livere sont universeles a tout le monde, selonc les propretés et les condicions des Amantz, qui sont diversement travailez en la fortune d'amour" (The *balades* from here to the end of the book are universal, for all the world, according to the qualities and conditions of lovers, who are in various ways afflicted by love's fortune). Gower doubtless selected rhyme royal for his *complainte de l'amant* because Chaucer had used the stanza so successfully in his philosophical tragedy of love, *Troilus and Criseyde*, which contains a lover's complaint (I.507-39) as well as letters of supplication to the lady (II.1065-70, in reported speech; V.1317-1421).[13] But we miss something important if we fail to recognize that, by breaking the octosyllabic rhythm of his narrative with rhyme royal, Gower also alludes to familiar techniques of French courtly poetry.

Venus's appearance to Amans must be judged in the context of Jean's *Roman*. Gower's portrayal of Amans, and his language at the close of the *Confessio*, are more subtle and archly comic than Jean de Meun's rather coarse depiction of Amant's plucking the Rose. Jean's *Roman* created a sensation in the later Middle Ages not just for its allegory and its attack on mendicancy but also for its indelicate language. Jean's Raison feels obliged to defend her mention of "coilles," "coillons," and "l'ains" (lines 7076-106)--roughly, testicles, testes, and penis--while Genius speaks frankly of testicles and castration ("escoillier") in the sequence on Jupiter's reign (see lines 20002-52); more important, Jean describes lusty copulation in Amant's consummation scene. Jean somewhat disguises the consummation in metaphor; hence, Amant's genitals become his "hernois" (line 21553), his "equipment" or "baggage," while his penis becomes his "bourdon" (line 21558), his pilgrim walking stick. Jean's language becomes blasphemous as Amant brings to a climax his idolatrous veneration for the Rose "conme bons pelerins" (line 21317), as a good pilgrim, by worshipping, eagerly and vigorously, at the shrine: "le biau saintuaire honorable" (line 21563). But then the metaphor shifts to include the storming of a castle (lines 21577-88) and to a jousting tournament (*bohourder*, line 21589; compare *bohort*). Such violent, profane language to a certain extent merely carries out the love-as-warfare metaphor-- the battle of the sexes. But there is more to it than that. The language is deliberately provocative--unmistakably sexual yet ironically veiled--and crafted at once to reveal and disclose, almost in the manner of fabliaux.[14] Amant does not merely enjoy his Rose in some abstract, vaguely sensual fashion: he tries to penetrate the virgin bud (lines 21607-16) or to "gather" the bud ("le bouton cueillir" [line 21642]; "le bouton prendre" [line 21668]). The action becomes ludicrous, as Amant describes the rape or "possession" of a flower--an *outré* mixed metaphor probably derived from Alain de Lille.[15] Nor does he stop there. Amant "seizes" his love object "Par les rains" (line 21675), by its branches, and "shakes" it, or her, without "pricking" himself:

> et quant a .II. mains m'i poi joindre,
> tretout soavet, san moi poindre,
> le bouton pris a elloichier. . . .
>
> (lines 21677-79)

> (and when I could attach myself to it with both hands, I began very softly, without pricking myself, to shake the bud. . . .)

In a final gesture, combining human and botanical "fertilization," so to speak, Amant releases his "seed" on the flower:

> A la parfin, tant vos an di,
> un po de greine i espandi,
> quant j'oi le bouton elloichié.
> Ce fu quant dedanz l'oi toichié
> por les fueilletes reverchier,
> car je vouloie tout cerchier
> jusques au fonz du boutonet. . . .
>
> (lines 21689-95)

(Finally, so much I will tell you, I scattered a little seed on the bud when I shook it. This was when I touched it within in order to pore over the petals. For the rosebud seemed so fair to me that I wanted to examine everything right down to the bottom.)

Amant's last act before waking is to "pluck" the Rose's flower.

Gower, in contrast to Jean, portrays his Amans and the love story's conclusion with exquisite tact and delicacy; and although he retains important features of Jean's conclusion--the distressed lover, Venus and Cupid, the courtly ambience--he emphatically alters the climax and dénouement. He also fails to reproduce--indeed, he might be said to repudiate--Jean's violent, sexual language, preferring a more refined and more euphemistically droll French diction mingled with forthright Anglicisms. Jean's language is euphemistic but only to camouflage, and somewhat mischievously to call attention to, Amant's sexual activity.

When Venus appears to Amans after the bill of complaint, she better resembles a courtly queen than the medieval goddess of luxury or cupidity (as she is so often depicted in medieval literature).[16] Amans's first gesture is to kneel, to address her as "Ma dame" (VIII.2321), and to beg her "forto do me grace" (VIII.2317). She says that she understands his complaint and adds that her court disdains those who behave contrary to nature:

> For al onliche of gentil love
> Mi court stant alle courtz above
> And takth noght into retenue
> Bot thing which is to kinde due. . . .

(VIII.2345-48)

This Venus is all sympathy and tact--polite and courteous--as befits the planetary influence described in Book VII as presiding over that man who

> . . . schal desire joie and merthe,
> Gentil, courteis and debonaire,
> To speke his wordes softe and faire.

(lines 784-86)

This beneficent, nurturing Venus contrasts sharply with Jean de Meun's Venus, who is characterized as attacking Chastée, chastity (lines 2834; 3402-03), as a notorious adulterer (lines 13805-44; 18031-99), as an inciter to lust (e.g., lines 20643-48), and as an Amazon-like assaulter of Jalousie's castle (lines 20681-766; 21221-36). Jean's Venus, a bow-wielding partisan, involves herself physically in Amans's erotic dilemma, whereas Gower's Venus presides over "gentil love" and maintains her court "above" other (earthly) theaters of conflict. Her agreeing to speak with Amans is, in Gower, a measure of her graciousness and approaches *noblesse oblige*.

When Venus speaks directly to Amans, she rebuffs him, at first gently:

> Bot as of that thou hast desired
> After the sentence of thi bille,
> Thou most therof don at my wille,
> And I therof me wole avise.

(VIII.2362-65)

Macaulay translates line 2365 as "And I will consider the matter," and comments that this is "practically equivalent to a refusal of the petition, as in the form 'Le Roy s'avisera'" (note

31

to line 2365). Venus later explains her decision with a mixture of French courtly words and Anglo-Saxon bluntness, the intermingling reminiscent of Chaucer:

> For loves lust and lockes hore
> In chambre acorden neveremore,
> And thogh thou feigne a yong corage,
> It scheweth wel be the visage
> That olde grisel is no fole. . . .
>
> (VIII.2403-07)

The proverb-like expression "olde grisel is no fole" is especially droll coming from the courtly goddess of love. (It may also echo or allude to the "proude Bayard" sequence from *Troilus and Criseyde* [I.218-31].) Rather than Amans's plowing ahead to pluck his Rose, he should, Venus suggests, effect a strategic withdrawal: "Betre is to make a beau retret" (VIII.2416). That French phrase--"beau retret"--is the most striking and arresting of the conclusion, and euphemistic or ironic in a way that French phrases sometimes were in Gower's day. I think of Chaucer's portrait of the Prioress, who was "symple and coy," who "spak ful faire and fetisly," and who was "ful plesaunt, and amyable of port" (I.119; 124; 138); of Alison's "Do wey your handes, for your curteisye!" (the Miller's Tale I.3287); of the Wife of Bath's "bele chose" (III.447; 510); or of Sir Thopas's horse, to which Thopas gives not only "good forage" but also "som solas" (VII.783; 782). In Gower's work, you know you are in amatory trouble when Venus herself advises face-saving retreat, even though she tries to soften the blow in courtly, gentle language. She adds:

> For thogh thou myhtest love atteigne,
> Yit were it bot an ydel peine,
> Whan that thou art noght sufficant
> To holde love his covenant.
>
> (VIII.2417-20)

Whereas Jean's Amant can make a binding "covenant" with

32

Cupid (line 1971), Gower's Amans is not so fortunate. Despite the good advice and visions of geriatric lovers, Gower clings desperately to his hope of love, of grace:

> I thoghte thanne how love is swete,
> Which hath so wise men reclamed,
> And was miself the lasse aschamed,
> Or forto lese or forto winne
> In the meschief that I was inne:
> And thus I lay in hope of grace.
>
> (VIII.2720-25)

Venus bids Gower a final, courtly "Adieu" (VIII.2940).

At the close of Gower's *Confessio Amantis*, there are no castles of Jalousie to be stormed, no Dangiers to be overcome, no Rose to be plucked. There is, however, a human truth in this situation that is not sufficiently explained by words such as *farce*, *mockery*, or *opera bouffe*. Those terms are too broad and clumsy to characterize the subtle, yet comic, portrayal of Amans's plight--*la condition humaine*. The human condition, in Gower's *Confessio*, suggests the human comedy, which includes both comic and tragic aspects. This mingling of mirth and pathos is why I want to characterize the ending of the *Confessio* as moral comedy. The situation of Amans--"John Gower"--at times verges on the ludicrous, especially in the disparity or incongruity between the French courtly language and Amans's unfortunate predicament. Yet on another level, a level made explicit in the moralistic outer narrative frame (Prol.; VIII. 2971-3172),[17] his condition may be said to express unfulfilled desire, absence, limitation, impotence, and mortality. This microcosm is now, like the greater world, "old and fieble and vil" (Prol. 887). Amans's plight finally occasions soul-searching for both the narrator and the reader in the interests of discovering what has gone wrong--and what it means that things have gone so very wrong.

*　　*　　*

The evidence from the ending of the *Confessio Amantis* demonstrates that Lewis was right in arguing for Jean's *Roman de la Rose* as Gower's original, at least on some level, but it is important to add that Gower by no means simply reproduced Jean's characters--the Lover and the Confessor--or the erotic ambience. Both Jean and Gower expose the difficulty of maintaining idealism in love--what Troilus calls *trouthe*--in a declining world, a world grown old.[18] But Jean opted to portray the Lover's gradual acceptance of mediation in his originally idealistic quest and in the idolatry of goal-oriented loving. Gower answered Jean by rejecting the brash comedy of Genius's exhortation to fecundity and Jean's consummation scene in favor of something like retirement, removal from the fray, and confession. In so doing he modernized the conclusion of his poem by bringing it into line with other fourteenth-century (and especially Ricardian) narratives that end on a penitential note, including DeGuilleville's *Pèlerinage*, Mandeville's *Travels*, Langland's *Piers Plowman*, and Chaucer's *Canterbury Tales*. Gower may not have been of "the newe jeet," yet he could manage comedy of a certain kind--comedy more fitting for reflection than for unqualified mirth. For Gower the famous spectacle of the French lover's "gathering his rosebud while he may" required an English reply, even at the risk of self-mockery. So he blunted the plow, reversed the plucking, and threw a fig leaf of French *politesse* over the Lover's retreat.

NOTES

[1]John H. Fisher, *John Gower: Moral Philosopher and Friend of Chaucer* (New York, 1964), has emphasized most of the categories, including the single long poem ("one continuous work," p. 135), the moral poet (pp. 187-204, 225-28, and passim), the poet of the common profit (pp. 178-80), and the poet of courtly love (pp. 187-204 and passim). The latter category, of course, derives chiefly from C. S. Lewis, *The Allegory of Love* (New York, 1936), who

also helped to define the "moral" in Chaucer's phrase "moral Gower." The category *ethical* (or *philosophical*) has received much critical attention recently, especially in *Gower's "Confessio Amantis": Responses and Reassessments*, ed. A. J. Minnis (Cambridge, 1983), and the essays by Minnis, Elizabeth Porter, and Charles Runacres, which develop arguments based in part on Judson B. Allen, *The Ethical Poetic of the Later Middle Ages* (Toronto, 1982); for Gower, see p. 102. Russell A. Peck, *Kingship and Common Profit in Gower's "Confessio Amantis"* (Carbondale and Edwardsville, IL, 1978), has highlighted Gower's concern with the Ricardian political ethos of the common profit.

[2]See David W. Hiscoe, "The Ovidian Comic Strategy of Gower's *Confessio Amantis*," *Philological Quarterly*, 64 (1985), 367-85. By "comic" Hiscoe seems to mean ironic in the sense of discrepancy. He says, for example, of Ovid's *Metamorphoses*: "The humor in the poem is largely created by the ever-present gap between the stories as the audience would already know them and the versions that are conjured up as one speaker or another bends myth to a multitude of shifty purposes" (p. 369). Hiscoe shows how Gower manipulates audience response to Ovid's stories, which were themselves manipulations. Linda Barney Burke offered a paper entitled "Genial Gower: Laughter in the *Confessio Amantis*" in the session "John Gower and Fourteenth-Century Poetics," 8 May 1987, at the Twenty-Second International Congress on Medieval Studies, Kalamazoo, Michigan; see her essay (same title) in the present volume. More representative of Gower criticism are two summaries of scholarship: Robert F. Yeager, "The Poetry of John Gower: Important Studies, 1960-1983," in *Fifteenth-Century Studies: Recent Essays*, ed. R. F. Yeager (Hamden, CT, 1984), pp. 3-28; and John H. Fisher, R. Wayne Hamm et al., "John Gower," in *A Manual of the Writings in Middle English*, ed. Albert E. Hartung, 7 vols. (New Haven, 1986), 7:2195-2210. Neither of these latter studies mentions humor or comedy in Gower's writings.

[3]James Dean, "Time Past and Time Present in Chaucer's Clerk's Tale and Gower's *Confessio Amantis*," *ELH*, 44 (1977), 411.

[4]*Old English and Middle English Poetry* (London, 1977), p. 210.

[5]Ed. Félix Lecoy, CFMA, 3 vols. (Paris, 1965-70), 3:90; trans. Charles Dahlberg, *The Romance of the Rose* (Princeton, 1971), p. 324. I modify Dahlberg's translation slightly for purposes of literalness.

[6]Quotations from the *Confessio Amantis* are from *The English Works of John Gower*, ed. G. C. Macaulay, 2 vols., EETS, e.s. 81-82 (Oxford, 1900-01).

35

[7]*The Allegory of Love*, p. 221.

[8]I do not mean to suggest direct influence, although Ralegh was a prodigious reader. The last stanza of *The Nymph's Reply* reads:

> But could youth last, and loue still breede,
> Had ioyes no date, nor age no neede,
> Then these delights my minde might moue,
> To liue with thee, and be thy loue.

In *The Poems of Sir Walter Ralegh*, ed. A. M. C. Latham (Cambridge, 1951), p. 17.

[9]*The Roman de la Rose: A Study in Allegory and Iconography* (Princeton, 1969), p. 6. Fleming has been part of a modern "Querelle" between those who regard Jean as an advocate of sexuality and those who understand him to denounce, through irony and allegory, the free exercise of sexuality as fornication. For an account of the early fifteenth-century controversy, see Pierre-Yves Badel, *Le Roman de la Rose au XIVe siècle: Étude de la réception de l'oeuvre* (Geneva, 1980), pp. 431-89.

[10]For a recent study of courtly love as an illness, see Mary Frances Wack, "The *Liber de heros morbo* of Johannes Afflacius and Its Implications for Medieval Love Conventions," *Speculum*, 62 (1987), 324-44. For the implications, see pp. 341-44.

[11]Of the *MED*'s six entries under *bewhapen*, four are from Gower's *Confessio*. Book VI, lines 78-80, for example, read, in language anticipating Bk. VIII: "The most wise / Ben otherwhile of love adoted, / And so bewhaped and assoted." The other two entries under *bewhapen* are to *Ferumbras* and *Beves of Hamtoun* ("Ðe porter was al bewaped. 'Allas!' queþ he, 'is Beues ascaped?'"). Chaucer uses the related word *awhaped*, and sometimes with French words, as in *Anelida and Arcite*: " . . . That turned is in quakyng al my daunce, / My surete in awhaped countenaunce" (*MED*, s.v. *awhaped*). For Gower's sensitivity to languages other than English in *Confessio Amantis*, see R. F. Yeager, "'Oure englisshe' and Everyone's Latin: the *Fasciculus Morum* and Gower's *Confessio Amantis*," *South Atlantic Review*, 46 (1981), 41-53.

[12]See, for example, Machaut's *La complainte de l'amant* in *La fonteinne amoureuse*, lines 235-1034, in *Oeuvres de Guillaume de Machaut*, ed. E. Hoepffner, SATF, 3 vols. (Paris, 1908-21), 3:151-80; and Froissart's *Complainte de l'amant* in *Le paradys d'amour*, lines 75-202, and *La complainte de l'amant* in *L'espinette amoureuse*, lines 1556-2354, in *Oeuvres de Froissart*,

ed. A. Scheler, SATF, 3 vols. (Brussells, 1870-72), 1:3-7 and 132-56 respectively. James Wimsatt claims that the genre of the lover's complaint derives from the *Roman de la Rose*; see *Chaucer and the French Love Poets* (Chapel Hill, 1968), p. 57.

Nicolette Zeeman has described Gower's debt to French authors, especially Machaut, in her talk "Love's Pleasure in the *Confessio Amantis*," delivered at the session "John Gower and Fourteenth-Century Poetics," 8 May 1987, at the Twenty-Second International Congress on Medieval Studies, Kalamazoo, Michigan. Fisher, however, says: " . . . it is Chaucer who reveals a profound influence from the French court poets, whereas Gower shows little, if any, knowledge of them" (*John Gower*, p. 74). On *fin amor* and Gower, see Fisher, pp. 76-77.

[13]Citations from Chaucer's work are from *The Riverside Chaucer*, 3rd ed., general editor Larry D. Benson (Boston, 1987). The implications of Gower's use of rhyme royal in the *Confessio* deserve further exploration. All of Gower's uses of this stanza postdate Chaucer's *Troilus*.

[14]R. Howard Bloch, *The Scandal of the Fabliaux* (Chicago, 1986), pp. 33-34 (on the clothing metaphor in Jean de Meun and in fabliau literature).

[15]See Jan Ziolkowski, *Alan of Lille's Grammar of Sex* (Cambridge, MA, 1985), esp. p. 30. For an amusing illustration of this plucking, see *The Romance of the Rose*, trans. Dahlberg, fig. 64 (from Bibliothèque Nationale Rothschild MS. 2800, fol. 137ᵛ).

[16]In medieval theory there were two Venuses, a "celestial" goddess and "the shameful Venus." See D. W. Robertson, Jr., *A Preface to Chaucer* (Princeton, 1962), pp. 125-26, esp. the reference to Bernard Silvestris, p. 126. See also *The Parliament of Fowls*, lines 260-84; the Knight's Tale I.1918-66; the Wife of Bath's Prologue III.604-13.

[17]For the distinction between outer and inner frame of the *Confessio*, see Alastair Minnis, "'Moral Gower' and Medieval Literary Theory," in *Gower's "Confessio Amantis,"* pp. 67-78.

[18]I develop the relation between old age in microcosm and macrocosm at greater length in my book, *The World Grown Old in Later Medieval Literature*, forthcoming with The Medieval Academy of America. For a discussion of "contradictory 'idealisms'" in Jean de Meun's *Roman*, see Marc M. Pelen, *Latin Poetic Irony in the Roman de la Rose* (Wolfeboro, NH, 1987), pp. 115-33.

GENIAL GOWER: LAUGHTER
IN THE *CONFESSIO AMANTIS*

Linda Barney Burke

Of the qualities which Chaucer valued in his friend John Gower, one of the most important must certainly have been his witty and self-deprecating sense of humor, so similar in many respects to Chaucer's own. For example, it is well recognized that both authors created portraits of themselves as comically inadequate lovers,[1] Gower in the *Confessio Amantis* and Chaucer in several of his works. Evidently the two poets sometimes bantered with each other in writing. For example, Chaucer most likely refers to himself and Gower when he savors a joke at the expense of "olde foles" who deny what is due to love.[2] In a more controversial passage, Chaucer apparently alludes to the *Confessio Amantis* in the Introduction to the Man of Law's Tale, where he places the following literary judgment in the mouth of his moralistic lawyer. Referring to Chaucer himself, the lawyer says:

> But certeinly no word ne writeth he [Chaucer]
> Of thilke wikke ensample of Canacee,
> That loved hir owene brother synfully--
> Of swiche cursed stories I sey fy!--
> Or ellis of Tyro Appollonius,
> How that the cursed kyng Antiochus
> Birafte his doghter of hir maydenhede,
> That is so horrible a tale for to rede,
> Whan he hir threw upon the pavement.

And therfore he, of ful avysement,
Nolde nevere write in none of his sermons
Of swiche unkynde abhomynacions,
Ne I wol noon reherce, if that I may.

(lines 77-89)

Of course, the tales of Canacee and Appollonius do appear in Gower's *Confessio Amantis*, so the Man of Law seems to be attacking the indecency of Gower's narratives while commending the morality of Chaucer's. These lines have usually been interpreted as some sort of humorous comment about Gower or the *Confessio*, but the point of the joke has been variously explained, often, and I believe inaccurately, as some kind of ridicule or parody of Gower. Some critics interpret this passage as Chaucer's own attack on the supposed immorality of the *Confessio*, perhaps delivered in snickering retaliation for Gower's alleged condemnation of Chaucer's racier stories.[3] However, given the unattractive personality of the lawyer, it is extremely unlikely that the latter's opinions represent Chaucer's own, and for that matter there is a total lack of evidence that Gower in fact did anything to provoke such a response from Chaucer. An even more surprising theory is that the Man of Law is himself a satirical portrait of Gower.[4] Exactly why this surrogate Gower would publicly defame his own writings on moral grounds is an irresolvable problem of such an interpretation. Donald R. Howard suggests what is much more likely to be the truth of the matter: the Man of Law represents not Chaucer or Gower, but those obtusely puritanical readers who "object to vice depicted in a work without considering the author's intention in depicting it."[5] If this view is correct, then the butt of Chaucer's humor in this passage is not his friend Gower but the confused sensibilities of certain readers who failed to understand either poet. Although Chaucer does not ridicule the *Confessio* in the Man of Law's Introduction, he does allude to his friend's major poem in a humorous context. To my mind, this fact suggests not a quarrel between the two poets, as some critics have alleged,[6] but rather Chaucer's assumption that Gower was not too stuffy to smile at a joke in which his most important work was mentioned.

While the evidence indicates that Chaucer appreciated his older contemporary's sense of humor, changing taste has obscured this element of the *Confessio* for many nineteenth- and twentieth-century readers. As an extended allegory and a sermon on the Seven Deadly Sins, the poem has often appeared to modern critics as a purely didactic work devoid of humanly appealing or aesthetically attractive qualities. Writing in 1964, scholar John H. Fisher traced the growth of the nineteenth-century stereotype of Gower as an insufferably dry and tedious poet. However, he contributed no new insight into the *Confessio* as literature, writing instead that its "dullness cannot be palliated, but must be recognized for what it is--not failure, but success in its intended genre [the moral complaint]."[7] Fortunately, other critics have noted and analyzed the more pleasurable qualities of the poem, including its elements of comedy and humor.[8] In her recent study, Frances McNeely Leonard points out the affinity of the *Confessio* with comedy as Dante defines the term: "The course of action in Gower's poem is loosely analogous to that in the *Divine Comedy*. It begins in a state of despair and ends in happiness, or at least peace and repose."[9] Leonard goes on to analyze the subtle humor evidenced by certain tales of the *Confessio*,[10] and, most important for the subject of this essay, she indicates the thematic significance of the Lover's first smile in the *Confessio*, which occurs only after he has regained his reason and thus his "unique human identity."[11] This essay will further investigate the poet's references to smiling and laughter in the *Confessio Amantis*. I will touch only incidentally on the subject of humor in the poem, in part because this issue has already been perceptively treated by other critics[12] and in part because laughter was not invariably associated with humor in medieval thought. Gower's attitude toward laughter *per se* as expressed in the *Confessio* has not been previously analyzed, and it provides important insight into the meaning and purpose of the poem as a whole. The essay will consist of two interwoven themes: a description of the traditional Christian attitudes which influenced the poet's treatment of the subject, and an analysis of the specific references to laughter in the *Confessio Amantis* itself. My findings will contribute to the emerging awareness that Gower, not unlike his great English contemporaries, used intelligence, artistry, and, where appropriate, humor and irony in his literary treatment of conventional moral themes.

It is best to begin with Gower's most explicit statement about the nature and physical origin of laughter. This appears in the discussion of human physiology which forms part of the encyclopedic summary of knowledge in Book VII of the *Confessio*. Explaining that each bodily organ has a rightful purpose to fulfill on behalf of the heart, the poet echoes the medical tradition of his day in locating the source of laughter in the spleen:[13]

> The Splen doth him [the heart] to lawhe and pleie,
> Whan al unclennesse is aweie:
> Lo, thus hath ech of hem [the organs of the body] his dede.
> (VII.473-75)[14]

Here the author asserts his belief in the essential purity and legitimacy of laughter, a view which was commonly though far from unanimously maintained in the Middle Ages. By writing a poem in which laughter is celebrated, John Gower aligned himself with a distinct current within the stream of medieval opinion on the subject. The religious and philosophical tradition which he inherited includes three sometimes contradictory approaches to the phenomenon of laughter. Two of these views, which I will call ascetic hostility and reluctant tolerance, are outlined by E. R. Curtius in an excursus to his *European Literature and the Latin Middle Ages*. Curtius cites the dictum of St. John Chrysostom that human beings ought to follow the example of Jesus, who never laughed;[15] he also quotes the prohibitions of St. Benedict and others against laughter in monasteries.[16] In the same excursus, Curtius also describes a more tolerant strain in the clerical approach to laughter. He notes that Hildebert and other twelfth-century authorities permitted a modicum of jesting to their monks; he also quotes Petrus Cantor to the effect that Jesus might possibly have laughed, although the Scripture omits to say that he did so.[17] Scholar V. A. Kolve's indispensable study provides much additional information on both of these attitudes toward laughter. He quotes certain medieval authorities who disparage every variety of mirth as incompatible with the imminence of the Last Judgment, as well as others who recognize the psychological necessity and didactic power of laughter.[18] Neither Curtius nor Kolve provided (or, for that matter, intended to provide) a full discussion of a third view which unreservedly affirms the inherent dignity of laughter, an attitude which has venerable roots in both the bible and the classics, and which plays an important role in some of the greatest literary works of the Middle Ages.

At this point it is useful to examine the medieval manuals of religious instruction, a group of treatises which extensively influenced the treatment of the Seven Deadly Sins in the works of Gower.[19] Although the manuals contain traces of ascetic hostility to laughter,[20] the dominant attitude of these works implies respect for the rightful place of mirthfulness in human life. For example, let us consider the Middle English *Mirroure of the World* (ca. 1465), a translation and combination of two influential treatises of religious instruction, one or both of which Gower certainly knew:[21] the anonymous *Miroir du Monde* (ca. 1280) and Frère Laurent's *Somme le Roi* (1279).[22] For our purposes, the *Mirroure* contains several statements on the subject of laughter. The treatise condemns all vicious and frivolous forms of mirth, particularly the vices of idle talk and laughter at mass.[23] However, the author implicitly acknowledges a legitimate and virtuous form of laughter in the following discussion of the deadly sin of envy:

> Also it [envy] is mooste unnaturell [of the vices]. For as
> seynt Denis seithe: It is good that of nature alle thyngys

loveth and desyreth, but thees of nature hateth goodnes. . . .
And because þat he [the envious man] maye not distroye al
the goodnes that he seeyth, thereof groweth soo grete a
sorowe to his herte that he is euer hevy withowte laughtyr.
His herte trembleth. His body rotith. Here he begynneth
helle, the whiche shalle never fayle him.[24]

By describing the envious man as unnatural and therefore without
laughter, the author recognizes the existence of a natural laughter which rejoices the hearts of those who are free of the cor-
rosive vice.

This view of envy as the pre-eminently mirthless state is a
commonplace in medieval analyses of the vices and virtues.
Like the *Mirroure*, the Parson's Tale connects the joylessness of
envy with its opposition to nature:

For wel unnethe is ther any synne that it ne hath som delit
in itself, save oonly Envye, that evere hath in itself angwissh
and sorwe. / The speces of Envye been thise. Ther is first,
sorwe of oother mannes goodnesse and of his prosperitee;
and prosperitee is kyndely matere of joye; thanne is Envye
a synne agayns kynde.

(lines 489-90)

Similar examples from medieval discussions of the Seven Deadly
Sins could be multiplied.[25] In drawing on traditional catalogues of
vices, Gower inherited the assumption that a virtuous human life
conforms to nature and therefore includes a legitimate form of
laughter and joy.

Turning to secular sources known to be used by Gower, we
find the same concept of envy as a condition without laughter,
or at best with only a corrupt and ironic form of mirth. In the
Roman de la Rose, the sin of envy is personified as a sickly and
dissatisfied woman:

Aprés refu portrete Envie,
Qui ne rist onques en sa vie
N'onques de riens ne s'esjoï,
S'ele ne vit ou s'el n'oï

Aucun grant domage retraire.

(lines 235-39)

(Envy was portrayed next. She never laughed in her life nor enjoyed anything unless she saw or heard a report of some disaster.)[26]

This passage derives its origin not only from the bible (Prov. 14:30), but from an influential description in Ovid's *Metamorphoses* of Invidia personified:

She never smiles [*risus abest*], save at the sight of another's troubles; she never sleeps, disturbed with wakeful cares; unwelcome to her is the sight of man's success, and with the sight she pines away; she gnaws and is gnawed, herself her own punishment.[27]

All of these examples imply the existence of a pure and blameless laughter which cannot be enjoyed by those who practice this most unnatural of sins.

In the treatise on the sin of envy which forms the second book of the *Confessio Amantis*, Gower makes artful use of the traditional association between envy and laughter in order to elucidate the spiritual condition of Amans. In the relevant passage, Genius inquires whether the Lover has ever been guilty of rejoicing at another man's grief. Yes, replies the penitent, he has laughed when other suitors of his beloved Lady have turned out to be as unsuccessful as he is:

Thanne am I fedd of that thei faste,
And lawhe of that I se hem loure;
And thus of that thei brewe soure
I drinke swete, and am wel esed
Of that I wot thei ben desesed.

(II.244-48)

The Lover quickly adds that he experiences such malicious pleasure only where his own Lady is concerned. When another woman is the object, he is indifferent to the success or failure of

45

a lover's suit (II.249-53). Genius replies that all forms of envious rejoicing are equally contrary to reason (II.278-90), and he proceeds to relate the story of the Travellers and the Angel, a vivid illustration of the folly of enjoying another man's harm for its own sake (see especially the reference to malicious laughter at II.362). Genius concludes the exemplum by returning to the familiar theme of envy as an unnatural sin (II.369-72).

This passage on envious laughter enriches its context in several ways. Here the Lover is sensitively portrayed as a human being afflicted by deadly sin, yet not so depraved as to desire another man's defeat where he and his counterpart are not competing for the same goal. This detail enhances the compassion of the audience for Amans and prepares us for his eventual repentance and restoration. At the same time, the Lover's confession of envious laughter adds a personal dimension to the traditional view of envy as the most unnatural of sins. As Venus reveals at the end of the poem, Amans is an old man who would be incapable of consummating his obsessive passion for the Lady (VIII.2412-39); his malevolent rivalry with the other suitors is particularly unnatural and irrational, as well as comic, in light of this fact.

For Gower and his predecessors, then, laughter can be natural and therefore virtuous. We can formulate a more positive definition of natural laughter by determining the connotations of the words *natural* or *kindely* for the moral writers of the Middle Ages. In their broadest sense, these terms refer to behavior which conforms to the God-given order of the world. Even animals participate in the natural order, and in so doing they often provide a good example for human beings to emulate.[28] When the word *natural* is specifically applied to human activity, it means primarily "in keeping with *lex naturalis* or natural law."[29] This law is defined by Thomas Aquinas in the following manner:

> Lex naturalis . . . nihil alius [est] quam impressio divini luminis in nobis. Unde patet quod lex naturalis nihil aliud est quam participatio legis aeternae in rationali creatura.[30]

46

> (Natural law is nothing other than the impression of the divine light in us. Whence it is obvious that natural law is nothing other than the participation of the eternal law in the rational creature.)

In other words, natural law is the innate sense of right and wrong which is present in all human beings, even those ignorant of Christian truth.[31] It is the law by which Adam and Eve were benignly ruled in paradise.[32] Although fallen man requires the additional guidance of revealed religion, he retains this divinely inspired capacity to discern that such acts as murder, false witness, and envious sorrow at another's joy are evil. Since natural law is the exclusive property of rational beings, an acceptable synonym for "natural law" would be "rational law." In keeping with the primary meaning of "natural" in the Middle Ages, I define as "natural" that form of laughter which is in harmony with man's original dignity, his faculty of reason, and his ultimate salvation.

The concept of innocent laughter is explicitly developed by Vincent of Beauvais (d. 1265), the encyclopedist who codified the accepted knowledge of his day in three volumes of the work which is now known as the *Speculum Quadruplex*. In the *Speculum Historiale*, Vincent repeats the dictum of Aristotle that man is the only animal who laughs,[33] and includes laughter among the distinctions bestowed by God upon the unfallen Adam and Eve:

> Animam verò ad imaginem, & similitudinem suam, de nihilo creans idem corpus vivificando, ac regendo inspiravit. Itaque sicut ait Aristoteles, nobilissimus, & altissimus, inter animalia terrestria est homo, solus ratione utens, cuius etiam corporis partes creatae sunt, & dispositae secundum creationem, & situm totius mundi. Unde etiam dicitur Microcosmus, id est minor mundus. Ipse solus inter animalia ridet. . . .[34]

> ([God] breathed in the soul [of man] in His own image and similitude, creating it from nothing for the vivifying and guiding of the same body. For this reason Aristotle said that

> man is the noblest and highest among the terrestrial animals.
> He is the only one who has the use of reason, and the only
> one whose body parts were created and arranged according
> to the creation and structure of the whole world. Whence he
> is called the Microcosm, that is, the lesser world. Man
> alone among the animals laughs. . . .)

This passage explicitly connects the gift of laughter with man's creation in the image of God and with the uniquely human faculty of reason.

In another chapter, one which deals with *gaudium* or joy, the same author invokes the authority of Seneca to affirm that mirthfulness necessarily belongs to the human life which is conducted in accordance with the rational order: "Et sapiens quidem nunquam sine gaudio est: gaudium autem hoc non nascitur, nisi ex virtutum conscientia, nec interrumpitur, nec definit. Quod enim non dedit fortuna, non eripit"[35] (Indeed the wise man is never without joy; for this joy is not born except from the consciousness of virtues, neither is it interrupted, neither is it ended. What fortune did not give, she does not take away). Elsewhere, Vincent explicitly associates laughter with virtue, in this case the morally commendable life of poverty:

> Compara inter se pauperum & divitum vultum, saepius
> pauper, & fidelius ridet; quia nulla ei solicitudo in alto est:
> etiam si qua incidet cura, velut nubes levis transit: horum
> autem qui felices vocuntur hilaritas ficta est, aut gravis; &
> supputata tristitia.[36]

> (Compare the faces of poor and rich men; the poor man
> laughs more often and more sincerely, because he has no
> serious cares; and if any care does assail him, it passes like
> a light cloud. The hilarity of those who are called fortunate
> is feigned or heavy, with concealed sadness.)

Of course, like other medieval moralists, Vincent also finds occasion to inveigh against the wicked, frivolous, and excessive manifestations of laughter and joy.[37] In summary, then, Vincent's statements indicate that joy and laughter are gifts of God, good in themselves though subject to misuse, and rightly to be enjoyed within the bounds of virtue and moderation.[38] This is essentially the attitude expressed in the *Confessio*. There is one instance in the poem of laughter treated pejoratively: when the magician Zoroaster laughed at his birth, it was a token that he would come to sorrow (VI.2370). However, as the following analysis will indicate, the poet almost invariably adhered to the positive beliefs about laughter which are outlined above.

In examining the *Confessio Amantis*, we find that Gower upholds a number of traditional beliefs on the subject of natural laughter. First, like Vincent and Dante before him, he recognizes laughter as one of God's original gifts to the unfallen Adam and Eve.[39] He alludes to this idea in the context of one of his favorite political themes: the evil of dissension in contemporary society. Referring allegorically to the prelapsarian world, Gower expresses nostalgic longing for the mythical Golden Age, when the divine harpist Arion brought peace to the living creatures of the world through the divine entrancement of his music:

> And therto of so good mesure
> He song, that he the bestes wilde
> Made of his note tame and milde,
> The Hinde in pes with the Leoun,
> The Wolf in pes with the Moltoun,
> The Hare in pees stod with the Hound;
> And every man upon this ground
> Which Arion that time herde,
> Als wel the lord as the schepherde,
> He broghte hem alle in good acord;
> So that the comun with the lord,
> And lord with the comun also,
> He sette in love bothe tuo
> And putte awey malencolie.
> *That was a lusti melodie,*
> *Whan every man with other low....*
>   (Prol. 1056-71, emphasis added)

The analogy between the music of the harp and a world in harmony was a medieval commonplace; Gower had himself employed the same image to describe King David's peaceable rule of Israel in his earliest poem, the Anglo-Norman *Mirour de l'Omme* (lines 22897-900). In the later passage quoted above, the poet enriched his musical metaphor by combining it with the theme of natural laughter in order to suggest in auditory terms the beauty and joy of the vanished Golden Age.

A second manifestation of natural laughter arises from the rightful happiness of an earthly society which conducts itself in accordance with God's plan for mankind. Very often, this form of merriment marks the release of tension following the restoration of the social order after a narrowly averted catastrophe. For example, in Book II of the *Confessio Amantis*, the emperor Constantine decides to cure his leprosy by taking a bath in the blood of little children (II.3187-221). When he observes the intended victims gathered with their mothers, he is seized with compassion, and although he is not yet a Christian he realizes that such a sacrifice of innocent human lives would be contrary to the spirit of charity which is inherent in natural law (II.3274-79). Instead of killing the children, he gives them presents and sends them safely on their way. The mothers laugh with relief at the emperor's change of heart:

> These wommen gon hom glade ynowh,
> Echon for joie on other lowh,
> And preiden for this lordes hele,
> Which hath relessed the querele,
> And hath his oghne will forsake
> In charite for goddes sake.
>
> (II.3319-24)

This laughter is inspired by and gives rise to the natural virtue of compassion; like much laughter in medieval literature, it is related to joyfulness rather than to humor or joking.[40]

Elsewhere in the *Confessio*, such an experience of shared laughter is enjoyed by Florent and his newly transformed bride as they recognize the end of their respective trials and the beginning of a happy married life together: "Tho was plesance and joye ynowh / Echon with other pleide and lowh" (I.1853-54). In a not dissimilar situation, the husband of Gower's Constance responds with a muted laugh when he recognizes his beloved wife whom he had given up for lost (II.1444). Also in the context of emotional relief, the Argonauts laugh as they accompany Jason returning victorious from his extremely hazardous quest for the Golden Fleece (V.3781). In all the passages just cited, communal or restored laughter reaffirms the natural and rational attachments within the family and society at large.

Turning to Gower's contemporaries, we note that Chaucer calls on the traditional idea of virtuous communal laughter in a subtle and ironic way. At the end of the Pardoner's Tale, an ugly dispute ensues between the Host and the Pardoner. Wishing to restore a modicum of good will, the Knight intervenes:

> "Namoore of this, for it is right ynough!
> Sire Pardoner, be glad and myrie of cheere;
> And ye, sire Hoost, that been to me so deere,
> I preye yow that ye kisse the Pardoner.
> And Pardoner, I prey thee, drawe thee neer,
> And, as we diden, lat us laughe and pleye."
> Anon they kiste, and ryden forth hir weye.[41]

(lines 962-68)

Chaucer's reference to natural laughter here has a joltingly mixed effect: it affirms that the pilgrims, for all their faults, are a Christian community[42] which enjoys a certain harmony and the laughter it brings; at the same time, this reference to laughter points up for us the vast disparity between the merriment of the pilgrims and the virtuous joy of a righteous man in Vincent or Gower. The Gawain-poet employs the same *topos* with equally challenging complexity. At the end of *Sir Gawain and the Green Knight*, the hero confesses with grief and contrition his less than perfect fulfillment of the terms of his adventure. All in the court respond by laughing loudly and offering to share with Gawain his badge of shame (lines 2514-18). Considered against the ideal of natural laughter, this example of communal mirth seems vacuous in the extreme. The poet gives no evidence that the courtiers ever achieve a rational appreciation of Gawain's experience; still, the laughter of Arthur's court is at least an attempt to welcome the stricken hero and to share his burden in a spirit of charity. This outburst of an imperfect approximation of natural laughter concludes the poem with yet another example of man's inability to conform himself entirely to his ideals, regardless of the loftiness of his intentions.

Likewise, in his tale of The Trump of Death, Gower also invokes the theme of natural laughter in order to create a disturbingly ironic effect. On a beautiful May morning, the king of Hungary rides out into the countryside, accompanied by all the young people of his court (I.2021-33). Suddenly the king notices two ancient pilgrims. He leaps from his chair, embraces and kisses the old men, and gives them presents, after which he returns to his seat. All the courtiers murmur against the king because they believe he has debased himself in honoring the two poor beggars. As the day progresses, however, they seem to forget their indignation: "Echon with othre pleide and lowh / And fellen into tales newe . . ." (I.2082-83). Later, the king's brother reprimands him for his supposed condescension, and the king responds by teaching his brother the lesson of humility through the device of the trump of death, and then by forgiving his presumption.

What are we to make of this apparent occurrence of natural laughter? Perhaps the courtiers' laughter belongs to the vain and foolish mirth which medieval moralists condemned. If so, the author creates a sharply ironic contrast by his exact repetition of a line from the Tale of Florent quoted above ("Echon with othre pleide and lowh"), which describes the natural and legitimate happiness of Florent and his bride. Just as possibly, the cheerful laughter of the young courtiers is sympathetically presented as a foreshadowing of the moral lesson, forgiveness, and return to harmony which occur at the end of the story. While the courtiers are certainly guilty of pride, at least they refrain from persistent or violent rage againt the king; their ability to laugh may be intended to signal the possibility of their eventual redemption.

Another major type of natural laughter in medieval literature is righteous derision of the wicked. This laughter springs from a rational apprehension of the futility and absurdity of evil. In the Old Testament, God is several times said to laugh at the puny machinations of his enemies (Ps. 2:4; 37:13; 59:8). Elijah derides the failure of the pagan god Baal to produce a miraculous fire (I [III] Kings 18:27). In the same spirit, Chaucer's St. Cecilia laughs when the pagan ruler Almachius orders her to sacrifice to Jupiter or be killed (Second Nun's Tale, line 462). Cecilia locates the source of her mirth in the ultimate impotence of her tormentors:

> "Youre myght," quod she, "ful litel is to dreede,
> For every mortal mannes power nys
> But lyk a bladdre ful of wynd, ywys.
> For with a nedles poynt, whan it is blowe,
> May al the boost of it be leyd ful lowe."

(lines 437-41)

The irrational blunderings of the sinful are frequently laughable in the comic sense, as are the personifications of gluttony and sloth in Langland's *Piers Plowman*.[43] Howard H. Schless points out that a similar response is evoked in the reader by the "ludicrously obstinate" behavior of the damned in Dante's *Inferno*. As Schless explains, the reader is required to accept the divine perspective from which the souls in hell are as absurd in their eternal obduracy as "some village ignoramus continually opting for the glittering bauble."[44]

The *Confessio* also includes several examples of such righteous or rational derision of sinful behavior. In two cases, such ridicule is as harsh and detached from its object as the examples in the preceding paragraph. For example, in the famous exemplum of Vulcan and Venus, Genius notes with approval that when Venus and Mars were trapped in bed together the gods derided Vulcan for his jealousy and "misgovernance" (V.696).[45] The story ends with no evidence that the gods' laughter served any compassionate or morally redemptive purpose. Quite different in tone is the Tale of the Courtiers and the Fool, in which the Roman emperor Lucius stands talking with his steward and his chamberlain, asking them whether his government is praised or blamed by the people. The steward answers untruthfully that the people hold their emperor in high esteem. Equally dishonest but more subtle, the chamberlain answers that the people believe Lucius would be a worthy ruler, if only his councillors were true. Unnoticed by the others, the emperor's fool overhears the entire conversation:

> And happeth that the kinges fol
> Sat be the fyr upon a stol,
> As he that with his babil pleide,
> Bot yit he herde al that thei seide. . . .
> . . . .
> The fol, which herde of al the cas
> That time, as goddes wille was,
> Sih that thei seiden noght ynowh,
> *And hem to skorne bothe lowh.* . . .
> (VII.3953-56; 3989-92; emphasis added)

The fool then contradicts the chamberlain, asserting boldly that if an emperor is good his councillors will not be bad. Lucius recognizes the grace of God in this answer, puts away his evil councillors, and reforms the government according to the dictates of peace and justice. In this narrative, the laughter of the wise fool exemplifies the gentle and forgiving spirit which prevails over most of the *Confessio*. No character in the story is made the butt of harsh or vindictive ridicule; instead, a moment of rational mockery serves the constructive purpose of immediate moral reform. Such an emphasis on the rational element in laughter is particularly appropriate to the character of Genius, who represents not only man's procreative drive but also his distinctively human faculty of reason.[46]

The same essentially compassionate spirit is characteristic of the special humor which pervades the *Confessio Amantis*. The poem has accurately been assigned to the genre of satire, in which human foibles are exposed with the serious purpose of inspiring the reader to recognize and correct his own faults.[47] To this end, Gowerian satire produces a form of humor which nearly always discourages the audience from assuming a detached or superior attitude to the person or situation being satirized. Instead, because we recognize ourselves in the object of satire, we laugh in a spirit not of derision but of empathy and community. A famous example of such comic effect is the portrait of Jonah in the alliterative *Patience*, a work nearly contemporary with the *Confessio*. Drooling in his sleep, oblivious to the storm which threatens the ship in which he is travelling, the prophet cuts a buffoonish figure as he vainly attempts to escape from the fulfillment of God's command (line 186). This scene naturally evokes laughter even as it calls on the reader to acknowledge the analogous absurdity of his own attempts to rebel against the God-given order of the world. Gower's humor is similar in nature and purpose. For example, in the exemplum of Nebuchadnezzar, the king is changed into an ox as punishment for his sin of vainglory. There is a poignant comedy in his inarticulate attempts to pray for forgiveness and restoration to human shape:

> And so thenkende he gan doun bowe,
> And thogh him lacke vois and speche,
> He gan up with his feet areche,
> And wailende in his bestly stevene
> He made his pleignte unto the hevene.
> He kneleth in his wise and braieth,
> To seche merci and assaieth
> His god, which made him nothing strange,
> Whan that he sih his pride change.
>
> (I.3022-30)

As Christopher Ricks makes clear in his analysis of this passage,

"Gower's art of admonition permits no easy superiority to his exemplary sinners."[48] For Ricks, the stricken king represents all of sinful humanity in comparison to the goodness and righteousness of God. Gower sets the example of such compassionate laughter by creating a comic self-portrait in the course of the poem and by smiling at his own foibles in order to signal his return to spiritual health (VIII.2958). This example is valid for the reader even if the fictional "John Gower" is not to be confused with the poet himself, and it is integral to the spirit of tolerance and charity which critics have rightly perceived in the *Confessio Amantis* as a whole.[49]

NOTES

[1]For references to the comic self-portrait in Chaucer and Gower, see E. Talbot Donaldson, *Speaking of Chaucer* (New York, 1970), pp. 9-10; Samuel T. Cowling, "Gower's Ironic Self-Portrait in the *Confessio Amantis*," *Annuale Medievale*, 16 (1975), 63-70; Masayoshi Ito, *John Gower: The Medieval Poet* (Tokyo, 1976), p. 243; Piero Boitani, *English Medieval Narratives in the Thirteenth and Fourteenth Centuries*, trans. Joan K. Hall (Cambridge, 1982), pp. 118, 130-31; J. A. Burrow, "The Portrayal of Amans in *Confessio Amantis*," in *Gower's "Confessio Amantis": Responses and Reassessments*, ed. A. J. Minnis (Cambridge, 1983), pp. 6, 9, where Burrow traces this device to the comic narrator-persona in the French *dits amoureux*, particularly Froissart's *Espinette Amoureuse*; and Elizabeth Porter, "Gower's Ethical Microcosm and Political Macrocosm," in *Gower's "Confessio Amantis,"* pp. 145-46.

[2]*The Legend of Good Women*, G text, line 315. All quotations from Chaucer in this essay are drawn from *The Riverside Chaucer*, 3rd ed., general editor Larry D. Benson (Boston, 1987).

[3]For such a reading of the Man of Law's Introduction, see John H. Fisher, *John Gower: Moral Philosopher and Friend of Chaucer* (New York, 1964), p. 289.

[4]See Alfred David, "The Man of Law vs. Chaucer: A Case in Poetics," *PMLA*, 82 (1967), 217-25; and Anne Middleton, "Chaucer's 'New Men' and the Good of Literature in the *Canterbury Tales*," in *Literature and Society: Selected Papers from the English Institute, 1978*, n.s. 3, ed. Edward W. Said (Baltimore

and London, 1980), pp. 15-56. I am indebted for these references and for further elaboration of the theory to Judith Davis Shaw, "*Lust* and *Lore* in Gower and Chaucer," *Chaucer Review*, 19/2 (1984), 116.

[5]See *The Idea of the Canterbury Tales* (Berkeley, 1976), p. 46.

[6]Richard Hazelton, "The *Manciple's Tale*: Parody and Critique," *Journal of English and Germanic Philology*, 62 (1963), 25. For a history of the theory that Chaucer quarreled with his friend Gower, see Fisher, pp. 31-34. Derek Pearsall, in *Gower's "Confessio Amantis,"* pp. 180-81, 193, gives an interpretation of the Man of Law's Introduction which differs from my own; however, he too rejects the theory that the two poets quarreled.

[7]Fisher, p. 2.

[8]See Derek Pearsall, *Gower and Lydgate*, Writers and their Work 211 (London, 1969), p. 14; Anthony E. Farnham, "The Art of High Prosaic Seriousness: John Gower as Didactic Raconteur," in *The Learned and the Lewed: Studies in Chaucer and Medieval Literature*, ed. Larry D. Benson (Cambridge, MA, 1974), pp. 161-73; Masayoshi Ito refers to humor in the description of the hag in the Tale of Florent and enumerates witty rhetorical devices in the *Vox Clamantis* and the *Confessio* (*John Gower*, pp. 18, 49, 54; 212, 243-46); Patrick J. Gallacher notes humor in the discussion of sacrilege in *Confessio* V.7032-75, in the Prayer of Cephalus, and in the witty answer of Diogenes to Aristippus (*Love, the Word, and Mercury: A Reading of John Gower's* Confessio Amantis [Albuquerque, 1975], pp. 57, 71, 125 respectively); Paul Miller notes that the *Confessio* is part of a tradition of humor used for a didactic purpose ("John Gower: Satiric Poet," in *Gower's "Confessio Amantis,"* p. 90); David W. Hiscoe argues that Gower, like Ovid, intentionally creates a humorous effect by distorting the traditional *moralitates* of well-known exempla ("The Ovidian Comic Strategy of Gower's *Confessio Amantis*," *Philological Quarterly*, 64 [1985], 367-85. It should also be noted that Gower evidently appreciated humorous works of literature: he borrowed extensively from a humorous work, the *Speculum Stultorum* (see Robert Raymo, "Gower's *Vox Clamantis* and the *Speculum Stultorum*," *Modern Language Notes*, 70 [1955], 315-20).

[9]See Leonard, *Laughter in the Courts of Love* (Norman, OK, 1981), p. 63. For an informative discussion of medieval theories of comedy, applicable to the *Confessio*, see Howard, *The Idea of the Canterbury Tales*, pp. 30-45.

[10]*Laughter in the Courts of Love*, pp. 73-75.

[11]*Laughter in the Courts of Love*, p. 63; referring to *Confessio* VIII. 2958.

[12]See above, nn. 1, 8, and 10. However, it should be noted that none of these treatments of humor in the *Confessio* is exhaustive; much remains to be investigated in this field.

[13]See "Religious Laughter," ch. 6 of V. A. Kolve, *The Play Called Corpus Christi* (Stanford, 1966), p. 126.

[14]All quotations from the *Confessio Amantis* are taken from *The English Works of John Gower*, ed. G. C. Macaulay, 2 vols., EETS, e. s. 81-82 (Oxford, 1900-01).

This passage may be related to the medieval belief in the medicinal value of laughter and joy; see Glending Olson, *Literature as Recreation in the Later Middle Ages* (Ithaca, NY, 1982), passim, esp. p. 61.

[15]*Patrologia graeca* 57.69; trans. and cited by E. R. Curtius in *European Literature and the Latin Middle Ages*, trans. Willard R. Trask (Princeton, 1953), p. 420.

[16]*European Literature and the Latin Middle Ages*, pp. 420-21.

[17]Petrus Cantor, *Patrologia latina* 205.203; quoted by Curtius, p. 421.

[18]*The Play Called Corpus Christi*, pp. 124-26; 127-34. Readers interested in the medieval controversy on the subject of whether Jesus laughed and on the legitimacy of laughter in general will enjoy Umberto Eco's popular treatment of the subject in his detective novel, *The Name of the Rose*, trans. William Weaver (New York, 1984). However, this book seems to be inaccurate in at least one detail. On p. 569, Eco assigns Aristotle's famous dictum that man is the only animal who laughs to his "book on the soul," whereas it is actually to be found in the *De Partibus Animalium*; see n. 36 below.

[19]For information on the subject of medieval religious manuals, see H. G. Pfander, "Some Medieval Manuals of Religious Instruction and Observations on Chaucer's *Parson's Tale*," *Journal of English and Germanic Philology*, 35 (1936), 243-58; also see P. S. Jolliffe, *A Checklist of Middle English Prose Writings of Spiritual Guidance* (Toronto, 1974).

For information on how these manuals influenced the works of Gower, see R. Elfreda Fowler, *Une Source Française des Poèmes de Gower* (Mâcon, 1905); J. B. Dwyer, "The Tradition of Medieval Manuals of Religious Instruction in the Poems of John Gower, with Special Reference to the Development of the 'Book of Virtues'" (Ph.D. diss., University of North Carolina at Chapel Hill, 1950); J. B. Dwyer, "Gower's *Mirour* and its French Sources; A Reexamination of the Evidence," *Studies in Philology*, 48 (1951), 482-505; for further bibliographical discussion, see Robert F. Yeager, "The Poetry of John Gower: Important Studies, 1960-83," in *Fifteenth Century Studies: Recent Essays*, ed. R. F. Yeager (Hamden, CT, 1984), p. 11. Another recent article on the subject is Gerald Kinneavy, "Gower's *Confessio Amantis* and the Penitentials," *Chaucer Review*, 19/2 (1984), 144-61.

[20]See, for example, Elaine E. Whitaker, ed., "A Critical Edition of the 'Mirroure of the Worlde'" (Ph.D. diss., New York University, 1971), 72, 83, 86. This treatise never condemns laughter *per se*, only the vices of frivolous laughter and laughter at mass. However, another religious manual flatly includes "laughter and grinning" among the sins of the mouth along with hideous oaths, lascivious songs, and various forms of lying; see Louise C. Lubbe, ed., "The Myrour to Lewde Men and Wymmen" (Ph.D. diss., University of California at Los Angeles, 1955), 166.

[21]For information on the date and sources of the "Mirroure of the Worlde," see Whitaker's Introduction.

[22]For the relationship of the "Mirroure" to an Old French treatise which combines the *Miroir* and the *Somme*, see Whitaker, pp. xix-xx. For a history of the two Old French treatises, see Whitaker, pp. xxiii-xxiv, and Edith Brayer, "Contenu, structure, et combinaisons du *Miroir du Monde* et de la *Somme le Roi*," *Romania*, 79 (1958), 1-38, 433-70. There is no satisfactory edition of the Old French *Somme le Roi*. One manuscript, the British Royal MS. 19cII of the British Library, is available on microfilm (no. 306 of the MLA Rotograph Collection, Library of Congress, Washington, DC) and has been transcribed in two parts: from the beginning to the virtue of humility, Ann Brooks Tysor, ed., "Somme des Vices et des Vertus" (M.A. thesis, University of North Carolina at Chapel Hill, 1949); and, from humility through the conclusion, Edward Herbert Allen, ed., "Somme des Vices et des Vertus, Part II" (M.A. thesis, University of North Carolina at Chapel Hill, 1951). The most accessible version of the *Somme* is its English Midland translation, *The Book of Vices and Virtues*, ed. W. Nelson Francis, EETS, o.s. 217 (London, 1942). An imperfect MS of the *Miroir du Monde* has been edited by Félix Chavannes, *Le Mirouer du Monde*, in *Mémoires et Documents publiées par la Société d'histoire de la Suisse Romande*, 4 (1845).

[23]Whitaker, pp. 72, 83.

[24]Whitaker, pp. 114, 116.

[25]See, for example, *Ancrene Wisse*, ed. J. R. R. Tolkien, EETS, o.s. 249 (London, 1962), p. 103; *The Book of Vices and Virtues* (n. 22 above), p. 23; Dante, *Purgatorio* 14.82-84; Pseudo-Vincent of Beauvais, *Speculum Morale* (in *Speculum Quadruplex sive Speculum Maius* [1624; rept. Graz, 1964-65]), Lib. III dist. I pars iv.

[26]French text as edited by Daniel Poirion (Paris, 1974); English translation from Guillaume de Lorris and Jean de Meun, *The Romance of the Rose*, trans. Charles Dahlberg (Princeton, 1971), p. 34.

[27]*Met.* II.778-82, trans. Frank Justus Miller, 3rd ed., rev. G. P. Goold, Loeb Classical Library (Cambridge, MA, 1977).

[28]For example, the *Book of Vices and Virtues* invokes the teachings of *kynde* in exhorting men and women to perform the corporal works of mercy; even the dolphin buries its dead, and the stork cares tenderly for his aged parents (ed. Francis, pp. 211, 213).

[29]See *OED*, "natural," I.1; also *MED*, "natural," I a and b.

[30]*Summa Theologica*, ed. Thomas Gilby, O.P. (London, 1966), "Law and Political Theory," I-II, q. 91, art. 2. Cited by Henriette Anne Klauser, "The Concept of *Kynde* in John Gower's *Confessio Amantis*" (Ph.D. diss., Fordham University, 1972), 43. For a quite different, much more detailed and technical analysis of natural law in the *Confessio*, see Kurt Olsson, "Natural Law and John Gower's *Confessio Amantis*," *Medievalia et Humanistica*, n.s., 11 (1982), 231-61.

[31]According to the *Book of Vices and Virtues*, even heathens and Jews conform to the precepts of *kynde* (p. 211). For more on natural law as man's innate moral sense, see Gareth W. Dunleavy, "Natural Law as Chaucer's Ethical Absolute," *Transactions of the Wisconsin Academy of Sciences, Arts, and Letters*, 52 (1963), esp. 177-78; George D. Economou, *The Goddess Natura in Medieval Literature* (Cambridge, MA, 1972), esp. pp. 93-96; and *Dictionnaire de Théologie Catholique*, vol. 9 (1926), "Lois. La Loi Naturelle," cols. 878-80; and Geoffrey Koziol, "Lord's Law and Natural Law," in *The Medieval Tradition of Natural Law*, ed. Harold J. Johnson, Studies in Medieval Culture 22 (Kalamazoo, 1987), pp. 103-17.

[32]For the role of natural law in paradise, see the Parson's Tale, line 920.

[33]*Speculum Historiale*, vol. 4 in *Speculum Quadruplex sive Speculum Maius* (see n. 25 above). See Aristotle, *De Partibus Animalium*, trans. Wil-

liam Ogle, vol. V, pt. I in *The Works of Aristotle Translated into English under the Editorship of J. A. Smith and W. D. Ross* (1912; rept. Oxford, 1958), Bk. 3, ch., 10, sect. 673a, lines 8 and 28.

Vincent's encyclopedia made Aristotle's ideas on natural science accessible to medieval readers; see Beryl Smalley, *The Study of the Bible in the Middle Ages* (1952; rept. Notre Dame, 1964), p. 312.

Helen Adolf notes other medieval allusions to the Aristotelian belief that man is the only laughing animal ("On Medieval Laughter," *Speculum*, 22 [1947], 251-53). In a later period, Rabelais alludes to the concept of laughter as natural to man in his "Advice to Readers" at the beginning of *Gargantua and Pantagruel*. When Montaigne seeks to humble mankind by building a case that man is not much different from the other animals, he observes that man is probably *not* the only animal who laughs; see "Apologie de Raimond Sebond," in *Oevres Complètes*, ed. Robert Barral and Pierre Michel (Paris, 1967), p. 190.

[34]*Speculum Historiale*, Lib. I cap. xxx, p. 12.

[35]Seneca, *Ad Lucillum* 59; quoted in *Speculum Doctrinale*, Lib. IV cap. cxi, col. 363b.

[36]Seneca, *Ad Lucillum* 80; quoted by Vincent, ibid.

[37]Vincent, ibid.; see also Pseudo-Vincent, *Speculum Morale*, Lib. I dist. XXIV pars i. The *Speculum Morale*, written by a fourteenth-century author, comprises one volume of the *Speculum Quadruplex*, cited in n. 25 above.

[38]The ideal of moderate and appropriate laughter is a commonplace in all times and cultures. See Ecclesiastes 3:4; Horace, *Odes* IV.12.28; and the medieval Muslim scholar Al-Jahiz, in Charles Pellat, *The Life and Works of Jahiz as edited and translated by D. M. Hawke* (Berkeley, 1969), p. 239. I am indebted to Denise Spellberg of Columbia University for the latter reference. Baldesare Castiglione, *The Book of the Courtier* II.42-97, provides an extended analysis of the permissible forms of joking and laughter; section 45 defines man as the animal who laughs. In the *Praise of Folly*, "Preface of Thomas More," Erasmus commends his friend's ability to enjoy a jest in season, referring to him as a new Democritus (Democritus was called "the laughing philosopher").

[39]See Pseudo-Vincent, cited in n. 25 above; and Dante, *Purgatorio* 28.96. Milton refers to the "smiles" and "mirth" of the unfallen Adam and Eve (*Paradise Lost* IV.337, 346).

Closely related to Edenic laughter in Christian thought is the belief that laughter will be restored to the saved after death. Consider the omnipresent "riso" of Dante's *Purgatorio* and *Paradiso*, as well as Whitaker, *"Mirroure of the Worlde,"* p. 339. Gower probably alludes to this belief when he notes laughter among the companies of famous lovers seen by Amans in his vision at the end of the poem (VIII.2491, 2685).

[40]For example, the "riso" of Dante's *Purgatorio* and *Paradiso* is almost invariably associated with joy rather than humor. At *Paradiso* 9.70-71, "riso" is explicitly associated with "letizia." This medieval association of laughter with joy is worth noting because it contradicts more recent ideas on the subject. For example, Charles Baudelaire, in his essay "On the Essence of Laughter," states that laughter arises from disgust and is based on a feeling of superiority to the thing laughed at; laughter is strictly postlapsarian; laughter is unrelated to joy; the joyful laughter of children is not really laughter; trans. Jonathan Mayne, in *Comedy: Meaning and Form*, ed. Robert W. Corrigan (San Francisco, 1965), pp. 449, 451, 453, 457.

[41]For a similarly ambiguous allusion to natural laughter, see also the Reeve's Prologue, line 3858.

[42]For the pilgrims as a viable though imperfect community, capable of moral progress and reconciliation, see, for example, Alfred David, *The Strumpet Muse: Art and Morals in Chaucer's Poetry* (Bloomington, IN, 1976), p. 72.

[43]*The Vision of William Concerning Piers the Plowman*, ed. Walter W. Skeat, 2 vols. (1896; rept. London, 1924), B text, Passus V.304-91, 392-464. Langland's portrayal of gluttony is analyzed in this connection by Howard H. Schless, "Dante: Comedy and Conversion," in *Versions of Medieval Comedy*, ed. Paul G. Ruggiers (Norman, OK, 1977), p. 146.

[44]Schless, pp. 139-40; Prof. Schless makes clear, however, that the *Divine Comedy* belongs to the family of "high comedy," not "risible comedy."

[45]For another example of derision of sin, see *Confessio* V.6931.

[46]For more on Genius as a spokesman for human reason, see, for example, G. D. Economou, "The Character Genius in Alan de Lille, Jean de Meun, and John Gower," *Chaucer Review*, 4 (1970), 208; Donald G. Schueler, "Gower's Characterization of Genius in the *Confessio Amantis*," *Modern Language Quarterly*, 33 (1972), 240-56; and Denise N. Baker, "The Priesthood of Genius: A Study of Medieval Tradition," *Speculum*, 51 (1976), 277-91.

[47]Paul Miller, "John Gower as Satiric Poet," in *Gower's "Confessio Amantis,"* p. 90.

[48]"Metamorphosis in Other Words," in *Gower's "Confessio Amantis,"* p. 32.

[49]See Linda Barney Burke, "Women in John Gower's *Confessio Amantis,"* *Mediaevalia*, 3 (1977), 253 n. 1; and Charles Runacres, "Art and Ethics in the Exempla of the *Confessio Amantis,"* in *Gower's "Confessio Amantis,"* p. 112.

CONSTANCE AND THE WORLD
IN CHAUCER AND GOWER

Winthrop Wetherbee

Most modern readers find the tale of Chaucer's Man of Law uncongenial, but it is hard to be sure whether one's dislike is a historical accident or an effect calculated by Chaucer. At one end of the critical spectrum Hope Phyllis Weissman has made a good case for viewing the tale as deliberately bad, arguing that its sentimentality is more to the point than its seriousness, and that in it Chaucer parodies and implicitly rejects the "Gothic pathos" inherent in the story he tells.[1] At the other, V. A. Kolve views it as a total success, poetry of the "fullest dignity" that affirms the possibility of "an uncompromised Christian life and true Christian society."[2] And there is the further question of how the tale is to be placed within the design of the *Canterbury Tales* as a whole. It is not clearly linked to other tales at either end, and one cannot even be certain about its relation to its putative narrator. There seems to be no way around the Man of Law's announcement, "I speke in prose," which suggests that his headlink was at some stage intended to introduce the Melibee, and there is no clear continuity between the headlink and the ensuing Prologue and Tale. We may, of course, assume that tale and introduction are mismatched.[3] Or we may try to discover the relationship of the elaborate literary excursus, with its long list of heroines whose lives were marked by unhappiness in love; the Prologue on the ills of poverty, which ends with praise of mer-

65

chants; and the tale itself, which contains no detail that enables us to assign it with certainty to the Man of Law.

In the present paper I will argue that a pattern of sustained allusion to the *Confessio Amantis* of John Gower provides an important index to the purpose of the Man of Law's Tale. The *Confessio*, too, contains a version of the Constance story, and Chaucer was well aware of Gower's narrative in composing his own. He departs from their common source, the *Chronicle* of Nicholas Trivet, at similar points, and explicitly invites comparison by making the Man of Law twice contrast his own narrative with the manner in which "some men" have told the story, in a way that clearly invokes Gower's version.[4] And these allusions are set in a broader context by the literary excursus in the headlink, where the Man of Law's long list of Chaucer's tales of women climaxes by contrasting them with two tales, both from the *Confessio Amantis*, that deal openly with incest.

Stories of "noble wives and lovers" have a strong hold on the Man of Law. His catalogue moves from mere enumeration ("In youthe he made . . . ," "And sitthen . . . " [lines 57-58]) to apostrophe ("the, queene Medea," "O Ypermystra" [lines 72, 75]), and several of the stories he recalls assume a new vividness in his hands, as in his gratuitous reference to the "woundes wyde" of Lucretia and Thisbe (line 63) or the wholly uncanonical suggestion that Medea's children died by hanging (line 73).[5] His embellishing tendency is particularly marked in the culminating references to Gower's tales of the love of Canacee, daughter of Aeolus, for her brother Machaire, and that of King Antiochus for his unnamed daughter. He mentions such stories only to repudiate them, but he brings them momentarily to life in passing:

> But certeinly no word ne writeth he
> Of thilke wikke ensample of Canacee,
> That loved hir owene brother synfully--
> Of swiche cursed stories I sey fy!--
> Or ellis of Tyro Apollonius,

How that the cursed kyng Antiochus
Birafte his doghter of hir maydenhede,
That is so horrible a tale for to rede,
Whan he hir threw upon the pavement.

(lines 77-85)

Most critics have taken the allusions to Gower as a good-natured joke, if not perhaps one Gower would have appreciated. Alfred David, the only critic to have considered them at any length, sees the humor as veiling a hint that Gower's work has about it something of the humorless pedantry of the Man of Law's literary criticism. "Moral Gower," he suggests, is just the sort of poet the Man of Law would like, if he could get around the problem of Gower's willingness to deal with topics like incest.[6] But while David has identified a fundamental trait of the Man of Law's imagination, a more important effect of the lawyer's allusions is to show him wholly failing to understand Gower's stories. Brief though his references are, the choice of detail and the intrusive inveighals ("wikke," "cursed," "fy!," "horrible") manage to convey a highly misleading impression of the stories cited, which in fact neither condone the incestuous acts they report nor dwell on their obvious sinfulness. Instead both use the theme of incest as a way of pointing to the importance of human culture in guiding and giving value to fallible natural impulse. In the tale of Canacee we are shown, not "wickedness," but a passion wholly unmediated by social form. The child-lovers, whose father is Aeolus, the god of storm, are a pair of *enfants sauvages*, and the most striking and terrible thing about their love is its sheer unmeaningness: in the utter absence of any "positive" or man-made law they are "taught" by Nature, and under her power they become, "as who seith, enchaunted" (III.170-78).[7] Where the Man of Law inveighs against Canacee's sinfulness, Gower communicates far more tellingly the horror of a moral void: his narrative ends, not with Canacee's suicide, but with the shockingly emblematic image of her baby playing in his mother's still-warm blood (III.312-15), and the mad impulse

67

of Aeolus, who causes the infant to be abandoned in a wild place "So that som beste him mai devoure" (III.327).[8]

Again, in the tale of Apollonius of Tyre, the function of the incest of Antiochus and his anonymous daughter (which Gower describes vividly but not graphically, and with no reference to the king's throwing his daughter to the pavement) is to provide an antithesis to the history of Apollonius himself, whose story is largely a vindication of the cultural institutions that sustain him. His one sure resource, in a life of wandering punctuated by misjudgments and near-disasters, is a thorough grounding in the values of his society, an education that encompasses everything from skill in games to a quasi-spiritual sense of the duties of kingship. The center of his life is his marriage, and his ultimate vindication seems to be due almost entirely to a conjugal love in which natural feeling and social obligation are perfectly integrated:

> Lo what it is to be wel grounded:
> For he hath ferst his love founded
> Honesteliche as forto wedde,
> Honesteliche his love he spedde
> And hadde children with his wif,
> And as him liste he ladde his lif.

> (VIII.1993-98)

I will have more to say later on about the broader implications of this complex invocation of the moral authority of Gower and the specific significance of the Man of Law's allusion to the story of Apollonius. For the moment it is enough to note that the stories recalled, by their common use of the motif of incest to illustrate the importance of culture in mediating and disciplining human behavior, call attention to this aspect of the *Confessio Amantis* as a foil to the performance of the Man of Law. And the emphasis on social values that is so prominent a feature of these tales is central also to Gower's own treatment of the story of Constance. Apollonius's story is a test of integrity which all lovers may apply to themselves: its lesson is "How ate laste it schal be sene / Of love what thei wolden mene" (VIII. 2001-02). The Constance story, too, ends by declaring itself an affirmation of "the wel meninge of love" (II.1599), and a number of its themes are developed in the tale of Apollonius. Gower's version preserves little or no trace of the theme of incest that seems to have been inherent in earlier versions of the story,[9] but its emphasis on Constance's active, public role points up by contrast an element of quasi-incestuous possessiveness in the Man of Law's attitude toward his heroine, a tendency to fetishize her helplessness and underplay her normal social relations, which points to the lurking presence of the traditional theme. In the context of Chaucer's repeated allusions to Gower, the tale provides a kind of running commentary on Chaucer's version, an example of dynamic and socially integrated sainthood that serves to expose the emptiness at the heart of the Man of Law's affirmation of order.

For the most remarkable feature of the Man of Law's treatment of the story is his consistent refusal to grant its heroine a full measure of earthly existence. It can be argued that this is a function of the tale's truth to its peculiar kind, the hagiographic romance, which aims at stimulating piety through pathos;[10] but in Chaucer's hands the tendencies of the genre become a means to expose the failure of the Man of Law as a spokesman for order. Though he is committed by his profession to the pursuit of social justice, and his choice of tale seems clearly intended to restore to the tale-telling game the emphasis established by the Knight's inaugural affirmation of social and cosmic order, his performance is pervaded by a deep anxiety, a distrust of earthly institutions, and a pessimism about the course of human life which make him adopt a stiflingly possessive attitude toward Custance herself. His emphasis on her passivity and the evils that continually threaten her does not simply cast her in a pathetic light, but rests in unresolved contradiction to his strident assertions of God's abiding care, and is at times flatly contradicted by the obvious facts of her situation. Even at moments when he is stressing the positive implications of his heroine's adventures, his affirmations of providence become an excuse for rendering her as nearly as possible inoperative in social terms, suppressing the realities of her role as wife, mother, and embodiment of the missionary Church in order to keep her insulated from any real involvement with social institutions. She remains invulnerable, and finally survives her misfortunes, but she inhabits a sort of limbo, suspended between hagiography and sentimental tragedy, thrall to the Man of Law's deeply divided view of life.

Conversely, what is most striking in Gower's Constance story, for one who comes to it with Chaucer's in mind, is the very active role played by the heroine. Where the Man of Law deploys his Custance as a sort of icon in a series of tableaux which set off her sorrow, her helplessness in the face of grief, and hence her suitability to serve as an example of God's providential concern, Gower's Constance is continually engaged with the world around her through the medium of social institutions. There is of course a radically spiritual *donnée* inherent in the story, and Gower makes no attempt to evade or suppress it: his Constance embodies the true faith, and her career is in many respects a representation of the mission of the Church. Wherever she goes, she carries with her the threat or promise of radical transformation, and despite the widely varying reactions she provokes she proves, like Chaucer's Custance, to be indestructible. But Gower takes great pains to establish a secular context for Constance's experience: the prevailing emphasis is on *how* she fulfils her evangelical mission, how her influence is mediated by the attraction her human presence exerts on others, and by the institutions of the different cultures with which she comes in contact. Her strength involves not only her constancy in faith but her humanity and intelligence, and it expresses itself best in situations which call her womanhood into action and enable her to function as daughter, wife, and mother as well as saint.

The sharp contrast between the two stories is clear from the outset. The Man of Law's heroine is offstage for the first 130

lines of her story, and the evangelizing of Surrye is wholly due
to her reputation. Gower's Constance is no sooner named and
labelled as "ful of feith" (II.597-98) than she sets to work con-
verting the barbarian merchants. This she accomplishes, characteristically, in the course of dealing with them on their own
terms; she first buys "worthily" of them, then teaches them
Christianity (II.604-10). Here and throughout, social acceptance
of Constance is a necessary precondition for religious enlightenment at her hands. In Barbarie her religious influence is never
apparent because she is perceived from the outset as a social
threat. Whereas in Chaucer and Trivet the Sultaness sees her
presence as a spiritual danger, Gower's "Sarazine" fears only
the loss of secular status ("astat" [II.649]) that Constance's marriage to her son would entail. The massacre she engineers is
aimed not at converts to Christianity but at all who have en-
dorsed the marriage (II.685-88), and Gower emphasizes the con-
tamination of the wedding-feast itself, a social sacrament which
is literally "torned into blod": "The dissh forthwith the Coppe
and al / Bebled thei weren overal. . ." (II.698-700). The gro-
tesque use of potentially sacramental imagery provides a measure of the alienation of the culture of Barbarie, not only from
Christianity, but from simply human *pietas*.

By contrast, when Constance sails to England Gower departs
from his source to dwell on the social values of the Northumbrians, whose worth and chivalry according to their lights
prepare a way for her (II.722-27). She gives no sign of her identity or religious role until she has been shown "worschipe" and
drawn into "felaschipe" on purely social terms (II.741-42). In
Chaucer's account the first Northumbrian convert, Hermyngheld, is won by the spectacle of Custance's tearful orisons, one
of several occasions on which "pitee" for her icon-like posturing
gives birth to faith; in Gower the conversion is the result of active but unobtrusive evangelizing, in the context of ordinary domestic intercourse ("spekende alday" [II.752]) between the two
women. The subsequent conversions of Elda and King Allee are

precipitated by their reflection on concrete, miraculous events rather than by any clear manifestation of Christian truth. When Hermyngheld, with a faith "enformed as Constance seith" (II.764), restores the sight of the blind man it is the miracle itself, "this open thing," that induces Elda first to reflect and finally to "obeie" the faith (II.776-78), and to commend Constance herself to the king. Allee, too, is provoked first to thought, then to love, and finally to religion by the report of the blinding of the knight who had accused Constance of the murder of Hermyngheld (II.892-900), an event which in Gower's version becomes a vindication of social justice as well as religion.[11] In every case the influence of Constance manifests itself socially before its religious significance is revealed.

Constance's roles as wife and mother, too, are given a measure of reality by Gower that they do not possess in the Man of Law's version. Her intimacy with Allee is indicated by her apparent involvement in the "lust" and "rage" of wedded love (II. 909-11), and perhaps also by the function of her Saxon name as a sort of code word ("Wherof somdiel smylende he lowh" [II.1404]) between them. Their closeness becomes clearly functional when, playing astutely on her husband's concern to conduct himself at Rome with due worship and honor, she proposes that he feast the Emperor her father (II.1457-62); the conversation occurs--a touch typical of Gower at his best--"as they lihe abedde and spieke" (II.1456). Motherhood, too, becomes important in practical terms at the low point of her career, the moment of her enforced departure from Northumbria, when, having prayed for divine protection, she swoons "as ded" (II.1063). God's aid takes the form of recalling her to a sense of the needs of her child: she is "strengthed for to stonde" (II.1077), and becomes totally absorbed in her maternal duties:[12]

> And tho sche tok hire child in honde
> And yaf it sowke, and evere among
> Sche wepte, and otherwhile song
> To rocke with hire child aslepe:

And thus hire oghne child to kepe
Sche hath under the goddes cure.

(II.1078-83)

Chaucer's tale contains much of the social reality of Gower's, but the Man of Law's strategy is consistently to suppress its implications, and he goes to extraordinary lengths to deny Custance any practical recourse in the face of her woes. At no point is she shown entering willingly into even the most ordinary social relations. From her inital reference to "thraldom and penance" (line 286) marriage is perceived as an intrusion on, even a violation of, her "hoolynesse" (line 713). Like the "fieble moone" whose conjunction with Mars is dominated by the malign influence of the "Crueel firmament" in the Man of Law's strange astrological gloss on her ill-fated first marriage (lines 295, 306-08), she responds to it in a wholly passive manner. Communication with the Northumbrians is inhibited initially both by a language barrier not present in other versions (Trivet's Constaunce, indeed, is at home in Saxon) and by her evasive claim to have "forgotten her mind" while at sea (lines 519-20, 526-27); she is cherished by the Northumbrians, but there is no clear suggestion that she reciprocates their love. The conversions of Hermyngeld and Alla are direct responses to the image of her tearful religiosity, unmediated by any social linkage. At no point is she a part of Northumbrian society. Other interactions, including her climactic reunions with her husband and father, will be fraught with fear and pain.[13]

Not only does Custance get no help from others, but the Man of Law does what he can to underplay her activity on her own behalf. An obvious difficulty is posed by the episode of the attack of the renegade Christian turned rapist, in the face of which some kind of action on Custance's part seems inevitable. Gower's treatment of this moment is characteristically balanced. He attributes the drowning of the intruder to "the mihti goddes hond" (II.1124-25), but only after he has shown Constance taking the initiative on her own behalf, pretending to acquiesce to

the lecher's address and persuading him to peer out at a porthole
and make certain that they are alone; there is room for at least
the speculation that she is inspired by God to give the sinner a
little push of her own. The Man of Law acknowledges that Custance struggled hard, and that the lecher fell overboard as a result (line 922). But the single line which records her stuggle is
surrounded by references to her "pitous" tears and the intervention of Christ and blissful Mary, and followed by three stanzas
at top volume, condemning lechery and affirming God's power
to aid the weak. Here as so often rhetorical elaboration seems
intended as much to dwarf Custance and her powers as to
celebrate the power of God.

Custance's inactivity is stressed again in the Man of Law's
treatment of the role played by her son Maurice in awakening her
memory in the minds of Alla and the Emperor. In the face of the
clear declaration of Trivet, who is followed by Gower, he refuses
to acknowledge that Custance could have deployed Maurice on
her own behalf, and when the child somehow appears at Alla's
feast he simply "stands" before his father to let himself be be-
held, reflecting in his posture the wholly passive exemplarity of
Custance herself (lines 1014-15). He is present again when Alla
visits the Emperor, though again the Man of Law will not admit
that this reflects any conscious purpose. In the apparent absence
of human agency his function is as nearly as possible that of a
symbol, rather than a link between Custance and the human
community.

The evasion or suppression of normal human relations in the
Man of Law's Tale and the importance of such relations in
Gower's narrative appear most strikingly in their very different
approaches to the element of pathos inherent in the Constance
story. Gower seems to go out of his way to avoid the pathetic.
There is no trace of the elaborate sorrow of Chaucer's Custance
when she first appears, reproaching her parents and resigning
herself to the thralldom and penance that are the lot of married
women (lines 275-87). Where Chaucer's heroine, on arriving in

Northumbria, first begs for death, then persists in her sorrow even after being accepted into the constable's household, Gower's experiences only an initial regret that the land is not Christian (II.744-46). In Gower, Constance's sorrowful moments are consistently those at which she is faced with situations rendered impossible in practical terms by clear manifestations of intractable human wickedness. He apologizes for her terror ("No wonder thogh sche wepte and cride" [II.702]) at the spectacle of the Sultaness's bloody feast; he allows her to swoon "ded for fere" when she is awakened by Elda's horrified cry to discover the bloody corpse of Hermyngheld (II.846), and again when she is on the point of being banished through the contrivance of Domilde (II.1062-63); and she makes an understandable attempt to hide when she finds her vessel drifting amid the vast Roman navy (II.1141-43). (Custance in the same situation "sit ful pitously" awaiting her fate [line 970].) Otherwise, apart from a persistent refusal to fully identify herself, she is unwavering and resourceful.

The extreme and bizarre pathos of the Man of Law's performance is its most remarkable feature. His heroine bathes in "pitee" at every opportunity, and at times this quality seems to be diffused at random. The forged letter ordering Custance's banishment from Northumbria is "pitous" (line 809), apparently because of the pathetic light in which it will allow the Man of Law to cast his heroine; even her show of maternal concern at the time of her departure from Northumbria has the effect of reducing her child to a prop for the purpose of allowing her to be compared, with elaborate poignancy, to the mother of God.[14] And when, having overcome her fear of new exile, she is reunited at last with her father, they experience a "pitous joye" (line 1114).

The Man of Law's indulgence in the pathetic reaches its high point in the elaborate trial scene, where the heroine is first shown out of her wits with terror, then with the "pale face" of one sentenced to death. The scene is wholly Chaucer's invention, intended by the Man of Law to dramatize Custance's help-lessness, but oddly self-contradictory in its attempt to do so. The Man of Law insists strenuously on the absence of any human witness on her behalf. The point of the episode, indeed, seems to be to deny the possibility of any good befalling the "sely inno-cent" through human agency:

> An Emperoures doghter stant allone;
> She hath no wight to whom to make hir mone.
> O blood roial, that stondest in this drede,
> Fer been thy freendes at thy grete nede!

> (lines 655-58)

But this stress on Custance's isolation is hard to reconcile with the description of the trial: popular sentiment on her behalf is so strong as to be taken seriously by Alla (lines 621-30), and he is already strongly disposed in her favor before the confirming miracle occurs. His behavior is so compassionate as to render utterly gratuitous the comparison of Custance, as she stands be-fore him, to a lamb being led to the slaughter (lines 617-18), and, when the narration of his scrupulous and humane conduct of the trial is juxtaposed with the elaborate portrayal of Cus-tance herself, centering on the famous "pale face" stanza (lines 645-51), it is as if we were listening to two separate stories. That Custance's role as the passive catalyst of violent emotion should be given such scope at a moment when her situation is in the process of being stabilized by institutional means points up the fundamental division in the Man of Law's attitude toward his story. It allows us to distinguish his ostensible, public role as a man of law and religion, celebrating the triumph of missionary Christianity, from a private design born of desperate anxiety in which his treatment of his heroine is so radically possessive, so exclusive of normal social intercourse, and so repressive of autonomous feeling that it amounts, as I have suggested, to something like incest.

A further confirmation of this palpable design is the radical contrast between the utter selflessness of Custance and the roles of her two feminine antagonists, the Sultaness of Surrye and Donegild, mother of Alla. Inescapably the villains in the story, these women evoke the Man of Law's most strenuous moral condemnation, but he also brings them powerfully and impressively to life, apparently in spite of himself. Thus while he inveighs against the mother of the Sultan as a "welle of vices" (line 323), whose femininity conceals a serpent in the service of Satan (lines 360-61), he simultaneously allows her both a compelling eloquence and serious arguments in defense of her religion. In contrast to the selfish motives of Gower's Sarazine, her scorn for the institutions of Christianity is real ("coold water shal nat greve us but a lite!" [line 352]), and there is real nobility in the speech with which she arouses her loyal followers to a kind of anti-crusade:

> What sholde us tyden of this newe lawe
> But thraldom to oure bodies and penance,
> And afterward in helle to be drawe,
> For we reneyed Mahoun oure creance?
>
> (lines 337-40)

Custance herself had complained to no avail of the "thraldom and penance" which are the lot of women (line 286), and it is difficult not to sympathize with the Sowdanesse in her repudiation of any passive acceptance of such a condition. By rendering her motivation so vividly, the Man of Law inevitably weakens the force of his own condemnatory eloquence.

The portrayal of Donegild reveals a similar tension between normal human motivation and a superimposed moral perspective. It is a basic weakness of the source-narrative that the role of Alla's mother largely duplicates that played by the mother of the Sultan, and Trivet had compounded the problem by endowing her with identical motives.[15] Chaucer plausibly imputes her behavior to a strong sense of insult at her son's marriage to a foreigner, in a passage in which the arbitrary intrusion of the single word "cursed" is the only moralizing note:

> Hir thoughte hir cursed herte brast atwo.
> She wolde noght hir sone had do so;
> Hir thoughte a despit that he sholde take
> So strange a creature unto his make.

(lines 697-700)

The narration of the exposure and punishment of Donegild's treason occupies a single stanza which acknowledges only the bare fact of Alla's agency in her death, and ends with the perfunctory comment, "Thus endeth olde Donegild, with meschance" (lines 890-96). The unemphatic, rather grudging report is in marked contrast to the elaborate invective of the earlier stanza that conveys the Man of Law's own condemnation of Donegild, whose "feendlych spirit" he professes himself incapable of representing (lines 778-84). As in his treatment of the Soldanesse, the disjunction between the effect of his narration and the moral he seeks to associate with it points up the arbitrariness of his moral stance. And his insistence on the "mannysh" and serpentine reality cloaked by the outward femininity of these women suggests that precisely their unwomanliness, their refusal to remain submissive in the face of thralldom or rejection, is the real focus of his moralizing. They are not really women at all, but vessels whose femininity has been appropriated by demonic agents. As such they pose a threat, not only to Custance, but to the Man of Law himself, representing as they do a dynamic, self-willed alternative to the wholly passive Custance, whom he can manipulate as he pleases and who constitutes womanhood as he wishes it to be. That both of these violently possessive mothers are to some extent spokeswomen for their cultures in their hostility to Custance points up by contrast the absence of social or religious purpose in the Man of Law's anxious shepherding of his heroine.

Custance's reunion with her father brings the Man of Law's private design to its appropriate culmination. Here again it is useful to compare his narration with Gower's. Where Gower makes the reunion the occasion for a beautifully measured unveiling of the meaning implicit in Constance's life throughout the story, for the Man of Law it is a private experience through which Custance gradually withdraws from the world. Describing the reunion of Alla and Custance, the Man of Law stresses the slow purging of Custance's fear and sorrow at the memory of Alla's earlier "unkyndenesse" (line 1057), and their reconciliation is reduced to little more than a step in the process of her reunion with her father the Emperor (lines 1075-83). Gower, in a rare departure from his customary decorum, is almost melodramatic in stressing the state of purgatorial anticipation in which Allee, having recognized Moris, awaits his meeting with Constance (II.1422-25), and the interval during which the couple recover conjugal intimacy is itself an episode of the story. Gower's Allee has recovered "the confort of his lond" (line 1562), his queen in the fullest and highest sense,

> Which ferst was sent of goddes sonde,
> Whan sche was drive upon the Stronde,
> Be whom the misbelieve of Sinne
> Was left, and Cristes feith cam inne
> To hem that whilom were blinde.
>
> (II.1567-71)

This first explicit confirmation of Constance's missionary role prepares us for the account of her return to Rome, where her father the Emperor dies in her arms, she herself is reclaimed by God from "this worldes faierie," and the empire descends to Moris, "the cristeneste of alle" (II.1593, 1598).

In these final forty lines Constance is effectively identified with the Church itself, and this new explicitness confirms the intuitive sense of her larger meaning that various characters have experienced in the course of the story. Charged with the duty of banishing Constance from Northumberland, Elda and Bishop Lucius feel as though they were being made to witness the death by fire of their own mother (II.1047-48), and the Emperor's wonder at recognizing her is compared to what he would feel if his mother were to emerge living from the grave (II.1524-27). For all of these figures Constance's "motherhood" symbolizes her role as a mediator of spiritual weal. And in her ministry to her dying father we can see that ideal relation between spiritual and temporal authority which it is one of the major projects of the *Confessio Amantis* to illustrate. The ideal is realized in the life of her child, Moris, wholly "abandoned" to the service of religion in a world prepared by his mother's militant faith (II.1596-97).

In the very different conclusion of the Man of Law's narrative the end of Custance's life appears as a gradual escape. After a brief reference to Maurice as emperor-to-be, the Man of Law reports her return with Alla to England, and a single line is devoted to their last happy year (line 1131). Then follows a long reflection on the brevity of earthly joys. The obvious occasion for this last is the death of Alla, which, however, is not announced until the Man of Law has given us this rather puzzling stanza, apparently intended as a reflection on the event:

> Who lyved euere in swich delit o day
> That hym ne moeved outher conscience,
> Or ire, or talent, or som kynnes affray,
> Envye, or pride, or passion, or offence?
> I ne seye but for this ende this sentence,
> That litel while in joye or in plesance
> Lasteth the blisse of Alla with Custance.

(lines 1135-41)

The Man of Law raises these questions only to dismiss them, and he never explains their bearing on either the marriage of Custance and Alla or the death of the latter. But, when encountered in the midst of a homily on the brevity of earthly joy, the passage is bound to create the impression that ire, envy, or some other source of "affray," rather than the normal course of nature, was the cause of the couple's separation. The passage just quoted is at one with earlier and equally irrelevant mutterings over marriage (lines 270-73, 710-14), a final expression of the Man of Law's obsessive anxiety about human relations.

The passage also marks Custance's final release to return to Rome. There, after a last burst of tears on being reunited with her father once and for all, in the final stanza of the tale she at last enters willingly into human fellowship, in a community where familial, social, and religious bonds are identical and absolute:

> In vertu and in hooly almus-dede
> They lyven alle, and nevere asonder wende;
> Til deeth departeth hem, this lyf they lede.
>
> (lines 1156-58)

But the uniting of Custance with family and friends is really a kind of merging, in the course of which she becomes indistinguishable from them. The Man of Law has preserved Custance through the course of her story immune to worldly accident, but he has done so largely by denying her a normal social existence; and his final gesture, the price of surrendering her to her father, is to rob her of her individual identity once and for all. Gower's Constance rises at last to become in effect the Church itself, but Chaucer's heroine flees the world without transcending it and ends by becoming simply invisible. Even the death which intrudes on her final communal life is wholly unspecified, a "departing" which seems to affect Custance only as one component of a collective organism. "Now is she scaped al hire aventure," the Man of Law proclaims (line 1151), and in the end she is allowed to escape invisibly from the story itself.

Considered as a literary performance, the Man of Law's Tale is a double failure, a betrayal of both the hagiographic and the romantic purposes of its source. Critics who stress its spiritual character are responding to something inherent in the story, but something the Man of Law's narration tends to dissipate or even suppress. It is Gower whose narrative conveys the energy of a primitive, missionary Christianity, while Chaucer, far from dramatizing "the austerity and conviction of the early Church,"[16] has created an elaborate anachronism, relocating the simple "historical" narrative of Trivet in a never-never land of pseudo-religious sentiment. Custance never comes into her own as an image of faith or constancy, and the real significance of the narrative centers in the strange combination of pietism and obsession that marks the Man of Law's attachment to his heroine.

The tale is equally unsuccessful as romance, rendered effectively stillborn on the level of social reality by the Man of Law's inability to allow his heroine to experience the world. Romance is properly a vehicle for testing the integrity of social institutions, of culture itself as a means of regulating and mediating human relations, and it is clear that the Man of Law has remarkably little faith in such mediation. Social justice appears almost exclusively in the violent deaths of Custance's accusors, and nowhere is there a trace of the sort of confidence that the Knight, for example, accords to the social order centered in Theseus.

But despite the completeness of the Man of Law's repudiation of the social norms proper to romance, they remain highly relevant to his performance. We may compare his tale with Boccaccio's story of the Babylonian princess Alatiel,[17] a narrative whose plot overtly mocks the governing power of social institutions by a *reductio ad absurdum* of conventional romance, and thus realizes the Man of Law's worst fears about the world. Shipwrecked while on her way to marry the king of Algarve, the beautiful Alatiel is possessed sexually by nine different men before being restored to her father. In the interval, like Custance, she is wholly cut off from her culture and its resources. Her initial seduction is brought about by drink, of which under Islamic law she has had no previous experience, and often in subsequent encounters the barrier of language prevents verbal communication with her lovers.

Like Custance, Alatiel is often the cause of violence in

others, and while it approaches her very closely, she remains, like Custance, immune to its effects. As Custance emerges tearful but unscathed from the bloody Syrian wedding-feast and the stratagems of Donegild, so Alatiel survives such moments as that in which the duke of Athens, having just murdered her previous lover, throws himself on her naked body while his hands are still covered with the blood of his predecessor. In the absence of cultural norms her sexual attractiveness assumes a magical power of protection and mediation that corresponds closely to that of the pathos-inducing piety of Custance. And as Custance in the end "escapes" her worldly experience to the haven of Rome, so Alatiel is finally restored to her father the Sultan, who marries her to her originally intended husband as if she were still a virgin. In both tales the exclusion of social reality and cultural values allows the fantasy element of romance to assume an extraordinary dominance, and the comparison sets off the peculiar workings of the Man of Law's narration. If Alatiel's story is the fantasy *par excellence* of innocent promiscuity, the anxious possessiveness of the Man of Law, which seeks to exclude the world itself from his narrative while imposing on the will and desire of his heroine a "providential" design that inevitably draws her home to her father in the end, exposes his tale as a disguised fantasy of incest.

This incestuous tendency in the tale corresponds to certain aspects of the Man of Law's social and professional role in the world of the *Canterbury Tales*, a role characterized by a similarly oblique and covertly subversive relation to cultural institutions which appears even in the way he defines his relation to the tale itself. He tells us that he learned his story from a merchant, and his Prologue commends merchants in general as wise and prudent men, widely travelled and thus in close touch with political shifts ("th'estaat / Of regnes" [lines 128-29]) and wars and rumors of wars ("tales, bothe of pees and of debaat" [line 130]). This knowledge enables them to trade well, avoid risk, and assure themselves of a secure existence (lines 123-26). The merchants within the story are in close touch with world politics and apparently serve as a sort of intelligence service for the Sultan, bringing him "tidynges of sondry regnes" (line 181). They also enjoy good relations with Rome. But their relation to the world is curiously hard to define: they keep themselves at a distance from political and religious issues, and their concerns are wholly private. Their purpose in coming to Rome is uncertain ("Were it for chapmanhod or for disport" [line 143]), though it seems clear that while there they trade extensively and successfully. They are commended as "sadde and trewe" (line 135), and are able to transmit an "earnest" and precise account of the excellences of Custance (lines 184-85), yet there is no indication that they themselves are affected by these tidings, which elicit so powerful a response from the Sultan, or even by the sight of Custance herself. Having seen her, they simply proceed about their business, setting sail with a fresh cargo for Surrye, where they continue to conduct their affairs "as they han doon yoore," and to live "in wele" (lines 174-75). In effect their tidings of Custance are just another item of the "chaffare" with which they habitually travel, and they bring this item forth only "amonges othere thynges" (line 183) in the course of their normal dealings with the Sultan. Having done so, they disappear from the story.

The antithesis to this self-regarding detachment is the behavior of the Sultan. His response to the "figure" of Custance, even at second hand, is to devote "al his lust and al his bisy cure" to love of her (lines 186-89), a radically subjective impulse with momentous political consequences (lines 233-38). The linkage between the merchants, who traffic in world affairs as an aspect of commerce while preserving a prudent detachment, and the Sultan, whose private passion provides the impetus for a world-transforming religious event, is significant. Neither merchant nor Sultan is concerned with the true meaning of Custance, and the collaboration between the former's "tidings" and the latter's desire is wholly unmediated by social or religious institutions. The merchants perhaps have no real culture. For them politics, religion, human virtue are only commercial resources to be deployed in the interest of maintaining good relations with prospective customers. The Sultan, properly the embodiment of Islamic law, is all too ready to betray his traditions in the interest of his wholly ungoverned need "to get" Custance (line 230), and literally shapes the world to his desire. The interaction of the two determines the fate of Custance. Though her proper function is as an agent of cultural transformation, she is excluded from ordinary social intercourse and relegated to the status, first, of an object of commerce, then of an essentially "strange" being who moves through the world as if under a curse, generating social conflict in spite of herself.

The collaboration between merchants and Sultan that launches Custance on her strange career is an image of the curious dual relation of the Man of Law to the tale itself, an empty commitment to its "official" significance that coexists uneasily with an intense engagement born of private, largely unfocussed need. The story exists to convey a message: Custance is an apostle to the English and mother of a Christian emperor, as it were, in spite of herself. But as the merchants promulgate Custance's "image" while remaining unaffected by it, the Man of Law pays lip-service to the story's affirmative message and at the same time, like the Sultan, infuses his tale with motives that contradict this message, evading the channels of normal cultural mediation to make Custance the object of his own possessive design.

The unwieldy combination of public and private motives in the Man of Law's performance expresses the dilemma of one of Chaucer's "new men."[18] His status in the social hierarchy is beyond question, but his prominence and affluence are also to a great extent a function of the needs of a changing society. Hence he feels compelled to assert and justify them, seeking to impress both by demonstrating legal, financial, and verbal skill and by presenting impeccable credentials. Beneath this surface lurks the impulse of self-aggrandizement that has led him to use his office

85

and knowledge for the purpose of the "purchasyng" noted in the General Prologue (lines 318-20). In his strenuous assertions of the power of God's providence to protect the weak and undo the effects of human injustice there are signs of a certain ambivalence about the combination of vested authority and material power that define his relation to his society, and perhaps also hints of a less conscious need for some sure belief beyond the certainties of wealth and worldly knowledge that he shares with the merchants who are his familiars. But his will to believe is stunted: whatever genuine piety is present in his performance is not strong enough to offset its spurious religiosity, a manipulation of sentiment that amounts to bad faith. Such a man, Chaucer suggests, may not fully know his own motives; his covetous impulses and the power that gratifies them can coexist, in his mind as in the rhetoric of his tale, with the officious sense of duty and high principle proper to his station. He is at once committed to an authoritarian view of life and better able than any of the pilgrims to appreciate the ease with which authority can be abused, a knowledge and a power which he both desires and fears.

This largely uncontrolled and covertly exploitative relation to moral and social authority is first revealed in the combination of fascination and repulsion with which the Man of Law responds to Gower's tales of incest. Both of the tales he evokes contain elements which mirror his own ambivalence. The tale of Canacee is a powerful exemplum of the horror of unmediated desire, but the violence with which Aeolus responds to the discovery of his daughter's incest by compelling her to suicide has strong incestuous overtones of its own. Like the pious tyranny of Virginius in the Physician's Tale, who feels his heart "stabbed" by paternal pity, yet persists in his exercise of paternal authority over one whose only recourse is to throw her arms around his neck, it reduces her to a mirror of his own distorted feelings. And Aeolus's extension of this violence to her child, whom he causes to be abandoned, is a further indication of his need to confine her within the sphere of his own desire, like the Man of Law's attempts to minimize the role of Maurice in the life of Custance.

The story of Apollonius, too, deals openly with the fact of incest at the outset, only to have it reenter as a covert element in the subsequent narrative. Apollonius exposes Antiochus's guilty relations with his daughter, but then, toward the close of his long wandering, unwittingly encounters his own long-lost daughter in a scene which deliberately evokes the dark guilt of Antiochus, and harbors the potential horror of those antecedents of the Constance story in which a royal heroine is driven into exile by the incestuous designs of her father.[19] Here, however, the implicit threat is neutralized by the essential integrity of the social values of the characters, and the encounter becomes Gower's climactic illustration of the role of culture in sustaining and vindicating "the wel meninge of love."

The crucial figure in the story is not Apollonius himself but his daughter, Thais, a Constance-figure in her own right. Her mother having apparently died in giving birth to her, Thais is gently reared and educated by foster parents until her brilliance arouses the envy of her foster mother, who arranges to have her murdered. Abducted to a deserted seacoast, she persuades her executioner to allow her a final prayer. As she prays, pirates appear and bear her away to be sold into prostitution at Mytelene. There her beauty attracts many clients, but all are rendered impotent to ravish her by the spectacle of her deep sorrow. She soon convinces the brothel-master that she can make him more money by keeping a school for young gentlewomen, which she does with great success.

As Apollonius, supposing Thais to be dead, is sailing despondently home to Tyre, he is driven by a storm to Mytelene. There he broods in the darkness of his cabin, refusing to acknowledge the good wishes of the lord of the city, until the renowned teacher Thais is summoned to "glad" him by her skill in the arts of music and language. In the dark cabin, unaware of her father's identity and unrecognized by him, she sings and tells stories, which elicit no response, and finally poses to him a series of subtle problems which arouse his interest but to which he again refuses to respond. When she persists, Apollonius, weeping and tossing his head like a mad man, angrily orders her away; but she still persists, bringing the episode to its crisis:

> And in the derke forth she goth,
> Til sche him toucheth, and he wroth,
> And after hire with his hond
> He smot: and thus whan sche him fond
> Desesed, courtaisly sche saide,
> "Avoi, mi lord, I am a Maide,
> And if ye wiste what I am,
> And out of what lignage I cam,
> Ye wolde noght be so salvage."
>
> (VIII.1691-99)

The confidence with which Thais continues to probe Apollonius's sorrow despite his angry reaction is a measure of the extent to which she is, in Genius's phrase, "wel grounded" (VIII. 1993). Sustained by her social values, and by the various arts which she deploys with such skill and resourcefulness, she is in effect the agent of courtly culture itself, the embodiment of a *gentilesse* which remains magnanimous and actively humane even in the face of potential violence. The critical significance of her confrontation with Apollonius is enhanced by its obvious recollection of the event which is the ultimate cause of Apollonius's long exile, the hidden relationship of Antiochus and his daughter. Thais's puzzling questions to Apollonius recall the riddle by which Antiochus had disguised his incest and confounded his daughter's suitors until Apollonius discovered the truth. The darkness of the cabin, the anonymity of father and daughter, the intimacy that threatens to issue in violence, all recall the horror of the rape itself. But Thais's clearsighted and "courtais" response to Apollonius's "desese" symbolically undoes the sin of Antiochus: private feeling and natural attachment are mediated by her affirmation of civilized values, and culture confirms "kynde":

> Non wiste of other hou it stod,
> And yit the fader ate laste
> His herte upon this maide caste,
> That he hire loveth kindely,
> And yit he wiste nevere why.
> Bot al was knowe er that thei wente;
> For god, which wot here hol entente,
> Here hertes bothe anon descloseth.
>
> (VIII.1704-11)

Apollonius's response to Thais closely echoes that of Allee when confronted with his exiled son Moris in Gower's tale of Constance (II.1381-82), and Thais in effect combines the function of Moris with that of Constance herself. The tale of Apollonius and the active role of Thais within it can be seen as reiterating the point of the Constance story in its social aspect. Her embodiment of the *gentilesse* of courtly society at its best provides a focus for Apollonius's "entente" as Constance's social instincts render those who love her responsive to her spiritual influence.

But in providing a broader context for the opposition between Gower's tale of Constance and Chaucer's Man of Law's Tale, and as Gower's clearest expression of a cultural ideal of which Constance is one of many earlier embodiments, the Apollonius-Thais story also points to a fundamental opposition between Gower's poem and Chaucer's. The tendency of the *Confessio* is always normative and conservative.[20] The Gower who in earlier works had inveighed like the Man of Law himself against social evils seeks in this poem to provide a gentler corrective, and shows himself much more willing than Chaucer to offer traditional social values and obligations as an antidote to the evils that concern them both. Genius's tales aim to inculcate a sense of the compatibility of "kynde" with the values of courtly-chivalric culture, and while the remedies they offer are limited in their efficacy--Gower tells no tale of an Antiochus transformed into an Apollonius--they assume that traditional culture is alive and valuable.

The *Canterbury Tales* dramatizes the problems of a society in flux in a more radical way. The Man of Law is only one of the more desperate of a social group for whom the telling of a tale is an occasion for seeking to position themselves in a world where traditional roles and values have apparently lost their authority. Chaucer's invocation of Gower at a point in his own poem when the question of the value and proper orientation of serious fiction is very much at issue is strong evidence of his respect for his friend's poetry, and suggests that he was capable of discovering in it the kind of stabilizing design he found in the poetry of Jean de Meun, Dante, or Boccaccio. But it is unlikely that he saw Gower's more affirmative social vision, with its faith in the public value of private virtue, as in itself a viable corrective to the world view he imputes to the Man of Law. Like the appeal to the "courtesy" of an implied audience which concludes the narrator's presentation of the pilgrims in the General Prologue, or the Knight's attempt to affirm the ideals of chivalry in the face of their inadequacy to sustain the order of the world of Theseus, the proffering of Gower's poetry as a foil to the desperate venture of the Man of Law seems to acknowledge a loss of control, to ask of us that we take responsibility for the preservation of a decorum the poet-narrator has been forced to abandon. The failure of the narrator of the General Prologue is elaborately dramatized as a failure of innocence; the Knight's is arguably the failure of one who has remained true to an obsolescent ideal; but the failure of the Man of Law is a failure of worldliness, a product of his knowledge of the nature of power and his own designs on it that expresses as effectively as the self-revelations of any pilgrim the dislocation of the social world of Chaucer's poem.[21]

NOTES

[1]Hope Phyllis Weissman, "Late Gothic Pathos in *The Man of Law's Tale*," *Journal of Medieval and Renaissance Studies*, 9 (1979), 133-53.

[2]V. A. Kolve, *Chaucer and the Imagery of Narrative. The First Five Canterbury Tales* (Stanford, 1984), pp. 297-300.

[3]Derek Pearsall, *The Canterbury Tales* (London, 1985), p. 259, declines to address the problem of continuity at all on purely practical grounds, and suggests treating the tale as if it were an independent poem. Kolve (pp. 294, 477-78 n. 77) suggests that headlink and Prologue represent two separate introductions to the tale and were never intended to appear together.

[4]The *Confessio Amantis* was substantially completed by 1390, and I assume the chronological priority of Gower's Constance story to at least the version we possess of Chaucer's. See the introduction to Patricia J. Eberle's explanatory notes on the Man of Law's Tale in *The Riverside Chaucer*, 3rd ed., general editor Larry D. Benson (Boston, 1987), pp. 854, 856-57, and her note on lines 77-89, p. 856; Margaret Schlauch, *Chaucer's Constance and the Accused Queens* (New York, 1927), pp. 132-34; Edward A. Block, "Originality, Controlling Purpose, and Craftsmanship in Chaucer's *Man of Law's Tale*," *PMLA*, 68 (1953), 600-02; Donald R. Howard, *Chaucer, his life, his works, his world* (New York, 1987), pp. 418-20.

The Man of Law's two references to how "Som men" have represented the role of Maurice (lines 1009-10, 1086-87) correspond much more closely to Gower's version than to Trivet's: Gower's Moris, like Chaucer's Maurice, is still a "child" (*Confessio Amantis* II.1381, 1386; MLT, lines 1010, 1086, etc.), whereas Trivet's Morice has entered his eighteenth year (*Chronicle*, ed. Margaret Schlauch, in *Sources and Analogues of Chaucer's Canterbury Tales*, ed. W. F. Bryan and Germaine Dempster [New York, 1941], p. 179); in Trivet Morice's presence at Alle's feast is taken for granted, whereas Gower makes plain Constance's agency in sending him (II.1364-69; compare MLT, lines 1009-10); and in Trivet it is Constaunce who entrusts Morice with the invitation to the Emperor (p. 180), whereas the Man of Law complains of a version in which, as in Gower's, he is commissioned by Allee (II.479-80; compare MLT, 1088-92).

[5]A list of such "mistakes" is offered by Rodney Delasanta, "And of Great Reverence: Chaucer's Man of Law," *Chaucer Review*, 5 (1970-71), 291-97. Quotations from the *Canterbury Tales* are from *The Riverside Chaucer*.

[6]Alfred David, "The Man of Law vs. Chaucer: A Case in Poetics,"

PMLA, 82 (1967), 220-21.

[7]Quotations from the *Confessio Amantis* are based on *The English Works of John Gower*, ed. G. C. Macaulay, 2 vols., EETS, e.s. 81-82 (Oxford, 1900-01).

[8]It is the presence of such details as these that leads me to disagree with the reading of this tale by C. David Benson, "Incest and Moral Poetry in Gower's *Confessio Amantis*," *Chaucer Review*, 19 (1984-85), 100-10, itself a valuable corrective to earlier readings.

[9]On the incest theme in the story see Schlauch, *Sources and Analogues*, pp. 156-57, 160; and the very full account in her *Chaucer's Constance and the Accused Queens*.

[10]Pearsall, pp. 258-63; Kolve, pp. 297-98; Helen Cooper, *The Structure of the Canterbury Tales* (London, 1983), pp. 122-23.

[11]Gower stresses the force and vividness rather than the doctrinal content of the divine intervention that exonerates Constance of the murder of Hermyngheld. He substitutes the more portentous "hond of hevene" (line 874) for the visible fist which rabbit-punches the false knight in Trivet's version, but the divine voice, which in Trivet and Chaucer protests in biblical language at an affront to the Church, is in Gower's version directed specifically at perjury and slander against Constance.

[12]For a very different reading of this scene see Weissman, pp. 148-49, who finds Gower's Constance more simply pathetic than Chaucer's, and wholly lacking in the fortitude of Trivet's.

[13]See Sheila Delany, *Writing Woman* (New York, 1983), pp. 37-43.

[14]See Weissman, pp. 149-53; Delany, p. 43.

[15]Both women see Constaunce as a threat to the custom or "law" of their society: the Sultaness is moved to treason "veaunte que sa ley estoit ia en poynt destre destrute par Cristiens" (*Sources and Analogues*, p. 167), and Doumilde is angered that Alle has come to love a "strange" woman, "sa primere ley gwerpi, quele touz ses auncestres auoient leaulment e enterement gardes" (*Sources and Analogues*, p. 172).

[16]Kolve, p. 297.

[17]*Decameron* 2.7.

[18]On this aspect of the pilgrim company see Anne Middleton, "Chaucer's 'New Men' and the Good of Literature in the *Canterbury Tales*," in *Literature and Society: Selected Papers from the English Institute, 1978*, n.s. 3, ed. Edward W. Said (Baltimore and London, 1980), pp. 15-18.

[19]See Schlauch, *Chaucer's Constance and the Accused Queens*, esp. pp. 35-47, 64-74.

[20]See Paul Strohm, "Form and Social Statement in *Confessio Amantis* and the *Canterbury Tales*," *Studies in the Age of Chaucer*, 1 (1979), 19-40.

[21]This essay is dedicated to the memory of Judson Boyce Allen.

GOWER, CHAUCER, AND THE CLASSICS: BACK TO THE TEXTUAL EVIDENCE

Götz Schmitz

I

Most of the knowledge medieval authors had of what we call the classics was limited and secondhand. There are many reasons for this: the scarcity of texts, the lack of competence in the ancient languages, and--not least--the fact that the notion of "the classics" in the sense of a set of standard Greek and Latin writers of antiquity is a fairly recent coinage. In England, it was not used in this sense before the seventeenth century, and was inflated to its present value only in the eighteenth.[1] For its modern meaning the Middle Ages lacked both critical and historical sense; what comparable terms they had (e.g., *veteres* or *antiqui*) were used to cover pagan and Christian authors indiscriminately, as even a casual glance at one of the contemporary lists or catalogues will prove.[2] Some of the writers canonized as school authors or invoked as authorities entered the lists on the strength of their names or obscure adaptations of their works only. The latter applies in particular to the Greek: at best, Chaucer knew "the gret Omer" he mentions in his *House of Fame* (1466) from Simon Aurea Capra's *Ilias latina*;[3] the "Philosophre" who presides over the seventh book, if not the whole, of Gower's *Confessio Amantis* is Aristotle as expounded by Brunetto Latini in *Li Livres dou Tresor*. With authors like

Homer and Aristotle this comes as no surprise because we know the Greek of Ricardian writers to have been less than Shakespeare's, but was their Latin really more than small?

In general, critics tend to assume that authors such as Chaucer and Gower were familiar with the Latin language and its masters. Chaucer, after all, translated the whole of Boethius's *Consolatio Philosophiae* and bits and pieces from Virgil and Ovid besides, and Gower wrote one of his major poems in a Latin dripping with phrases from classical works. It seems only natural to imagine them, as William Connely does with Chaucer and his *Legend of Good Women*, scribbling away at their poems with a Latin model literally at their fingertips: "So there sits Chaucer, left forefinger running down the pages of Publius Ovidius Naso, right hand busy with his own manuscript."[4] The recent surge of interest in *Chaucer and Pagan Antiquity* (to name but one, and the most thorough, book-length study of the matter of Greece and Rome, by Alastair Minnis)[5] has not led to a substantial revision of this picture--not, that is, as far as the most prominent Latin classics, Virgil and Ovid, are concerned.[6] As T. R. Lounsbury wrote about "Chaucer's Learning" as early as 1892: "There are two great classic authors with whom not merely Chaucer's acquaintance, but also the intimacy of his acquaintance, cannot be disputed. These are Virgil and Ovid."[7]

On the whole, Lounsbury's conclusion has indeed stood undisputed, at least as far as literary criticism is concerned. John M. Fyler, author of the book *Chaucer and Ovid* (New Haven, 1979), takes Chaucer's intimate acquaintance with all of Ovid's writings for granted and does not bother about the textual side of their relationship at all. Such reticence, if not simply thoughtless, may be based on the assumption that the philological ground has been cleared and we are free to build our critical constructs on it. It is certainly supported by the fact that most of us have less Latin than critics used to have and that, spoiled as we are by modern critical editions (if not translations) of the classics, we feel ill prepared for the sort of groundwork our positivist forbears did. I have become suspicious of this comfortable attitude for reasons which I shall presently give and, once alerted to its dangers, have realized that it grew with the distance that developed between scholars and critics in the course of this century. There have been warnings and misgivings about this attitude. In fact, the closer the scholars looked at the textual evidence for the transmission of classical texts to the later Middle Ages the more cautious their assessments tended to be, even with regard to such standard authors as Virgil and Ovid. "It is somewhat remarkable that more lines and phrases of Virgil do not appear in Chaucer," Dorothy Hammond wondered in 1908.[8] In 1974, Bruce Harbert, having examined a composite Latin manuscript which may have been available to Chaucer, concluded: "The extent of his classical knowledge has, I believe, been overestimated."[9] It is time, I think, that critics reconsider their position in the light of such evidence.

Being more of a critic than a scholar myself, I based my earlier work on Chaucer and Gower on some of the same assumptions I would question now. In my book on the *Confessio Amantis* I traced Gower's plain style to Aristotle's *Ars rhetorica*, and some of his tales to Ovid's *Metamorphoses*, giving little thought to the fact that in both cases he made use of French translations.[10] In a more recent study of "Complaints by Unfortunate Women" I went straight back to classical models again, trying to establish an elegaic mode of telling a story: to distinguish it from the epic, I chose as an example Ovid's reshaping of Virgil's Dido episode in the seventh letter of his *Heroides*. I then followed this narrative mode through the Middle Ages and the English Renaissance and, of course, did not miss the opportunity of including Gower's and Chaucer's treatments of heroines like Dido.[11] They both show a predilection for the elegaic mode and the concomitant plain and passionate style, and this is no doubt due to the overwhelming influence that Ovid, and in particular his elegaic writings, had on the later Middle Ages.

This predilection in itself is somewhat surprising if one

bears in mind that most critics (and some scholars) would give pride of place to Virgil if asked to name the most important and most influential Latin poet and would certainly prefer his serious version of the Dido story--the only Roman tragedy, as it has been called by Friedrich Leo[12]--to the juggling manner of Ovid. Gower and Chaucer, however, apparently never doubt Ovid's authority in what we would call the woman question and take his treatment of stories like Dido's straight. They both were, as we know, easily affected by the plight of maids and wives forlorn--with regard to Chaucer, this was pointed out as early as about 1500 by Gavin Douglas; with respect to Gower, as recently as 1966 in Derek Pearsall's article, "Gower's Narrative Art."[13] Both poets adopt Dido's point of view wholeheartedly, and both are, I believe, sincere in retelling it along Ovidian lines, but without his sidesteps.[14] There is none of Ovid's equivocal, highhanded dealing with his heroine, and no trace of what Charles Martindale has called "the knowing Ovidian innuendo."[15] They either missed or omitted a great many of the subtleties of Ovid's style, not least his ironies with their terrible and on occasion tasteless connotations. Much of this may be due to misunderstandings resulting from either deficient learning or deficient texts. The overall effect of their plain view of history is scarcely less deflating than the irony which brought Ovid into disgrace, if not into exile. To a great extent this is a matter of perspective. The fall of Troy and the founding of Rome take on a different coloring if looked at from the point of view of Penelope or of Dido instead of Ulysses or Aeneas, and the contrast is deepened if viewed with innocent eyes as in Gower and Chaucer--tears are no less effective in undermining an heroic attitude than laughter. I will try to substantiate this critical point by looking more closely at Gower's and Chaucer's treatment of the Dido story before moving on to the material basis for their essentially Ovidian position.

II

Gower tells Dido's story near the beginning of the fourth book of his *Confessio Amantis* as an example of *lachesce* or negligence in matters of love (IV.77-137).[16] Aeneas is rebuked for being slow--not because he lingers in Carthage and is negligent of his supreme task of founding an empire but because he fails to return to Carthage as he promised his lady when he left for Italy. In thus stretching the time span, incidentally, Gower makes Dido's complaints more plausible and less hysterical than Virgil and particularly than Ovid, whose heroine writes her letter of reproach with Aeneas's fleet still in sight. On the whole, of course, this is Ovid's Aeneas rather than Virgil's, a classical hero and forsworn knight as seen through the eyes of a medieval love poet.[17] Like Ovid, Gower is sceptical of the business of founding empires beyond the sea. Ovid's Dido is allowed to repeat the sneers she hurls at her lover in the *Aeneid* "pete regna per undas" (IV.381; in Dryden's translation, "Go seek thy promised Kingdom through the Main" [IV.549]), with a vengeance. In Virgil's epic these sneers are counterpoised by an apology from Aeneas, by the command of the gods, and, above all, by the weight of eight more books of epic action culminating in the foundation of the promised empire. In Dido's letter they remain unanswered. Gower's view of the question appears to be nearly as narrow as that of Ovid's letter writer. He does not mention the mission of Aeneas, who is said to have left for Italy "as it be scholde" (IV.92). The Latin gloss on the margin adds an equally vague "bellaturum." Moreover, there is a passage in the same book of the *Confessio Amantis* where the idea of military exploits "over the grete Se" (IV.1626)--in their medieval guise of crusades, "Somtime in Prus, somtime in Rodes, / And somtime into Tartarie" (IV.1630-31)--is rejected by both Amans and Genius. Like Ovid, Gower concentrates on questions of private rather than public conduct. No imperial calling is to overrule this prime responsibility.

With a poet like Chaucer, such domestication of imperial values would come as less of a surprise. I need not expound the way he reduces the elevating power of Virgil's epic and strengthens its pathetic impact; this has been demonstrated most eloquently with regard to the *House of Fame* by Wolfgang Clemen and to the *Legend of Good Women* by Robert Worth Frank.[18] Suffice it to point out in the *House of Fame* his ingenious and engaging method of changing the sorceress of the *Aeneid* into a silly maid "that loved al to sone a gest" (line 288) --"silly" here retaining some of the original meaning which is preserved in the German cognate *selig*, that is, *blessed*; or, in the *Legend of Good Women*, his conversion of Dido from the courtly figure of the beginning of her legend ("of alle queenes flour" [line 1009]) to the lost maiden who would be her false lover's slave ("His thral, his servant in the leste degre" [line 1313]), a conversion which traces in medieval terms Dido's fall from Virgil's epic heights to Ovid's elegiac humbleness.[19] Chaucer may have known what he was doing when he took sides with Ovid against Virgil, or with Dido against Aeneas. "He was evir (God wait) all womanis frend," as Gavin Douglas put it in his "Prologus in Virgilii Eneados" (line 449) in mild exasperation over Chaucer's treatment of a lady who, for all he knew, was rightly burned. But what about "moral" Gower, Chaucer's stern friend and even sterner mentor of the realm? Surely he might be expected to take sides with Virgil and Aeneas and imperial piety (as, in fact, Douglas did)?

There is, of course, the question of the framework of the *Confessio Amantis*, and Gower is at times very much aware of the narrowing of perspective this imposes on his poem: it is Genius, the priest of love, who tells Dido's story, and he is obliged to plead the amorous cause *ex officio*. To all those, however, who have taken the so-called code of courtly love at all seriously, tarrying in the service of *fin amour* meant the temptation of the knight-at-arms to forget about his martial duties in the arms of a Circe-like seductress, and Virgil's Dido episode might have served as an example of how to avoid this kind of sloth. Instead, Gower puts Aeneas in a row with Ovidian heroes, or rather anti-heroes such as Demephon and Protheselaï, both treated in Book IV, whose knighthood is called into doubt from the point of view of their forsaken ladies. To him, Aeneas is the seducer, and a traitor to boot (Gower mentions his fine words and his false thoughts in IV.89, 118), and he makes him, as he always does with his heroes, personally responsible. There is no intervention from Venus, Jove, or Mercury; the "as it be scholde" (IV.92) is no more than a tag.

Ovid, then--"the grete Clerk Ovide" (III.736)--presides over the fate of Gower's Dido and Aeneas as he does over so many parts of the *Confessio Amantis*. He is frequently invoked as an authority in matters of love; there are half a dozen tales taken from the *Heroides*, and more than two dozen from the *Metamorphoses*. His subtle and softening influence made itself felt in the *Confessio*, perhaps in spite of its author, and Ovid may well have been the force that drove him towards "the middel weie" he mentions in the Prologue (line 17) and formed the mellowed style of his later years.

Gower appears to have had Ovid's poems close to hand, if not by heart; he repeatedly quotes from or refers to specific passages from the *Heroides*, for instance, particularly the more memorable opening and closing lines--occasionally mixing them up in a very quaint and telling manner. A delightful example is the way he handles the famous simile of the dying swan at the beginning of Dido's letter. In Ovid's *Heroides* they run like this: "Sic ubi fata vocant udis abiectus in herbis / ad vada Maeandri concinit albus olor" (VII.1-2; in Dryden's translation, "So, on *Maeander's* banks, when death is nigh, / The mournful *Swan* sings her own Elegie"). Maeander, of course, is a river meandering into the Aegean Sea. Gower turns this into a wistful death-scene, remembered by a King Menander and predictive of the death of Dido. His swan kills herself for love of her mate by pushing a feather into her brain, and Dido warns Aeneas that she might do the same:

> Sche scholde stonde in such degre
> As whilom stod a Swan tofore,
> Of that sche hadde hire make lore;
> For sorwe a fethere into hire brain
> She schof and hath hireselve slain;
> As king Menander in a lay
> The sothe hath founde, wher sche lay
> Sprantlende with hire wynges tweie,
> As sche which scholde thanne deie
> For love of him which was hire make.
>
> (IV.104-13)

A lovesick swan, killing herself with the quill of a feather; this might serve as an emblem of the letter-writing tragic heroine of Ovidian descent, and it might look like an ingenious invention or the kind of creative misunderstanding that indicates congeniality (as opposed to the mere verbal misunderstanding that follows, the confusion of the river Maeander with King Menander). Both these misunderstandings, however, are probably based on good authority and textual evidence, as far as such things go in medieval times. The Maeander-Menander confusion is quite common in manuscripts of the *Heroides*,[20] although in some of those preserved in the British Library it is cleared up by interlinear glosses such as *fluvius* or just *flu* above the hard word--e.g., in the Harley MS. 2709 and the Additional MS. 21169 (both of the thirteenth century).

The touching death-scene of the swan, however, is a reminiscence of ancient animal lore. Gower may have found it in the *Speculum naturale* of Vincent of Beauvais, which he certainly knew; chapter 50, "De cigno," provides the following information: "Instante morte pennam in cerebro figit, & sic dulciter canit. naturaliter enim mortem suam in cantu laetitiae iubilationisque praeit."[21] Or he may have come across a note on the margin of a manuscript edition of the *Heroides*. There is an extended sidenote, e.g., in the Burney MS. 219 opposite the first lines of Dido's letter, stating, among other things, that it is in the nature of the swan not only to sing but also to shove a quill into her brain when she feels death approaching: "natura est cigni ut morte sibi imminente dulce cantet. dicent enim quidam quod penna traiicit in cerebro eius" (fol. 12^v). An almost identical gloss is to be found on the margin of folio 7^r opposite the same passage in Additional MS. 21169. Gower's seemingly idiosyncratic rendering of the opening lines of *Heroides* VII is only partly "due to his imagination," not "chiefly," as Macaulay suggested in a somewhat bewildered note on the lines I quoted from Book IV of the *Confessio Amantis*.[22] Apparently original are Gower's inference that the swan kills herself out of grief for her lost mate--a characteristic sentimental touch--and the structural use he makes of the comparison: Dido will kill herself in a manner similar to that of the swan by shoving not a quill but a sword and not into her brain but "unto hire herte rote" (IV.134).

It is possible, then, that Gower worked from an annotated Latin manuscript of Ovid's *Letter of Dido* when writing his short exemplum of Dido and Aeneas, cutting it to his purposes with much freedom and little regard for its original form. There is no reference to his source in the *Heroides* and no sign that he knew Virgil's epic version of the story at all. With Chaucer, the situation appears to be exactly the reverse. He used and named both authorities in his Legend of Dido, but it is uncertain whether he worked from Latin or vernacular manuscripts.[23] Chaucer translated the first lines of Ovid's *Letter of Dido* fairly literally and worked them into his rendering of Virgil's Dido episode as a coda. Their dying fall comes as an anticlimax to the splendid courtly scenes of the opening of the "Legend of Dido" and cannot be taken as an unqualified sign of a more scholarly or reverential attitude towards either Virgil or Ovid. Rather, Chaucer plays one authority off the other: he begins in the light of "Virgil Mantoan," whom he hails in his opening lines and ends in the Sulmonian--or rather, Ponto-Caspian--shade of Ovid. The shadowy impression is the one that lasts.

With Gower, this preference for the Ovidian point of view may have been due to the simple fact that he lacked the opportunity to read Virgil's high-minded epic as he did the irreverent echo it found in Ovid's letter. There was a marked decline in the production of manuscripts containing classical material during the fourteenth century, and Gower, though well-read in the scholastic compilations which replaced it, may have missed Virgil altogether. There is no indication that he knew his poems anywhere near as well as Ovid's. Indeed, in the *Confessio Amantis*, Virgil is mentioned only twice: first as a sorcerer in the story of Virgil's Mirror which Gower adapted from a French romance (V.2031-2224); second as *senex amans* outwitted by the Emperor's daughter (VIII.2714-17), an anecdote which he may well have found in such medieval florilegia as British Library Additional MS. 18459, which contains Virgilian anecdotes and a few lines from his works among a mass of Ovidian and patristic material.

In fact, such florilegia could have provided Gower with all he knew of Virgil's works. This impression is confirmed by the evidence contained in his major Latin poem *Vox Clamantis*, which is in small parts laid out to a plan that might have been modelled on the opening books of the *Aeneid*. In chapters XIII to XV, the Peasants' Revolt and their march on London is explicitly compared to the destruction of Troy. London is called Troynovant, and some of the rebels are named after their ancient forbears. The archbishop of Canterbury is called Helenus, the queen mother Hecuba, and Richard II, somewhat incongruously, Priam. The whole of the visionary poem is sprinkled with classical phrases--not, however, as might have been expected, from Virgil or some other epic, but almost exclusively from Ovid. According to Eric Stockton's tally, there are some five hundred borrowings from Ovid's works in the *Vox Clamantis*; according to F. C. Mish's thesis, there are over 750.[24] That most of these are taken from Ovid's epistles can be attributed to the elegiac meter employed in the *Vox Clamantis*; meter does not, however, account for the total absence of Virgilian material in the poem. The most plausible explanation would be that Gower had no access to such material.

III

These are rather strange findings, not only with regard to Gower, who was called the Virgil of his age by a contemporary, possibly the "philosophical Strode," but also with respect to the question of classical learning in the Ricardian age as a whole. If Gower, who certainly was well-versed in several languages, had no firsthand knowledge of Virgil, what about Langland, who treats him--very much like Gower in his motley procession of lovers in VIII.2714-17--as a frustrated wooer of the Emperor's daughter (see *Piers Plowman*, B-text, Passus XII.43-44); what about the *Gawain* poet, who refers to the destruction of Troy in an even more devious way than Gower does and yet is supposed to have read the *Aeneid* (*Sir Gawain and the Green Knight*, lines 3-5); and what, indeed, about Chaucer, whose faltering attempts to follow Virgil's lantern take on a different coloring as well in the light of this evidence? Chaucer, also, appears to be steeped in Ovidian, but no more than sprinkled with Virgilian, lore, and he shook off Virgil's influence more easily than did Augustine or Boccaccio, who questioned the *Aeneid* for scholastic or for scholarly reasons. Chaucer bent it to his purposes; he rewrote it in the terms of a domestic tragedy centered, like Gower's exemplum, around the heroine. For this purpose one of the French historical romances, which sometimes contained material related to the fall of Troy drawn from both the *Aeneid* and the *Heroides*, would have served as well as any original. Such use would further explain both the occasional Romance spelling of proper names like "Lavyne" (*Book of the Duchess* [line 331]) for Lavinia or "Sytheo" (*Legend of Good Women* [line 1005]) for Sychaeus, and why there are so few references in Chaucer's works to the second half (or even two thirds) of the *Aeneid*:

Dido kills herself in Book IV, her last appearance is in the underworld of Book VI.[25]

Chaucer's predilection for Books I, II, IV, and perhaps VI of the *Aeneid* will be shared by all but the most assiduous Latinists. The first Englishman, or rather Scotsman, to show no such preference and to approach the poem in the true philological spirit was Gavin Douglas, who, however gently, rebuked both Chaucer and Gower for their handling of the Dido story. In the "Proloug of the first buke of his Eneados," he pokes fun at Chaucer's claim that he follows Virgil's poem word for word by pretending that this procedure is beyond his own means and then, of course, by going on to deliver one of the most conscientious translations in the English language. A few lines later, he firmly refutes Chaucer's allegation that "Eneas to Dydo was forsworn" (line 414)[26]: "Thus, wenyng allane Ene to haue reprevit, / He has gretely the prynce of poetis grevit" (lines 417-18). His is the attitude of a Renaissance scholar, while Chaucer and Gower felt under no obligation to respect the texts of their authorities. Theirs is the Manciple's approach:

> But for I am a man noght textueel,
> I wol noght telle of textes never a deel;
> I wol go to my tale. . . .
>
> (Manciple's Tale, lines 235-37)

The scholars and critics of our age have, perhaps too readily, assumed that Ricardian writers were as familiar with their Augustan forbears as Chaucer's and Gower's name-dropping way of referring to such authors as Virgil and Ovid suggests. The basis for such assumptions has to be reconsidered in every single case and in the light of positive, or negative, textual and paleographical evidence. Positivist and revisionist investigations of this kind are gaining ground, at least in the field of historical studies, if one may take the papers read at the 1981 Bristol Symposion on English Court Culture as a sign.[27] By implication, some of these papers have revived the theory of a virtually bookless fourteenth century first raised by Samuel Moore in 1913 and supported on the evidence of several thousand wills enrolled at the Court of Hustings by Margaret Deanesly in 1920.[28] These wills are much closer to Chaucer and Gower than those mentioned by Laura Loomis or Elizabeth Salter to refute the theory of a bookless century.[29] They were laid down by London citizens (including members of the Chaucer family), minor clergymen, and a few members of the gentry or the court. Scarcely any books containing secular literature are mentioned in these testaments. An examination of R. R. Sharpe's *Calendar of Wills* (1889), which reprints about two thousand of the more interesting of them, produced not a single reference to a classical text. The bequests mentioned by Laura Loomis and Elizabeth Salter come from a different sphere altogther: aristocratic households on the one hand, and clerical institutions (monasteries, colleges, cathedral schools) on the other. The aristocratic libraries (if *libraries* is not too flattering a term) held mainly the sort of Frenchified literature that both Chaucer and Gower repeatedly ridicule in their poems (the "rum, ram, ruf" romances and courtly "balades, roundels, virelays"). Elizabeth Salter fixed her attention on the revival of alliterative poetry and searched for evidence of a literary culture in provincial courts, but her results apply to the royal household as well. What non-practical and non-devotional literature she searched out is of the light entertainment sort. In fact, one sometimes wonders if King Richard, when he ordered a love-poem from John Gower, did not get more than he had bargained for. As for clerical institutions, there is little evidence that Chaucer was closely connected with any of them--apart perhaps from the almonry or grammar school attached to St. Paul's Cathedral where he may have received his early education. Almost all the manuscripts assembled at St. Paul's were removed to Sion College under Cromwell and perished in the Great Fire of 1666.[30] Some booklists have come down to us, the most interesting a bequest made by the schoolmaster William de Ravenstone to the almonry containing an Ovid--which Edith Rickert in her study of the will identifies as Chaucer's "owne book"--but, significantly, only the *Georgica* of Virgil.[31] Concerning Gower, though he was closely attached to St. Mary Overeys for the latter part of his life, the evidence is even more scarce. What manuscripts we know to have belonged to the monastery are of an ecclesiastical order. None of those listed by Ker in his *Medieval Libraries* contains a classical text, and the inventory lists inserted in the Cotton Faustina MS. A VIII and the Harley MS. 670 have only the usual missals, psalters, and portifories.

After so much deconstruction, one is left with the question of what exactly remains of the physical basis on which writers such as Chaucer and Gower worked if they had none at the court nor in the cloisters where we imagined them to be. We will have to find out, and in the meantime had rather be more careful with such ill-founded terms as *courtly culture* or *classical influence*. This need not lead us back to highbrow judgments like that of Matthew Arnold, who deplored the lack of "high poetic seriousness" in Chaucer because he missed the heroic element in his poetry. Such verdicts can be turned to good, as J. A. Burrow has shown when he described the "middle-aged" and unheroic quality of Ricardian poetry.[32] What both critics noticed in the fourteenth-century literature, its lack of classical standards, may in part be due to the fact that Ricardian poets were very much men of the Middle Ages and hardly knew one of the bearers of such standards, Virgil's Aeneas.

NOTES

[1]The earliest instances the *OED* gives are of 1607 (for *classical*) and 1627 (for *classic*). E. R. Curtius follows the vacillations of such terms in ch. 14, "Classicism," of his *European Literature and the Latin Middle Ages*, trans. Willard R. Trask (New York, 1955), pp. 247-72.

[2]Curtius gives several such lists in a paragraph on the set reading of medieval schools ("Curriculum Authors," *European Literature*, pp. 48-54).

[3]See Albert C. Friend's article, "Chaucer's Version of the *Aeneid*," *Speculum*, 28 (1953), 317-23, which presents the *Ilias latina* as not only Chaucer's Homer but also his Virgil.

[4]"Imprints of the *Heroides* of Ovid on Chaucer, *The Legend of Good Women*," *Classical Weekly*, 18 (1924), 9.

[5]A. J. Minnis, *Chaucer and Pagan Antiquity*, Chaucer Studies 8 (Woodbridge, Suffolk, and Totowa, NJ, 1982).

[6]Doubts have been expressed about Chaucer's firsthand knowledge of, among others, Lucan, by J. L. Lowes (see F. N. Robinson's note to line 400 of the Man of Law's Tale in *The Works of Geoffrey Chaucer* [London, 1957], p. 694); Statius, by F. P. Magoun (in "Chaucer's Summary of Statius' *Thebaid*, II-XII," *Traditio*, 11 [1955], 409-20); and Seneca, by R. A. Pratt ("Chaucer and the Hand that Fed Him," *Speculum*, 41 [1966], 619-42).

[7]*Studies in Chaucer: His Life and Writings*, vol. 2 (New York, 1892), p. 250.

[8]*Chaucer: A Bibliographical Manual* (New York, 1908), p. 105.

[9]"Chaucer and the Latin Classics," in *Geoffrey Chaucer*, ed. Derek Brewer (London, 1974), p. 142.

[10]*"the middel weie"*: *Stil- und Aufbauformen in John Gowers "Confessio Amantis"* (Bonn, 1974).

[11]*Die Frauenklage. Studien zur elegischen Verserzählung in der englischen Literatur des Spätmittelalters und der Renaissance* (Tübingen, 1984); an English version of this study is being prepared for the European Studies in English Literature series at the Cambridge University Press.

[12]Quoted by Karl Büchner in "P. Vergilius Maro," *Realencyclopädie der classischen Altertumswissenschaft*, 2nd ser., vol. 16 (Stuttgart, 1958), col. 1373.

[13]*PMLA*, 81 (1966), 475-84.

[14]Despite repeated claims to the contrary I doubt if the *Legend of Good Women* is a work of pervasive irony. In the case of the legend of Dido, Chaucer's other treatment of the story in the *House of Fame* asserts his basically sympathetic view of the heroine.

[15]In his Introduction to *Virgil and His Influence*, ed. Charles Martindale (Bristol, 1984), p. 6.

[16]Quotations are from G. C. Macaulay's edition of *The English Works of John Gower*, 2 vols., EETS, e.s. 81-82 (London, 1900-01).

[17]For the medieval Aeneas see Carl Vossen's unpublished doctoral dissertation, "Der Wandel des Aeneasbildes im Spiegel der englishchen Literatur" (University of Bonn, 1955), and compare L. B. Hall, "Chaucer and the Dido-and-Aeneas Story," *Medieval Studies*, 25 (1963), 148-59.

[18]W. Clemen, *Chaucer's Early Poetry*, trans. C. A. M. Sym (London, 1963), pp. 79-87; R. W. Frank, *Chaucer and "The Legend of Good Women"* (Cambridge, MA, 1972), pp. 57-78.

[19]Chaucer quotations are taken from *The Riverside Chaucer*, 3rd ed., general editor Larry D. Benson (Boston, 1987).

[20]See Heinrich Dörrie's article on medieval manuscripts of the *Heroides*, "Untersuchungen zur Überlieferungsgeschichte von Ovids Epistulae Heroidum," *Nachrichten der Akademie der Wissenschaften in Göttingen aus dem Jahre 1960*, Philologisch-historische Klasse (1960), 113-230 and 359-423.

[21]*Speculum naturale*. Liber decimsextus. Cap. L, fol. 201^b, quoted from *Speculi Maioris Vincentii Burgundi Praesulis Belvacensis* (Venice, 1541). John Trevisa has a similar passage in his translation of Bartholomaeus Anglicus's *De proprietatibus rerum* XII.xii (*On the Properties of Things*, vol. 1 [Oxford, 1975], p. 623): "And whan sche schal dye and a fethir is ipight in the brayne, thanne sche syngeth and agenst the usage of othir beestis in stede of gronynge the swan syngeth, as Ambrose seith." So has Brunetto Latini in his *Livres des Tresor*, I.161. The ultimate source is a misreading of two lines from Ovid's *Fasti* (II.109-10), as Florence McCulloch has shown in her article, "The Dying Swan - A Misunderstanding," *Modern Language Notes*, 74 (1959), 289-92.

[22]*The English Works of John Gower* 1:502.

[23]There are reasons, presented by Sanford Meech some time ago, to assume that he made use of Filippo Ceffi's Italian translation of the *Heroides* (S. B. Meech, "Chaucer and an Italian translation of the *Heroides*," *PMLA*, 45 [1930], 110-280). This example may have prompted Conrad Mainzer to adduce Italian comments on the Phyllis-and-Demephon story to prove that Gower had access to a similar edition; see his "John Gower's Use of the Medieval

Ovid in the *Confessio Amantis*," *Medium Aevum*, 41 (1972), 215-29.

[24]*The Major Latin Works of John Gower: The Voice of One Crying and the Tripartite Chronicle*, trans. Eric W. Stockton (Seattle, 1962), p. 27; F. C. Mish, "The Influence of Ovid on John Gower's *Vox Clamantis*," *Dissertation Abstracts International*, 34 (1974), 7198 A.

[25]For Chaucer's reading in the *Aeneid*, see John Koch, "Chaucers Belesenheit in den römischen Klassikern," *Englische Studien*, 57 (1923), 68. There has been a controversy as to which sources besides the *Aeneid* Chaucer tapped for his portraits of Dido and Aeneas; see E. B. Atwood, "Two Alterations of Virgil in Chaucer's Dido," *Speculum*, 13 (1938), 454-57, and D. R. Bradley, "Fals Eneas and Sely Dido," *Philological Quarterly*, 39 (1960), 122-25; that he first went to Virgil was not called into doubt.

[26]Quoted from David F. C. Coldwell's edition, *Virgil's Aeneid Translated into Scottish Verse* (Edinburgh, 1957).

[27]*English Court Culture in the Later Middle Ages*, ed. V. J. Scattergood and J. W. Sherborne (London, 1983).

[28]Samuel Moore, "Some Aspects of Literary Patronage in the Middle Ages," *The Library*, 4 (1913), 369-92; Margaret Deanesly, "Vernacular Books in England in the XIVth and XVth Centuries," *Modern Language Review*, 15, (1920), 349-58.

[29]L. H. Loomis, "The Auchinleck Manuscript and a Possible London Bookshop of 1330-1340," *PMLA*, 57 (1942), 595-627; Elizabeth Salter, "The Alliterative Revival," *Modern Philology*, 64 (1966), 146-50; 233-37.

[30]See N. R. Ker, *Medieval Manuscripts in British Libraries. I. London* (Oxford, 1969), p. 240.

[31]Edith Rickert, "Chaucer at School," *Modern Philology*, 29 (1932), 257-74.

[32]J. A. Burrow, *Ricardian Poetry: Chaucer, Gower, Langland and the 'Gawain' Poet* (London, 1971), p. 129; the reference to Arnold is given on p. 45.

DID GOWER WRITE *CENTO*?

R. F. Yeager

A history of *cento* verse, were one to be written, must needs focus on two periods of European cultural development. The first is, of course, antiquity, when the form--from Latin "patchwork," a poem comprised of lines and line-parts selected from the work of a renowned poet of an earlier time--was defined and initially practiced. Aristophanes offers us several examples using Homer, and we may cite as well a "very funny song," said by Lucian to contain a mixture of extracts from other Greek poets.[1] The *Iliad* and the *Odyssey*, however, remained the favorites for *centos* in Greek through at least the fifth century A.D., when the Byzantine empress Eudocia herself reportedly composed *Homerokentrones*.[2] Among Latin writers, Virgil replaced Homer as the source most often quarried for *centos*; we have extant the *Medea* of Hosidius Geta from the second century A.D., employing passages from the *Aeneid* throughout, and some suggestion as well of earlier effort.[3] The Virgilian tradition lasts into the fourth century, as is represented by the *Cento Nuptialis* of Ausonius, and by the Christian *centos* of Anicia Faltonia Proba, Pomponius, Luxorius, and perhaps Sedulius.[4] During these years, too, the practice was broadened to include works of other poets such as Ovid and Statius. Subsequently, the construction of *centos* seems to have fallen off. Although we may agree with F. J. E. Raby that "the *centos* continued . . . to be admired and read" and that "the Carolingians can hardly have overlooked them,"[5] scholars have commonly held that only the tenth-century *Ec-basis Captivi* remains, along with one or two other pieces, to establish medieval interest in the form.[6] The second great period in our history of *cento* literature, then, is the Renaissance, with numerous examples both ancient and freshly composed appearing in print from the late fifteenth through the seventeenth centuries.[7]

Looking only at this pattern and attempting a general explanation, one might well find in it the broad cartography of the Renaissance phenomenon itself. Erratically supplied with texts, and thus cut off frequently from classical poetic models, the Middle Ages could not reproduce so allusive a way of writing, one so dependent on a sophisticated literary culture, as the *cento*. Not until the rebirth of that antique culture and the renewed currency both of models and--especially--of the idea of a continuity of letters, intrinsic to the *cento*, was the form attempted again.[8] Thus, predictably, we discover significant interest rekindled in *cento* poetry in Italy first, and in the shadow of the great Humanist pioneers such as Erasmus.[9]

Yet to so dismiss the later Middle Ages as lacking awareness or practice of the *cento* may prove over-hasty, and a mistake. Strands of the tradition exist to be found throughout the period, woven into its fabric obviously enough to be noticed and unravelled by men of learned habits. One such, very possibly, was John Gower, author of prodigious works in Anglo-Norman, in Latin, and in his native English. "Schoolboy plagiarism," in Gower's Latin poetry particularly, has long been remarked by many readers. G. C. Macaulay, for example, commented in his definitive edition of Gower's Latin works that in the *Vox Clamantis*, a poem of 10,265 elegiac verses, Gower "repeatedly takes not lines or couplets only, but passages of eight, ten, or even twenty lines from the *Aurora* of Peter Riga, from the poem of Alexander Neckham *De Vita Monachorum*, from the *Speculum Stultorum* [of Nigel Wirecker], or from the *Pantheon* [of Godfrey of Viterbo], so that in many places the composition is entirely made up of such borrowed matter variously arranged and combined."[10] Subsequent studies have helped to identify other sources for Gower's borrowing, and to clarify his practices. John H. Fisher, while pointing out the frequency with which excerpts from Ovid turn up in the *Vox Clamantis*, has argued against considering them merely copying. In Gower's poem, Fisher observes, the lines "do not express any experience or sentiment taken from Ovid. The . . . quotations . . . come from such a variety of contexts and are so tailored to fit their positions that if the passage [in the *Vox*] has any meaning, it must be that of the immediate author."[11] Another recent scholar, Paul Beichner, who has examined Gower's treatment of Peter Riga, reached conclusions similar to Fisher's about Gower's use of Ovid. In Beichner's view, whether Gower

> . . . created a mosaic from slightly changed passages separated by hundreds of thousands of lines in the *Aurora*, or whether he used a long excerpt from one place, his context is original. And the general context of the *Vox Clamantis* . . . gives originality even to passages borrowed without change by removing them from the plane of the exegete's timeless moral interpretation of Scripture to the reformer's criticism of his own day.[12]

Certainly, Macaulay, Fisher, and Beichner are correct in their description of Gower's interpolation of material from other texts into his own writing. What they (and other scholars who have addressed this aspect of Gower's poetry) have not noticed is a possible explanation for such concentrated borrowing in the strong correspondence between Gower's practices and the formal lineaments of *cento* verse.[13] As Ausonius described it, *cento* was the fitting together of "scattered tags . . . into a whole," to "harmonize different meanings, to make pieces arbitrarily connected seem naturally related, to let foreign elements show no chink of light between, to prevent the far-fetched from proclaiming the force which united them. . . ."[14] This is precisely what Gower has accomplished, as the following example illustrates. In these nineteen lines from Book I of the *Vox Clamantis*, Gower's work appears first; below each line and indented is his Ovidian source.

Qui prius attulerat *verum michi semper amorem*
    nam cum praestiteris *verum mihi semper amorem*
                (Ex Ponto, 4.6.23)

Tunc *tamen aduerso tempore* cessat *amor*:
    hic *tamen adverso tempore* crevit *amor*
                (Ex Ponto, 4.6.24)

Querebam fratres tunc fidos, non tamen ipsos
    quaerebam fratres, exceptis scilicet illis
                (Tristia, 3.1.66)

Memet in insidii semper locuturus habebam,

Verbaque sum spectans pauca locutus humum:
    verbaque sum spectans pauca locutus humum
                (Fasti, 1.148)

Tempora cum blandis absumpsi vanaque verbis,

Dum mea sors cuiquam cogeret vlla loqui.

Iram multociens frangit responsio mollis,

Dulcibus ex verbis tunc fuit ipsa salus;

Sepeque cum volui conatus verba proferre,

Torpuerat gelido lingua retenta metu.
    torpuerat gelido lingua retenta metu
                (Heroides, 11.82)

Non meus vt querat noua sermo quosque fatigat,

Obstitit *auspiciis lingua* retenta *malis*;
    substitit *auspicii lingua* timore mali
                (Heroides, 13.86)

Sepe meam mentem volui dixisse, set hosti

Prodere me timui, linguaque tardat ibi.

Heu! *miseram tristis fortuna tenaciter vrget,*
    an miseros tristis fortuna tenaciter urget
                      (Heroides, 3.43)

Nec venit in fatis *mollior hora* meis.
    nec venit inceptis *mollior hora* malis
                      (Heroides, 3.44)

Si genus est mortis male viuere, credo quod illo
    si genus est mortis male vivere, terra moratur
                      (Ex Ponto, 3.4.75)

Tempore vita mea morsque fuere pares.[15]

A comparison of Gower's lines with the original contexts of his extracts will show how much he has taken Ausonius's dictum "harmonize different meanings" to heart. As Gower composed it, the passage may be translated:

> One who before had *always borne a sincere love for me--* even his love had ceased *in this time of adversity.* I then *made search for faithful brothers, not those whom their father wished he had never begotten.* Whenever I was on the point of speaking, I considered myself to be in ambush; *and looking upon the ground, I uttered only a few words.* When my lot forced me to say something to somebody, I passed the time idly with glib talk. Again and again a soft answer turned away wrath, and my very safety depended upon agreeable words to convey my inclinations; *my halting tongue grew numb from a chilling fear.* In order that my talk might not consist of complaint about recent happenings and become burdensome to people, *my tongue remained firmly tied because of the hostile circumstances;* I was often inclined to declare my mind, but I was fearful of handing myself over to the enemy, and then my tongue grew hesitant. Alas! *A sad fate was persistently dogging me in my wretchedness, and an easier hour did not enter into my destinies. If to live in misery is a kind of death,* I believe

that at that time my life and death were just alike.[16]

These verses form part of a description of the poet's dream, a lightly-veiled allegory of the Peasants' Revolt of 1381. Speaking here as if in his own person, Gower relates in lines preceding those quoted above how he hid in the woods beneath a pile of loose grass, weeping and in fear for his life should he be discovered by the marauding bands of rebels, which he portrays--not inappropriately--as wild beasts. In contrast, Gower found the phrase "verum michi semper amorem" (always a sincere love for me) in a letter addressed by Ovid to his otherwise unidentified friend Brutus; ironically, however, Brutus, "tamen adverso tempore" (in this time of adversity), had stood by Ovid; Gower's nameless comrade does not. The larger context is as follows, from the *Ex Ponto*:

> I can swear with a clear conscience that you too utter the same prayer, Brutus--you whom I know from indubitable proof. For although you have *ever granted me sincere love*, yet your love has increased *in this time of adversity*. One who saw your tears that matched with mine would have believed that both were about to suffer punishment.[17]

The difference in meaning of the lines is, if anything, increased by viewing the contexts. Comparison of the next two lines as they appear in the *Vox Clamantis* and in Ovid's *Tristia*, where Gower found them, yields the same results. The "querebam fratres" ([faithful] brothers) for whom Gower sought, "quos suus optaret non genuisse pater" (not those whom their father wished he had never begotten), are difficult to identify in the *Vox*--though perhaps Gower intended a religious allusion.[18] No obscurity exists in Ovid's poem, however. There, the first-person narrator is Ovid's latest book, come home to Rome in search of poetical "brothers" whose "father"--the exiled Ovid himself--regrets writing, since they have cost him dear. The book describes a search through the library in the temple of Apollo on the Palatine:

> Then with even pace up the lofty steps I was conducted to the shining temple of the unshorn god, where alternating with the columns of foreign marble stand the figures of the Belids, the barbarian father with a drawn sword, and all those things which the men of old or of modern times conceived in their learned souls are free for the inspection of those who would read. *I was seeking my brothers, save those indeed whom their father would he had never begot,* and as I sought to no purpose, from that abode the guard who presides over the holy place commanded me to depart.[19]

Clearly, however Gower meant us to understand his *fratres*, it could not correspond to the sense of the word in these Ovidian lines on which he drew so specifically. Similar juxtaposition of the remaining borrowed verses in the foregoing example against their original contexts is unnecessary to make the point here. Nor need we cite further composite passages to do so, though this is quite possible: approximately one-third of the *Vox Clamantis* contains splicings from other sources, altered very slightly in the manner of those just examined and put to serve a meaning wholly new.[20] What Gower attempted with these expropriations appears to be heavily influenced by *cento* style as defined and practiced by the writers of antiquity and the Renaissance and is not, in any strict sense, plagiarism.

If Gower seems to have been aware of the *cento* form and to have employed it, deliberately and with near-classical skill, as an ornament to his verse, he stands unique amidst his times. Perhaps this itself should make us suspicious of crediting too much to what may be merely coincidence, and to the proof of a single--albeit lengthy--poem.[21] Certainly for the second efflorescence of *cento* writing in Italy nearly a century after Gower's death, there was a community of humanism to support and direct interest, as well as the ready availability of antique manuscripts from which to learn by imitation. Before concluding that Gower was indeed a maker of *centos*, we must therefore ask additionally whether it would have been possible for him, working alone and with resources extant in England during the latter 1300s, to discover the *cento* and understand its characteristics.

A variety of factors combine to suggest a positive answer. From what we may ascertain of Gower's biography and cast of mind, he appears a bookish man, deeply and widely read, who had access to a significant collection of texts. Whether these were his own possessions, the property of the library at St. Mary Overeys Priory in Southwark where he lived for many years, or borrowed from friends and libraries in and about London is impossible to say.[22] The results of his extensive study are clear, nevertheless, from the many sources, medieval and ancient, which back his poems. In addition to names already mentioned--Ovid, Peter Riga, Nigel Wirecker, Alexander Neckham--a long list of others whose work influenced Gower can be cited, including Virgil, Statius, Livy, Hyginus, Boethius, Lucretius, the Church Fathers, the major rhetorician Geoffrey of Vinsauf, Brunetto Latini, Vincent of Beauvais, Jean de Meun, Alain de Lille, Dante, Martianus Capella, John of Garland, Nicholas Trivet, Peter Lombard, John of Salisbury, Jacobus de Voragine, and Geoffrey of Monmouth, to name but some.[23] Nor should we forget Chaucer, whose friendship with Gower is variously attested, and whose reading Gower must have shared, at least vicariously, in many ways.[24] Gower's thorough knowledge of his books can be stressed, too. Unlike many medieval writers who seem to have relied primarily on florilegia, Gower gives evidence again and again of a close acquaintance with his manuscripts from beginning to end, in a search not only for narrative material and rhetorical ornament, but also for the learning they contained. Reading habits such as these, then, might have brought Gower in contact with *cento* verse, if any were to be found in England; moreover, his customary thoroughness with texts would have been suited to absorbing, as well as practicing, the style.

Determining what examples of *cento* Gower could have seen in England is problematic work at best, given the state of surviving records. Nevertheless, certain conclusions may be drawn, some of them helpful and illuminating. It is intriguing, for example, to entertain the possibility that Gower was familiar with the *Ecbasis Captivi*, an extensive beast-allegory which bears several kinds of affinity with Book I of the *Vox Clamantis*; but there are good reasons to consider his knowledge of the poem unlikely. Manuscripts of the *Ecbasis* are rare (two are believed to exist today), and they appear to have circulated only in Germany.[25] More convincing still is the absence of any reference to the *Ecbasis*, or quotation from it, in Gower's poetry. With Ausonius we are on somewhat firmer ground; Gower might indeed have come to know Ausonius's *Cento Nuptialis*. Manuscripts of Ausonius's work existed in England, at Peterborough and Glastonbury at least, and perhaps there were others.[26] Because of Ausonius's fame as a rhetor and the consequent ornamentation of his work and of Gower's demonstrable interest in classical writers, the Bordeaux schoolmaster is an author Gower would have read (if hardly enjoyed) had the opportunity been available. Still, Gower seems not to have borrowed from Ausonius in his Latin poems or elsewhere, nor does he follow Ausonius's expressly-stated opinion that the best *centos* are constructed of partial lines, never of a whole line or more taken intact.[27] If Gower were using Ausonius as a model, it could only have been loosely, since he frequently incorporates lines in clusters, as Macaulay noted long ago. Such individualistic variation upon so little-known a form must be deemed improbable, were Ausonius Gower's only authority. As for Sedulius's supposed *cento*, the *De Verbi Incarnatione*, or the writings of Pomponius, Luxorius, and others, we have no report which places them within Gower's reach, or among his proven reading. While it is at least possible that Gower read Sedulius in some form--for his poems were often combined in manuscript with widely familiar poets such as Venantius Fortunatus--no proof exists to confirm or deny the supposition.[28]

Where then might Gower have encountered *cento*? All factors considered carefully, the work and reputation of A. Faltonia

Proba offer the strongest likelihood of being Gower's source. Although Gower neither mentions Proba nor quotes from her directly, a number of signs point toward his having known of her *Cento Virgilianus*. It was the most famous of the *centos* composed in the early Middle Ages, with many manuscripts--quite a few of late provenance--surviving as evidence of its popularity.[29] Importantly for our purposes, some of these manuscripts were in England in Gower's time, though whether he was aware of them we cannot say.[30] One intriguing possibility is offered by Trinity College, Cambridge, MS. 0.7.7, however. This manuscript, from the early thirteenth century, contains a dozen pieces in addition to Proba's *Cento*, nearly all by writers familiar to Gower.[31] Of these pieces, two are especially striking: the anonymous "Letter of Alexander to Aristotle from India," and part of the *Res Gestae Alexandri Macedonis* of Julius Valerius. Alexander stories were popular with Gower. They appear in nearly all of his writings and often figure prominently, as in the *Confessio Amantis* where the entirety of Book VII is said to represent Aristotle's program of education for Alexander--though the source is actually Brunetto Latini's *Tresor*--and where the long central narrative of Book VI relates the apocryphal sireing of Alexander by the Egyptian magician Nectanabus, the prince's upbringing, and the mistaken killing of Nectanabus by his royal son.[32] For this tale, Julius Valerius's *Res Gestae* served as one of Gower's three sources.[33] Since the *Res Gestae* was a relatively popular piece in the Middle Ages, Gower did not have to use the Trinity College manuscript to read Valerius; but it is worth noting nonetheless that this manuscript, while now fragmentary, appears never to have contained the entire *Res Gestae*, but only the first few sections treating Nectanabus and Alexander.[34] If Gower had known Trinity College MS. 0.7.7, then, it would have provided him with precisely the part of the *Res Gestae* on which he drew--as well as the *Cento Virgilianus* of Proba from which to learn the practice of that verse form.

Gower might, therefore, have read Proba directly; but most certainly he knew her name and possessed a clear enough idea of her achievement for her to have been his inspiration, even if such knowledge came to him secondhand. This is because Proba, and the manner of the *cento* form, are prominently discussed by two writers well known to Gower--Isidore of Seville and Giovanni Boccaccio.[35] In his *De Viris Illustribus*, Isidore commends the ingenuity with which Proba linked "selections" from Virgil into *centos* honoring Christ (*componens centonem de Christo, Virgilianis cooptatum versiculis*).[36] Again, in the first book of the *Etymologies*, Isidore mentions Proba. This is an especially valuable *locus*, since Isidore here includes *cento* as one of the possible forms of writing available to authors; it is therefore in just that place to which, if a poet like Gower were looking for stylistic definitions, he would turn for reference. After a succinct description of *cento* as a poem from many sources "patched together into one whole" (*ex multis hinc inde compositis in unum sarciunt corpus*), Isidore goes on to cite Proba as his first example of those who turn the work of the great pagans Homer and Virgil into songs with Christian worth.[37]

Boccaccio obviously read Isidore and borrowed certain biographical details from him; however, in chapter 95 of *De Claris Mulieribus*, devoted to Proba, he goes much beyond Isidore's brief paragraphs and delineates Proba's achievement and the stylistic aspects of it.[38] Because Boccaccio's statements are significant, it is useful to examine them at some length. After noting that "Proba became so well informed and familiar with Virgil's poems through continuous devotion to them that she seemed to have them always present in her mind," Boccaccio continues:

> Perhaps some time when she was reading these works with more careful attentiveness, the idea came to her that with them one could write the history of the Old and New Testaments in calm, graceful verses full of vigor. . . . Carrying out her pious thought, she searched here and there through

the *Bucolics*, the *Georgics*, and the *Aeneid*, sometimes taking entire lines from one place or another, and at times,
parts of lines. She collected them for her purpose with such
great skill, aptly placing the entire lines, joining the fragments, observing metrical rules, and preserving the dignity
of the verses, that no one except an expert could detect the
connection. . . . This distinguished woman wanted the book
which she had composed to be called *Cento*, and I have
seen it several times.[39]

Various points here are worthy of comment. First, there is
the description of the *cento* method as involving borrowed lines,
as well as line-fragments. This, as we have seen, is characteristic of Gower's practice, though it is condemned by some makers
of *cento*, notably Ausonius. Second, Boccaccio strongly implies
that Proba's *Cento*, seen by him "several times," is a book of
wide familiarity, at least in Italy. His statement may not be true,
of course; he may be attempting to lend his claims greater
authority through an impression of substantial erudition. And it
is the case as well that books common in Italy in the fourteenth
century were not then always available to Englishmen in such
numbers. Thus, what was familiar to Boccaccio--assuming that
he speaks truly of Proba here--might not have been so to Gower.
Yet, if Gower read Boccaccio (and we can be certain that he
did), statements such as these about Proba and the dissemination
of her *Cento* could only have given him the impression that the
style was known to serious men of letters, and was an admired
one, at that. Third, we should observe here the tone of reverence
with which Boccaccio speaks of Proba's achievement: hers are
"graceful verses full of vigor," the product of "continuous devotion" to the work of Virgil and the bible, turned out with
"great skill" in "aptly placing the entire lines, joining the fragments, observing the metrical rules, and preserving the dignity
of the verses. . . ." Boccaccio makes the description of *cento* almost challenging, a note he strikes more firmly further on:

> But I ask if anything more praiseworthy has been heard
> than that a woman scanned the verses of Virgil and Homer
> and, taking those suitable for her work, put them together
> so marvelously. And let learned men consider how, in spite
> of their being distinguished in the profession of sacred let-
> ters, it would be difficult and arduous to select parts here
> and there from Holy Scripture, which is very long, and put
> them together in a series to give the life of Christ in prose
> or verse, as she did with the verses of poets who were not
> believers. . . . But, being zealous in her sacred studies, she
> removed from her intellect the rust of sloth and achieved
> eternal fame. . . . And let them realize how much difference
> there is between seeking glory with praiseworthy works
> and having one's name buried together with one's corpse,
> leaving this life as if he had never lived.[40]

Such warm treatment of the *cento*, and of the potential honor
derived from constructing it, would hardly have discouraged a
poet from attempting to make his own, if he felt secure of the
formidable resources necessary. As the only late medieval
English poet to compose major works in three languages, one of
them Latin, Gower seems as likely as any to have had such confidence, as well as such ambition. Finally, there is Proba's matter, alongside her method, to commend her as a model for
Gower. Unlike Ausonius, whose *Cento Nuptialis* was famous in
part because it was salacious, Proba possessed a spirit kindred to
Gower's own in her concern to treat Christian subjects in her
verse. To see her lauded by Isidore and Boccaccio for successfully exploiting the ancient poets for the glory of Christ would,
therefore, have been attractive to Gower, the more so because of
the high purpose toward which her skill was directed.

Carefully examined, then, there appears to be evidence both
internal and external to support the likelihood that John Gower's
"plagiarised" lines in his *Vox Clamantis* and elsewhere are in
fact applications of *cento* techniques rather than an attempt to
copy clandestinely, or to swell illegitimately his own insufficient product. Very likely modelling himself on the Christian
poet Proba, whose work he could have known either in the origi-

nal or from the descriptions of Isidore and Boccaccio, Gower appears in this as in other ways a thoughtful innovator. Whether he stands, on the eve of the fifteenth century, as the last medieval practitioner of a classical style, or the earliest English poet to see a new potential in this antique form, is perhaps beyond our ability to determine, given the absence of any *ars poetica* from Gower's hand. Yet the experiment seems to have been his to make--and make it he did, *mutatis mutandis*, as now we may come to appreciate more clearly.

NOTES

[1]For Aristophanes's mention of the *cento*, see *Peace* 1090-94; Lucian's "song" is by one "Histiaeus the grammarian" and includes Hesiod, Anacreon, Pindar, and Homer. See *Convivium* 17.

[2]Discussed by Eduard Stemplinger in *Das Plagiat in der griechischen Literatur* (Leipzig and Berlin, 1912), pp. 193-210.

[3]On Hosidius, see August Pauly, *Real-Encyclopädie der classischen Altertumswissenschaft, Neue Bearbeitung, unter Mitwirkung zahlreicher fachgenossen*, ed. Georg Wissowa, 2nd ser., 67 vols. (Stuttgart, 1894-1972), 6: col. 1932. Possible early *centos* of Pindar are mentioned by Petronius, *Satyricon* 2; the parodies of Aelius Donatus, *Vita Vergiliana* 43, should also be compared.

[4]Pauly-Wissowa, *Real-Encyclopädie* 6:cols. 1931-32.

[5]F. J. E. Raby, *A History of Secular Latin Poetry in the Middle Ages*, 2nd ed., 2 vols. (Oxford, 1957), 1:44-45.

[6]See Maximilian Manitius, *Geschichte der lateinischen Literatur des Mittelalters*, 3 vols. (Munich, 1911-31), 1:618; and see also O. Delepierre, *Revue analytique des ouvrages écrits en centons, depuis les Temps anciens, jusqu'au XIXième Siècle* (London, 1868), pp. 107-36, 141-47, for one or two additional, anonymous *centos* of late Latinity and the thirteenth century. See further Raby, *A History of Christian-Latin Poetry from the Beginnings to the Close of the Middle Ages*, 2nd ed. (Oxford, 1953), pp. 138-39, who notes that "reminiscences of Virgil, Ovid, Horace, Juvenal, Claudian, and Sallust, to say nothing of Prudentius" are to be found in the prose and poetry of Columban.

[7]Delepierre, *Revue analytique*, pp. 148-363, prints a number.

[8]This, at least, is the opinion of Rosa Lammachia, "Dall'arte allusiva al centone," *Atene e Roma*, n.s., 3 (1958), 193-216.

[9]On early editions of *centos*, see Delepierre, *Revue analytique*, p. 148; Sister Marie José Byrne, *Prolegomena to an Edition of the Works of Decimus Magnus Ausonius* (New York, 1916), pp. 81-83; and Filippo Ermini, *Il centone di Proba e la poesia centonaria latina* (Rome, 1909), pp. 68-70.

[10]*The Complete Works of John Gower*, ed. G. C. Macaulay, 4 vols. (Oxford, 1899-1902), 4:xxxii-xxxiii. All quotations from the poetry of Gower are taken from this edition.

[11]John H. Fisher, *John Gower: Moral Philosopher and Friend of Chaucer* (New York, 1964), p. 149.

[12]Paul E. Beichner, "Gower's Use of the *Aurora* in the *Vox Clamantis*," *Speculum*, 30 (1955), 592.

[13]For other studies of Gower's Latin borrowings, see Robert Raymo, "Gower's *Vox Clamantis* and the *Speculum Stultorum*," *Modern Language Notes*, 70 (1955), 315-20; and *The Major Latin Works of John Gower: The Voice of One Crying and the Tripartite Chronicle*, trans. Eric W. Stockton, (Seattle, 1962), pp. 26-32.

[14]" . . . colligere et integrare lacerata . . . pari modo sensus diversi ut congruant, adoptiva quae sunt, ut cognata videantur, aliena ne interluceant: arcessita ne vim redarguant. . . ." *Ausonius*, ed. and trans. Hugh G. Evelyn White, 2 vols. (Cambridge, MA, and London, 1968), 1:370, 374.

[15]*Vox Clamantis*, lines 1501-20. Ovidian quotations are taken from the Loeb Library editions of Arthur Leslie Wheeler, *Tristia and Ex Ponto* (1953); Grant Showerman, *Heroides and Amores* (1914); and Sir James George Frazer, *Fasti* (1951).

[16]The translation is primarily that of Stockton, *Major Latin Works*, p. 82. I have, however, changed some punctuation and one or two words.

[17]   te quoque idem liquido possum iurare precari,
      o mihi non dubia cognite Brute nota.
    nam cum praestiteris verum mihi semper amorem,
      hic tamen adverso tempore crevit amor.

quique tuas pariter lacrimas nostrasque videret,
passuros poenam crederet esse duos.

The lines and their translation are from Wheeler, Loeb edition, p. 442.

[18]John Fisher has suggested the *fratres* here may be intended to signify "the faithful brothers of St. Mary Overeys"; see *John Gower*, p. 148.

[19]
    inde tenore pari gradibus sublima celsis
      ducor ad intonsi candida templa dei,
    signa peregrinis ubi sunt alterna columnis,
      Belides et stricto barbarus ense pater,
    quaeque viri docto vetercs cepere novique
      pectore, lecturis inspicienda patent.
    quaerebam fratres, exceptis scilicet illis,
      quos suus optaret non genuisse pater.
    quaerentem frustra custos e sedibus illis
      praepositus sancto iussit abire loco.

Lines and translation are from Wheeler, Loeb edition, p. 104.

[20]Other significant *cento* sections in the *Vox Clamantis* include: Bk. III, ch. 26 (primarily Peter Riga and Ovid); Bk. IV, lines 395-486 (primarily Alexander Neckham); Bk. V, lines 957-76 (primarily *Remedia Amoris*); Bk. VI, lines 937-92 (primarily Peter Riga). See Stockton, *Major Latin Works*, notes and index, for many others.

[21]Gower may be using *cento* techniques--or at least techniques *cento*-inspired--in his French verse as well. Compare, for example, lines 11407-09 from the *Mirour de l'Omme*:

    Houstez voz troeffes et voz gas,
    Car tiel me couve soubz ses dras
    Q'assetz guide estre fortz et siens . . .

with XV.10-12 from MS. Bibliothèque Nationale latin 14958 of *Les Vers de la Mort* of Hélinant de Froidmont:

    Laissiez voz trufes et voz gas!
    Car me cueve desoz ses dras
    Qui cuide estre tous forz et sains.

The editors of Hélinant, Fredrik Wulff and Emmanuel Walberg (Paris, 1905), do not offer these lines exactly as I do, since for their edition they rely on a different manuscript; but see their textual notes to these lines. It is likely that Gower used a manuscript more like Bib. Nat. lat. 14958 than like the "better" version of Wulff and Walberg. Gower is quoting directly here, but the pastiche technique has obvious parallels with *cento*. Also suggestive of this influence are some of Gower's *balades* in both the *Cinkante Balades* and the *Traitié*, where lines appear to be taken from French poets such as Deschamps and also from the troubadours. On this problem, see E. Koeppel, "Gowers französische Balladen und Chaucer," *Englische Studien*, 20 (1895), 154-56; Jean Audiau, *Les Troubadours et l'Angleterre* (Paris, 1927), pp. 103-28; G. Kar, *Thoughts on the Medieval Lyric* (Oxford, 1933), pp. 55-63; and Fisher, *John Gower*, pp. 76-77, 83-88.

[22]Gower helped rebuild St. Mary Overeys Priory and dwelt for much of his later life within its walls, availing himself of the library. See Macaulay, *Works* 4:lix-lxxi, and Fisher, *John Gower*, pp. 59-61.

[23]No single study attempts to deal with all of Gower's sources. Useful, however, are discussions by Maria Wickert, *Studien zu John Gower* (Cologne, 1953; now also translated by Robert J. Meindl as *Studies in John Gower* [Washington, DC, 1981]); Patrick J. Gallacher, *Love, the Word, and Mercury: A Reading of John Gower's "Confessio Amantis"* (Albuquerque, 1975); Russell A. Peck, *Kingship and Common Profit in Gower's "Confessio Amantis"* (Carbondale and Edwardsville, IL, 1978); and Macaulay's notes, *Works*, passim. See also the Subject Index in my *John Gower Materials: A Bibliography through 1979* (New York, 1981).

[24]Chaucer's dedication of *Troilus and Criseyde* to "moral Gower" (V. 1856) is well known, as is Gower's original greeting of Chaucer (later cancelled) in the *Confessio Amantis* (VIII.2941*-57*); such exchanges suggest close literary and personal ties between them, as does in a different way Gower's holding power of attorney for Chaucer when the latter travelled to Italy in 1378 (see *Chaucer Life Records*, ed. Martin M. Crow and Clair C. Olson [Ann Arbor, 1966], p. 120; and also Fisher, *John Gower*, p. 207).

[25]Both manuscripts of the *Ecbasis*, now in the Royal Library at Brussels, very likely came from the monastery of St. Eucharius in Trier and seem to have remained close by; see *Ecbasis cuiusdam Captivi per Tropologiam*, ed. Karl Strecker, in *Scriptores rerum Germanicarum in usum Scholarum ex Monumentis Germaniae Historicis, separatim editi* (Hanover, 1935), pp. viii-x.

[26]On the manuscripts of Ausonius, see *Decimi Magni Ausonii Burdigalen-*

sis, Opuscula, ed. Rudolf Peiper (Leipzig, 1886), pp. xviii-lviii; and Manitius, *Geschichte* 1:307 n. 6.

[27]A debt to Ausonius has nowhere been determined; see Macaulay, *Works,* vol. 4, and Stockton, *Major Latin Works,* Introduction, passim.

[28]Ermini, *Il centone,* lists contents of various manuscripts including Sedulius, pp. 65-66; see also Pauly-Wissowa, *Real-Encyclopädie,* 2nd ser., vol. 3 (1921), cols. 1025-26.

[29]Manuscripts of Proba are listed by Ermini, *Il centone,* pp. 63-65.

[30]See Ermini, *Il centone,* pp. 63, 65, who notes manuscripts at Peterborough and at Cambridge; also M. R. James, *Western Manuscripts in the Library of Trinity College, Cambridge: A Descriptive Catalogue,* 3 vols. (Cambridge, 1902), 2:348-50.

[31]Trin. Col. Camb. 0.7.7 contains work by Bernard Silvestris, Ovid, Seneca, and Jerome's *Ad Jovinian,* among others; see James, *Western Manuscripts* 2:349-50.

[32]*Confessio Amantis* VI.1789-2366; see also III.1201-1330 and III. 2363-2417.

[33]Gower's other sources were the *Roman de toute Chevalerie* by Thomas of Kent and the *Historia Alexandri de Preliis* by the archpresbyter Leo; see Macaulay, *Works* 3:519, n. to line 1789; and Peter G. Beidler, ed., *John Gower's Literary Transformations in the "Confessio Amantis": Original Articles and Translations* (Washington, DC, 1982), p. 119.

[34]Trin. Col. Camb. MS. 0.7.7 has seventy-seven leaves in its present state, with the *Res Gestae* beginning on fol. 76: see James, *Western Manuscripts* 2:349-50. James's description of the quires also indicates very little missing from the end of the manuscript (p. 349), enough probably to complete the Nectanabus-Alexander story, but not the entire *Res Gestae.* In the edition of Bernard Kuebler, *Res Gestae Alexandri Macedonis, Translate ex Aesopo Graeco* (Leipzig, 1888), this story occupies the first nine pages, and could be completed in the manuscript on another page or two. The remainder of the *Res Gestae* in Kuebler fills 168 pages.

[35]For Gower's reading of Isidore, see Stockton, *Major Latin Works,* pp. 420 n. 6 and 451 n. 2. For his reading of Boccaccio, see Macaulay, *Works,* vols. 2-3, nn. (esp. to Prol. 389); Dorothy A. Dilts, "John Gower and the *De Genea-*

logia Deorum," Modern Language Notes, 57 (1942), 23-25; Charles L. Regan, "John Gower and the Fall of Babylon: *Confessio Amantis* Prol. 670-86," *English Language Notes*, 7 (1969), 85-92 (on Gower's use of the *De Casibus Illustrium Virorum*); Fisher, *John Gower*, pp. 226-27, argues Gower's involvement with Chaucer's *Troilus and Criseyde*, based on Boccaccio's *Filostrato*, and also connects the *Confessio* with Chaucer's *Legend of Good Women*, based in part on Boccaccio's *De Claris Mulieribus*, pp. 235-50.

[36]Isidore of Seville, *De Viris Illustribus*, cap. 18; in *Patrologia latina* 83.1095 (hereafter *PL*).

[37]Isidore of Seville, *Etymologiae*, Lib. I, cap. 39, 25-26; text in *PL* 82.121.

[38]Boccaccio's description of Proba as "Adelphi coniuge" derives from Isidore; see *Giovanni Boccaccio, Opere in versi*, ed. Pier Giorgio Ricci, La Letteratura Italiana, Storia e Testi 9 (Milan and Naples, 1964), pp. 764-66, n. 4. All quotations from Boccaccio are taken from this edition.

[39]   Verum, inter alia eius studia, adeo pervigili cura virgiliani carminis docta atque familiaris effecta est, ut, fere omni opere a se confecto teste, in conspectu et memoria semper habuisse videatur. Que dum forsan aliquando perspicaciori animadvertentia legeret in existimationem incidit ex illis omnem Testamenti Veteris hystoriam et Novi seriem placido atque expedito et succipleno versu posse describi. . . . Operam igitur pio conceptui prestans, nunc huc nunc illuc per buccolicum georgicumque atque eneidum saltim discurrendo carmen, nunc hac ex parte versus integros nunc ex illa metrorum particulas carpens, miro artificio in suum redegit propositum, adeo apte integros collocans et fragmenta connectens, servata lege pedum et carminis dignitate, ut nisi expertissimus compages possit advertere. . . . Voluit insuper egregia femina labore suo compositum opus vocari *Centonam*, quod ipsi persepe vidimus.

For the Latin text, see Ricci, *Opere in versi*, p. 766. The translation is that of Guido A. Guarino, *Concerning Famous Women* (New Brunswick, NJ, 1963), pp. 219, 220.

[40]   Sed queso nunc: quid optabilius audisse feminam Maronis et Homeri scandentem carmina, et apta suo operi seponentem? Selecta artificioso contextu nectentem eruditissimi

prospectent viri, quibus, cum sit sacrarum literarum insignis professio, arduum est et difficile ex amplissimo sacri voluminis gremio nunc hinc nunc inde partes elicere et ad seriem vite Cristi passis verbis prosaque cogere, uti hec fecit ex gentilitio carmine. . . . Sed quantum sedula studiis sacris ab ingenio segniciei rubiginem absterxit omnem, in lumen evasit eternum. . . . Quantum differentie sit inter famam laudandis operibus querere, et nomen una cum cadavere sepelire et tanquam non vixerint e vita discedere!

Latin text from Ricci, *Opere in versi*, p. 768; trans. Guarini, *Famous Women*, p. 220.

GOWER'S SOURCE MANUSCRIPT
OF NICHOLAS TREVET'S *LES CRONICLES*

Robert M. Correale

Les Cronicles is a compilation of world history, from the Creation to the early fourteenth century, written by the English Dominican friar Nicholas Trevet for his patroness, Princess Mary of Woodstock, fourth daughter of Edward I and Eleanor of Castile, who was a nun at Amesbury.[1] Trevet's book survives in eleven Anglo-Norman manuscripts, two of which contain only portions of the chronicle copied in post-medieval times. The other nine are all written in English scripts, and all but one belong to the fourteenth century. They are as follows:[2]

A	London, British Libr., Arundel 56, fols. 2-77	ca. 1375
M	Oxford, Magdalen Coll. 45 (138), fols. 1-97^v	ca. 1335-40
F	Oxford, Bodleian, Fairfax 10 (S.C. 3890), fols. 1ra-106ra	XIV^m
T	Cambridge, England, Trinity Coll. 0. 4. 32, fols. 1ra-101va	XIV^m-1360
S	Stockholm, Kungliga Bibl., D. 1311a (III), pp. 1-276	ca. 1400
P	Paris, Bibl. Nationale, franç. 9687, fols. 1va-114va	ca. 1340-50
R	Oxford, Bodleian, Rawlinson B. 178 (S.C. 11545), fols. 1-66	ca. 1335-50
L	Leyden, Universiteitsbibl., Voss. Gall. F. 6, fols. 1-93^v	XIV 4/4
D	Oxford, Bodleian, Douce 119 (S.C. 21693), fols. 1 (=1^a)-69^v	XV 1/4

There is also a Middle English translation made in the early fifteenth century[3]:

E	Cambridge, Mass., Harvard f MS. Eng. 938, fols. 9ra-91rb	XV^2

The first five of the French MSS, and the Middle English version, end with Trevet's account of the disputed election in 1330 of Louis of Bavaria as Holy Roman Emperor. The others--with the exception of D, which breaks off incomplete during the reign of Richard the Lionheart--have a lengthy continuation describing Louis's struggles with the papacy and his condemnation on charges of heresy, and then conclude with the decision of Edward II of England to invade Scotland. The manuscripts of this second group also share differences in the presentation of material relating to early British history as well as other textual variants. On the basis of this evidence, as well as the examination of several test passages, Professor Ruth Dean has proposed that Trevet's book, as we have it, exists in two separate redactions, one represented by MSS. A M F T S (Family A), and the other by P R L D (Family B)--either of which might have been presented to Princess Mary before her death in 1332, though the chronicle itself goes beyond 1334 and may have been finally interrupted by Trevet's own death.[4]

Les Cronicles has never been printed, but an edition of it based on five manuscripts (A M T R D) was prepared as a doctoral dissertation over fifty years ago.[5] Using this edition as a copy text, I have collated all the extant manuscripts in their entirety and found that on the basis of shared errors, shared omissions, and other common variants the manuscripts do indeed align themselves into the two families representing the two separate redactions that Professor Dean postulated. These collations also confirm the existence of subgroups A M, F T, and P R that she also noticed. S, which also belongs to the same sub-group as F T, has such a large number of unique readings and additions of words and phrases as to suggest that either the scribe's exemplar contained readings found nowhere else in the manuscript tradition or, what I think more likely, the scribe himself edited it quite freely.[6] There are several large gaps in D--including the omission of most of Trevet's story of Constance--but textually D is closely related to P R. L, the other member of this family, appears to have been contaminated in a number of places by readings from Family A type manuscripts, although there is not much evidence of conflation in the story of Constance.

That Trevet's story of Constance in *Les Cronicles* is the principal common source of both Chaucer's Man of Law's Tale in the *Canterbury Tales* and Gower's Tale of Constance in the *Confessio Amantis* (II.587-1598) was discovered in the middle of the last century.[7] Since then, the French version has been edited twice--mainly for the benefit of Chaucerians--first by Edmund Brock for the Chaucer Society in 1872, and then by Margaret Schlauch in 1941. Brock printed the text found in A, corrected at times by readings from S, and provided a modern English translation. He learned about the existence of four other manuscripts (M T R D) only after his edition was set in type.[8] Miss Schlauch used M as her base text and printed variants from all the manuscripts except L, which Professor Dean discovered in the Leyden University Library in 1948.[9]

Despite their obvious inadequacies, these are the texts scholars have had to rely upon to study and assess Chaucer's and Gower's debt to Trevet and to each other. Several comparisons of both poets' versions of the story of Constance with Trevet's account and with each other have amply demonstrated the artistic superiority of Chaucer's tale over Gower's.[10] A number of scholars have also attempted to discover whether Gower, as he followed Trevet, also used Chaucer as a source or vice versa, and--with the notable exceptions of Skeat and Macaulay--they have concluded that Gower probably wrote first and that Chaucer's work most likely contains some verbal borrowing from his friend's poem.[11]

None of these scholars, however, tried to identify either Gower's or Chaucer's source manuscript of *Les Cronicles*, nor, until recently, did anybody think to inquire whether either poet read other sections of the book besides the life of Constance. Then in 1969 Professor Robert A. Pratt pointed out that Chaucer did know various other parts of Trevet's chronicle and used

135

phrases and ideas from scattered portions of it in several of his works, including the tales of the Pardoner, Physician, Monk, Squire, and the Wife of Bath in the Canterbury collection.[12] Gower, too, as I have discovered, read considerably more of *Les Cronicles* than just the story of Constance, and borrowed material from several of Trevet's *estoires* for some of his own stories of biblical figures and events elsewhere in the *Confessio Amantis*.[13]

Clearly, then, a new edition of Trevet's whole book is needed, one that will help to reveal the total indebtedness of both poets to this source; and, in keeping with the aims and ideals of the Chaucer Library, I have been preparing such an edition based on the surviving manuscript that most nearly resembles the one Chaucer knew and used. To find this manuscript, I have followed the method used by Professor Severs to identify the Latin and French source manuscripts of the Clerk's Tale. Each passage in which one or more of the French texts diverge from the others has been compared with the corresponding passage in the Man of Law's Tale and any other place in Chaucer's works where Trevet's influence can be detected. The manuscript containing the largest number of correspondences and requiring the fewest emendations will be the one that best represents Chaucer's manuscript.[14]

The manuscript that is probably closest to Chaucer's, as I have shown elsewhere,[15] is the Paris MS (P) of Family B, and it has been selected as the base text for the new edition of *Les Cronicles* in the Chaucer Library series. The subject of this investigation, however, is Gower's use of Trevet; and, using the method just described, the main question I will try to answer in this essay is which of the surviving French manuscripts comes closest to representing Gower's text of Trevet's story of Constance.

When he wrote his tale of Constance, Gower followed Trevet much more closely than Chaucer did in the Man of Law's Tale. But he made enough deletions, additions, and other kinds of changes that when his poem is compared with its source it is clear, as Macaulay has observed, "that Gower treated the story with some degree of freedom" (*Works*, 2:483). When his version is placed side by side with the French texts it also becomes clear that fewer than twenty passages--excluding places where there are differences in the forms of proper names--provide any evidence which can be used to help identify Gower's source manuscript, and some of this evidence is either ambiguous or inconclusive, as shown by the comparisons in the first four passages below.

(1-2)	Gower[16]		Sche hath hem with hire wordes wise
		607	Of *Cristes feith* so full enformed,
			That thei therto ben all conformed,
			So that baptesme thei receiven
			And alle here false goddes weyven.
		611	Whan thei ben of the *feith* certein,
			Thei gon to Barbarie ayein
	Trevet	165[17]	E quant ele entendi qil estoient paens, lour prescha la *fey Cristien.* E puis qil auoient assentu *a la fey,* les fist baptizer e enseiner parfitement en la *fei Iesu Crist.* Puis retournerent a lour terre.
	All MSS		prescha la *fey* Cristien
	All MSS		assentu a la *fey*
	A M S P R L		*fei* Iesu Crist
	F T		*ley* Iesu Crist
(3)	Gower		'Mi Sone, I am be double weie
			With al myn herte glad and blithe,
			For that miself have ofte sithe
			Desired thou wolt, as men seith,
		660	Receive and take a newe *feith*
	Trevet	167	la mere le soudan . . . mout mercier e loer dieu qel auoit le purpos de la *ley Cristien,* e lui iura qe par grant tenps auoit ele este en mesme la volunte priuement. . . .
	A M F T S L		*ley* Cristien
	P R		*foi* Cristien

137

In the French manuscripts both *fei*, *foi* (faith) and *ley*, *loi* (law) refer to the Christian and pagan religions, and the scribes use both words with considerable freedom, sometimes even switching for no apparent reason from one word to the other in the same sentence. Gower also employs both words, but with much greater consistency. He uses *lawe* in only three lines (587, 727, 769) where it is needed for the rhyme; in all the other thirteen references to the different religions of his characters, he uses *feith*--whether he is adding material of his own to the story (lines 1160, 1313) or translating a part of his source where most of the manuscripts have *fey* (lines 607, 611) or where most of them read *ley* (line 660). In light of these facts, then, the variant readings of F T in the first two passages and those of P R in the third produce evidence that is obviously ambiguous and should be disregarded.

(4)	Gower		And therupon to make an ende
		632	The Souldan hise hostages *sende*
			To Rome, of Princes Sones tuelve:

| | Trevet | 166 | Puis apres poy de iours le soudan *maunda* mesmes cesti admiral e solempnes messagers dez plus grantz de sa terre e en lour conduyt duzze enfauntz Sarazins fitz a grauntz Sarazins, hostages a Thiberie, en fourme de seurte pur sa fille. |

A M P R L	e soudan *maunda* mesmes cesti admiral
F T S	le soudan mesmes cesti admiral

Gower's manuscript probably had *maunda* in the French sentence quoted here. But in his very next sentence Trevet mentions that the Souldan conveyed (*maunda*) his assent to the terms set by the Romans for his marriage to Constance, and that he also sent (*enuoya*) sealed letters assuring peace between the Christians and his people. Since all the manuscripts have both verbs in this second sentence, Gower would have had two French equivalents for his word *sende* literally right under his eyes if he were looking at any one of the surviving copies of his source while writing this part of his poem. In this context, therefore, I think the omission in F T S is not very significant and the evidence in this passage is inconclusive.

Several other comparisons, however, provide more convincing evidence that Gower's manuscript was unlike the F T S manuscripts of Family A.

(5)	Gower	636	*Tuo Cardinals* he hath assissed With othre lordes many mo, That with his doghter scholden go, To se the Souldan be converted.
	Trevet	166	En cele veiage estoit enueye *vn euesqe cardinal* e *vn prestre cardinal* oue grant noumbre de clergie e vn senatour de Rome oue noble cheualerie. . . .
	A M S P R L		*vn euesqe cardinal e un prestre cardinal* oue grant noumbre de clergie
	F T		*vn euesqe cardinal* oue grant noumbre de clergie
(6)	Gower	712	Vitailed full for yeres fyve, Wher that the *wynd* it wolde dryve, Sche putte upon the wawes wilde.
	Trevet	167-68	Dount ele fist estorer vne neefs de vitaile, de payn. . . . E issint la fist mener par autres neefs tanqe a la haute meer, e ou nule terre lour apparut; e issint les mariners la lesserent soule e la comaunderent a quatre *ventz*.
	A M P R L		a quatre *ventz*
	F T S		a quatre *nefze*

Gower changed his source in this first exile scene (passage 6) so that the wicked mother of the Souldan, and not her navy, is directly responsible for putting Constance upon the "wawes wilde." He was also obviously following a copy of Trevet that had the right reading *ventz* (winds) instead of the erroneous *nefze* (boats) in F T S.

> (7)   Gower   1031   That ye the same Schip *vitaile*,
> In which that sche tok arivaile,
> Therinne and putteth bothe tuo,
> Hireself forthwith hire child also

> Trevet   174   e, pur ceo comaunda a Elda . . .
> apres lez lettres luez feit apparailer
> *vne neef e vitaile* pur cync aunz de
> manger e boire pur Constaunce, e
> en la neef mettre mesme le tresor
> que fu en sa primere neef troue, e
> qe en mesme la manere en cele neef,
> sauntz sigle e sauntz enviroun, ou
> saunz nul autre engyn, fut oue son
> enfaunt Moris de la terre exile, come
> ele en la terre entra.

> A M S P R L   vne neef e *vitaile*
> F T   vne neef e *viande*

At this point in the tale, Constance is about to undergo a second exile at sea, this time because of the treachery of Domilde, her second evil mother-in-law, and Gower's use of *vitaile* instead of *viande* to describe the stores of food and drink being put into her boat is another clue that his manuscript was different from F T. But in the first exile scene (passage 6 above) Gower uses the same word *vitailed* (line 711) to describe the provisions Constance is given, and in the corresponding passage in his source all the manuscripts have *vitaile*. Of course it is possible, especially if we are willing to grant that he did not handle his source too mechanically, that when Gower was writing this second exile scene he simply repeated a word he had borrowed earlier from Trevet, and so perhaps the evidence against F T in line

1031 is not as strong as it might at first appear. But the parallel is still impressive.

(8)	Gower	952	And sche with *feigned* joie it herde And yaf him yiftes largely
	Trevet	172-73	Avint que le messager maunda par Elda e Lucius, ala par Knaresbourch pur porter e nuncier a la mere le rey bone nouele, com il quidoyt par resoun. E ele, oye la nouele, *feynt* trop grant *ioye* en agard de gentz, e al messager dona trop grauntz dounz e riches en moustraunce de ioie.
	A M P R F T S L		*feynt* trop grant ioye *fist* (*fesoit* S) trop grant ioye

When the messenger tells Domilde that Constance has given birth to a son, Gower's comment that the queen pretended to be happy at the news provides unmistakable evidence that his manuscript had the word *feynt* (feigned) instead of *fist* or *fesoit* (made). In this passage, therefore, F T S L get negative votes and A M P R, positive ones.

In the next few passages, however, there are indications that Gower's text of Trevet differed from *all* the Family A texts--including A M--and that it more closely resembled the Family B texts.

(9)	Gower		Constance, as the Cronique seith,
		598	*Sche hihte*, and was so ful of feith
	Trevet	165	cist Tyberie Constantin . . . engendra de sa femme Ytalie *vne fille Constaunce*
	A M F T S P R L		vne fille Constaunce vne fille *apele* Constaunce

Gower's phrase "as the Chronique seith" calls attention to the fact that he is following his source closely at the beginning of his poem, and so the word *apele*, present only in the B manuscripts, surely accounts for the words "Sche hihte" in line 598.

(10)	Gower	824	*This* false *knyht* upon delay Hath taried til thei were aslepe
	Trevet	171	puis que Hermyngild e Constaunce estoient forment endormies apres longes veiletz e oreisouns, *cist*, que tut estoit pris en la mayn al diable, trencha la goule Hermingild. . . .
	P R L		*cist chivaler*, que tut estoit pris en la mayn al diable
	A M F T S		*cist*, que tut estoit pris en la mayn al diable

The little piece of evidence in this passage may not seem too convincing, especially since the whole paragraph from which the French sentence is taken begins with the phrase "vn cheualer Sessoun de la meyne Elda" (Trevet, p. 170). But its significance as part of a larger stylistic pattern is not lost upon anybody who has collated the entire text of *Les Cronicles* and noticed with what monotonous regularity the scribes of P R L cite or repeat nouns like *chivaler* after demonstrative pronouns, while the scribes who copied the Family A manuscripts do not usually follow this practice.[18]

There is of course much more important evidence in the following lines from the same murder scene.

(11-12) Gower		And in his hond a rasour knif He bar, with which hire throte he cutte, And prively the knif he putte
	833	*Under* that other beddes side,
	834	Wher that *Constance lai beside*

Trevet	171	cist, que tut estoit pris en la mayn al diable, trencha la goule Hermingild, sa dame, *e coste Constaunce*, qe fu forment endormie en mesme le lyt. E quant il auoit parfait la felonie, musca le coteil senglaunt *en Constaunt lorier* la pucele.

P R L	*en coste* Constaunce
F T S	*a cost* Constaunce
M	*e coste* Constaunce
A	*e ceste* Constaunce

P R L	*desouz* le oeiler Constance
A M	*en* Constaunt lorier
F T	*et* Constance lorir
S	*aderer* loriler Constaunce

When describing the murder of Hermyngheld, Gower follows Trevet by saying that the false knight cut the lady's throat while she and Constance were sleeping in the same bed. But whereas Trevet mentions the pillow of Constance as the place where the felon hides his bloody knife, Gower, in his version, puts it underneath her bed. Here the French manuscripts, as the variant readings indicate, divide themselves very neatly into the main families and sub-families of the entire recension, and it is clear that, even though Gower was altering his source somewhat, he had his eye on one of the B manuscripts containing the phrase "*desouz* le oeiler Constaunce" when he wrote "*Under* that other beddes side" (line 833).

In the variants for line 834, the phrase *a cost* in F T S is close enough to the reading of P R L as to suggest a similar meaning, and presumably the exemplars of A and M had (or were meant to have) a horizontal bar over *e*, so that M's present reading, with the lost n-stroke restored, would be identical to the reading of P R L. In any event, it is certain that Gower could not be following A, where the phrase *e ceste Constaunce* creates the impossible meaning that Constance was also murdered by the knight.

From Gower's point of view, A is also in error in the three following passages:

(13) Gower

                      This olde fend, this Sarazine,
                      Let take anon this Constantine
707   With *al the good* sche thider broghte

Trevet 168 E en cele neef fist mettre *tote la richesse e le tresour* que lempire Tyberie aueit maunde

M F T S P R L mettre *tote* la richesse e le tresour
A mettre la richesse e le tresour

(14) Gower

                      For the seconde day a morwe
891   *The king cam*, as thei were acorded

Trevet 172 Et pur ceo que *la venue le rey* fu pres, pur ceo ne voleit Elda iugement doner sur la tresoun iesqes a sa venue; et mist le feloun en prisoun.

M F T S P R L pur ceo *la venue le rey* fu pres . . . iesqes a sa venue; et mist le feloun en prisoun. . . .

A pur ceo *la venue*; et mist le feloun en prisoun

(15) Gower 1520 And whanne *he wiste* it was Constance, Was nevere fader half so blithe.

Trevet 180 E puis qe lemperour out sa fille oy *e bien conu*, ia de si sudeyne ioye auoit le qoer suppris que a poy estoit de son destrer tresbuche. . . .

F T S P R L D lemperour out sa fille oy et *bien conu*
M lemperour out sa fille oy et *bien com*
A lemperour out sa fille oy et *vieu com*

The omissions in A of *tote* in passage 13 and of *le rey* (by homeoteleuton) in passage 14 are both marks against this manuscript, but the next comparison provides much stronger evidence against it. When Constance is reunited with her father at the end of the story, according to A's reading the Emperor is filled with sudden joy after he has heard and seen (*vieu*) his daughter. But in Gower and most of the other French texts the Emperor is made joyful as soon as he has heard his daughter's greeting and "wiste" (*conu*) it was Constance. As far as Gower is concerned, A is obviously in error, and so is M, although the exemplar of M might have had the correct reading which has been corrupted by the scribe's omission of a final minim that changed the phrase *bien conu* to *bien com*.

Almost all the passages examined up to this point have readings that are negative for one or more of the manuscripts of Family A, and at the same time a few passages (9-12) have readings that are positive for Family B. On the basis of this evidence it is clear that Gower's manuscript was closer to P R L D than any of the others. Of this group, D, as mentioned earlier, lacks most of Trevet's story. It has only the final portion in which Constance, after having been rescued by the Roman navy from her second exile at sea, lives unrecognized in Rome with her son for many years before she is finally reunited there with her husband and her father. D is, in fact, a good witness for this part of Trevet's story--it has the correct reading, for example, in passage 15--and the leaves that are missing from it today might have been present in the fourteenth century, so that Trevet's entire story could have been available to Gower in this copy. In its present state, however, D obviously cannot represent Gower's manuscript; the only real contenders are P R L and, as the next comparisons reveal, there is not much evidence against any one of them.

(16)	Gower		And hath ordeined, as sche thoghte,
		709	A nakid Schip *withoute stiere*,
			In which the good and hire in fiere

Trevet	168	e en cele neef fist la soudane mettre la pucele saunz sigle e *sauntz neuiroun* e sauntz chescune manere de eide de homme.
RL		saunz sigle e *sanz viron* et sauntz chescune manere de eide
AMFTS		saunz sigle e *sauntz neuiroun* et sauntz chescune manere de eide
P		sanz sigle et sanz chescune manere de eide

In this passage we are back again to the first exile scene, and Gower's words "withouten stiere" mean "without a rudder" or "without a steering oar." Trevet's phrase *sanz viron* or *sauntz neuirous* (*naviroun*), therefore, was presumably in Gower's source text, and its omission here is a mark against P. But our attitude concerning how much weight should be given to this omission will depend again, as in passage 7, upon our view of how mechanically or slavishly Gower followed his source as he crafted his poem. When Constance is exiled for the second time in the "same Schip" (line 1031), Gower does not mention that her boat lacks a rudder. But Trevet's account of the second exile scene contains the exact same phraseology that he had used earlier to describe the boat in which she is cast adrift, and in this second scene P has the right reading, *sanz viroun*.[19] If Gower had read all of Trevet's story, or both of the exile scenes, before he began his translation, he might easily have remembered the detail about the rudderless boat from either scene, and so its omission from the first scene in P would be much less significant than it now appears.

The same line of reasoning is applicable, I think, in deciding how much weight to give to the error in P R in the following passage:

| (17) | Gower | 954 | Bot in the *nyht* al prively Sche tok the lettres whiche he hadde, Fro point to point and overradde |

146

Trevet   173   qar *cele nuyt* enyueri taunt le
                     messauger de vn maliciouse
                     beyuere. . . . Puis, par lassent e le
                     conseil le soun clerc, ouery la
                     boiste le messager e ouery les
                     lettres maundes al rey. . . .

A M F T S L   *cele nuyt*
P R   *ele mit*

Soon after King Allee marries Constance, he is obliged to go to war against the Scots, and he leaves his pregnant wife in the care of Elda, "the kinges Chamberlein." In both Trevet and Gower, there are two scenes in which a messenger from Elda, carrying letters to and from the king about Constance and the birth of their son Moris, stays overnight in the castle of the queen mother Domilde, who counterfeits the letters on the same night. In the first scene, P R have the erroneous reading *ele mit* for Trevet's phrase *cele nuyt*. But in the second scene, which occurs shortly thereafter in both stories (Gower, line 1005; Trevet, p. 174), P R have the correct reading that is found in all the manuscripts. The fact that Gower could have found this detail in both of Trevet's scenes, therefore, also diminishes the weight of the evidence against P R in this passage.

So far, then, the score is about even. There are two votes against P in passages 16 and 17, and one each against R in passage 17 and against L, as we saw earlier, in passage 8. With so little evidence against these B texts, it is difficult to decide which one of them is closest to Gower's manuscript. But the task is made even more difficult because of the way Gower uses proper names from Trevet's story.

There are only a few place names in Gower's tale, and none of them gives any definite indication of the kind of manuscript he consulted. He refers to *Northumberlond* (line 717) and *Wales* (line 904) in lines where he follows Trevet rather closely, and these forms are found in P R L, as opposed to *Northumbre* and *Gales* in A M F T S. But the B manuscripts do not deserve positive votes in these places because Gower certainly did not need to consult a French source for such common English names.[20] Besides, such factors as the demands of meter (line 717) or personal preference undoubtedly influenced his choices. A more interesting place name in the story is that of *Knaresburgh* Castle, home of the treacherous Domilde. Chaucer does not mention the castle by name in the Man of Law's Tale, probably for good political reasons, since it had been associated with treasonous persons and events from the time it harbored the assassins of Thomas Becket in 1170-71 down to the 1380s when its owner John of Gaunt was accused of treason by the government.[21] Gower, by contrast, mentions it four times--twice when he tells how Domilde duped the messenger and changed his letters as part of her plot against Constance (lines 943, 1001), and twice by adding it to material in Trevet, when he recounts how the king discovered the plot and had his mother killed (lines 1265, 1273). One wonders why Gower refers to the castle so often, for he also could easily have learned of its reputation and its association with the unpopular Gaunt who found refuge there during the Peasants' Revolt. Whatever his motive, if he borrowed the name from Trevet he would have found the form he uses only in A F T S L, a fact that would seem to give L a helping hand against P R, as well as suggest the influence of the A manuscripts on his source text. But the variants in the other manuscripts--*Knaresbourch*, *-bourgh*, *-burg*--were all commonly used English spellings,[22] so that Gower might have seen any one of them in his manuscript and simply substituted the form he preferred.

Some of the other names Gower uses, however, do suggest the influence of the A manuscripts on his source. As readers of these stories know, Gower and Chaucer employ different names for several of the main characters. Thus, Gower's heroine is *Constance*, her husband is King *Allee*, and the king's mother is *Domilde*, whereas Chaucer names these persons *Custance*, King *Alla*, and *Donegild*.[23] In addition, Gower, unlike Chaucer, re-

148

tains many of Trevet's names for the minor characters. He keeps *Theloüs*, for example, as the name of the lecherous steward who tries to seduce Constance after she arrives in Spain, and he uses *Elda* as the name for King Allee's chamberlain, who figures so prominently in the plot.[24]

Constance's husband corresponds to the historical King Aelle of Deira in Northumberland (d. 588), and earlier in the chronicle, when Trevet is trying to distinguish between him and King Aelle of Sussex (d. 514?), the name of the Northumbrian monarch is spelled differently in the two families of manuscripts.

> Et fu le primer rei de Sussex *Alle*, noun pas *Alle*, le rei de Northombre. (M, fol. 46ᵛ)

All MSS	Sussex *Alle*

| A M F T S | *Alle* le rei de Northombre |
| P R L | *Alla* le rei de Northombre |

This same pattern is followed in the first part of Trevet's story of Constance. From the time when the king meets and marries Constance to the point where he orders his mother's execution, the scribes of the A manuscripts in every instance spell his name *Alle*, while in the B texts the scribes invariably use *Alla*. But later when he makes his pilgrimage to Rome to receive the pope's absolution, and there finds Constance again, the scribes of the B manuscripts, except for a few places in L, switch from *Alla* to *Alle*. Gower's exact form *Allee* survives only in the two final references to the king in S, but even so it is more likely that his name comes from a manuscript in which *Alle* forms appear at the beginning of the story and are used throughout, instead of one like P R L (D) where *Alla* forms appear first and are changed at the end. The evidence may be somewhat conflicting, but it suggests that Gower's name for the king came from an A manuscript.

Gower mentions the name of the king's mother only once, and he says her "rihte name was *Domilde*" (line 947). Trevet uses the name five times, but it is difficult to determine how he intended it to be spelled because the scribes use several different forms. Gower could have chosen *Domilde* to rhyme with *spilde* (line 948), or he might be telling his audience the manuscript he worked from had other forms and he has chosen the correct one. *Domilde* appears only in F T S, which also have *Domigild(e)*; and *Domylde* is found in A M, which also have several other forms including *Deumylde* and *Dounylde*. In P R L, it is spelled *Dowmld(e)*. Gower also refers to *Theloüs* only once (line 1092), but does not use the name as a rhyme word. Trevet uses the name six times, and, while there is not great variation in the scribal spellings, only three texts--A M S--have the form Gower uses. In P R L it is *Telous, Tylous*.

But the best evidence that Gower's manuscript had some names found only in the A texts is his use of *Elda* as the name of the king's chief nobleman. Trevet refers to this lord some forty times, and in every single instance the spelling *Elda* is found only in A M. Everywhere else it is *Olda*. Gower mentions *Elda* fourteen times, more often than any other name except *Constance*, and so there can be no doubt that Gower's form came from a manuscript like A M.

By now it is clear that none of the surviving manuscripts of *Les Cronicles* preserves the text of Trevet's story in the form Gower used as his source of the Tale of Constance, and it should be just as apparent that it is difficult to identify the French text that comes closest to representing Gower's. But at least we have a good idea of the *kind* of manuscript he used. As shown in the accompanying table, the results of the comparisons in the first seventeen passages provide solid evidence for believing that Gower's text more closely resembled those of Family B than those of Family A. There are more correspondences between the words and phrases of Gower's poem and the readings of the B manuscripts than between it and the readings of the others, and, conversely, fewer emendations would be required to change P R or L into Gower's hypothetical source manuscript than would be needed to produce the same result for A M F T or S.

Leaving aside those passages where the evidence is either ambiguous or inconclusive, R and L correspond to Gower in twelve places, and each would need to be changed in only one place, R in passage 17 and L in passage 8. The next closest manuscript is P, which agrees with Gower eleven times, and would need to be emended in passages 16 and 17. Of the A manuscripts, M is the closest, agreeing with Gower in nine places and differing in four (9, 10, 11, 15), followed by S, which agrees in eight places and differs in five (6, 8, 9, 10, 11). The farthest removed from Gower's text are A F T, each agreeing with it in six places and differing in seven--A in passages 9 through 15; F T in passages 5 through 11.

The evidence produced by comparing the proper names in the two stories, however, points in the opposite direction. In fact, if each manuscript were given positive or negative votes depending on whether or not it had the spelling Gower uses for the last four names in the table, then M would have thirteen agreements and four disagreements and would appear to be slightly closer to Gower than either R or L, both of which would continue to have twelve correspondences, but need five emendations. However, when we consider how Gower treated all the proper names in his poem, we must assume, I think, that other factors such as the demands of rhyme and meter, the customary spellings of place names in his time, perhaps even previous reading and personal preference, also contributed to his choices of forms. Admittedly, *Domilde*, *Theloüs*, *Allee*, and *Elda* are uncommon names, and Gower most likely borrowed them from Trevet. But it is also true that we know very little about Gower's usual ways of treating the names he took from his sources, especially the kinds of changes he might make in them for his own artistic purposes, and so I am inclined to put this evidence in a separate category and consider it less important than the other. In short, I believe that, taken collectively, the evidence in the first seventeen passages outweighs the evidence derived from

151

the comparisons of proper names; in particular it strongly favors the B manuscripts in passages 9, 11, 15, where the readings of P R L are clearly those of Gower's source, and where M and the other members of Family A are obviously in error from Gower's point of view.

It is difficult to decide which of the B manuscripts has the better claim to represent Gower's source manuscript because, as mentioned earlier, there is so little evidence that tends to eliminate any one of them. Only the omission of one phrase (*sanz viron*) in passage 16 keeps P from having the same number of correspondences with Gower that R and L have, and that omission, for the reasons given above, may not be very significant after all. Moreover, in the three passages (8, 16, 17) where P R L do not have the same readings, the strongest evidence for or against any one of them is found in passage 8 where the language of P R--*feynt trop grant ioie*--accounts for Gower's phrase, *feigned joie*, and where L's reading is plainly incorrect from Gower's point of view. In a contest between R and L, then, perhaps the nod should go to R. However, since Gower's manuscript had the forms of several proper names that survive only in the A texts, it might have looked less like P R. and more like L, which in several parts of the chronicle is contaminated by readings from Family A.

Thus, the evidence at our disposal is finally inconclusive, and, apart from the spellings of some names, Gower's copy of Trevet's story probably was not very much different from Chaucer's, which, as already indicated, appears to have been closer to P than any of the surviving manuscripts. Since P will be used as the base text for the new edition of *Les Cronicles* in the Chaucer Library series, students of Gower will be able to consult this edition with confidence, whether they are reconsidering Gower's handling of the story of Constance, re-examining the question of whether Chaucer or Gower used the other's poem, or looking elsewhere in the book for further evidence of Gower's indebtedness to Trevet. The discovery of such evidence may, in turn, also shed more light on the kind of manuscript Gower used. In any event, with an edition of Trevet's whole book before them, scholars will have the opportunity to study and assess the extent to which Trevet's popularized account of world history helped to shape some of Gower's thought and his art.

Passage	Line	Gower's reading	Positive MSS	Negative MSS
1-2	607-11	feith	Ambiguous	
3	660	feith	Ambiguous	
4	632	sende	Inconclusive	
5	636	Tuo Cardinals	A M S P R L	F T
6	712	wynd	A M P R L	F T S
7	1031	vitaile	A M S P R L	F T
8	952	feigned	A M P R	F T S L
9	598	Sche hihte	P R L	A M F T S
10	824	This knyht	P R L	A M F T S
11	833	Under that beddes	P R L	A M F T S
12	834	lai beside	M F T S P R L	A
13	707	al the good	M F T S P R L	A
14	891	The king	M F T S P R L	A
15	1520	he wiste	F T S P R L D	A M
16	709	withoute stiere	A M F T S R L	P
17	954	nyht	A M F T S L	P R
--	714	Northumberlond	Inconclusive	
--	904	Wales	Inconclusive	
--	943	Knaresburgh	Inconclusive	
--	722 (etc.)	King Allee	A M F T S	P R L
--	947	Domilde	A M F T S	P R L
--	1092	Theolüs-Theloüs	A M S	F T P R L
--	726 (etc.)	Elda	A M	F T S P R L

ROBERT M. CORREALE

NOTES

[1]Medieval scribes spell the author's name in a variety of ways including *Trivet*, the form that has been in general use among modern scholars. I follow Professor Ruth J. Dean's practice of spelling it *Trevet*, the form he himself used in an acrostic in his treatise on the Mass. Four of the surviving MSS (A M P R--see list below) contain a title which reads, with some variation among the four, "Ci commencement les cronicles qe frere Nichol Trivet escrit a ma dame Marie, la fille le roi d'Engleterre Edward le fitz Henri." For a summary of the contents and purpose of the work, see Dean, "Nicholas Trevet, Historian," in *Medieval Learning and Literature, Essays Presented to R. W. Hunt*, ed. J. J. G. Alexander and M. T. Gibson (Oxford, 1976), pp. 339-46, and M. Dominica Legge, *Anglo-Norman Literature and Its Background* (Oxford, 1963), pp. 298-302.

[2]I print the list of MSS (with the same sigla but in a different order) that is found in Dean, "Nicholas Trevet, Historian," pp. 351-52. For fuller descriptions of them, see Dean's articles, "The Manuscripts of Nicholas Trevet's Anglo-Norman *Cronicles*," *Medievalia et Humanistica*, 14 (1962), 95-105; and "An Essay in Anglo-Norman Palaeography," in *Studies in French Language and Mediaeval Literature presented to Professor Mildred K. Pope* (Manchester, 1939), pp. 79-87.

[3]Two editions of this Middle English translation have been prepared as doctoral dissertations in American universities--"Nicholas Trevet's Chronicle: an early fifteenth-century English translation, edited with an introduction, notes and glossary," by William V. Whitehead (Harvard University, 1961) and Christine M. Rose, "An Edition of Houghton Library f MS 938: The Fifteenth Century Middle English Translation of Nicholas Trevet's Anglo-Norman *Les Chronicles*, with *Brut* Continuation" (Tufts University, 1985), the latter with the "Brut Continuation" from the same manuscript.

[4]Dean, "Nicholas Trevet, Historian," pp. 346-48.

[5]Alexander Rutherford, "The Anglo-Norman Chronicle of Nicolas Trivet" (Ph.D. diss., University of London, 1932).

[6]Some of this "editing" in the story of Constance occurs in the following sentences, where the italics indicate words and phrases found only in S. "Donc quant Thelous par dures manaces la voloit afforcer, *et* ele *luy* respount par *resouns sages et bels si dit* lenfaunt Moris, qi ia estoit de ii aunz entiers puis qil estoit exile dengleterre, poet avoir entendement et memoire de chose fait en sa presence. *Puit avenir grant peril ceste* fu sa colour soy defendre de

154

pecche" (Stockholm MS, p. 167).

[7]That Chaucer's tale is based on Trevet's story was first pointed out by the Swedish scholar P. O. Bäckström in *Svenska Folkböcker: Sagor, Legender och Äfventyr*, 2 vols. (Stockholm, 1845), 1:221-28. (See Schlauch, *Sources and Analogues*, n. 9 below, p. 155). Gower's indebtedness to Trevet was first mentioned by Thomas Wright in his edition of *The Canterbury Tales of Geoffrey Chaucer*, vol. 1 (London, 1847), p. 206.

[8]See *Originals and Analogues of Some of Chaucer's Canterbury Tales*, ed. F. J. Furnivall, E. Brock, and W. A. Clouston, Chaucer Society, 2nd ser., nos. 7, 10, 15, 20, 22 (London, 1872), pp. iii-xii, 1-53. The Middle English version of Trevet's story is printed in the same volume, pp. 221-50.

[9]Margaret Schlauch, "The Man of Law's Tale," in *Sources and Analogues of Chaucer's Canterbury Tales*, ed. W. F. Bryan and Germaine Dempster (1941; rept. New York, 1958), pp. 155-206.

[10]"It is worth while to read the simpler versions of Trivet and Gower, if only to realize afresh from the contrast how far Chaucer stands above them" (Schlauch, *Sources and Analogues*, p. 161). In addition to the works cited in n. 11, see also Edward A. Block, "Originality, Controlling Purpose, and Craftsmanship in Chaucer's *Man of Law's Tale*," *PMLA*, 68 (1953), 572-616; and Masayoshi Ito, *John Gower: The Medieval Poet* (Tokyo, 1976), pp. 25-38. Two recent discussions of Gower's artistic purposes and achievements in retelling the tale can be found in Patrick J. Gallacher, *Love, the Word, and Mercury: A Reading of John Gower's "Confessio Amantis"* (Albuquerque, 1975), pp. 91-102; and Russell A. Peck, *Kingship and Common Profit in Gower's "Confessio Amantis"* (Carbondale and Edwardsville, IL, 1978), pp. 63-69.

[11]See W. W. Skeat, ed., *The Complete Works of Geoffrey Chaucer*, 2nd ed., vol. 3 (Oxford, 1900), pp. 409-17; G. C. Macaulay, ed., *The Complete Works of John Gower*, vol. 2 (1901; rept. Grosse Pointe, MI, 1968), pp. 483-84. Those who think that Chaucer borrowed from Gower include E. Lücke, "Das Leben der Constanze bei Trivet, Gower und Chaucer," *Anglia*, 14 (1892), 77-122, 149-85; J. S. P. Tatlock, *The Development and Chronology of Chaucer's Works* (1907; rept. Gloucester, MA, 1963), pp. 172-88; Margaret Schlauch, *Chaucer's Constance and Accused Queens* (1927; rept. New York, 1969), pp. 132-34 (which also contains a summary of the earlier arguments); and John H. Fisher, *John Gower, Moral Philosopher and Friend of Chaucer* (New York, 1964), pp. 290-92.

[12]"Chaucer and *Les Cronicles* of Nicholas Trevet," in *Studies in Lan-*

guage, Literature, and Culture of the Middle Ages and Later, in Honor of Rudolph Willard, ed. E. B. Atwood and A. A. Hill (Austin, 1969), pp. 303-11.

[13]Trevet's influence can be detected, for example, in the tales of Nebuchadnezzar's Punishment (I.2785-3042), Jephthah's Daughter (IV.1505-95), and Ahab and Micaiah (VII.2527-2685). I intend to treat this subject more fully elsewhere.

[14]J. Burke Severs, *The Literary Relationships of Chaucer's "Clerkes Tale"* (1942; rept. Hamden, CT, 1972), pp. 108, 191-92.

[15]"Chaucer's Manuscript of Nicholas Trevet's *Les Cronicles*," forthcoming in *The Chaucer Review*.

[16]Citations from Gower are from Macaulay, *Complete Works* (see n. 11 above). Italics are mine.

[17]The passages from Trevet are cited by page number from Schlauch's edition in *Sources and Analogues*. In recording variants from the other manuscripts I have kept the spelling of M (Schlauch's base MS) whenever possible. Three of Schlauch's sigla for the MSS are different from those I have adopted: she uses Ar for A, G for T, and Fr for P. To avoid a great deal of confusion, the reader should also note that, although Schlauch was "not able to include variants from the text of F" (p. 162), she uses the sigil F when citing variants from Fr or P.

[18]Other examples from Trevet's story of Constance are *Cist Morice, Cist Telous, Cist messager, Cist Arsenius*. Schlauch also notices this pattern in the B manuscripts (*Sources and Analogues*, p. 163).

[19]F T have *saunz mariner* for *saunz naviroun* in the second exile scene.

[20]See P. H. Reaney, *The Origins of English Place Names* (London, 1964), pp. 83, 100. Other place names for which Gower needed no source are *Humber* (River), line 720, and *Engelond*, line 1581; and the MSS have no significant variants for *Bangor* (Wales), line 905, *Spaigne*, line 1088, or *Capadoce*, line 1332. Gower invents the name *Barbarie* (line 599) to replace Trevet's *Sarazine*, the home of the Souldan and his mother.

[21]A. C. Edwards, "Knaresborough Castle and 'The Kynges Moodres Court'," *Philological Quarterly*, 19 (1940), 306-09.

[22]See *MED*, s.v. *burgh*; and A. H. Smith, *The Place Names of West Rid-*

ing and Yorkshire, English Place-Name Society, vol. 34 (Cambridge, 1961), pp. 110-11.

[23]Gower's name *Constance* is found in both A and B manuscripts. A M usually have *Constaunce* (and in a few places *Custaunce*, which is closer to Chaucer's spelling), but the name was common in Gower's time and his spelling was obviously dictated by his own preference. See P. H. Reaney, *A Dictionary of British Surnames* (London, 1961), p. 76.

[24]Gower's names for the other minor characters not mentioned by Chaucer include: Tiberie Constantin (II.590), Ytalie, (II.591), Lucie, (II. 905); Salustes (II.1199); Heleine (II.1200); Pelage (II.1316); Edwyn (II. 1319); and Arcenne (II.1332). Some of these are his own adaptations of Latin forms in Trevet--*Lucius, Salustius, Pelagius, Arcemius*. For the others there are no variants in the MSS that give positive clues about his source text.

JOHN GOWER AND THE BOOK OF DANIEL

Russell A. Peck

"As you watched, O king, you saw a great image. This image, huge and dazzling, towered before you, fearful to behold. The head of the image was of fine gold, its breast and
arms of silver, its belly and thighs of bronze, its legs of
iron, its feet part iron and part clay. While you looked, a
stone was hewn from a mountain, not by human hands; it
struck the image on its feet of iron and clay and shattered
them. Then the iron, the clay, the bronze, the silver, and the
gold, were all shattered to fragments and were swept away
like chaff before the wind from a threshing-floor in summer, until no trace of them remained. But the stone which
struck the image grew into a great mountain filling the
whole earth. That was the dream."

(Dan. 2:31-36[1])

Nebuchadnezzar's dream of the composite statue defines an
apocalyptical view of history which biblical commentators and
medieval writers seized upon to analyze what they saw to be the
wretched decline of human enterprise. The golden head, silver
breast, belly of bronze, and feet of iron mingled with clay desig-
nate the progressive degeneration of earthly kingdoms, Daniel
explains, as human endeavor, despite its pristine beginning, dis-
integrates into dust. The great stone not carved by human hand,
which crushes the statue like a millsone and grinds it to bits, is
indicative of God's might which will establish its authority on
the last day in one cataclysmic swoop. Although the eschatology
of the vision was generally interpreted in terms of nations in

159

decay, a more psychological implication lies hidden in the dream as well. The ruptured statue suggests the disintegrative progress of sin, for which there will ultimately be an accounting. Dante expands upon this latter idea in *Inferno* XIV.103-20, where Nebuchadnezzar's monster is placed on Crete, the desert isle of the ancient world. Virgil tells Dante of the monster to explain the blood-red stream flowing from a wood across the barren wastelands of the Seventh Circle (the circles of the violent against God, nature, and art), prior to their entering the deepest regions of Hell and human folly. All the rivers of Hell flow like tears from the cracks in the composite statue, down through a crevasse, ultimately to form Cocytus. The numerous cracks and the several rivers--Acheron, Styx, and Phlegethon (all prior to Cocytus)--suggest the divisive waste of sin, a very draining of the ancient monster's substance. All sins, it seems, exude from the statue's fissures and are compounded as they converge in the deadly pool. As if to comment on the very condition of sin, what had begun internally becomes the external ice-block which imprisons Satan and his tribe.

Gower draws upon the dream of the composite statue in both the *Vox Clamantis* and the *Confessio Amantis* with the intent of creating apocalyptic effects. With greater subtlety than is usually acknowledged by his modern readers, albeit without the genius of Dante's creative application, he adapts the dream to establish an apocalyptic mood which is crucial to the overall effect of both long poems. Like Dante, he uses the dream to suggest the divisive consequences of sin, as we shall see, and also to imply internal causes of the human psyche's imprisonment, whether within the chaos of contemporary history or within the wilful individual. He will do so, moreover, with a deliberately eschatological moral in mind. But with Gower, as with Dante, the matter of historical perspective is complex, including possibilities of redemption as well as judgment and condemnation. In the *Confessio Amantis*, Gower uses the second of Nebuchadnezzar's dreams (Dan. 4), the dream of the proud king humbled like a beast, grazing at the stump of a once proud tree, to establish a complementary view of history which is, nonetheless, distinctly different from the apocalyptic view embodied in the first dream. This second approach observes history as a perpetual sequence of exempla from which an individual, making right use of his critical abilities, can learn and improve himself through penitential acts. This combination of the redemptive along with the eschatological constitutes the basis of Gower's concept of history and its uses. What is of interest here is that both approaches to history, at least insofar as Gower identifies his models, derive from the Book of Daniel. Daniel is, as we shall see, Gower's exemplary historian.

The Book of Daniel is a collection of pseudo-historical materials assembled as "a pacifistic manifesto" of the Hasidim in the mid-second century B.C., with particular reference to the last years of Antiochus IV Epiphanes's reign.[2] According to Bernard McGinn, "almost every apocalyptic text can be related to some time of crisis,"[3] and that is certainly the case with Daniel, which was compiled at a time contemporary with the Maccabean revolt and intense persecution of the Jews.[4] (It is this voice in crisis which will appeal so strongly to Gower.) Structurally, Daniel falls into two parts, with a deuterocanonical coda, namely, the story of Susanna and the Elders (chap. 13), which became the basis of the charmingly thrilling *Pistill of Susan* in the later fourteenth century, and the stories of Bel and the Dragon (chap. 14).[5] The first six books consist of independent midrashic stories exemplifying the power of God to care for his people despite the worldly arrogance of pagan kings--the stories of God's favoring those who eat properly (chap. 1); Daniel and Nebuchadnezzar's dream of the composite statue (chap. 2); Shadrach, Meshach, and Abednego in the fiery furnace (chap. 3); Nebuchadnezzar's dream of the great tree and his subsequent humiliation and madness (chap. 4); Belshazzar's disastrous feast (chap. 5); and Daniel and the lions' den (chap. 6). In all these stories those who heed God's signals and learn from them thrive. Those who do not are doomed.

Apart from the apocalyptic overtones of the dream of the composite statue,[6] the attitude toward history in this section of the book is exemplary, as if history exists to teach us. This pedagogical view is akin to the apocalyptical insofar as it presupposes that all acts pertain to a divine plan and are purposeful according to God's larger vision. But it differs from the apocalyptical in that it views time as a means toward correction rather than an eschatological foreclosure. That is, the proud kings learn from the trial of the three in the fiery furnace and from Daniel's patient survival in the lions' den. Even the foolish Belshazzar sees and comes to accept the writing on the wall, albeit to no avail. He learns nothing and is destroyed. Indeed, it is the second of Nebuchadnezzar's dreams (chap. 4), where Nebuchadnezzar suffers for seven years before regaining his kingly stature, which appealed most strongly to medieval writers as an example of the penitential way. Chaucer's Parson cites the passage as an exemplum of penance,[7] and in Book I of the *Confessio Amantis* it defines one of Gower's fundamental beliefs, that history is penitentially instructive, "a storehouse of exempla, full of warning and encouragement to mankind."[8] The first dream, the dream of the composite statue, differs from the other stories in this first half of the treatise in that it is distinctly apocalyptical as well as penitential. (This is doubtless one reason why Gower liked it.) Every penitential act embodies some element of the apocalyptic, insofar as a well-determined end (an elevating satisfaction) is sought in accord with God's plan. As Lee Patterson has suggested, Penance is apocalypse on a personal level.[9]

The second half of Daniel, chapters 7-12, consists of four enigmatic visions, all of which prophesy the destruction of pagan kingdoms--the vision of the four beasts, the vision of the horn and the he-goat, the revelation of seventy weeks of years, and the revelation of the fall of Cyrus and the men clothed in linen. It is this part of the text which establishes Daniel as the apocalyptic prophet.[10] More than any Old Testament work, with

the possible exception of Ezekiel, Daniel defines the mode out
of which New Testament apocalyptical writing, as well as rab-
binical eschatology, devolves,[11] a fact readily acknowledged by
medieval commentators on the Apocalypse.[12] McGinn notes that
"Daniel's vision forms a classic presentation of an eschatological pattern of present crisis-coming judgement-final vindication
that will become central to apocalypticism."[13] Dream vision,
prophecy through interpreted historical events, symbolic language, admonitory voice, and a structured view of historical
process become the rhetorical properties of eschatology, even as
Daniel had used them. His voice differs from that of earlier
prophets in that his is deliberately a *written voice*--the voice of
writings dictated by a divine presence, with hidden meanings to
be pondered.[14] This is a feature of apocalypticism to which
Gower was particularly alert and which he uses as his opening
premise in the *Vox Clamantis*.[15] The written word presides as
commentary on present conditions, both for now and for the future. Fascination with the obscurity of Daniel and his obsession
to work out the time remaining until judgment and the resurrec-
tion[16] provoked commentaries by several influential Christian
exegetes, including St. Jerome, Richard of St. Victor, Peter
Comester, Albert the Great, and Nicholas of Lyra.[17]

But the fact is that Daniel is not a major inspiration for secular writers in England, which makes Gower's extensive use of
his book all the more remarkable. A number of continental writers besides Dante drew upon Daniel for the creating of popular
literature, the twelfth-century liturgical plays of Daniel being
the most spectacular.[18] Murray Roston notes that

> the development of the *Ordo prophetarum* . . . provides the
> earliest dramatic example of the expansion and elaboration
> of the Old Testament stories at the expense of those from
> the New. The portion of the sermon that found its way into
> the liturgy was a lengthy prose passage addressed to the
> recalcitrant Jews and introducing the testimony of Isaiah,
> Jeremiah, Daniel, Moses, David, and Habakkuk, followed
> by the New Testament witnesses Simeon, Zacharias, Eliza-

beth, and John, and concluding with the pagan testimonies of Virgil, Nebuchadnezzar, and the Erythraean Sybil.[19]

It was through this form that many of the details of the "prophet" plays entered the cycles, in England as well as on the Continent.

In the English mystery plays, however, Daniel is not one of the more prominent prophets. He never has a play of his own, which is too bad, since his several episodes have so much potential for good theater. Daniel is mentioned in the York *Purification* play as one who in his holiness foretold the birth of Jesus, "borne of a woman and maiden free."[20] (Daniel's holiness is often his dominant praiseworthy trait which writers single out.) In the Towneley cycle he is one of four prophets in the *Procession of the Prophets* play, a play in fragmentary condition.[21] Daniel is the last to speak, and thus it is his lines which are missing. The play breaks off after his prophecy of the virgin birth, allowing him only seventeen lines as opposed to ninety for Moses, seventy-two for David, and fifty-four for Sybil.

The most interesting treatment of Daniel in the English plays occurs in the clothworkers play of *The Prophets of Antichrist* in the Chester cycle.[22] In this play Daniel speaks in his apocalyptical voice, foretelling the birth of the Antichrist through the metaphor of the horn with mouth to speak and eyes to see on the head of the fourth beast. The Expositor explains how the little horn which springs up in the middle of his forehead and spreads over the other ten horns signifies Antichrist himself, who will slay three of the ten kings represented by the other ten horns and put the remaining seven in his grace. In this play, Daniel joins the company of Ezekiel and Zacharias, who precede him, and John the Evangelist (i.e., John of the Apocalypse) who follows, as prophets of the last day when the seals are at last opened and history brought to its conclusion.

In England Daniel's influence on literature other than the dramatic remained relatively obscure until the latter part of the fourteenth century. Mary W. Smyth, in her *Biblical Quotations in Middle English Literature before 1350*, cites only one direct quotation from Daniel, that being in the *Pricke of Conscience*.[23] She notes four instances of paraphrase from Daniel in *Handlynge Synne*, though three of the four are from the same episode (Daniel in the lions' den). *Juliana*, the *Life of St. Katherine*, *Vices and Virtues*, and the *Aʒenbite of Inwit*, between them, include half a dozen allusions to Daniel, and that is about it.

Late in the century Chaucer and Langland make more extensive use of the prophet, Chaucer mainly in the Monk's Tale, where Nebuchadnezzar and Belshazzar provide two of his seventeen tragedies. In the Man of Law's Tale, the allusion to Daniel in the lions' den in the sequence of rhetorical questions on God's underlying conservation of mankind reflects with some subtlety Chaucer's perception of the prophet's apocalyptic voice.[24] Usually, however, he cites Jacob and Joseph as his patriarchial authorities on dreams, though Chauntecleer mentions Daniel as the "Olde Testament" authority on dreams in the Nun's Priest's Tale (VII.3128); the Parson (as we have noted) cites Nebuchadnezzar's dream of the tree as an example of penance (X.126), and, in the Proem to Book II of *House of Fame*, Geoffrey rattles off the dreams of Isaiah, Scipio, Nebuchadnezzar, Pharaoh, Turnus, and Elcanor for their prophetic content. But, unlike Gower, Chaucer never uses Daniel as a definitive spokesman within his literary consciousness. At most he lurks on the fringes.

Although Langland has been acclaimed *the* apocalyptic writer of the later fourteenth century, he makes even more sparse use of Daniel that Chaucer does. *Piers Plowman* includes only two references: B.VII.151-58 mentions Daniel's interpretation of Nebuchadnezzar's dream, though which dream is unclear.[25] (Skeat thinks Langland is mistakenly remembering the Belshazzar episode.[26]) In B.XV.589 Langland quotes Daniel 9: 24, 26 in Latin, the passage on the coming of the Holy of Holies, a passage he repeats in B.XVIII.108. But these two allusions (three if we include the repetition) hardly bespeak prominence, despite the fact that Daniel is the apocalyptic prophet and an apocalyptic tone is important to the poet's conception of his voice.

Apart from the *Pistill of Susan*, which is neither a prophetic nor penitential work but rather a romance based on one of the tales affiliated with Daniel, the most important treatment of material from the apocalyptic prophet--besides Gower's treatment, that is--is the concluding section of *Cleanness*, where the poet uses the story of Belshazzar's feast as the poem's culminating image of defilement. The story is elaborately introduced through "historical" remarks on Nebuchadnezzar found in what the poet calls "Danyel in his dialokes."[27] Actually, the material for this section of the poem comes mainly from 2 Chronicles and Jeremiah.[28] It seems that Nebuchadnezzar materials have become so strongly linked to Daniel that anything about the Babylonian king gets attributed to Daniel as well. It is not until about three hundred lines later that the narrator moves into material actually found in the fifth chapter of Daniel, which contains the account of the feast. Even there the narrative is richly embellished with borrowings from other biblical writings,[29] as well as flashbacks to Daniel 4:27-33, recounting Nebuchadnezzar's transformation into an ox. The *Cleanness*-poet knows his Bible well, however, and makes highly intelligent use of his materials. But although he is remarkably sensitive to the innuendoes of the biblical text, his voice in *Cleanness* lacks the apocalyptic fervor characteristic of the second half of Daniel. Of the several major English writers of the later fourteenth century to draw upon Daniel, only Gower takes advantage of the prophet's apocalyptic voice, as if he were aware that Daniel lies behind such political prophesies in the Latin tradition as Geoffrey of Monmouth's *Prophecy of Merlin* and its descendents.[30]

In discussing Langland's apocalyptic view of history Morton Bloomfield observes that Langland was "fundamentally apocalyptically-minded in a way many of his distinguished contemporaries were not . . . neither Occam nor Chaucer, Richard Rolle nor Bradwardine, John Gower nor Richard Bury."[31] Although

Bloomfield's conclusion may be generally sound, Gower shoud be removed from the list of exceptions to apocalyptical-mindedness, at least if the *Vox Clamantis* is to be included in the works under consideration. The tone of the *Vox* is heavily apocalyptic. Gower pays allegiance to Daniel in several instances in his great Latin poem, but of especial importance is the citation of Daniel in the Prologue to Book I on the value of meaningful dreams and in the conclusion, Book VII, which is based largely upon Nebuchadnezzar's dream of the composite statue. As he puts his poem together the whole of the vision in *Vox Clamantis* is framed by the perspective of Daniel. It is generally thought that Book I of the poem was written after the other six books had been completed,[32] in which case Gower came to his "beginning" after having composed his elaborate application of Daniel's account in Book VII of the degeneracy of time through his explication of the tyrant's dream. Indeed, it is just that figure of degenerative time implicit in the clay feet of the statue that lurks so boldly in Gower's mind as he composed the nightmarish vision of the Peasants' Revolt, that time of crisis which precipitates Book I. It may be, in fact, that it was not until after completing Book VII that Gower conceived of the apocalyptic tone in which to cast Book I. If that is so the Prologue to Book I, with its allusion to Daniel, would have stood as introduction to what is now Book II, as it does in the Laud 719 manuscript.[33] The poem would still have been framed by Daniel materials, but the apocalyptic emphasis would have been less. Without Book I the Daniel allusions function more as ominous embellishments than as a fully articulated prophetic voice.

Gower's Prologue, nonetheless, incorporates several distinguishing features of apocalyptic literature into its statement, namely, the notion of a guardian angel (compare the protector of the children in the fiery furnace and of Daniel in the lions' den) and an enigmatic narrator-commentator who cries out against the overwhelming magnitude of evil which engulfs society. Gower explains that in visions such as Daniel's, a good angel, keeper of the inner-man, always protects God's servant with watchful love, visiting his mind and sustaining its strength,[34] providing auspicious portents so that man may better have knowledge of the issues of the times ("monstrat prenostica visu, / Quo magis in causis tempora noscat homo" [Prol. 13-14]). After identifying himself enigmatically by means of a riddle (Prol. 19-26), Gower invites careful study of his vision, warning that "one who looks further into the work and into the present time will find nothing consoling in the whole poem" (Qui magis inspiciet opus istud, tempus et instans, / Inueniet toto carmine dulce nichil [Prol. 41-42]).[35] So corrupt is the present time, he says, that if he had many mouths and as many tongues he still could not relate all the evils which pervade the wicked present time. His Prologue concludes with an invocation to John of Patmos, author of the Apocalypse and Gower's own namesake, to guide his writing. This combination of Daniel, John of the Apocalypse, the enigmatic author, and the guardian angel, establishes an apocalyptic perspective out of which Gower's political and social commentary grows. The prophetic pose is enhanced by the title of the work--the *vox clamantis*, the voice of one crying, presumably as a lone voice in the wilderness--a biblical phrase which echoes throughout the treatise.[36]

So we see that the apocalyptical mode of the poem is well-established, even without the allegorical account of the Peasants' Revolt. But with that vision the apocalyptical point of view is not only established, it is dominant. Like Daniel, the first book of *Vox Clamantis* draws extensively on animal symbolism to portray its potent vision of the moral chaos of the contemporary scene.[37] The setting for the nightmare vision is cleverly introduced. Gower begins with a sequence of Ovidian allusions to spring and summer which not only tell the month in which the revolt occurred but establish the idea that England is (or could be) "the ornament of the globe, the flower of the world, the crowning glory of things, containing every delight that enjoyment seeks" (Hic decus est orbis, flos mundi, gloria rerum / Delicias omnes, quas petit vsus, habet [I.i.75-76])[38]--in short, a second Paradise. Gower's aureate description echoes the classical idea of a Golden Age, when every creature rejoiced in its peaceful season. That is, the two dozen or so Ovidian allusions to the springtime world not only define the time and kingdom in which the destructive revolt occurred; but they also anticipate Gower's use of Daniel's degenerating monster with its golden head and clay feet in the last book of the poem. Here, in Book I, the nightmare which befalls the end of day combines Ovidian metamorphoses with apocalyptic doom as the narrator arises in his dream, hoping to gather flowers in the fields, but encounters instead countless rascally peasants who are suddenly changed into wild beasts--asses, fierce oxen, swine, savage dogs, cats and foxes, ravenous birds, and plagues of flies and frogs--an apocalyptically numbered seven bands in all. I need not fully rehearse here the dreamer's dreadful fright, his escape to a rudderless ship, his landing on the Isle of Brut, his swooning and then coming to in a desert, and the voice from heaven commanding him to awaken and write down all he has seen. These passages are well-known, perhaps the most often cited in all of Gower. My point here is simply to emphasize the apocalyptical rhetoric of the first book and its affiliation with both Daniel and Apocalypse--the animal imagery, the ominous outcries of disappointment and admonition, the enumerative techniques as disaster after disaster unfolds, the pseudo-historical teleology, and the otherworldly journey[39]--all in anticipation of the dream of the composite statue which governs the poem's conclusion.

The middle books of *Vox Clamantis* include a number of allusions to the Book of Daniel. Usually they are more of the exemplary sort--the *speculum vitae* variety--rather than the specifically apocalyptical, though they are an important part of that larger movement within the poem. Although they are not systematically arranged they are sufficiently numerous and from different chapters of the sacred writing to suggest that Gower worked directly from the Vulgate and its commentaries. Gower knew the Bible very well.[40] Book II of the *Vox* is loaded with biblical allusions, several of which come from Daniel: men dependent upon Fortune are contrasted with such just men as the three in the fiery furnace or Daniel himself or Susanna (II.v. 256-72; V.vi.309); followers of Fortune are more like Nebuchadnezzar, who was forced to change his shape because of his pride. In Book III, when discussing how clergy should be gentle and patient in their love of God and neighbor, he cites Daniel together with Joel as holy men who girded themselves with patient virtue against the foe.[41] And in Book VI, in his consideration of avarice and deceit amongst lawyers, he quotes Daniel 13:5 to the effect that evil dwells among old men (VI.vii.573-74). Now, he says, Babylon (i.e., Nebuchadnezzar's kingdom) is venerated above all cities (VI.xix.1207).

Indeed, it is Nebuchadnezzar's dream of the composite statue in Book VII which exemplifies life in Babylon and provides the culminating metaphor of the poem, a metaphor we can understand, Gower says, *because* of our sins: "We are able to discover from present day evils," he begins, "what is wont to lie concealed in ancient symbols" (Quod solet antiquis nuper latitare figuris, / Possumus ex nostris verificare malis [VII.i.1-2). "The last age, that of clay, is at hand throughout the world. / The feet of the statue furnish me signs of it" (Vltima per terras superest modo fictilis etas, / Vnde pedes statue dant michi signa fore [VII.iii.1-2]). The ancient writings stand as commentary, and we perceive through our own experience. In his summary assessment of man's corrupted nature Gower puts the blame largely on lechery (a topic he will explore at greater length in his next poem). The French sins prevail everywhere: the female has become lord and master of the male; virtue lies prostrate (see Book I of *Confessio Amantis*, where Amans lies prostrate in his wood).[42] Then, for a moment, the clamorous voice becomes more gentle, recalling man's golden state of innocence, when he stood upright, perceiving the pristine beauty of the world around him and recognizing within his feeling of admiration the love of God, his author (VII.vi). The passage is reminiscent of the opening prologue with its Ovidian golden age prior to the nightmare of rampaging animals. The springtime mood leads to reflections upon God's generosity toward man (VII.vii) and upon sympathetic analogies between the greater and lesser worlds (VII.viii). But then, having contrasted the upright man with the monster of degenerating time, the voice returns to the evils of the modern day which are proclaimed everywhere by the *vox populi*.[43] Just as man causes the outbreak of this world's corruption, so will he suffer corruptibility in death. After a gruesome diatribe on rotting bodies, the apocalyptic voice declaims the Seven Deadly Sins, emphasizing the horrors of death repeatedly (VII.ix-xx), reminding England that the sinner suffers a twofold death. The diatribe concludes on an eschatological note: "Behold, the days [of judgment] which Christ foretold are come, / And the fearful words of God are made clear" (Ecce dies veniunt, predixit quos fore Cristus, / Et patuere diu verba timenda dei [VII.xxii.1203-04]), when "the earthen foot rages against the golden head" (Hinc puto quod seuit pes terreus in caput auri [VII.xxiv. 1379]), and the land is left barren of virtue (O sterilis terra morum [VII.xxiv.1383]).

This cursory sketch of the Daniel materials in the *Vox Clamantis* should be sufficient to conclude that Gower, like Langland, is an "apocalyptically-minded" poet (the phrase is Bloomfield's), at least in his long Latin poem. But the *Vox Clamantis* is not the only poem in which Gower uses Daniel to create an apocalyptic vision of history. Many years later he maintained a similar voice in the *Tripartite Chronicle*, albeit more feebly, with its ominous beast fable of the Swan, Bear, and Horse. And apocalypticism marks likewise the tone of the Prologue to the *Confessio Amantis*, which was the next poem he undertook after the *Vox*.

In the Prologue to the *Confessio Amantis* Gower uses a greatly elaborated version of Nebuchadnezzar's dream of the monster with clay feet to demonstrate from the outset how history has declined and yet how it can, nonetheless, guide mankind in the present day. The importance of this story to the overall structure of the poem is evidenced in the earliest manuscripts, such as MS. Fairfax 3, by an illumination depicting the dream, an illumination the subject matter of which may have been selected by Gower himself. In those manuscripts which have illuminations it is normally the first and is placed either at the beginning of the poem or midway in the Prologue where the account of the dream begins.[44] As Jeremy Griffiths points out, "The Precious Metals picture seems to have been the one constant illustration to the text."[45] More than half of the illuminated manuscripts have a second illustration at or near the beginning of Book I depicting a kneeling figure confessing to his priest.[46] The precise placement of this second illustration varies somewhat from manuscript to manuscript, enough so that Griffiths suggests that "the confessor picture may not have originated from Gower himself."[47] Nonetheless, the two characteristic illuminations--Nebuchadnezzar's dream and the confession of the Lover--define the two perspectives of the narrative which are crucial to Gower's literary scheme in the poem: namely, the apocalyptic view in the Prologue which moves from an analysis of history to an assessment of the ills of the present day; and the more gentle fictive device of confession whereby priest Genius's admonitory stories illustrate to the Lover how he might, through right penitential choices, return, mentally at least, from his prostrate captivity in the woods to a peaceful relationship with God, history, and England.[48] The Fairfax 3 manuscript and others akin to it have only these two illuminations. In the Fairfax drawing of Nebuchadnezzar, which is placed at the beginning of the manuscript, the king lies sleeping in a well-blanketed bed which is drawn horizontally across the bottom of the picture. At the foot of his bed, in the right side of the drawing, the monster in his dream stands in the conventional pose of the counsellor.[49] The picture is not very skillfully drawn, though some effort is made to represent the ideas in the dream, that is, the golden head, silver torso, bronze belly and thighs, iron legs, and splayed feet of iron and clay. The stone which will crush the statue hovers in the background. The point of the drawing here, as in other manuscripts which include it and the several which have left spaces for it to be included, is to focus attention on the primary topic of the Prologue, namely the progressive decline of human glory in history.

Gower introduces the dream near the midpoint of the Prologue. Up to that moment he has discussed the perilous condition of the three estates to conclude that it is plainly evident that the fault of earthly chaos lies not with God "bot plenerliche upon ous alle, / For man is cause of that schal falle" (Prol. 527-28). Some people, he says, blame Fortune for the world's ills, but that is a false opinion. Fortune and the world may be untrue, but only as they always have been:

> The world arist and falth withal,
> So that the man is overal
> His oghne cause of wel and wo.
> That we fortune clepe so
> Out of the man himself it groweth.
>
> (Prol. 545-49)

The history of Israel, especially from the Babylonian captivity onward, illustrates the thesis of man's blameworthiness and the need for holiness. That history is the subject of the Book of Daniel, especially as Gower presents it. Although several details of Gower's retelling of Nebuchadnezzar's dream differ from the Vulgate, Gower appears to be working directly from the Bible. The opening lines on God's eternal foresight (Prol. 585-92) echo Daniel's initial prayer to the name of God blessed from all eternity, who through his wisdom and power brings about all changes, setting up one king and deposing another (Dan. 2:20-21). Gower has shifted the voice of the prayer from Daniel to himself, but the point of underscoring "hou that this world schal torne and wende" (Prol. 591) is the same.

The next change occurs in the narrative itself. In the Bible Daniel intuits the content of the king's dream directly from God. We learn of the dream from Daniel as he tells Nebuchadnezzar what the dream literally contained. He then proceeds to gloss it. In Gower, the king tells Daniel what he dreamed, and then Daniel explains. One effect of this change in voice is to give the king a larger role in the event, as if his choices were more real and consequential, a notion Gower will accentuate in his second extended borrowing from Daniel, in Book I (the account of Nebuchadnezzar's second dream). This change is consistent with Gower's subtle shift at the end of the Prologue from an apocalyptic voice to a penitential one as he shifts his biblical text from Daniel to Isaiah to imagine a more comfortable ending--a peaceable kingdom. This shift in texts strongly dampens the apocalyptic voice in favor of the penitential. But more on that in a moment.

The third and most important alteration Gower makes in his presentation of Nebuchadnezzar's first dream occurs in its explication, which Gower greatly expands. Having told the dream and glossed it as Daniel did, Gower goes over it a second time, bringing it up to date. The belly of brass signifies that period from Alexander to Julius Caesar, and the feet of iron mingled with clay signify the enfeebled kingdoms after Caesar up through Charlemagne to the present. Gower's vision of the decline of the ancients and their once glorious city is almost worthy of Gibbon:

> The wall and al the Cit withinne
> Stant in ruine and in decas,
> The feld is wher the Paleis was,
> The toun is wast; and overthat,
> If we behold thilke astat
> Which whilom was of the Romeins,
> Of knyhthode and of Citezeins,
> To peise now with that beforn,
> The chaf is take for the corn,

As forto speke of Romes myht.

(Prol. 836-45)

The cause of this progressive degeneration from grandeur to chaff Gower attributes to division within the nations and within the minds of the people, a division symbolized by the amalgamated feet of the monster (Prol. 889-909). Like Dante, Gower uses the statue to comment on the progress of sin and its fatal capacity to fragment and confine. Sin, he says, is "moder of divisioun" (Prol. 1030), a sign of man's severance from God.[50] Such division is the cause of all evil that "makth the world to falle" (Prol. 972): it drove man from Paradise, provoked God to destroy the world by flood, and brought the Tower of Babel to destruction. The clay feet betoken the destruction of the world at the last Judgment, when

> Pes and acord awey schol wende
> And alle charite schal cesse
>
> . . . .
> and whan these toknes ben befalle,
> Al sodeinly the Ston schal falle,
> As Daniel it hath beknowe
> Which al this world schal overthrowe.

(Prol. 1034-40)

(Compare Dan. 2:34-35.) The stone is God's judgment which shall grind the feet and all the statue to dust, to be blown like chaff from the threshing-floor in summer.

But although the eschatological threat of the stone is strongly emphasized in Gower's projection of the Last Judgment when man will know at last where he is going, whether "straght to hevene or straght to helle" and such "descord / That ther may be no loveday" (Prol. 1044-47), in his conclusion to the Prologue Gower imagines a different end through a projected wish that a visionary peacemaker like Arion might guide men in brotherly love--"Bot wolde god that now were on / An other such as Arion" (Prol. 1053-54). In view of Gower's use of Golden Age *figura* in the *Vox Clamantis* as a means to accentuate his apocalyptical doom-saying, his choice here of Arion is apt: would that the classical artist, who through music could charm the beasts, might restore even now, after such prolonged decline, a peaceable kingdom, bringing "good acord" to

> . . . the comun with the lord,
> And lord with the comun also.
> He sette in love bothe tuo
> And putte awey malencolie.
> . . . .
> To make pes wher now is hate.
>
> (Prol. 1065-75)

This happier ending than the stone's grinding blow is not altogether unexpected in the Prologue, for even in the midst of his most apocalyptical mode Gower was embellishing his review of man's dastardly decline with questions of free choice, a theme more appropriate to the penitential voice than the apocalyptic. (One thinks of Jonah where the doomsday prophet spoke so eloquently that apocalypse was transformed to penance, albeit to the prophet's disappointment, for which he got *his* penance as well.) Although man's frustration may seem to be the effect of adverse fortune or some entropic determinism, the cause, Gower repeatedly insists, is man's own divisive choices:

> The man himself hath be coupable,
> Which of his propre governance
> Fortuneth al the worldes chance.
>
> (Prol. 582-84)

Gower's juxtaposition of Fortune and free choice as part of his introduction of Nebuchadnezzar's dream of the composite statue is similar to an idea he explored at the beginning of *Vox Clamantis*, where he explained fatedness as a condition determined by free choice.[51] This notion of the interlocking of sin and fate is the essence of Gower's moral premises and is the crux of his interfacing modes--the apocalyptic and the penitential, the judgmental and the redemptive. As he moves into Book I, with its picture of the confessor addressing the acolyte, the penitential mode becomes dominant, and Gower shifts his text from Nebuchadnezzar's first dream to the second, the dream of the tree and the beast eating grass, which sets the tone of the remainder of the *Confessio* and brings Book I to its conclusion.

Genius evokes Nebuchadnezzar's second dream to exemplify vainglory, the fifth and last aspect of Pride. Like the hewn-down tree, the king, having ignored Daniel's warning, is cut down in his false glory and transformed

> Fro man into a bestes forme;
> And lich an Oxe under the fot
> He graseth, as he nedes mot,
> To geten him his lives fode.
> Tho thoghte him colde grases goode
> That whilom eet the hote spices,
> Thus was he torned fro delices.
>
> (I.2972-78)

The tale exemplifies admirably how an individual who sins divides himself from his life source and is thus doomed to bestiality. But it also illustrates how, even when fallen, he may choose to reshape destiny.

Penelope Doob's discussion of the episode offers the most eloquent appraisal of the fallen king's restoration:

> Gower has admirably filled out the concise biblical account. Each thought, each feeling of the king in his gradual return to sanity, is fully and brilliantly conceived, from his initial yearning for finery to improve his appearance to his realization--perhaps brought about by the sight of his unorthodox but penitential "Cote of heres"--that prayer is the only hope. Where the biblical Nebuchadnezzar merely acknowledged God's power and praised him, Gower's conducts himself in more specifically Christian fashion, confessing his sin, asking mercy, and pledging amendment. . . . The picture of the miserable but engaging beast raising his hooves and braying its appeal to God is charming, . . . a

stroke of genius on Gower's part.[52]

Nebuchadnezzar's right use of his wits in getting out of his mess underscores Gower's theory of the interconnectedness of choice and determinism and admirably introduces the concluding tale of Book I, the Tale of Three Questions, a tale which shows how intelligence, humbly applied, can bridge apparently irreparable divisions.

In short, Gower has used the two dream passages from the Book of Daniel at the outset of the *Confessio* to emphasize two esential features of his moral rhetoric:[53] first, the apocalyptic reminder that in keeping with God's well-designed plan, a plan announced in the writings of old, history has something to teach us, namely, that men who set themselves against God's laws are doomed to destruction; and second, the psychological inference that by learning from history we can do something about our fallen situation through right use of our wits. History provides the example; our wits offer the means. The markedly apocalyptic tone of the Prologue which culminates in the extended survey of human history in light of Nebuchadnezzar's dream of the statue with clay feet, an idea first introduced in the best manuscripts through a drawing of the statue, establishes the need to take the exemplary nature of history and its stories seriously. The subsequent instruction of the fallen Lover in the proper use of his will and wits, an instruction which culminates in Book VII on the education of the prince, shows how stories and history can instruct. The two modes converge in Book VIII where the fatuous Lover achieves a kind of personal apocalypse when, after his final confession, he faints and is visited by an apocalyptic vision, awakens to view himself in a mirror, and then recognizes the old man he has become. Venus and Genius disappear in a past tense along with his fatuousness, and he discovers a new voice and a new relationship with time (or, rather, his former voice, the prophetic voice of the Prologue when he viewed the full sweep of time). As he turns his attention back to the welfare of the state of England, he once again looks upon history as "the field of God's activity," which becomes comprehensible only in light of the last end.[54] Gower's conclusion is apocalyptic in that it removes veils and projects a future that will be determined by human choices according to God's plan. God has given a great gift of "intelligence / In mannys soule resonable" (VIII.2974-75) so that he might stand in virtue "above alle erthli creature" (VIII. 978). But if the three estates, which Gower reviews one last time, fail to "desire pes" (VIII.2991) or to act responsibly, their end will be destruction. As he did in the Prologue, Gower reiterates here the idea that division between the estates "is cause of mochil synne" (VIII.3040). But, like the Prologue's conclusion, Book VIII projects a happier end as well: if division is amended,

> . . . mechil grace ther uppon
> Unto the Citees schulde falle,
> Which myghte availle to ous alle.

> (VIII.3046-48)

Time may end in disaster or it may end well. It is up to men to decide.

It is noteworthy that the Latin tag which Gower appends to the Fairfax 3 manuscript, beginning "Quia vnusquisque . . . ,"[55] singles out three features of the *Confessio* which define its scope: first, the prophecy of Daniel which marks off the times from King Nebuchadnezzar even until now; second, the training of King Alexander in the government of himself even as in the governance of others; and third, the exploration of such rule through the fatuous passions of lovers.[56] At first it might seem odd that Gower would give the biblical dream of the Prologue, along with Book VII, which many have deemed a digression, such prominence in his assessment of the three main points of the poem's ideological scheme. It is only through analysis of his use of the Daniel materials in *Vox Clamantis* and in *Confessio Amantis* that the implication of such a rationale becomes evi-

179

dently just. At the foundation of both poems is Gower's apocalyptic view of history blended with the penitential whereby the progressive events of time hold meaning and instruction for the careful observer. But ultimately the tone of *Confessio Amantis* is different from that of *Vox Clamantis*. The *Confessio* is essentially confessional, as its title implies, with apocalyptical rhetoric functioning principally as a threat, with penitence as the goal. Although Gower is still "apocalyptic-minded" in the *Confessio*, he is not an apocalyptic prophet. Chaucer's epithet--"moral Gower"--seems more appropriate.[57]

NOTES

[1]*New English Bible* (Oxford and Cambridge, 1970), p. 1071.

[2]On the "pacifistic manifesto" see *The Book of Daniel*, trans. with notes and commentary by Louis F. Hartman and Alexander A. DiLella; the *Anchor Bible*, vol. 23 (Garden City, NY, 1978), pp. 43-45. On the relationship of Daniel's apocalyptic religious attitudes to the shattering crises under Antiochus, see Amos N. Wilder, "The Rhetoric of Ancient and Modern Apocalyptic," *Interpretation*, 25 (1971), 436-54.

[3]Introduction to *Apocalyptic Spirituality: Treatises and Letters of Lactantius, Adso of Montier-en-der, Joachim of Fiore, the Franciscan Spirituals, Savonarola*, trans. Bernard McGinn (New York, 1979), p. 8.

[4]See Hartman and DiLella, pp. 43-45, 104, on the juxtaposition of Daniel and Maccabees.

[5]See Hartman and DiLella, pp. 9-24, on the structure of the Book of Daniel. For a text of the *Pistill of Susan*, see *Susannah: An Alliterative Poem of the Fourteenth Century*, ed. Alice Miskimin (New Haven, 1969).

[6]On apocalyptical elements in Daniel 2, the dream of the composite statue, see Bernard McGinn, "Early Apocalypticism: The Ongoing Debate," in *The Apocalypse in English Renaissance Thought and Literature: Patterns, Antecedents, and Repercussions*, ed. C. A. Patrides and Joseph Wittreich (Ithaca, 1984), p. 8.

[7]Parson's Tale (X.126). All references to Chaucer's works are taken from *The Riverside Chaucer*, 3rd ed., general editor Larry D. Benson (Boston, 1987), and are hereafter cited by work and line number in the context of the argument.

[8]The phrase is from Morton Bloomfield, *Piers Plowman as a Fourteenth-Century Apocalypse* (New Brunswick, NJ, 1962), p. 176, in his discussion of *speculum vitae* literature in its relationship to the apocalyptical.

[9]Patterson's comment was made during the discussion following delivery of a version of this paper at the Twenty-First International Congress on Medieval Studies, Kalamazoo, May 1986. See n. 57 below.

[10]Hartman and DiLella, pp. 62-71, and Michael E. Stone, "Lists of Revealed Things in Apocalyptic Literature," in *Magnalia Dei: The Mighty Acts of God (G. E. Wright Memorial)*, ed. F. M. Cross, W. Lemke, and P. D. Miller (New York, 1976), p. 439.

[11]McGinn, "Early Apocalypticism," pp. 10-12, on Jewish features of apocalypticism; "Paul did not invent the antichrist" (p. 20). For Jewish apocalypses see Martha Himmelfarb, *Tours of Hell: An Apocalyptic Form in Jewish and Christian Literature* (Philadelphia, 1983).

[12]"The key apocalyptic sections of the New Testament were consciously based on the classical Jewish apocalypses, such as the Book of Daniel" (McGinn, *Introduction*, p. 100). Marjorie Reeves, "The Development of Apocalyptic Thought: Medieval Attitudes," in *The Apocalypse in English Renaissance Thought and Literature*, ed. Patrides and Wittreich, p. 49, notes the enormous popularity of Beatus of Liebana's *Commentary on Apocalypse*, written in the second half of the eighth century, which draws heavily upon Daniel materials. The Beatus Commentary regularly was accompanied by a commentary on Daniel. Richard Kenneth Emmerson and Suzanne Lewis, "Census and Bibliography of Medieval Manuscripts Containing Apocalypse Illustrations, c. 800-1500," *Traditio*, 40 (1984), 337-79, describe thirteen manuscripts which attach Jerome's commentary on Daniel to the Apocalypse and Beatus Commentary, usually with Daniel illustrations.

[13]McGinn, "Early Apocalypticism," p. 9.

[14]On apocalypticism as a "scribal phenomenon" which addresses its audience as the written rather than the spoken word, as if writing had more authority, see Jonathan Z. Smith, "Wisdom and Apocalyptic," in *Religious*

Syncretisms in Antiquity, ed. Birger A. Pearson (Missoula, 1975), p. 154.

[15]"Scripture veteris capiunt exempla futuri, / Nam dabit experta res magis esse fidem" (Writings of antiquity contain examples for the future, / For a thing known by experience will afford greater faith): *Vox Clamantis, Prologus libri primi*, 1-2, in *The Complete Works of John Gower*, vol. 4: *The Latin Works*, ed. G. C. Macaulay (Oxford, 1902), p. 20. All subsequent references to *Vox Clamantis* are taken from this edition and are cited by book, chapter, and line number in the context of my argument.

[16]McGinn, "Early Apocalypticism," p. 9.

[17]See St. Jerome, *Commentariorum in Danielem*, in Corpus christianorum: Series Latina, 75A (Turnhout, 1964); Richard of St. Victor, *De eruditione hominis interioris: Occasione accepta ex somnio Nabuchodonosor apud Danielem, Patrologia latina* 196.1229-1366 (hereafter *PL*); Peter Comester, *Historia scholastica, PL* 198.1447-76; Albertus Magnus, *Commentaria in librum Danielis, Opera Omnia*, vol. 18 (Paris, 1890-99); Nicholas de Lyra, *Biblia sacra cum glossa ordinaria et postilla Nicolai Lyrani*, vol. 4 (Paris, 1590). Walafrid Strabo inserts Jerome's commentary into his *Glossa Ordinaria*. For discussion of the relationship of Jerome's commentary on Daniel to Hebrew commentaries, see Jay Braverman, *Jerome's Commentary on Daniel: A Study of Comparative Jewish and Christian Interpretations of the Hebrew Bible* (Washington, DC, 1978). For a modern translation of Jerome's commentary, see *Commentary on Daniel*, trans. Gleason L. Archer, Jr. (Grand Rapids, MI, 1958).

[18]On the Daniel plays by Hilarius and by the students of Beauvais, see Karl Young, *The Drama of the Medieval Church*, 2 vols. (Oxford, 1933), 2:276-77. See also *The Play of Daniel: A Thirteenth-Century Musical Drama*, ed. Noah Greenberg (New York, 1958). Greenberg's text is based on BL Egerton 2615. The play focuses on the episodes of Belshazzar's feast and Daniel in the lions' den. The play draws upon a popular moral treatise, the *Acta Prophetarum*, for many of its details.

[19]*Biblical Drama in England from the Middle Ages to the Present Day* (Evanston, IL, 1968), p. 34.

[20]*The York Plays*, ed. Richard Beadle (London, 1982), line 107, p. 151.

[21]*The Towneley Plays*, ed. George England with notes by Alfred W. Pollard, EETS, e.s. 71 (London, 1897), pp. 56-64.

[22]*The Chester Mystery Cycle*, ed. R. M. Lumiansky and David Mills, EETS, supp. ser. 3 (London, 1974), pp. 396-407.

[23]Yale Studies in English 41 (New York, 1911), p. 195. See p. 259 for paraphrases and allusions. David C. Fowler, *The Bible in Middle English Literature* (Seattle, 1984), p. 116, notes a penitential allusion in "The Maid and the Palmer" (Child 21A), which may derive from Dan. 4:25. Fowler also notes, in *The Bible in Early English Literature* (Seattle, 1976), pp. 221-22, that the *Cursor Mundi* and the *Polychronicon* see in Daniel allegorical foreshadowing of the Redemption and apocryphal narratives of the life of the Virgin and the childhood of Jesus.

[24]Man of Law's Tale II (B$_1$) 472-76. The sequence of questions (lines 470-504) is designed to imply divine conservation of man as he is sustained by God throughout history. The mystery of such sustenation is heightened by the interrogatory mode.

[25]All references to *Piers Plowman* are taken from Skeat's three-text edition, *The Vision of William Concerning Piers Plowman*, ed. W. W. Skeat, 2 vols. (Oxford, 1886; rept. 1954), and are cited by text, passus, and line number in the context of the argument.

[26]Skeat, *Piers Plowman* II:129.

[27]*The Poems of the Pearl Manuscript: Pearl, Cleanness, Patience, Sir Gawain and the Green Knight*, ed. Malcolm Andrew and Ronald Waldron (Berkeley and Los Angeles, 1979), line 1157, p. 160.

[28]See 2 Chron. 36:11-14, and Jer. 52:4-19.

[29]E.g., the account of Solomon's Temple, lines 1285-90 (cf. I Kings 5-7 and 2 Chron. 2-5), Solomon's brass altar, lines 1443-50 (cf. 2 Chron. 1:5), and the mention of Solomon's candlestick, lines 1478-80 (cf. 2 Chron. 4:7, 1 Kings 7:27-37, and Exod. 25:31-36 and 37:17-24). See Andrew and Waldron's extensive notes on the matter (pp. 164-71).

[30]See Rupert Taylor, *The Political Prophecy in England* (New York, 1911) for discussion of *The Book of Merlin* and its progeny. Taylor sees Daniel as the source of Geoffrey's apocalyptical mode (ch. II.iv). The tradition has Middle English manifestations in *The Prophecy of John of Bridlington* (ca. 1362-64) and its imitators (*The Cock in the North* and the *Prophecy of the Fishes*), as well as the Thomas of Erceldoun cycle (*The Romance and Prophecies of Thomas of Erceldoun*, EETS, 62 [London, 1875]). It is doubtful that Gower knew these later writings, however.

[31]*Piers Plowman as a Fourteenth-Century Apocalypse*, p. 178.

[32]E.g., see Macaulay, *Latin Works*, pp. xxxi-ii, and Eric W. Stockton, trans., *The Major Latin Works of John Gower: The Voice of One Crying and the Tripartite Chronicle* (Seattle, 1962), pp. 12-13.

[33]On the layout of the poem in this manuscript Macaulay observes: "There is really something to be said for this arrangement. . . . The first book, with its detailed account of the Peasants' Revolt though in itself the most interesting part of the work, has something of the character of an insertion" (p. xxxii).

[34]"Angelus immo bonus, qui castos interioris / Est hominis, vigili semper amore fauet" (Prol. 9-10).

[35]Stockton's translation, p. 50.

[36]The phrase *vox clamantis in deserto* originates in Isa. 40:3; it is used by the Gospel writer Mark to identify John the Baptist (Mark 3) and then also by Matthew (3:3), Luke (3:46), and John (1:23), who all probably drew upon Mark, though each of the four attributes the line to Isaiah.

[37]On the relationship of Daniel and apocalyptic animal imagery see Francis Klingender, *Animals in Art and Thought to the End of the Middle Ages*, ed. Evelyn Antal and John Harthan (Cambridge, MA, 1971), pp. 36, 202-37 (esp. 206-10), and 298-300 on Beatus MSS.

[38]Stockton's translation, p. 52.

[39]On the features of apocalyptical literature, see McGinn, "Early Apocalypticism," pp. 4-10; John J. Collins, ed., *Apocalypse: The Morphology of a Genre*, *Semeia* vol. 14 (Missoula, 1979), pp. 1-19; and Stone, "Lists of Revealed Things."

[40]A detailed study of Gower's use of the Bible remains to be done. A cursory reading of Stockton's notes to *Vox Clamantis* provides a good starting point. Marie E. Neville did a Ph.D. dissertation on "The Vulgate and Gower's *Confessio Amantis*" (The Ohio State University, 1950), though as far as I know none of that study was ever published. Gower made extensive use of Peter Riga's *Aurora*, as well as the Vulgate. See Paul E. Beichner, "Gower's Use of the *Aurora* in the *Vox Clamantis*," *Speculum*, 30 (1955), 582-95.

[41]III.vii.422. Chaucer's Parson likewise singles out Daniel to exemplify

JOHN GOWER AND THE BOOK OF DANIEL

the holy man as opposed to Samson the strong man, or Solomon the wise man (X[I].954). St. Jerome emphasizes Daniel's holiness in his prefatory epistles (*The Middle English Bible: Prefatory Epistles of St. Jerome*, ed. Conrad Lindberg [Oslo, 1978], p. 79).

[42]For further discussion of the prostrate lover as victim of his own cupidity, see *Confessio Amantis*, ed. Russell A. Peck (New York, 1968; rept. Toronto, 1982), pp. xii-xiii.

[43]The phrase *vox populi* or *vox plebis* recurs frequently in Bks. II-VII (e.g., see III.Prol.11-12; III.xv.1267; VI.i.20; VI.i.15; VI.vii.545; VI.vii.577; VII.xxv.1470). The phrase does not occur in Bk. I. One wonders if it would have been so prominent a phrase at all if Bks. II-VII had been written after the Peasants' Revolt.

[44]Of the twenty-seven illustrated manuscripts listed in Jeremy Griffith's "'Confessio Amantis': The Poem and its Pictures," in *Gower's "Confessio Amantis": Responses and Reassessments*, ed. A. J. Minnis (Cambridge, 1983), pp. 163-78, sixteen place the miniature of Nebuchadnezzar's dream either at the beginning or near the middle of the Prologue (i.e., between Prol. 578-95) and another seven leave blank spaces at the same places, presumably as scribal provision for an illustration which never got drawn. Of the twenty-three manuscripts which include or seem to have planned to include the drawing, seven place it at the head of the Prologue, three after Prol. 578, one after Prol. 594, one beside the summary at line 591, ten after the summary at line 591, and two in the initial to Prol. 595. See Griffiths's Table, p. 177.

[45]Griffiths, p. 172.

[46]See Griffiths's Table, p. 177: seventeen include or leave space for the confessor drawing--one in the initial to Prol. 1, three at the head of Bk. I, twelve after line 202 or before line 203, and one in the initial to I.203.

[47]Griffiths, p. 174.

[48]Two manuscripts include author portraits in the initial to the Prologue instead of confessor drawings in Bk. I, which suggests to Griffiths that the manuscript editor was wanting to emphasize Gower-the-poet's voice rather than the voice of Gower in the guise of lover or priest.

[49]E.g., the placement of Lady Philosophy in the *Consolation of Philosophy*, both in the text and in the many illuminations of the scene; or in the appearance of King Seyes as counsellor to Alcione in her dream (*Book of*

the Duchess, line 199) and the placement of the dreamer at the Black Knight's feet in the same poem (line 502).

[50]Cf. Prol. 575-78, where Gower introduces the dream as an example of "divisoun," whereupon "no worldes thing may laste"; the point is reiterated in line 872, where "divisioun" is labelled "moder of confusioun"; then again after completing the survey of disintegrating kingdoms which leave men throughout the world divided against themselves (Prol. 966); and finally, in the extended discussion of division leading up to the assertion that sin is "moder of divisioun" (Prol. 967-1052), where the disintegrative effect of division, symbolized by the clay feet, is reiterated nearly a dozen times more. Gower brings up the idea one last time in the poem's conclusion, VIII.3040-41, after he has returned to the voice of the Prologue to admonish the three estates for their divisiveness. The moral point is akin to that made by Dante's heavily fissured statue on Crete which exudes the rivers of Hell.

[51]
Set sibi quisque suam sortem facit, et sibi casum
Vt libet incurrit, et sibi fata creat;
Atque voluntatis mens libera quod facit actum
Pro variis meritis nomine sortis habet.

(*Vox Clamantis* II.iv.203-06)

(Yet each man shapes for himself his own destiny, incurs his own lot according to his desire, and creates his own fate. In fact, a free mind voluntarily claims what it does for its various deserts in the name of fate.)

[52]*Nebuchadnezzar's Children: Conventions of Madness in Middle English Literature* (New Haven, 1974), p. 89.

[53]N.B., there are other references to Daniel in the *Confessio Amantis* besides the extended treatments of the two dreams, which, like the several references in the interior books of *Vox Clamantis*, suggest careful reading of the prophet but need only to be mentioned as footnote to my main analysis here. In Bk. V Genius takes three examples from "tholde lawe" to illustrate the culpability of sacrilegious princes, namely Antiochus, Nabuzardan, and a combination of Nebuchadnezzar and his son Baltazar (lines 7007-25); Nebuchadnezzar is a culprit for seizing the temple, though it is his heir who pays the penalty "whan Mane, Techel, Phares write / Was on the wal" (lines 7023-24). No specific mention of Daniel is made in the passage, though he is source for at least part of the allusion. Gower's treatment of Antiochus in the Tale of Apollonius may also bear some kinship to Daniel.

[54]The phrase is Marjorie Reeves's, in her definition of what constitutes

apocalypticism ("The Development of Apocalyptic Thought," p. 40).

[55]Macaulay, *Confessio Amantis* II.550. In addition to appearing in *Confessio Amantis* manuscripts, the note appears in similar form in two *Vox Clamantis* manuscripts. See *Latin Works*, pp. 418-19.

[56]The pertinent passage reads: "Tercius iste liber qui ob reuerenciam strenuissimi domini sui domini Henrici de Lancastria, tunc Derbeie Comitis, Anglico sermone conficitur, secundum Danielis propheciam super huius mundi regnorum mutacione a tempore regis Nabugodonosor vsque nunc tempora distinguit. Tractat eciam secundum Aristotilem super hiis quibus rex Alexander tam in sui regimen quam aliter eius disciplina edoctus fuit. Principalis tamen huius operis materia super amorem et infatuatas amantum passiones fundamentum habet. Nomenque sibi appropriatum Confessio Amantis specialiter sortitus est" (*Confessio Amantis* II, p. 480).

[57]I am indebted to Lee W. Patterson and Lynne Staley Johnson for comments on an earlier version of this paper which I presented 9 May 1986 at the Twenty-First International Congress on Medieval Studies at Kalamazoo, Michigan, and to David L. Jeffrey, who read the essay in rough draft.

GOWER'S METAETHICS

Michael P. Kuczynski

Confessio Amantis has been situated--indeed, situates itself--in the tradition of medieval penitential manuals such as Peraldus's *Summa vitiis* and such exempla collections as Bromyard's *Summa predicantium*. Here I want to place the poem in a somewhat different tradition, that of medieval metaethics--the branch of moral philosophy concerned with the nature of moral language, the meaning of moral terms. Unlike normative ethics, which states what is right or wrong (by prescribing or proscribing certain types of behavior, giving advice, etc.), metaethics investigates what we mean when we use such terms as *right* and *wrong*. That is, whereas normative ethics is largely directive, metaethics is primarily analytical.[1]

For many twentieth-century philosophers, metaethics precludes normative ethics.[2] This is not the case in medieval ethics, where questions of moral language and behavior are inseparable. Medieval moralists take this inseparability for granted, and at least one medieval poet, John Gower, followed their lead by making the inseparability of ethics and metaethics a literary concern.

The discussion is in two parts: a review of the metaethical tradition as represented in Peter Abelard's treatise *Scito te ipsum* and in some anonymous fourteenth- and fifteenth-century prose treatises of religious instruction written in English; and a discussion of Gower's indebtedness to this tradition, especially in Book

IV of *Confessio Amantis*, in which Genius and Amans consider the sin of sloth. In particular, I discuss Amans's use of the term *bisinesse* in his confession and Genius's response to his use of that term in the story of Pygmalion and his statue.

I. Traditions

Despite its title, Abelard's *Scito te ipsum* (*Know yourself*) is neither an oracular pronouncement on morals nor a Polonius-like list of moral do's and don'ts. Abelard's main interest in *Scito te ipsum* is intentionality and the extent to which ignorance of the nature of one's acts reduces moral culpability. In pursuing this point, Abelard insists on a distinction between two ethical terms which are sometimes confused, *vice* (*vitium*) and *sin* (*peccatum*). Vice, Abelard explains, is simply a mental--and natural-- inclination to sin; sin itself involves actual consent to this inclination:

> And so vice is that by which we are made prone to sin, that is, are inclined to consent to what is not fitting so that we either do it or forsake it. Now this consent we properly call sin, that is, the fault of the soul by which it earns damnation or is made guilty before God. For what is that consent unless it is contempt of God and an offense against him?[3]

Abelard's distinction between vice and sin is complicated by his use of the term *uoluntas*, or *will*, which usually denotes desire and thus consent to sin in a particular way. Abelard explains that sometimes the term *uoluntas* is inaccurate to describe certain kinds of consent, such as consent constrained by circumstances beyond one's control. At this point in *Scito te ipsum* Abelard uses a hypothetical example to illustrate the inseparability of moral language from practical questions of moral behavior:

> But perhaps you will say that the will to do a bad deed is also sin. . . . For just as we please God by willing to do what we believe to please him, so we displease him by willing to

do what we believe to displease him and we seem to offend him or hold him in contempt. But I say if we consider this more carefully, our conclusion should be very different from what it seems. . . . For consider: there is an innocent man whose cruel lord is so burning with rage against him that with a naked sword he chases him for his life. For long that man flees and as far as he can he avoids his own murder; in the end and unwillingly he is forced to kill him lest he be killed by him. Tell me, whoever you are, what bad will he had in doing this. If he wanted to escape death, he wanted to save his own life. But surely this was not a bad will? You say: not this, I think, but the will he had to kill the lord who was chasing him. I reply: that is well and cleverly said if you can show a will in what you claim. But, as has already been said, he did this unwillingly and under compulsion; as far as he could he deferred injury to his life; he was also aware that by this killing he would put his own life in danger. So how did he do willingly what he committed with danger to his own life as well?[4]

We may be tempted to dismiss the style and concerns of this passage as narrow and casuistical. Abelard himself, however, points out the dangers of casuistry when he admits that one of his imagined opponent's arguments is "well spoken and cleverly put forward" (Bene et argute dicis) but fallacious. And Abelard's exemplum, particular but hardly over-imaginative, establishes a believable moral context for his metaethical distinctions between the terms vice, sin, and will. Questions of moral language and concerns about moral behavior here impinge directly on each other.

In what sense, however, is Abelard's discussion of vice, sin, and will relevant to Confessio Amantis? Abelard's use of exempla to ground questions about moral language in practical moral concerns recalls Gower's own persistent and very complicated use of exempla in his poem.[5] Abelard's exempla, like many of Gower's, do not usually contain clear statements of their moralitates. Rather, they are frequently the kind of stories described by Peter von Moos in his discussion of exempla in John of Salisbury's Policraticus:

> . . . the *exemplum*, like any other written testimony, requires
> interpretation. The ability to read and understand *exempla*,
> John emphasizes, depends on the level of literary knowledge.
> Whereas the "ignorant mulititude," always curious of spec-
> tacles, takes the representation of vice at its face value and
> even wishes to imitate it, the wise man, trained in herme-
> neutics, is able to differentiate between positive and nega-
> tive, persuasive and dissuasive *exempla*. . . .[6]

Exempla used indirectly rather than directly, as parts of an argument, von Moos calls (after John of Salisbury) *strategematica*,
ways of generating, focusing, and directing moral arguments.
Von Moos's distinctions between types of exempla in the
Policraticus illuminate Abelard's and Gower's use of stories.
Abelard and Gower both use exempla argumentatively rather
than straightforwardly. Unlike the moralist, they are not primarily concerned with deriving from their stories simple *moralitates*. Rather, they use their stories to examine the nature of
moral terms. *Scito te ipsum* contains several exempla like the
story of the man pursued by his enraged lord, and in each instance the imagined story Abelard tells focuses or directs the
discussion of moral terms being conducted at that point in the
treatise. Gower achieves a similar effect in his version of the
Pygmalion story, as I shall show later.

Abelard's use of dialogue is another literary technique that
associates *Scito te ipsum* with Gower's *Confessio Amantis*. Dialogue is, of course, an ancient literary form. But Abelard's use
of it in the context of questions about moral language is more
like Gower's use of the Genius-Amans dialogue in *Confessio
Amantis* than is, for instance, a dialogue between the soul and
the body. Also, the admixture of dialogue and argumentative exempla in *Scito te ipsum* makes Abelard's and Gower's approaches to moral discourse seem even more analogous.

Unfortunately there is no evidence that Gower read Abelard
on ethics. Only five manuscripts of *Scito te ipsum* are known to
survive. Three of these are fourteenth- or fifteenth-century. One,
owned by William Gray, bishop of Ely, when he died in 1478

and now in the library of Balliol College, Oxford, was almost
certainly copied in England, perhaps before Gower finished
Confessio Amantis, but that Gower saw this manuscript is unlikely.[7] Gower need not have known Abelard's work to have
learned his method, which became the foundation of scholastic
discourse. It is much more likely that Gower encountered metaethical habits something like Abelard's in the many anonymous
prose treatises of moral instruction written and widely circulated
in England throughout the fourteenth century. Most of these
treatises, which are written in English, remain unedited. I have
examined several of them in manuscript, and certain similarities
between their language and concerns and Gower's in *Confessio
Amantis* suggest that the poet knew and used works like them.

The sorts of moral terms these prose writers scrutinize are
not the more general kinds Abelard attends to (*vice, sin,* and
will), but what Bernard Williams has recently called "'thicker'
or more specific moral notions . . . such as *treachery* and *promise* and *brutality* and *courage*, which seem to express a union of
fact and value."[8] One such moral notion addressed often in the
prose treatises and in Book IV of *Confessio Amantis* is *bisinesse*.

In one of these treatises, in Cambridge University Library
MS. Ff.6.71 (2),[9] the author begins his discussion of the term
bisinesse with a translation of Matthew 6:25-34:

> . . . Therefore I sey to ȝou þat ȝe be not bisy to ȝoure lif--
> what ȝe schulen ete, eþer to ȝoure bodi--wiþ what ȝe
> schulen be cloþid. Whenne ȝoure lif is not more þen mete,
> and þe body more þen cloþ? Biholde ȝe þe fleyng foulis of
> þe air, for þei sowen not ne ripon, neþer gadere into bernes,
> and ȝoure fadir of heuen fediþ hem. Whenne ȝe ben not
> more worþi þen þei?

The prose writer translates Latin *sollicitus* with Middle English
bisi; but he does not, therefore, imply that *bisi* simply means
"anxious." Rather, he pursues the definition of *bisi* immediately
after his translation of the gospel verse, attempting to explain
exactly what Christ meant by his injunction. In the manuscript,

the following passage begins with its key-word, *bisi*, written in large red letters:

> . . . BISY. Al out we ben deliuered from cure or bisyness of þis þing, whom kynde ʒiveþ comoun to alle grete beestis. . . . But it is comaundid to vs þat we be not bisy what we schule ete, for we make redy bred to vs in swot of chier. Body traueyl is to be hautid, but bisynes is to be put away. Đis þat is seid, þat ʒeþ "be not bisy to ʒoure lif--what ʒe schule ete, neþer to ʒoure body--wiþ what ʒe schule be cloþid," we schule vndirstond of fleischly mete and cloþ, fforwhi we owen euere be bisy of gostly metis and cloþis.

The writer makes two important distinctions about the terms of Christ's injunction. First, he specifies that *bisness* in the gospel verse does not refer to that physical labor necessary for life, but only to an excessive preoccupation with worldly goods. This restriction on the definition already implies the writer's second point, with which he concludes the passage--that the word *bisness* can actually denote two antithetical activities or concerns, excessive pursuit of or preoccupation with the things of the world; or, avid pursuit of spiritual goods. Behind this dual definition is the assumption that the objects of one's industry, as well as the degree of it, will determine whether it is morally commendable or not.

The writer returns to the same sort of distinction later in his treatise, when he analyzes the injunction from Matthew's gospel in connection with another divine command, alluded to earlier--God's charge to Adam in Genesis that he make his bread by the sweat of his brow ("In sudore vultus tui vesceris pane" [Gen. 3:19]):

> . . . Crist seide noʒt "nyl ʒe trauel," but "nye ʒe be bisy." Đerfore we ben forbeden to be bisy, but we ben comaundid forto trauel. God speking to Adam seide not, "þu schalt make bred to þee wiþ bisynes," but "wiþ trauel and swot of þi face." Đerfore, noʒt in gostly bisynes but in bodily trauelis bred is to be geten, so good worching bred is plentyous to men worching, for mede of diligence. But bred is wiþdrawe

fro men slepyng and necligent for peyne of necligence.

Especially notable is the writer's remark that man must not get his bread by spiritual busyness, but by the work of his hands, or physical busyness. As before, the writer draws attention to the different, even opposite, meanings the word *bisinesse* can have in moral statements, and thus the different types of behavior the term can signify. This sort of glossing, I would argue, is in the same tradition as Abelard's distinctions concerning moral terms in *Scito te ipsum*, although the kinds of terms these practical treatises discuss differ from the sort with which Abelard is concerned. Like Abelard's distinctions, these glosses are not casuistical. They are attempts to dispel moral ignorance by being more precise about the language of moral statements.

Before discussing Gower's indebtedness to the tradition represented by Abelard and these anonymous moral writers, it would be useful to indicate how widely known metaethical discussions of the word *bisinesse* were by looking briefly at where the tradition appears in the work of Gower's contemporaries. Langland and Chaucer are not interested in using the tradition as a basis for poetic composition, as Gower is in *Confessio Amantis*. However, their awareness of the tradition appears at points in their work. For instance, at the beginning of Passus I of *Piers Plowman*, after Will's vision of the fair field full of folk, Holy Church appears to him and interprets the significance of the vision for him:

> ". . . sone, slepestow? sestow þis peple,
> How bisie þei ben about þe maȝe?
> The mooste partie of þis peple þat passeþ on þis erþe,
> Haue þei worship in þis world þei [kepe] no bettre;
> Of ooþer heuene þan here holde þei no tale."
>
> (lines 5-9)[10]

The activity of the people in the field may strike the modern reader simply as an expression of the bustle of medieval life-- that is, as a cliché:

> . . . houed þer an hundred in howues of selk,
> Sergeantʒ it [s]emed þat serueden at þe barre,
> Pleteden for penyes and pounde[d] þe lawe
> [Ac] noʒt for loue of oure lord vnlose hire lippes ones.
> . . . .
> Baksteres and Brewesteres and Bochiers manye,
> Wollen webbesters and weueres of lynnen,
> Taillours, Tynkers and Tollers in Markettes,
> Masons, Mynours, and many oþere craftes;
> Of alle kynne lybbynge laborers lopen forþ somme.
>
> (Prol. 211-14; 219-23)

Holy Church's comments, however, suggest that there is something morally suspicious about the activity of the people in the
field. In their preoccupation with the things of this world, they
neglect the next, which ought to be their true concern. In Holy
Church's remarks, the word *bisie* cannot be translated in so morally neutral a way as "engaged in vigorous activity." It must be
translated more strongly, as something like "engaged in spiritually debilitating activity." Unlike the sleeping Will, these people may seem more virtuous because they are more industrious.
Paradoxically, though, they may in fact be just as slothful, insofar as their activity is not spiritually useful. In other words,
Langland relies in Holy Church's speech on a double meaning
of *bisinesse*. The reader's ability to distinguish between these
two meanings is crucial to the success of the satire.

Similar instances of the word *bisinesse* appear in Chaucer's
poetry. For instance, in the description of the Sergeant of Law in
the General Prologue to the *Canterbury Tales*: "Nowher so bisy
a man as he ther nas, / And yet he semed bisier than he was"
(lines 321-22).[11] Jill Mann has pointed out that in these two
lines Chaucer implies a criticism of the Sergeant of Law but
does not make his criticism explicit.[12] The Sergeant of Law's
busyness may be interpreted simply as the necessary activity of
his profession; however, it may also be a façade, and, if it is, it
is spiritually harmful because it wastes time and distracts his attention from spiritual concerns. Chaucer, then, like Langland in

Passus I of *Piers Plowman*, relies on his audience's understanding of the double meaning of *bisinesse*. If his audience does not recognize the double meaning, and if it does not understand the distinction between spiritual and physical busyness, it will miss the implied irony in the Sergeant of Law's portrait.

Chaucer's use of the double meaning of *bisinesse* is more explicit in the Second Nun's Prologue:

> The ministre and the norice unto vices
> Which that men clepe in Englissh Ydelnesse,
> That porter of the gate is of delices,
> To eschue, and by hire contrarie hire oppresse--
> That is to seyn, by leveful bisynesse--
> Wel oghten we to doon al oure entente,
> Lest that the feend thurgh ydelnesse us hente.

(lines 1-7)

"Leveful" or commendable busyness necessarily calls to mind its opposite, "unleveful" or condemnable busyness--the sort which does not combat sloth but encourages it. Thus for the Middle Ages not all busyness was commendable, and the word *bisinesse* denoted different patterns of behavior. Langland and Chaucer rely on these denotations for poetic effect and in doing so acknowledge the medieval metaethical tradition.

II. Applications

Gower's use of the metaethical tradition is much more thoroughgoing than either Langland's or Chaucer's. In the different meanings for *bisinesse* he identifies a verbal paradox he can use to express a moral one. Langland and Chaucer recognize this paradox too, but neither represents it in any particular character as directly as Gower does in Amans. If *bisinesse* can mean both an excessive preoccupation with the things of this world and an avid pursuit of spiritual goods, it is possible to imagine someone so ignorant of the nature of his moral condition that he represents himself as virtuous simply because he is constantly active, when in fact his activity conceals the condition of sloth. In speaking of his condition, such a character would confuse, or mistakenly attempt to combine, the two contrary meanings of *bisinesse* in a single, literal one, defining *bisinesse* simply as activity in pursuit of his end.

This is Amans's verbal and moral dilemma in Book IV of *Confessio Amantis*. During Genius's discussion of sloth, Amans admits his guilt in terms of only one branch of the sin, *lachesse*, or procrastination: though he continually pursues his lady, he cannot always bring himself to speak with her openly, because he is tongue-tied. Normally, Amans appeals to his busyness in pursuing the lady as evidence that he is not slothful:

> . . . I am so simple of port,
> That forto feigne som desport
> I pleie with hire litel hound
> Now on the bedd, now on the ground,
> Now with hir briddes in the cage;
> For ther is non so litel page,
> Ne yit so simple a chamberere,
> That I ne make hem alle chere,
> Al for thei scholde speke wel:
> Thus mow ye sen mi besi whiel,
> That goth noght ydeliche aboute.
>
> (lines 1187-97)[13]

Amans here defines busyness as any behavior, however trivial, which will please his lady and further his suit. Idleness, conversely, he defines as any sort of behavior that frustrates this end. According to the value system of *fin amor*, these definitions are normative. On a more transcendent scale of value, however, Amans's definitions of what is busy, and therefore commendable, and what is idle, and therefore condemnable, actually confuse the moral norms, because they do not take into adequate account the object of his industry.

Gower invokes this transcendent scale of value, and points up Amans's moral confusion, at two important moments during the Lover's confession in Book IV. Immediately after Amans describes the trivial things he does to please his lady, Gower has him relate how he pursues her on pilgrimage:

> And if hir list to riden oute
> On pelrinage or other stede,
> I come, thogh I be noght bede,
> And take hire in min arm alofte
> And sette hire in hire sadel softe,
> And so forth lede hire be the bridel,
> For that I wolde noght ben ydel.
> . . . .
> And thus I ryde forth mi weie,
> And am riht besi overal
> With herte and with mi body al,
> As I have said you hier tofore.
> My goode fader, tell therfore,
> Of Ydelnesse if I have gilt.

(lines 1198-1223)

Like Chaucer's Wife of Bath, Amans knows a lot about wandering by the way. He is not a virtuous pilgrim, with his eyes set on the heavenly city. He centers his attention and behavior on the things of this world.[14] His language is the best indication of his misdirected attitude. For instance, he does not distinguish between pilgrimages and other journeys on which he follows his lady ("On pelrinage or other stede"); as long as he is in her presence, he attends to nothing else, least of all his spiritual welfare. He goes on pilgrimage--that is, he describes himself as having engaged in a form of spiritual busyness. But he is not a genuine pilgrim because his concerns are misdirected. His concluding remark to Genius in this passage may carry a note of vain self-confidence: "Tell me then, good father, if I'm at all guilty of idleness."

Toward the end of his confession in Book IV, Amans expresses frustration to Genius at his lady's continued indifference. Amans's terms invoke a spiritual standard of value which qualifies his own implied definitions of busyness and idleness. As the Lover finally laments to his Confessor:

199

> . . . if a sinful wolde preie
> To god of his foryivenesse
> With half so gret a besinesse
> As I have do to my ladi,
> In lacke of askinge of merci
> He scholde nevere come in Helle.

(lines 3490-95)

In this complaint Amans himself compares the two value systems, Christianity's and *fin amor*'s, highlighting as he does so two different senses in which the word *bisinesse* can be construcd. He misunderstands the distinction between these senses; but, by unwittingly raising this distinction as an issue in the poem, Amans focuses the reader's attention on Gower's meta-ethical concerns. "I can say for certain," Amans remarks earlier in Book IV,

> . . . of dede and thoght
> That ydel man have I be noght:
> For hou as evere I be deslaied,
> Yit evermore I have assaied.
> Bot thogh my besinese laste,
> Al is bot ydel ate laste,
> For whan theffect is ydelnesse,
> I not what thing is besinesse.

(lines 1753-60)

Gower's rhyme in the last two lines of this passage, "For when theffect is *ydelnesse*, / I not what thing is *besinesse*" (my emphasis), is a verbal correlative to the moral confusion afflicting Amans. His definition of *bisinesse* is too limited, too literal. It fails to account for a kind of physical activity which can be spiritually debilitating--the kind of busyness that is in fact, not just in rhyme, the equivalent of idleness.

At another point earlier in Book IV Amans had come close to recognizing the verbal and moral paradox in which he is caught, when he remarked, "I seche that I mai noght finde, / I haste and evere I am behinde" (lines 289-90). Gower's allusion to Matthew 7:7 ("quaerite et invenietis") encourages the reader to set the certain rewards of spiritual busyness against the uncertain and insubstantial rewards of physical busyness. In admitting the fruitlessness of his efforts, Amans almost realizes that he should leave off his current activity and reconsider his definition of the word *bisinesse* itself. This, however, is the closest Amans can come to moral enlightenment without the assistance of Genius.

Amans's enlightenment is not complete in Book IV of *Confessio Amantis*. Four more books of the poem remain before he finally asks Venus for release from love and is given his beads to pray upon. But in Book IV Genius continues the process begun in the first book largely by way of the moralized stories he tells to Amans. These exempla, as I have already suggested, are often indirect rather than direct. Unlike the language of traditional exempla, Gower's language suggests more than it seems to mean; it requires careful interpretation. Genius's indirection forces Amans, and the reader, to scrutinize the terms of his stories and thus to become more conscious of the nature of moral language itself.

One of the stories Genius tells Amans in Book IV is the tale of Pygmalion and his statue, from Book X of Ovid's *Metamorphoses*. Genius tells the story ostensibly as an illustration of the rewards that come to those who persist in love. As such the exemplum might be thought to encourage rather than to discourage Amans's limited definition of *bisinesse*. Is this, in fact, how Genius intends the story?

It clarifies Genius's intentions to note some of the changes Gower made in Ovid's story. For example, Gower eliminates the initial motive behind Pygmalion's fashioning his ideal statue, his outrage at the prostitutions of real women: "Pygmalion had seen these women spending their lives in shame, and, disgusted with the faults which in such full measure nature had given the female mind, he lived unmarried and long was without a partner of his couch" (X.243-46).[15] In Ovid's story, this detail excuses somewhat Pygmalion's infatuation with his creation. Ovid likewise absolves Pygmalion by remarking directly to the reader that the statue was indeed so lifelike that anyone might have mistaken it for a real woman, so that it is not surprising that Pygmalion fell in love with it: "virginis est verae facies, quam vivere credas" (X.250). Again, Gower excludes this detail from his story. Apparently, he was not interested in having Genius tell a story which Amans could read as encouragement of his behavior.

In fact, Gower adds details to Ovid's story, driving home the point that Pygmalion's love for the statue springs from his fancy alone. Genius remarks quite directly,

> . . . thurgh pure impression
> Of his ymaginacion
> With al the herte of his corage
> His love upon this faire ymage
> He sette, and hire of love preide.

(lines 389-93)

Genius's view that Pygmalion is at the mercy of his fantasy recalls a similar comment Amans makes about himself elsewhere in Book IV. After he has seen his lady in church and thought how pleasant it would be to hold her by the arm, Amans laments:

> Bot afterward it doth me harm
> Of pure ymaginacioun;
> For thanne this collacioun
> I make unto miselven ofte,
> And seie, "Ha lord, hou sche is softe,
> How sche is round, hou sche is smal!
> Now wolde god I hadde hire al
> Withoute danger at mi wille!"

(lines 1142-49)

Amans, like Gower's Pygmalion, is a slave to fantasy. Given Gower's changes to Ovid, which point up this aspect of Pygmalion's character, it is reasonable to assume that Amans ought to understand more from Genius's story than that he can hope for success if he continues pursuing his lady.

Another way in which Gower points up Pygmalion's enslavement to fantasy is by emphasizing in his version of Ovid's story that Pygmalion takes his statue to bed. Ovid simply tells the reader that Pygmalion lays the statue on his couch; Gower has Pygmalion actually sleep with the image:

> . . . whan the nyht was come,
> He leide hire in his bed al nakid.
> He was forwept, he was forwakid,
> He keste hire colde lippes ofte,
> And wissheth that thei weren softe,
> And ofte he rouneth in hire Ere,
> And ofte his arm now hier now there
> He leide, as he hir wolde embrace,
> And evere among he axeth grace,
> As thogh sche wiste what he mente.
>
> (lines 402-11)

Ovid does tell us that Pygmalion kisses his statue as if she were alive and caresses her, imagining for a moment that the marble yields to his touch, like the marble thigh of Persephone in Bernini's Pluto and Persephone in the Galleria Borghese. It is only in Gower's version, though, that all this happens in bed. Also, Gower, unlike Ovid, suggests Pygmalion's own pathetic embarrassment at his behavior: he has his servants carry the statue into his bedroom at night after dinner ("And whan the bord was taken uppe, / He hath hire into chambre nome," [lines 400-01]); he himself, once the sun goes down, takes the statue to bed with him ("And after, whan the nyht was come, / He leide hire in his bed al nakid" [lines 402-03]). Gower even has Genius, in concluding the story, make a pun which provokes laughter at Pygmalion as much as joy in his pleasure when the statue comes alive:

Bot for he hath his word travailed
And dorste speke, his love he spedde,
And hadde al that he wolde *abedde*.

(lines 428-30, my emphasis)

Pygmalion has both all that he has longed for, and all that he wanted *in bed*. In other words, Gower not only emphasizes the debilitating power of Pygmalion's imagination, but also the carnal nature of his motives, which Ovid suggests but does not emphasize.

Of course, Amans's chances for success with his lady are not strengthened simply because Genius tells him a story about the rewards that come to those who persist in love. In fact, two additions which Gower makes to Ovid's story suggest that Genius does not want Amans to interpret this exemplum too optimistically. There are no references to Fortune's role in Pygmalion's situation in Ovid. There are two, however, in Gower's version of the story. Genius introduces the story explaining that it is about how Fortune

. . . yifth hire happi chance
To him which makth continuance
To preie love and to beseche.

(lines 367-69)

But he qualifies this beneficent view of Fortune's role only a few lines later, when he explains that Fortune was also responsible for Pygmalion's initial grief; it was she who caused him to make the statue in the first place and to fall hopelessly in love with it:

. . . thurgh fortune it fell him so,
As he whom love schal travaile,
He made an ymage of entaile. . . .

(lines 376-78)

The story turns out happily for Pygmalion: Cupid turns the statue into a real woman. But Genius implies clearly that Fortune is fickle. Because things worked out for Pygmalion does not necessarily mean they will for Amans. To this point, Amans has had absolutely nothing to show for his efforts. The nature of his reward--suffering--might move him to interpret Genius's story of Pygmalion as cause for moral re-evaluation, not hope.

Genius's status in *Confessio Amantis* is itself paradoxical. He represents himself, early on in the poem, as the agent both of Venus and of God. In this dual role, he can only address Amans's problems indirectly, lest he offend either the goddess of love or his heavenly lord. But the very fact that Genius must proceed by indirection involves the reader in Gower's metaethics, by forcing him to scrutinize the terms of Genius's comments and exempla with the same care Amans must exert. In his insistence on such scrutiny, Gower shows himself to be sometimes as subtle a poet as Chaucer, and as interested as Chaucer (or Abelard) in the relationship between how we behave and how we talk and write about how we behave.

NOTES

[1]For a clear discussion of the differences between metaethics and normative ethics, with remarks on ethics and literature, see Stephen E. Toulmin, *The Place of Reason in Ethics* (Cambridge, 1950; rept. Chicago, 1986).

[2]For a discussion of this view and a powerful response to it, see Bernard Williams, *Ethics and the Limits of Philosophy* (Cambridge, MA, 1985). Briefly, Williams insists that the concerns of metaethics and normative ethics are always inseparable, a view medieval moralists and poets would have found congenial.

[3]Quotations and translations from *Scito te ipsum* are from *Peter Abelard's "Ethics,"* ed. and trans. D. E. Luscombe (Oxford, 1971): "Vitium itaque est quo ad peccandum proni efficimur, hoc est, inclinamur ad consentiendum ei quod non conuenit, ut illud scilicet faciamus aut dimittamus. Hunc uero consensum proprie peccatum nominamus, hoc est, culpam animae qua dampnationem meretur, uel apud deum rea statuitur. Quid est enim iste consensus nisi Dei contemptus et offensa ipsius?" (pp. 4-5).

[4]"Sed fortassis inquies, quia et uoluntas mali operis peccatum est. . . . Quemadmodum enim uolendo facere quod Deo credimus placere ipsi placemus, ita uolendo facere quod Deo credimus displicere ipsi diplicemus, et ipsum of-

fendere siue contempnere uidemur. Sed dico quia si diligentius adtendamus, longe aliter de hoc sentiendum est quam uideature. . . . Ecce enim aliquis est innocens in quem crudelis dominus suus per furorem adeo commotus est, et eum euaginato ense ad interimendum persequatur, quem ille diu fugiens et quantumcunque potest sui occisionem deuitans, coactus tandem et nolens occidet eum ne occidatur ab eo. Dicito mihi quicumque es, quam malam uoluntatem habuerit in hoc facto. Volens siquidem mortem effugere uolebat propriam uitam conseruare. Sed numquid haec uoluntas mala erat? Non, inquies, haec arbitror, sed ille quam habuerit de occisione domini persequentibus. Respondeo, Bene et argute dicis, si uoluntatem possis assignare in eo quod asseris. Sed, iam ut dictum est, nolens et coactus hoc fecit, quod quantum potuit uitam incolomen distulit, sciens quoque ex hac interfectione uitae sibi periculum imminere. Quomodo ergo illud uoluntarie fecit, quod cum ipso etiam uitae suae periculo commisit?" (pp. 6-9).

[5]For a discussion of Gower's use of exempla, see Charles Runacres, "Art and Ethics in the *Exempla* of *Confessio Amantis*," in *Gower's "Confessio Amantis": Responses and Reassessments*, ed. A. J. Minnis (Cambridge, 1983), pp. 106-34.

[6]"The Use of *Exempla* in the *Policraticus* of John of Salisbury," in *The World of John of Salisbury*, ed. Michael Wilks (Oxford, 1984), pp. 207-61.

[7]Luscombe, *Abelard's "Ethics,"* pp. xxxviii-lxi.

[8]Williams, *Limits of Philosophy*, p. 129.

[9]I am grateful to the Syndics of the Cambridge University Library for access to and permission to quote from the manuscript. All punctuation is my own.

[10]Quotations from Langland are from *Piers Plowman: The B Version*, ed. George Kane and E. T. Donaldson (London, 1975).

[11]Quotations from Chaucer are from *The Riverside Chaucer*, 3rd ed., general editor Larry D. Benson (Boston, 1987).

[12]*Chaucer and Medieval Estates Satire* (Cambridge, 1973), pp. 90-91.

[13]Quotations from Gower are from *The English Works of John Gower*, vol. 1, ed. G. C. Macaulay, EETS, e.s. 81 (Oxford, 1900).

[14]On bad pilgrims of this sort, see Christian K. Zacher, *Curiosity and Pilgrimage: The Literature of Discovery in Fourteenth-Century England* (Baltimore, 1976).

[15]"Quas quia Pygmalion aevum per crimen agentis viderat, offensus vitiis, quae plurima menti femineae natura dedit, sine coniuge caelebs vivebat thamique diu consorte carebat." Quotations from Ovid are from *Metamorphoses*, vol. 2, ed. and trans. Frank Justus Miller (Cambridge, 1976).

GOD'S FAITHFULNESS
AND THE LOVER'S DESPAIR:
THE THEOLOGICAL FRAMEWORK OF
THE IPHIS AND ARAXARATHEN STORY

David G. Allen

I

Although it normally progresses in a stately, exceedingly un-hurried way, the frame structure of *Confessio Amantis* occa-sionally seems to lurch to a halt. Every now and again, Amans comes up with an objection to Genius's teaching serious enough, it would appear, to call the entire confession into question. Just such a moment occurs prior to the final story of Book IV. Despondent over his lack of progress toward winning his lady, Amans interrupts--in a respectful way, of course--Genius's flood of good advice:

> And natheles this dar I seie,
> That if a sinful wolde preie
> To god of his foryivenesse
> With half so gret a besinesse
> As I have do to my ladi,
> In lacke of askinge of merci
> He scholde nevere come in Helle.
>
> (lines 3489-95)[1]

While he does not yet follow up on his insight, Amans makes

something of a breakthrough here, as Patrick Gallacher has shown.[2] As far as he still may be from repudiating earthly love, he does seem to intuit the flaw in the analogy between earthly and heavenly love upon which his entire confession is based. He is overwhelmed by this rather belated recognition that, unlike God, his lady lacks any obligation to her petitioner. While Jesus may have said, "Ask, and it shall be given you: seek, and you shall find: knock, and it shall be opened to you" (Matt. 7:7, Douay version), neither Amans's lady nor the gods of love who could inspire her have made such a promise. Indeed, as Amans himself acknowledged in Book I, the opposite is true, for love

> . . . yifth his graces undeserved,
> And fro that man which hath him served
> Fulofte he takth aweye his fees.

> (lines 51-53)

Amans's suit has drawn him into the trap (to lapse into our own vernacular) of literally mistaking his lady for someone who gives a damn.

To suppress Amans's challenge and, therefore, to keep the confession moving along, Genius tells a very much altered version of Ovid's story of Iphis and Anaxarete, whom he calls Araxarathen. By closing with this tale, Gower accomplishes two significant tasks. First, he gives balance to Book IV, for a very different story about another Iphis plays an important role near the beginning of the book. Second, using these two tales of Iphis, Gower draws our attention to the late medieval debate on God's faithfulness. Explored in the universities by William of Ockham (d. 1349) and other nominalists and developed poetically by contemporaries such as Chaucer, this important late medieval issue surfaces here to frame the close of Gower's consideration of the sin of sloth. A consideration of how this final Iphis story differs in thrust not only from its source in the *Metamorphoses* and its customary allegorizations, but also from its precursor in Book IV, will reveal the significant influence of this debate.

Genius begins his refutation of Amans's objection to love's unpredictability by mildly uttering some consoling words. "Mi sone," he says, there's nothing to do about the lady's stand-offishness until "love his grace wol thee sende" (lines 3502-04). But, rather than venture a prediction of when that longed-for event will occur, Genius tells the gloomy story of the deaths of Iphis and Araxarathen so as to emphasize the dangers of losing hope. This puzzling decision to respond to Amans's despairing remark about his lady's unreliability with the story of Iphis and Araxarathen particularly demands our attention. For Genius's story only seems to affirm the very unpredictability that Amans finds so disturbing.

Genius's story concerns the love which King Theucer's son Iphis has for Araxarathen, "a Maide of lou astat" (line 3521). As much as Iphis might beg and pray for her favor, Araxarathen knows that she is not a suitable match for him. So she refuses all of his gifts, plunging him into despair. Bereft of the "delit / Of lust, of Slep, of Appetit" (lines 3543-44), Iphis goes in the night to Araxarathen's house and hangs himself outside where she will be sure to find him in the morning. When she sees the body, Araxarathen blames herself for Iphis's death and calls on the gods to place a judgment on her:

> For I ne dede no pite
> To him, which for mi love is lore,
> Do no pite to me therfore.
>
> (lines 3628-30)

The perversely agreeable gods turn her into stone.

To be sure, this story shows the dangers of despondency. But in its bleakness it provides no overt remedy to the dilemma that is driving Amans to despair--his uncertainty over his lady's willingness ever to grant him grace, regardless of how hard he strives to purify himself of the sins of love. In fact, the story overwhelmingly suggests that, depending on the lady, a miserable uncertainty may be a lover's only long-term partner. The epitaph on Iphis's tomb says only that he was too soft when his lady was too hard (line 3681). So while Iphis may have been incapable of accepting Araxarathen's unwillingness to do him grace, perhaps Amans is made of sterner stuff. And if he is not, then there may be a noose in his future; for in the final analysis a lover simply cannot *make* his beloved return his affection. But is Genius's counsel, that spurned lovers must be tough, really the last word on handling despair?

A change in the story from its source suggests that Gower had advice of a more consoling sort in mind. Ovid tells the story of Iphis and Anaxarete in the fourteenth book of the *Metamorphoses*. There, however, Anaxarete is King Theucer's offspring, and Iphis is a poor boy of common birth. This alteration may seem, at first glance, to be simply another of Genius's garblings of classical narrative. But as Götz Schmitz has shown, Gower's reversal of the social classes of his two main characters seems intended to illustrate how morally wrong his Iphis is in surrendering to despair.[3] Where Ovid focuses on the "crudelis et inpia" Anaxarete in her disdain for Iphis, Gower in Book IV calls attention to his Iphis's immoral repudiation of all of the advantages and responsibilities he possesses. This in turn permits Genius to make his point with Amans, and Gower, on another level, to make the same point with the reader.

By pointing out this congruence between narrator and author, Schmitz has contributed significantly to our understanding of Gower's procedures here. But there are also other, less obvious, results of the alteration of Ovid which we should consider. By changing the social classes of the characters, Gower creates the occasion for Iphis to make the following allusion-laden remarks, which he addresses to the absent Araxarathen immediately before he kills himself:

> Thogh I no deth to the deserve,
> Hier schal I for thi love sterve,

> Hier schal a kinges Sone dye
> For love and for no felonie.
>
> (lines 3577-80)

The story of Iphis, a king's son who dies not because he is guilty of any crime but because he loves his tormentor, a woman of lesser birth, recalls another "kinges Sone," Christ, who similarly died showing his love for an inferior, humanity. While the very idea that Iphis's suicide could be used to recall Christ's sacrifice might seem forced or bizarre to a modern reader, it is nonetheless very much in accord with medieval mythographic interpretation of the story. In the *Ovide moralisé*, for instance, Anaxarate is glossed as God the Father whose "devin corage" is full of anger against man for his base sins. But:

> Jhesus . . . por nous enricher
> Fu povres et por nous franchir
> Devint sers plains d'umilite
> Et sougiez a la deite
> Pria la devine amistie.
>
> (XIV.5601-05; 5.152)[4]

> (In order to enrich us, Jesus made himself poor and in order to free us he wholly humbled himself and, subject to the divinity, he besought divine friendship.)

In the *Ovide*, then, the death of Iphis becomes Christ's payment of the "rigid satisfaction" that regains the Father's blessings. And in Bersuire's *Ovidius moralizatus*, the reader is instructed to "say allegorically that this girl is the soul, this young man Christ who was hung on the gibbet of the cross for love of her."[5]

Thus, by reversing the social classes of the two characters, Gower connects his version of the story with the mythographic tradition. But where Bersuire and the poet of *Ovide moralisé* bring Iphis and Christ together in order to fuse them, in *Confessio Amantis* the gloomy story is not metamorphosed into the good news. Unlike Christ, who is resurrected and causes all who believe in him to be reborn, Gower's Iphis remains in his richly decorated tomb, and Araxarathen herself turns to stone. By implicitly juxtaposing the hope Christ brings with Iphis's despair, Gower suggests despair's true medicine. While it is unsafe to count on an idolized beloved who may turn out to be as immovable as Araxarathen was before Iphis hanged himself, Christ is, in contrast, perfectly reliable.

II

The consequences of this lesson are several. By adding an allegorical layer of meaning to Ovid's story, Gower essentially reinforces the insight that drove Amans to complain of his lady's remoteness. Genius, on the literal level, fails to help Amans, but Gower does more than simply respond to Amans's halting step towards spiritual growth. By emphasizing the concept that God's favor is predictably attainable while an adored and idolized human's may or may not be, he touches on a network of theological issues concerning man's responsibility and God's reliability that the later Middle Ages found to be of paramount importance. As Heiko Oberman and Gordon Leff, among others, have shown, late medieval orthodoxy stressed that "all virtue and vice have their source in volition."[6] This emphasis on the intentions behind actions led to a preoccupation with the purification of a person's will. While this struggle for good intentions was necessarily aided by God's grace, one also had to intend to struggle, to do what was within oneself (*facere quod in se est*) so as to receive the grace necessary to struggle successfully.[7] In other words, every sinner also had to be a suitor actively pursuing God's grace, dedicating him or herself, as a most critical Martin Luther would claim at the end of the period, to a religion preoccupied with works.[8]

In centering on man's will, this essentially voluntarist theology also had to face the issue of God's will; if a person actually does what is within himself to be saved, can he be confident that God will save him? Following the 1277 Paris condemnations of a theology that overemphasized secondary causes, late medieval theologians such as William of Ockham consistently stressed the extreme dependence of creation upon its maker.[9] No future contingent, Ockham maintains, ever happens out of a necessity in itself. When even a divinely inspired prophet foretold an event, for instance, the prophecy did not necessarily determine the event's coming to pass; rather, the event ultimately happened or not according to God's will.[10] Even salvation was so contingent, as Marilyn McCord Adams has pointed out:

> In defining his position about grace, acceptance, and merit, Ockham is intent on preserving divine freedom and sovereignty over the redemptive process. The keystone of his view is the assumption that worthiness of eternal life or eternal punishment are not values natural to any created thing . . . but are conferred solely by divine institution or legislation.[11]

But while God is completely free to shape future contingents, he does not do so arbitrarily or whimsically. Instead, he has freely made himself predictable. For, according to Ockham and others, he forbears from exercising his absolute power and conducts himself instead according to the covenants he has ordained with mankind. So, in Adams's words, "a wedge is driven between what He can do with respect to His absolute and ordered power": by his absolute power, God could certainly save a person without first infusing him or her with saving grace, but he refuses to act in this unpredictable way. Instead, he invariably saves through grace.[12] The same observation has been made by Gordon Leff:

> Only God decides the worth of a person or an action, and nothing is meritorious save by God's acceptance. That does not mean that he acts arbitrarily or in defiance of his own canons. By his ordained power his saving love is reserved for the baptized who having been thus disposed to eternal life do not subsequently fall away from him into mortal sin.[13]

Thus, while God is perfectly free, he has made his freedom reli-

able insofar as a Christian's salvation is concerned. Heiko Oberman summarizes Ockham's notions of man's responsibility and
God's interconnected reliability succinctly:

> God is committed to give his grace to all who do what is in
> them. This does not detract from his sovereignty, since in
> eternity God was free to establish totally different laws; he
> was free to act with absolute power, the *potentia absoluta*,
> subject only to the law of non-contradiction or the law of
> consistency. Out of sheer mercy and grace, he freely decided
> in eternity to establish the law that he would convey grace to
> all who make full use of their natural capacities. Though the
> law as such is freely given, and therefore an expression of
> God's *potentia absoluta*, God is now committed to it, in the
> order chosen by him, the order of his *potentia ordinata*,
> and he therefore gives his grace "necessarily."[14]

Since God has freely and reliably obliged himself not to act
whimsically, man can rely on "the trustworthiness of God's
will."[15]

Articulated first in less-than-accessible scholastic writings,
it was inevitable that the complex network of ideas about God's
absolute and ordained powers and about his faithfulness and forbearance would enter the wider realms of public discourse as the
fourteenth century progressed. Chaucer, for one, was aware that
these issues are crucial, invoking the high stakes of eternal salvation or reprobation.[16] Although he relies mainly on Boethius in
framing Troilus's speech on predestination in the fourth book of
Troilus and Criseyde, Chaucer indeed displays such a keen interest in the questions of God's power and freedom that he
seems predestined to enter into the late medieval scholastic
dialogue. He has Troilus speak most anachronistically of being
baffled by the "argumentes" of the "grete clerkes many oon,"
those experts "that han hire top ful heighe and smothe yshore,"
who lead his maunderings over whether his misfortunes with
Criseyde happened to him because God had foreseen them or if
God has foreseen them because they were bound to happen
(IV.968-69, 995-96, and passim).[17] In a serio-comic passage in

the Nun's Priest's Tale, Chaucer displays a greater ease than
Troilus ever was able to manage in dealing with the arguments
of the shorn clerics, despite his claim that issues of God's
foreknowledge and necessity are largely beyond him:

> But I ne kan nat bulte it to the bren
> As kan the hooly doctour Augustyn,
> Or Boece, or the Bisshop Bradwardyn,
> Wheither that Goddes worthy forwityng
> Streyneth me nedely for to doon a thyng--
> "Nedely" clepe I symple necessitee--
> Or elles, if free choys be graunted me
> To do that same thyng, or do it noght,
> Though God forwoot it er that I was wroght;
> Or if his wityng streyneth never a deel
> But by necessitee condicioneel.
>
> (VII.3240-50)

In mentioning the thoughts of "Bisshop Bradwardyn," that is,
Archbishop Thomas Bradwardine of Canterbury (d. 1349) on
predestination, Chaucer alludes to the great debate with Ockham
and the other so-called *moderni Pelagiani* who, Bradwardine
argued, denigrated God's control over his creation by overem-
phasizing the capacities of contingent creatures to achieve salvation by doing what they had within themselves.[18] But probably
the most profound use Chaucer ever made of nominalist theology is in his characterization of Walter in the Clerk's Tale as
"an embodiment of possibilities which God never has and never
will actualize. In that sense and only in that sense can Walter be
said to be an embodiment of the *potentia dei absoluta*."[19]

III

The significant presence of the interconnected issues of
God's reliability and man's responsibility in Chaucer's work
prepares us to notice them in *Confessio Amantis*.[20] So to return
to the close of the fourth book, if we use the nominalist distinction between ordained and absolute power we can see that, by

slavishly devoting himself to a lady who has made no corresponding commitment to him, Amans has given himself over to
a being possessed of absolute power. But, struggling to purify
his will of any sins against love, he continues to act as though
the lady has ordained a way for him to win her favors. Amans
will not recognize the illogic of his position for quite a while,
but the end of Book IV marks an important point in his development. Taken together, his outburst that God is much more
reliably approached than is his lady and the underlying layer of
meaning of the story that that outburst occasions serve to orient
Amans in the right direction.

This reorientation becomes obvious when we look back in
Book IV to a story of a different Iphis. Towards the beginning of
his consideration of sloth, Genius sets out optimistically to prove
that, since "The god of love is favorable / To hem that ben of love
stable" (lines 443-44), Amans should persevere in doing what he
can to win his lady. Take the case of the child of King Ligdus,
says Genius. When his wife was pregnant, the king demanded that
she give birth to a son, since he would order a baby daughter to
be slain. The queen did give birth to a girl, but she managed to
deceive her husband about the baby's sex. Called Prince Iphis, the
girl was raised as a boy, and all went well even after he/she was
given in marriage as a child to Iante, a duke's young daughter.
The couple got along splendidly as playmates, but as they grew
up together they found that something was missing in their marriage. Horrified that they might act against nature, Cupid "Tok
pite for the grete love" and answered their prayers, transforming
Iphis into the boy she had been raised to be (lines 488-505). Thus,
"mi Sone," Genius concludes,

> . . . with thi grete besinesse
> Thou miht atteigne the richesse
> Of love, if that ther be no Slowthe.

> (lines 513-15)

Or in other words, if Amans continues doing all he can, he too may receive his just reward.

Doing battle against the sin of sloth, Genius presses home the point that persistent effort can bring good results. But the "besinesse" the Confessor endorses here is a far cry from "leveful bisynesse" such as Chaucer offers as a true *remedium* for "ydelnesse" in the Prologue to the Second Nun's Tale (VIII. 1-25). Just how idly futile Amans's busy pursuit really is will become clear towards the end of the book. Gower's pairing of the two Iphis stories, one cheerful and the other gloomy, underscores his point about the fundamental unreliability of earthly love. One Iphis finally achieves a union with his lady, but the other dies unfulfilled. There seems to be no compelling reason why one would find grace while the other would not. Thus Amans stands fixed in a state of complete contradiction: he recognizes that he can best achieve a connection with his stand-offish lady only when he indulges in a form of slothful sin. When he busily pursues her and does all he can to win her, she draws back from him. But when he goes to bed alone and thinks of her, he has considerably better luck. His heart leaves him and steals into her bed,

> And softly takth hire in his arm
> And fieleth hou that sche is warm,
> And wissheth that his body were
> To fiele that he fieleth there.
>
> (lines 2885-88)

Delighted by such pleasant thoughts, Amans drifts off to a "slepi hevene," and, as Russell Peck points out, ironically covers himself with the sin he is supposed to be learning to avoid.[21]

The way out of this apparently inescapable predicament is available to us through nominalist argument. As John Bowers has pointed out in his recent book on *Piers Plowman*, the sin of sloth was seen as sapping the will's strength and diverting it from those basic pursuits that could lead to, and result in, the infusion of salvational grace.[22] A slothful person would resist doing all he could to be saved. Viewed from an Ockhamist perspective, then, Genius is right to counsel Amans to persist in battling sloth, even though the goal of this battle may be inadequate. The position is supported by the mythographic interpretations, also, where both Iphis stories are given a single allegorical resolution in the *true* "besynesse" of Christ. In the *Ovide moralisé* where Anaxarete's harshness reflects God the Father's bitterness toward sin, King Ligdus's willingness to kill a girl child reflects God the Father's

> . . . sentence amere et dure
> Contre femeline nature,
> C'est contre l'ame pecherresse.
>
> (IX.3201-03; 3.298)

> (. . . bitter and harsh sentence against feminine nature, that is against the sinful soul.)

The two stories end happily in the moralizations, for Christ is a reliable intercessor in both.

In the course of Book IV, then, Gower explores the ramifications of this fundamental question of what reliability or certainty a lover can find as he purifies himself in his quest for his beloved's favors. By showing, particularly in the story of Iphis and Araxarathen, how an unpredictable, fundamentally uncommitted object of adoration strips the adorer of any stable ground for action regardless of how devotedly the adorer does what he can to win the beloved, the poet prepares his work's conclusion. When the time comes, an old, worn Amans will turn to God for the certainty he could never find in his lady. Gower's quite sophisticated use of late medieval theology pushes his reader to grasp fully the uncertainty inherent in earthly love and to intuit its opposite in the love of God.

NOTES

[1]All quotations from the *Confessio* are taken from *The English Works of John Gower*, ed. G. C. Macaulay, 2 vols., EETS, e.s. 81-82 (1900-01; rept. London, 1969). Book and line numbers appear in the body of the essay.

[2]Patrick J. Gallacher, *Love, the Word, and Mercury: A Reading of John Gower's "Confessio Amantis"* (Albuquerque, 1975), pp. 74-75.

[3]Götz Schmitz, *"the middel weie": Stil- und Aufbauformen in John Gowers Confessio Amantis* (Bonn, 1974), pp. 122-24.

[4]*Ovide moralisé: Poème du commencement du quatorzième siècle publie d'apres tous les manuscrits connus*, ed. C. De Boer et al. (1931; rept. Wiesbaden, 1966). Book and line numbers, as well as volume and page numbers, are given in the body of the essay.

[5]William Donald Reynolds, *The Ovidius Moralizatus of Petrus Berchorius: An Introduction and Translation* (Ann Arbor, 1985), p. 414.

[6]Gordon Leff, *William of Ockham: The Metamorphoses of Scholastic Discourse* (Manchester, 1975), p. 477.

[7]Heiko Augustinus Oberman, *The Harvest of Medieval Theology: Gabriel Biel and Late Medieval Nominalism* (1963; rept. Durham, NC, 1983), pp. 131-39.

[8]For a discussion of Luther's gradual repudiation of the by-then completely orthodox notion of *facere quod in se est*, see Heiko A. Oberman's essay "*Facientibus Quod in se est Deus non Denegat Gratiam*: Robert Holcot, O.P. and the Beginnings of Luther's Theology," *Harvard Theological Review*, 55 (1962), 317-42. When a man does what is within himself, Luther would come to argue, he sins.

[9]For the importance of the 1277 Condemnations, see Gordon Leff, *The Dissolution of the Medieval Outlook: An Essay on Intellectual and Spiritual Change in the Fourteenth Century* (New York, 1976), pp. 27-31, 127-44, passim.

[10]See William Ockham, *Predestination, God's Foreknowledge, and Future Contingents*, trans. Marilyn McCord Adams and Norman Kretzmann (New York, 1969), p. 44.

[11]Marilyn McCord Adams, *William Ockham*, 2 vols. (Notre Dame, 1987), 2:1295.

[12]Adams, *William Ockham* 2:1295-96. Throughout her lengthy discussion of Ockham's theology, Adams consistently emphasizes the forbearance of Ockham's God. Although he is omnipotent and, therefore, capable of being the sole immediate cause of all proper effects, God predictably refrains from being such so as to allow the ordained secondary causes to have their own immediate effects. "It does not follow," she writes, "that if God is a total immediate cause of Isaac that Abraham could not simultaneously be a total immediate cause of Isaac." God cooperates with nature, then, so as to give nature a predictable role in his plan. See Adams, 2:1228-31.

[13]Leff, *Ockham*, p. 473.

[14]Oberman, *Harvest*, pp. 245-46.

[15]Steven Ozment, *The Age of Reform, 1250-1550: An Intellectual and Religious History of Late Medieval and Reformation Europe* (New Haven, 1980), p. 39. In refuting previous claims that so-called nominalist theology is essentially sceptical inasmuch as it highlights an unknowable God's absolute power, contemporary scholarship has emphasized God's faithfulness. Perhaps the greatest argument for this emphasis comes from the study of the Reformers and how their views were received. Ozment argues that the Reformers found widespread acceptance because late medieval orthodoxy, with its insistence on *facere quod in se est*, placed too much of a burden on an ordinary believer's conscience. How could anyone, Luther would fruitfully ask, ever know when he or she has done enough? The Reformers' quarrels with nominalist theology, then, stemmed not from any sense that it presented God as an unknowable, unpredictable being. The Reformers objected, instead, to the nominalist sense that God's favor could be won by an individual *working* according to an ordained plan. In fact, Ozment argues, the central religious problem of mainstream Protestantism became the certitude of salvation--not the rationality of faith or the proof of God's existence, but the trustworthiness of God's word and promise. "It is not farfetched," he concludes, "to see here the legacy of Ockham" (Ozment, *Age of Reform*, p. 244). See also Steven Ozment, *The Reformation in the Cities* (New Haven, 1975), pp. 22-32, 49-56, and passim.

[16]See Adams, *William Ockham* 2:1300.

[17]All quotations from Chaucer are taken from *The Riverside Chaucer*, 3rd ed., general editor Larry D. Benson (Boston, 1987). Book and line numbers appear in the body of the essay.

[18]For background on this dispute, see Gordon Leff, *Bradwardine and the Pelagians: A Study of His "De Causa dei" and its Opponents* (Cambridge, 1957), pp. 1-20. Although its assessment of nominalist theology as being essentially sceptical severely limits the usefulness of this book, it nonetheless remains important if for no other reason than that so much subsequent work addresses its overstatements. For some of the most extreme of these, see particularly pp. 127-39.

[19]David C. Steinmetz, "Late Medieval Nominalism and the *Clerk's Tale*," *Chaucer Review*, 12 (1977), 44. For the prior association of the tale with nominalist theology (there perceived as essentially sceptical), see Robert Stepsis, "*Potentia Absoluta* and the *Clerk's Tale*," *Chaucer Review*, 10 (1975-76), 129-46.

[20]It should be noted here that nominalist theology seems to play a very significant part in *Piers Plowman*, a work by another of Gower's great contemporaries. See Robert Adams, "Piers's Pardon and Langland's Semi-Pelagianism," *Traditio*, 39 (1983), 367-418.

[21]John Bowers, *The Crisis of Will in Piers Plowman* (Washington, DC, 1986), pp. 63-77.

[22]Russell A. Peck, *Kingship and Common Profit in Gower's "Confessio Amantis"* (Carbondale and Edwardsville, IL, 1978), p. 96.

ASPECTS OF *GENTILESSE*
IN JOHN GOWER'S *CONFESSIO AMANTIS*,
BOOKS III-V

Kurt Olsson

Readers of John Gower's extended tribute to *gentilesse* in Book IV of the *Confessio Amantis* will recognize in its basic doctrine a medieval *topos*: true *gentilesse* is based on virtue, and on nothing else that a person "can, / Ne which he hath, ne which he mai" (lines 2276-77).[1] Because many earlier writers had expressed a like doctrine, one may be tempted to pass over this statement as mere commonplace and to dismiss the excursus in which it is developed as a mere pastiche of traditional ideas. A closer examination of the tribute and of Gower's other references to *gentilesse* in the middle books of the confession will reveal, however, that these ideas are genuine *topoi*, devices of poetic discovery or invention that open Gower's subject, giving his fuller treatment of the concept a meaningful complexity that neither the *topoi* nor the references alone provide. In this essay, I shall explore that fuller statement as it evolves in the relationship between the excursus and other sections of the middle confessional books, with a view to identifying aspects of *gentilesse* that have a significant impact on the meaning of the *Confessio* as a whole.

Initially I shall be concerned with the setting, form, and content of the tribute in Book IV. Gower places this discussion of *gentilesse* in a portion of the book organized around the concept of *otium* and interrelated ideas of idleness, leisure, and busyness. The meaning the poet ultimately assigns to the concept will be influenced by that setting, as well as by his strategy of creating his statement about *gentilesse* out of *demandes* resembling the questions of love that often inspired refined "conversacion" in late medieval courts and courtly fictions: a brief examination of one such fiction, the *Trésor Amoureux*, a *dit* tentatively attributed to Froissart, will help elucidate that strategy. The poet's approach to *gentilesse* is not limited by forms of courtly fiction, however. The tribute in Book IV also offers to the lover and Gower's readers a new way of perceiving the moral topics that organize the confession, and in that regard it has a distant, yet suggestive analogue in Dante's *Purgatorio*. The latter work also provides *topoi* of faculty psychology which, together with Gower's own statements about "entencion," the will, imagination, the heart, and reason, illumine the treatment of the concept outside the excursus, in other passages of the middle books of the confession. These *topoi* and statements also help explain why Genius, the priest in the fiction, guides the Lover to certain exercises of "gentil love." Four key exemplars of the gentle woman, or models of the beloved, organize the priest's counsel, delimit the field of *gentilesse*, and reveal a certain faculty psychology in the speakers who invent them. In those speakers' uses of imagination, I shall finally argue, lie the elements of what is perhaps the most significant contribution of the concept of *gentilesse* to the creation of meanings in the work.

I

Polite behavior associated with *gentilesse* is obviously a central concern in Gower's poem. Amans's conduct in love, modelled on the behavior of lovers in the *dits amoureux* of French court poets, is supposedly gentle, and Genius, in the course of his instruction, repeatedly addresses questions of good manners, or gentle conduct, grace, and courtesy, befitting those not merely in "loves court" but more broadly in courtly society. In all the confessional books Genius urges behavior that is genteel and refined. His dialogue with the Lover on matters of courtesy provides a basic "language" of the confession, and after its own fashion it also supports and confirms values that Gower shares with his courtly audience.

Nevertheless, that dialogue also crystallizes an ambiguity in the confession and especially in the stance of Genius. Gentle behavior, as perceived and celebrated by speakers in the poem, may express different kinds of *gentilesse*, and it is not enough to applaud it without examining what the poet reveals about its origins and "entencion." On the one hand, such behavior may be based upon "vertu moral" or the *gentilesse* praised in the excursus in Book IV. According to Genius, the "verrai gentil man" follows "resonable entencion" (line 2270), practices virtue, and manifests charity,

> Which hath the vertus forto lede,
> Of al that unto mannes dede
> Belongeth. . . .

(lines 2327-29)

A priest might well advocate such *gentilesse*, of course, and it is not surprising that this Confessor, against his own background of courtly service, should adapt it to the teaching and shriving of Amans.[2]

On the other hand, gentle behavior may be based upon "kinde" and, more specifically, a *gentilesse* that prevails in love's court and is championed by Venus, called the goddess not only of love, "worldes lust," and "plesance," but "ek of gentilesse" (V.1442-43). Near the end of the poem, the goddess identifies her court's distinction:

> For al onliche of gentil love
> Mi court stant alle courtz above
> And takth noght into retenue
> Bot thing which is to kinde due.

(VIII.2345-48)

Throughout the confession, being "gentil" always means to be courteous and "debonaire" (III.601), and, more generally, "soft in compaignie" (III.2734): such behavior, we shall find, is based upon and is wholly consistent with the lore of "kinde." As Venus's own behavior reveals, however, nature itself does not provide a sufficient warrant against promiscuity or self-indulgence,[3] and that is the danger in the gentle love and *gentilesse* the goddess sponsors. Setting no limits on natural appetite or the work of the "gentil" affectus, she blurs the very distinction of being gentle: as Genius in his more priestly function notes, she puts all danger aside to advance her own carnal pleasure, and she also allows every woman to

> . . . take
> What man hire liste, and noght forsake
> To ben als comun as sche wolde
>
> (V.1427-29)

This *gentilesse* is finally self-interested, and as such it is obviously contrary to the *gentilesse* celebrated in Book IV. As we might expect, Genius attacks it, but curiously, because he also serves Venus, he frequently defends, even champions, it as well.

Gower clarifies the contradiction, or the terms of Genius's ambivalence, by placing the tribute to *gentilesse* in Book IV, a book whose topic is sloth. This decision is an appropriate one, given what the poet and medieval tradition tell us about the gentle Venus. In contrast to the *gentilesse* or virtuous busyness displayed by the "verrai gentil man," the *gentilesse* that the goddess prefers is a form of sloth consistent with her own excessive regard for fleshly comfort and her desire "to live the soft life of barren ease."[4] This conflict comes to a head in the subdivision of Book IV dealing with idleness and its remedies. The subdivision is broken into three sections by Gower's Latin verses. The first of these introduces idleness, the fifth species of sloth, and attends to one of its cures, love-busyness; the next two sections feature other remedies: "chivalerie" and "gentilesse," and the "studies" producing knowledge whereby "We be now tawht of that we kunne" (line 2390). Especially relevant to the poet's statement about *gentilesse* in this setting is a turn given to the content of each of the three sections by the rich medieval concept of *otium* or *otiositas*, in meanings ranging from "idleness" or "laziness," through "leisure," to "the fruit of leisure" (i.e., authorship).[5]

The third section celebrates the labor and study of ancient inventors who, through the full exercise of their natural ability or *ingenium*,[6] discovered the arts and sciences:

> Here lyves thanne were longe,
> Here wittes grete, here mihtes stronge,
> Here hertes ful of besinesse.
>
> (lines 2353-55)

Such terms of praise are typical of late medieval encomia on the surpassing excellence of the ancients.[7] Following in that tradition, and also observing a convention in a didascalic literature more narrowly understood, Genius describes the ingredients of learning or discovery: natural ability, busyness, commitment, discipline; also implied throughout is *otium*, the very leisure that allows one

> . . . to studie and muse,
> As he which wolde noght refuse
> The labour of hise wittes alle.
>
> (lines 2385-87)

In the context of the entire *Confessio*, this tribute to the inventiveness of the ancients is the first in a series of didascalic excursuses culminating in Book VII, a book that actually organizes a program of study. In providing a catalogue of inventors and a context for invention, however, even this early section bears a likeness to chapters of a very important work in this tradition, the *Didascalicon* of Hugh of St. Victor. Hugh, after treating inventors,[8] describes the *ingenium*, discipline, and practice necessary for study and then the condition necessary for discipline: "Quiet of life--whether interior, so that the mind is not distracted with illicit desires, or exterior, so that leisure [*otium*] and opportunity are provided for creditable [*honestis*] and useful [*utilibus*] studies--is in both senses important to discipline."[9]

The prospect of *otium* as leisure for disciplined study sets a point of reference for Genius's treatment of *gentilesse*. The value of such a freedom to learn will later become apparent to Amans; indeed, he will discover that "the love of truth makes one seek a holy leisure."[10] Now, however, he has other things on his mind, and thus, when Genius encourages him to read a useful invention in "poesie," Ovid's *Remedia amoris*, his is an expected response: "It were an ydel peine / To lerne a thing which mai noght be" (IV.2678-79). Amans has hardly achieved the quiet of life that will allow him to "studie and muse" or, at another level, enable him to clutch his beads *por reposer*, engage in contemplation, or "bidde and preie" (VIII.2961). Leisure will become meaningful and profitable--indeed, possible--only after he is released from the inner quarrel of his "gentil love."

As the last of these sections hints at a world beyond the *negotium* that vexes Amans, the first places us squarely in that business and busyness: this is a world filled with distraction, where the major confusion centers on a major ambiguity in the concept of *otium*. The subject is idleness--*ocium* in the Latin sidenotes--and especially a refusal to love. The cure, obviously, is love, but, as all Ovidian poets recognize, certain kinds of love exist because of idleness. Ovid's advice in the *Remedia*--"fugias otia" (flee idleness), and "da uacuae menti, quo teneatur, opus" (give the idle mind necessary work)[11]--might be the priest's own counsel, except that Genius really argues the contrary: making love the needed occupation, he essentially reverses Ovid's senses of idleness and work. It is perhaps baffling enough that he should here oppose the stance of a book he will recommend to Amans a short time later. What makes his argument even more confusing is his notion of "besinesse." Ovid's doctrine becomes a medieval *topos*: "Venus otia amat,"[12] the ancient poet writes, and Chaucer thus makes Ydelnesse the porter of her garden and principal abode (Knight's Tale, line 1940). His model for this figure, Oiseuse, the porter of the garden of Deduit in the *Roman de la Rose*, has attracted a scholarly controversy that itself reflects the ambiguity of the Latin root. Some argue that Oiseuse represents a "genteel and courtly relaxation," a cultivated leisure that allows a gentle love to mature. Others, including John Fleming, maintain that she represents both idleness and *luxuria*.[13] This ambiguity provides one context for judging Genius's counsel.

In his own argument, the priest never expressly addresses the distinction between idleness and leisure or "relaxation." What makes his argument suspect, nonetheless, is the kind of busyness he champions. Medieval spiritual writers issue a warning:

> ydelnesse . . . is a synne þat dopþ moche harm, as holy
> bookes tellen; for whan a man is ydele and þe deuel fyndeþ
> hym ydel, he him setteþ a-swiþe to werke, and make hym
> . . . to desire foule harlotries, as lecheries, and þus lese his
> tyme and moche good þat he myȝt doo þat he myȝt wynne
> þer-þorw paradis.[14]

Genius seems to encourage work of this kind, and with it a loss of time and much good, when he justifies love as the means to preserve one's comforts:

> Love is an occupacion,
> Which forto kepe hise lustes save,
> Scholde every gentil herte have.

> (IV.1452-54)

Even this statement is potentially self-interested and idle, for, as a marginal gloss explains, its doctrine "is not the truth, but the opinion of lovers."[15]

It may be "vilenie" to see "lecheries" or "foule harlotries" in the love Genius advocates--it is, after all, "gentil love"--and certainly the language of this judgment seems ill-suited to the genteel rhetoric adopted by Gower in the poem. Nevertheless, Genius's advice, though it befits the priest of a gentle Venus, remains questionable, and not merely in the context of an external spiritual tradition. In this very section, Genius attacks love according to "Cupides lawe" (IV.1471) and offers his first defense of honest, chaste, or married love. The language of the external judgment aside, misguided or idle busyness remains a key moral issue in the *Confessio*, and in this section it surfaces because of Genius's own apparent unsureness about the love he is advocating. In its ambiguities, the section exemplifies the trying work, for speakers and Gower's audience alike, of sorting through meanings in the *negotium* of the shrift.

The middle section of this "treatise" on idleness represents a state between the taxing business of the confession and the leisure that comes at its end. It promises to have practical value for Amans, since it will address the question of love-profit, and it also includes a modest confessional element; here too the lover "wol speke upon [his] schrifte" (IV.1683). At the same time, it has other features that distinguish it from the sections that precede and follow it, separating it from the *negotium* of Amans's love-quarrel and from "studie" that is not, for the most part, directly related to that business.

Leisure or *otium* can be perceived as the goal of work: in antiquity, such a state of retirement or fulfillment permitted a devotion to cultural pursuits; in medieval monastic settings, it occasioned contemplation.[16] "Studie," in Genius's tribute to inventors, looks ahead to that state of leisure. The middle section of the treatise on idleness also involves leisure, but not as a goal. Its field, instead, is the leisure of recreation, what Glending Olson describes as a rest or relaxation that enables a person to return to work; it is a "re-creation, a re-constituting of one's normal . . . mental health."[17]

This section of Book IV provides such recreation in a courtly or genteel setting. Its topics--chivalry, love, *gentilesse* -- obviously belong to the court, and in treating them Genius uses a specifically courtly mode of "argument." Undoubtedly, the subjects of the excursus form serious issues for any late medieval court and court poet, and it can hardly be said that in the tales, or the content of the section, we see "rest from work." Nevertheless, all of this material is presented in a format and setting of leisure. Next to the distracting "reality" of the confession proper, the section organizes experience as might a literary creation at one remove from real experience: it becomes a gentle "tale," fitted to a setting of "worschipe and ese," and offering an enabling rest.

A hint of the procedure of the section is indicated at another point in Book IV, where Amans describes some of the courtly recreations he might engage in, at the pleasure of his mistress:

> And whanne it falleth othergate,
> So that hire like noght to daunce,
> Bot on the Dees to caste chaunce
> Or axe of love som demande,
> Or elles that hir list comaunde
> To rede and here of Troilus,
> Riht as sche wole or so or thus,
> I am al redi to consente.

(lines 2790-97)

Asking "som demande" about love is the informing principle of Gower's treatment of chivalry and *gentilesse*, and it is so in a sense distinct from that of interrogation in a lover's confession. As is well-known, the posing of *demandes d'amour* or questions of love was a very popular activity in medieval courtly literature.[18] The form orders love cases presented in Andreas Capellanus's *De amore* and in many later works. Often such *demandes* are introduced in a quasi-legal setting, sometimes by two litigants of equal merit or with pleas of comparable worth, each seeking a favorable verdict. Such is the case in Machaut's *Jugement dou Roy de Behaingne*. The *demande* is also familiar to readers of Chaucer, who has several tellers of noble tales ask a question pertaining to cases of individual characters: in the

Knight's Tale, "Who hath the worse, Arcite or Palamoun?" (line 1347) or, of characters in the Franklin's Tale, "Which was the mooste fre, as thynketh yow?" (line 1622).[19] In this tradition, the question is sometimes presented in the abstract--without reference to a particular case--and that will be so in Gower's text and in a work I shall propose as having a special relevance to it. Whatever form the *demande* takes, however, it is introduced most frequently in a courtly setting to open conversation and especially "amoureuse conversacion": it organizes courtly leisure profitably, "en joieuse recreation."[20]

A useful model to guide our examination of Genius's procedure might be found in the *Trésor Amoureux*. This poem ends with a series of *demandes*: both for the content of those questions and for the possible opposed responses to them--prefigured in the work by Love and Congnoissance--the *Trésor* merits our attention. Late in the poem, Congnoissance seeks to win Love's favor for her charge, the poem's narrator, but Love refuses the request because the lover and Congnoissance each betrays a divided loyalty, the lover because of his devotion to Congnoissance, and Congnoissance because of her devotion to Reason; neither character has submitted wholly to Love. This conflict is really a conflict of principle, of course, and Love and Congnoissance, to settle their differences, agree to ask readers for a verdict on seven questions involving the relative worth of love and arms, of conflicting means for securing high status or degree, and of biological nature or "blood" and nobility of character.[21] Effectively, the work ends with these questions, and thus the poem, itself a recreation, potentially effects another recreation-- a conversation--in its courtly audience. Genius's excursus is designed to resolve these very issues; it is itself re-creative. More over, because its statements appear to contradict arguments the priest offers elsewhere in the confession, the excursus, together with the enveloping shrift, evolve *demandes* that help make the entire *Confessio* a recreation.

One of the distinctions of the *Confessio*, in fact, is that the opposed voices in its "debate" are Genius's own. Thus, in responding to the various *demandes* implied in the major question of this section--how a person "schal be take / The rathere unto loves grace" (lines 2194-95)--Genius does what he often does elsewhere in the poem by arguing on both sides of an issue, speaking sometimes as a "clerk / Of love" (VIII.2053-54), sometimes as a priestly advocate of reason. Effectively, he thereby moves between stances represented by Love and Congnoissance in the *Trésor*. What distinguishes this section of the work is its clear conceptual order and the resolution of the *demandes*. Genius finally arranges various kinds of gentle activity according to a hierarchy of worth.

The courses to love's grace, he argues, are worthiness of "manhode," or the prowess of those who "dar travaile" at arms, and worthiness of "gentilesse." His opening topic is "Hou love and armes ben aqueinted" (IV.2137), a subject which, as Froissart argued elsewhere, provided the enduring themes of conversation in courtly society.[22] Later Genius will integrate this subject into his discussion of *gentilesse*, but here, in defending the honor of arms for a "worthi kniht," he focuses on the more immediate issue and responds to several relevant *demandes* of the *Trésor*. One of these questions is especially important to Amans: in order to live always in delight--and with a true hope of deserving reward--is it better to serve love faithfully or to pursue arms honorably?[23] Amans's own preference is clear: "who as evere pris deserve / Of armes, I wol love serve" (lines 1685-86). "What scholde I winne over the Se, / If I mi ladi loste at hom?" (lines 1664-65), he asks, and then answers, "It were a schort beyete / To winne chaf and lese whete" (lines 1709-10). Responding to Amans's pleasure, Genius tells many stories to prove that travail in arms can effect "decerte" in love. But when he also argues that "betre it were honour to winne / Than love" (lines 1867-68),[24] he begins to set new priorities: "chivalerie" serves the common profit, and the love to which honor is preferable does not; that love, we might note, is not the love Genius will advocate when he comes to define *gentilesse*.

The excursus builds a case out of Amans's concern, but it advances to better senses of profit and "loves grace" than he can anticipate. That will become apparent when Genius shifts the topic to *gentilesse*. In denying that "blood" and wealth can be the sources of distinction or true *gentilesse*, the priest responds to three more questions in the *Trésor*.[25] At one point in this argument, however, his statement seems ambivalent, and that is when the *demande* bears directly on Amans's wish for preferment. What better places a person in high status, good knowledge adorned by conscience, or good fortune in the "aventure" of every court?[26] The priest rejects wealth as a source of *gentilesse* because, unlike virtue, it provides no "sikernesse" (lines 2214-15, 2267-68), but in love's court, he later argues, a "povere vertue schal noght spiede" (line 2280). Good fortune is Amans's concern, and Genius here appears to yield to what ensures it: in his opinion, the person "riche and vertuous" is "wel the more worth" (lines 2286-87).[27]

This gesture to success in love's court is not conclusive, however. In the way Genius introduces it, immediately after he has defined the "verrai gentil man," there is a slight hint of disdain: "Bot for al that yit nou aday, / In loves court . . ." (lines 2278-79). He has just pointed out that a success that depends on "worldes good" is extremely precarious, both now and in the future:

> The lord is more forto charge,
> Whan god schal his accompte hiere,
> For he hath had hise lustes hiere
>
> (lines 2242-44)

Even more important, the priest devalues such success immediately after he describes it, when, at the next stage of his argument, he defends a love that yields a secure and truly gentle profit. "Honeste" love, he argues,

> . . . in sondri weie
> Profiteth, for it doth aweie
> The vice, and as the bokes sein,
> It makth curteis of the vilein,
> And to the couard hardiesce
> It yifth, so that verrai prouesse
> Is caused upon loves reule
> To him that can manhode reule.
>
> (lines 2297-2304)

In this progression, the excursus not only arranges goods hierarchically, but also works to interiorize "worthinesse." The good deemed superior in the first part of the argument--knighthood of arms "oghte ferst to be desired" (line 1881)--displaces the "sotie of love," but it is surpassed in the second part by a "gentilesse" that might include chivalry but is not limited to it. Love "honeste" is then deemed superior to external success in love's court. Because it inspires courtesy and "verrai prouesse" and thereby changes for the better those who submit to it, it helps redefine chivalry, and it also forms the substance of a response to another *demande* of the pseudo-Froissart: whether a person can be born so elevated in virtue that he can serve both love and arms well.[28] In the tribute to "love honeste," Genius also rephrases his earlier assertion that the "gentil herte" must love "forto kepe his lustes save," now in a more traditional, acceptable form[29]: "love hath evere hise lustes grene / In gentil folk" (lines 2309-10); this answers the one remaining question in the *Trésor*, why Love works to better effect with one of his subjects than with a hundred others.[30]

As the argument draws to its conclusion, even that honest love, praised in mere "bokes," is superseded by a love taught in "holi bokes wise": concerning it, and it alone, Genius claims to speak "After the vertu moral" (line 2321). Having answered the *demandes* of the *Trésor*, Genius now goes beyond them in this final encomium on love, identified by a marginal gloss as *amore caritatis*. With this shift, he moves into another sense of *gentilesse*, one espoused, for example, in late medieval handbooks of

237

religious instruction: "For verrey nobleie comeþ of a gentel hert. For-soþe, þer is no gentel herte but it loue God; þer is no nobleye but to serue God . . . ne vilenye but þe contrarie þer-of."[31]

The entire excursus, as it clearly unfolds to the praise of this supreme virtue, a virtue that transcends *gentilesse* in all forms that lack "sikernesse," becomes profitably reconstitutive, setting a standard for judging other behavior, especially "gentil" behavior, in the work. In reordering the idea of profit according to a model of true *gentilesse*, the excursus clears opacities of the confession proper. It offsets the great danger in *otium* as leisure--"not being occupied with profitable, serious activities"[32]--but it does so in a setting of "ese." In that courtly setting, in fact, it exemplifies a classical precept: "Leisure, which seems most contrary to industry and study, ought especially to be subjoined to them not to the extent that virtue dies away, but to the extent that it is revived [*recreatur*]."[33] The *otium* of this section, though not a goal in itself, is in that particular sense re-creative.

II

As the concept of *gentilesse*, with various potential conflicts built into it, reveals central concerns of the poem, the placement of the excursus in the middle confessional book seems to have a special significance.[34] The power of the topic, as fitted to Genius's double role, is that it might well occasion a shift in the focus of the entire confession away from Amans's love-quarrel to the more stable ground of virtue. The effect, though never so obviously the intent, of Genius's argument concerning *gentilesse* could be a new perception in Amans of a great good that he has manifestly loved too little. In that regard, the relevance of this excursus to the entire *Confessio* is potentially like the relevance of the central cantos of Dante's *Purgatorio* to that work in its entirety. On the cornice of sloth, in an episode Dante recounts in Cantos XVII and XVIII, Virgil notes that "The love of good which comes short of its duty is here restored" (XVII.85-86)[35]:

as souls here recover a love of good, so Virgil, seizing the moment of an enforced rest from a difficult ascent, instructs Dante in that love; and as Virgil on love, so Genius on *gentilesse*, each to his respective pupil.

Genius's excursus does more than present an ideal busyness to overcome what Virgil describes as the "lukewarm love" (XVII.130) of sloth. The implications in the pattern of idleness, recreation, and leisure reach far beyond the three sections of Book IV. Once "John Gower" is restored to himself in the final vision of the poem, he sets out "to take reste" (VIII.3142) and looks ahead to "thilke place / Wher resteth love" (VIII.3170-71); leisure, now a repose, occasions prayer and contemplation. A similarly comprehensive pattern obtains in the *Purgatorio*. In Canto II, the pilgrim, his teacher, and gathered spirits, idly enthralled by Casella's singing of a *canzone* Dante himself had written, must be wakened by Cato's interruptive "What stay is this?" (II.121); in the middle cantos, Virgil offers his re-creative instruction; in Canto XXVII, the poet walks through the fire that purifies the lustful; he dreams of Leah and Rachel, exemplars respectively of virtuous busyness and contemplation,[36] who also prefigure what Dante will experience in the Earthly Paradise and later; Virgil's final act, crowning and mitering the pilgrim lord of himself, anticipates Dante's future repose. The point I wish to emphasize here is that in both texts the middle episode "orders" the progress of the central figure from idleness to self-recovery and the leisure and repose available only to those of cleansed heart and rightly ordered will.

In that larger framework, Genius's stay in the "besinesse" of the confession to expound *gentilesse* may provide an especially enabling rest, re-creative in the enlarged sense of organizing the topics of confession and potentially the whole of the lover's experience. The principle of that larger program has a parallel in Virgil's teaching that love is the source of all human actions: "love must needs be the seed in you of every virtue and of every action deserving punishment" (XVII.103-05). By a distinction of

239

loves, Virgil offers an explicit rationale of *sufficientia* for the sins,[37] a rationale that also serves to "map" Purgatory. Genius does not attempt anything precisely like this in his excursus, and yet, implicit in his ideal of *gentilesse*, including especially the love that orders "al that unto mannes dede / Belongeth," is a drawing together of virtues that elsewhere in the confession form remedies for the sins.

I have argued in another essay that the remedies proposed during the course of the *Confessio* are based upon increasingly complex medieval notions of the *jus naturae* or the law of nature that include, but are not limited to, Genius's distinction of "kinde" and "reson."[38] That distinction is itself relevant to classifying virtues linked with *gentilesse* at various places in the confession. Associated with "kinde" and the "gentil herte," for example, are "frendlihede," pity, grace, compassion, mercy, and kindness.[39] Such virtues, based on a sensitivity to a shared humanity, offset what Virgil describes as the love of another's evil (XVII.113). Associated with "reson" and the "mesure" of *gentilesse*, on the other hand, are virtues such as chastity, discretion, sobriety, restraint: these check what Virgil calls love "in faulty measure" (XVII.126). Virtues of both kinds, displayed singly or in groups at various points of the confession, become remedies for the separate vices. Ultimately more important than their separate uses, or their being grouped into virtues of "kinde" and "reson," however, is their integration. Charity, the supreme virtue in Genius's ideal *gentilesse*, unites "kinde" and "reson," and, as a love ordered by "resonable entencion" that allows a person to realize the fullest potential of his or her nature, it becomes the principle of all other virtues. As those virtues originate in it, of course, they also originate in true *gentilesse*.

Genius's excursus does more than merely open out into a universe of virtues: it implicitly draws the virtues into itself, specifically into its model of the gentle person who, in advancing to the rest and holy leisure that Amans himself will discover at the end of the *Confessio*, engages in a just and charitable "besinesse" in all things pertaining to "mannes dede." At the end of the excursus Genius maintains, on the basis of scriptural precept, that love is a necessity (IV.2325), and the effect of that point is to suggest, for the entire section, the Augustinian doctrine that "the necessity of love [*caritatis*] makes one undertake a righteous business."[40]

Given the strength of this ending, there is good reason to hope that the excursus will stabilize the confession by ordering the speakers' discursive and imaginative busyness. In fact, it does not. If the tribute to *gentilesse* is re-creative, offering an ideal that enables us to return to work with mental health restored, the "reality" of the confession seemingly works to cancel its value, making it appear the product of an idle leisure: it seems too neat or tidy to account for the complexities of the Lover's experience or the priest's confessional doctrine. Its failure to effect a lasting change in the perspective of either speaker may be attributed to a distinction of faculty psychologies. The priest and Lover will continue to follow a "psychology" at odds with the one ordering the righteous busyness of the "verrai gentil man." Our immediate task, then, is to note the difference, to see how the psychology championed in the excursus is not the psychology advocated and practiced in the confession proper.

III

In evolving his doctrines of *gentilesse*, Genius relies on *topoi* of medieval cognitive psychology which, for our purposes, are conveniently summarized by Dante's Virgil, again on the cornice of sloth. Once Virgil has established, in Canto XVII, that "Each one apprehends vaguely a good wherein the mind may find rest, and this it desires" (lines 127-28), and that such a craving is love, he goes on, in Canto XVIII, to describe the process of advancing toward that good: "Your faculty of apprehension draws an image from a real existence and displays it within you, so that it makes the mind turn to it; and if, thus

turned, the mind inclines toward it, that inclination is love, . . ."
(lines 22-26). Of course, such a love must be evaluated, as Virgil warns when he remarks, "how far the truth is hidden from
the people who aver that every love is praiseworthy in itself, because perhaps its matter appears always to be good: but not
every imprint is good, although the wax be good" (XVIII.34-
39). For judging that imprint and making every will conform to
a primal will,

> ". . . there is innate in you the faculty that counsels and that
> ought to hold the threshold of assent. This is the principle
> wherefrom is derived the reason of desert in you, according
> as it garners and winnows good and evil loves."
>
> (XVIII.61-66)

The complete process described by Virgil will emerge in the
composite of Genius's exemplars of *gentilesse*; but in the excursus the Priest begins at the stage where good and evil loves
are garnered and winnowed:

> . . . after the condicion
> Of resonable entencion,
> The which out of the Soule groweth
> And the vertu fro vice knoweth,
> Wherof a man the vice eschuieth,
> Withoute Slowthe and vertu suieth,
> That is a verrai gentil man.
>
> (IV.2269-75)

In this model, intention follows an ideal of willing, "a tending
towards an object within the plan of reason."[41] Peter Abelard's
treatment of intention in *Scito te ipsum*[42] sheds some light on
Gower's strategy in introducing this notion in the excursus.
Specifically, several of the analogies or instances Abelard uses
to build the case that "an action does not bear anything good in
itself" but "is good by reason of a good intention"[43] pertain directly to Genius's setting up his definition of the "verrai gentil
man." The first is a simile of lineage or birth: "a man is said to

be good by his own goodness, but when we speak of the son of the good man by this nothing good is indicated in him"; similarly, "anyone's intention is called good in itself, although the work is not called good by itself but because it proceeds from a good intention."[44] The second is the example of wealth. Genius, it will be recalled, remarks that wealth is valued in love's court, where it makes a person "more worth." To Abelard, however, it is unthinkable that "a great amount of money ... could contribute to merit or the increase of merit," or that it could "make anyone better and more worthy."[45] What is critical to him, once again, is good intention, and that would seem to be Gower's position as well. Even Genius, in describing love's court, keeps riches separate from the *gentilesse* originating in "resonable entencion." That distinction of "entencion" alerts us to an importance which the doctrine will also have in the arguments of the confession proper.

Gower is certainly not unique in working past the specious external signs or the accidents of *gentilesse* to its substance, "vertu set in the corage" (IV.2261), but he is unique in drawing the doctrine of intention into his definition of the concept. He thereby warns us about the false images of *gentilesse*, about the conventional ones of "hih lignage" and "richesse," to be sure. But he also forces us to recognize that even deeds and words that seem truly "gentil" are not always what they seem: the appearance of an honest love, for example, does not necessarily betoken an honest "entencion" or true gentility. Outside the excursus, that becomes relevant as Genius tests the *gentilesse* of characters not only by their external behavior but by their internal acts of knowing and willing. Even then, however, the accuracy of judgment is not assured. Applying the standard of "entencion" is extremely difficult, even in a fiction where it might seem possible, because, as Abelard noted, "men do not judge the hidden but the apparent."[46] The "psychology" Genius invents for characters in his fictions is, as we shall see, finally superficial: the priest works with the apparent; Gower would have us remain sensitive to the possible, to the hidden. If this effectively renders all judgments tentative, it also further opens the poet's subject. What is finally most important to Gower in the exercise of judgment is not the testing of another, but the forming in oneself of a "resonable entencion." To that end, all that Genius records is significant.

Outside the section of the *Confessio* where he introduces this standard, Genius is especially interested in the stages of the knowing and willing process that precede consent or the formation of an intention. One of his *topoi* is the analogy used by Dante's Virgil of softened wax, a metaphor of the imagination or heart impressed or imprinted[47] by images, or even by "virtue": thus Foryetelnesse "noght mai in his herte impresse / Of vertu which reson hath sett" (IV.542-43). Medieval poets, as J. D. Burnley has recently shown, also identify a special power of imagination with the "gentil herte,"[48] for such a heart is "neysshe" and therefore particularly susceptible to impressions. To soften the heart or to make it "gentil" is, in a good sense, to make it particularly receptive or sensitive to the good imprint, or to virtue. It is to such an end, in the larger idiom of the period, that God "makeþ þe herte nesche . . . as wex tempred."[49] Heightened sensitivity and perception associated with the heart also incline the "gentil" to love, of course, and this notion underlies Genius's assertion that "love evere hath his lustes grene / In gentil folk." The idle Rosiphelee presumably belongs to the "gentil nacion," for though initially no imagination "mihte sette hire in the weie / Of loves occupacion" (IV.1256-57), she is deeply affected by the images of a vison, and because of that experience she changes "al hire ferste entente / Withinne hire herte" (IV.1444-45).

If a heart is truly "gentil," of course, it will be most deeply affected by a good love. A tale about Ulixes near the outset of Book IV reveals more fully how such a love is ordered by "resonable entencion." In this exemplum, a much revised version of a story in Ovid's *Heroides*, Penolope writes to Ulixes in Troie, lamenting his slackness in returning to her. Genius's chief interest is the effect of that letter. When it reaches Ulixes,

> . . . he, which wisdom hath pourveied
> Of al that to reson belongeth
> With gentil herte it underfongeth.

(lines 204-06)

Ulixes's imagination then identifies the goal of a reasonable intention: "love his herte hath so thorghsesed / With pure ymaginacioun" (lines 210-11) that he is unable to "flitt his herte aside" (line 214) from Penolope's concern, and thus he applies his whole "corage" to shaping his homeward journey. Genius does not mention Ulixes's tardiness or wandering on the journey itself: once the war ends, this hero makes "no delaiement" and hastens home, "Wher that he fond tofore his yhe / His worthi wif in good astat" (lines 228-29). Intent on magnifying the virtue of his exemplar, Genius also foreshadows what he will later say about "honeste love" and "gentilesse," for Ulixes represents in his journey to Penolope a response to the sloth that "hindreth many a cause honeste" (line 233). This case makes clear how the "gentil herte," seized by imagination, is quickened to purposive, reasonable activity.

Elsewhere in Book IV, Genius represents in the imagination a power to organize the busyness he has established as the chief antidote for sloth. Therein lies a difficulty, however. Whereas this faculty might quicken the heart to pursue a great and noble good, it might, when not ordered by reason, encourage promiscuity, at root fostering the opinion that "every love is praiseworthy in itself": this is the danger to the pliant, soft, or tender heart of "gentil folk," a reluctance to judge rationally whether the impression--the image--is good. The excursus on true *gentilesse* discourages such indulgence by providing a mechanism for garnering and winnowing. The other prospect for imagination, however, is a reality in the *Confessio*, and even Ulixes is not exempted from it.

The exemplum of that hero in the opening section of Book IV is preceded by another story drawn from the *Heroides*, the tale of Dido's response to Aeneas's leaving Carthage. Unlike the story of Ulixes, which finally praises busyness, this tale is written exclusively to condemn sloth. Shortly after Eneas departs for Italy, Dido writes a letter threatening suicide if he tarries in returning to her. With "thoghtes feinte / Towardes love and full of Slowthe" (lines 118-19), however, Eneas lets time pass, and Dido kills herself after she issues a final complaint: "Ha, who fond evere such a lak / Of Slowthe in eny worthi kniht?" (lines 128-29). This story, like that of Ulixes, creates obvious problems for those who know it in other versions. To stress Eneas's sloth, the priest gives little warrant for the trip to Italy, only hinting at a reason in an almost parenthetical "it scholde be." In Virgil's epic, of course, Aeneas displays "a lak / Of Slowthe" in a sense neither Dido nor her creator in the *Confessio* intends: he displays a virtuous busyness in obeying the gods' behest that he leave Dido for the sake of a great "cause honeste": to remain with Dido, or to return to her, in this frame of reference, would constitute *lachesce*. Given the emphasis in Gower's possible sources, however, Genius's opposed perspective is perhaps understandable: in the *Heroides* and relevant medieval versions of the story, the divine purpose in Aeneas's mission tends to be understated. Even more germane to the context of Amans's concern, of course, the omission makes the tale a better exemplum *in causa amoris*. The same might be said of changes in the second narrative. By having Penolope send the letter to Troie while Ulixes is still there, Genius effectively cancels the questions that even the Ovidian Penelope has about the reasons for Ulysses's delay. Her letter in Ovid has no clear destination. The war has ended; most of the Greek survivors have returned; but no one really knows the whereabouts of Ulysses, and Penelope is forced to give a copy of her letter to every sojourner in Ithaca who might later encounter him. Her uncertainty about what causes his delay, about where hard-heartedly [*ferreus*] he hides, and her fear that, free to return, he wills to be absent,[50] make her complaint and appeal all the more poignant. Genius's tale is psychologically simpler, and had he stuck to its point throughout Book IV, centering imagination and *gentilesse* on the honest cause, this tale, like the first one, might have retained the power of its simplicity.

In the long reach of argument, however, Genius rarely does things simply. Later in Book IV--in setting arms against a slothful ease--he finds occasion to reverse the status of his two exemplars: Eneas now becomes the positive, Ulixes the negative figure. Eneas, Dido's earlier testimony notwithstanding, is a "worthi kniht" who wins Lavinia because he fights Turnus, thereby engaging in the travail expected of a person of his estate. Ulixes, on the other hand, exemplifies deferred busyness once again, in this case before he joins the Greek campaign: now, however, his eventual activity is called into question by virtue of his "entencion." At home on Ithaca, he has "his herte fyred / Upon his wif" (lines 1882-83) and devises a trick to stay there--to avoid the war--so that he might "welde his love at wille" (line 1828). Tricked in turn by his recruiters, he is then taught a lesson in the "gret schame to a king" who

> . . . wolt in a querele of trowthe
> Of armes thilke honour forsake,
> And duelle at hom for loves sake.
>
> (lines 1864-66)

Eventually, the chastened Ulixes, with "tamed . . . herte," joins the Greek forces, leaving behind "al the sotie / Of love for chivalerie" (lines 1887-88). The context for these tales reveals that a busyness narrowly focused *in amoris causa*, though obviously purposive, need not be reasonable or as worthy as a "vertu moral" which opens out to a greater world, a social context.

Even more important, however, is the revision in Genius's opinion of these figures, and especially of Ulysses. Certainly the Greek hero is not the exemplar we might have initially thought:

given the "sotie" of his love before the Trojan War, we must now doubt his "resonable" intention in two directions, asking whether he truly aspires to honor in battle or is merely shamed into action, and whether, on later receiving Penolope's letter, he truly seeks the honest love of a worthy wife or merely craves once again to indulge the foolish "lustes [he] sette above" (line 1878) chivalry. His gentle heart, in other words, may be too soft, too susceptible to impressions. Ulixes is quickly persuaded to join the assault, then to return to Penolope: we are not much assured that he follows the counsel of the wisdom he is supposed to possess. And lest we think that Genius, in these retrospective tellings, sees Ulixes changed for the better by his experience at Troie--that the first tale in this sequence does establish an ideal of the better man--we need only observe that later in the confession the priest, drawing on still other sources, reveals that his hero after the war does not actually return to Penolope in all haste as he had earlier claimed. No longer impressed by "knihthod" or his "worthi wif," Uluxes pauses to dally with Circes and Calipsa, and, while he avoids their "Art magique" and deception, "He tok of hem so wel his part, / That he begat Circes with childe" (VI.1460-61). Uluxes knows what he is doing--"He kepte him sobre and made hem wilde" (line 1462)--and yet, much as he has lost sight of the "cause honeste" imprinted on his imagination and "gentil herte," he also soon forgets this child by Circes; for him, that lapse of memory will be fatal. These tales together reveal that the gentle Uluxes attends only to what pleases him at the moment. Quick to "flitt his herte aside," he clearly lacks the stability that virtue alone provides, indeed does confer, on the "verrai gentil man."

IV

The exemplar of Ulixes (Uluxes), I shall later argue, has a special relevance to Genius, to the gentle make-up of his character, to his gentle busyness, and to the kind of activity he encourages in his charge. To Amans, however, Ulysses has less relevance, and the tales about him would appear to offer little solace, for, as the lover complains, "me was nevere assigned place, / Wher yit to geten eny grace" (IV.271-72). In response to such complaints, Genius provides other tales of gentle love, better designed to console him and to inform his amorous busyness. The exemplum of Pygmaleon and the Statue is one such tale. It begins in the strong imagination of Pygmaleon, a "lusti man," who creates an image

> Wherof that he himself beguileth.
> For with a goodly lok sche smyleth,
> So that thurgh pure impression
> Of his ymaginacion
> With al the herte of his corage
> His love upon this faire ymage
> He sette. . . .
>
> (IV.387-93)

Pygmaleon's creation of the image and his busyness in asking grace, itself grounded upon an indefatigable hope, lead to "loves spede." In late medieval poetry, of course, Pygmalion is typically presented as an exemplar of idolatry, and yet at least one scholar has seen exceptions: whereas Jean de Meun uses the tale to represent "idolatrous love at once foolish and sensual," Machaut, in the *Fonteinne amoureuse*, uses it to display "faithful conjugal love," and Gower, it appears, follows in the tradition of Machaut: "Most examples of good love in Gower lead to marriage and offspring," and the English poet "extends the illustration [of good love] to Pygmalion,"[51] presumably because his love leads to marriage and offspring.

Such an outcome, however, does not suddenly make the love "honeste" or good. By his prayers, Pygmaleon "wan a lusti wif" (line 424) and she "obeissant was at his wille" (line 425). If the vivid account of Pygmaleon's busyness prior to this event is not enough to disclose the nature and intent of his will--or to allow us to determine whether his is a "resonable entencion"--we need only continue reading: because Pygmaleon "dorst speke" his prayers, a happy Genius concludes, "his love he spedde, / And hadde al that he wolde abedde" (lines 429-30). Thus the story ends, unless we wish to take its one remaining sentence, on the begetting of a knave child, as further proof of honesty, legitimizing all of Pygmaleon's earlier labor as work in an honest cause.

The narrative of Pygmaleon becomes a model to inform Amans's busyness. Amans never wavers in loyalty to his lady's "faire ymage," and in that refusal to turn his heart aside he, like Pygmaleon, better exemplifies a truth embodied in Ulysses than does Ulysses himself. The outcome of his own tale is not assured, of course, but with Genius's support he will continue to follow Pygmaleon, who profits because "he axeth grace" (line 410).

Through most of the confession, a hope nourished by imagination is all that sustains Amans; he has succumbed to the "gentil" counsel of will:

> Reson seith that I scholde leve
> To love, wher ther is no leve
> To spede, and will seith therayein
> That such an herte is to vilein,
> Which dar noght love and til he spede,
> Let hope serve at such a nede. . . .
>
> (III.1179-84)

This hope, though presumably gentle, never achieves the status for Amans that Esperance can have for the gentle lovers in the *dits* of French writers, including especially the poetry of Machaut. There, Douglas Kelly argues, hope enables a lover "to grow inwardly by [the lady's] example" and to be "content with less than might satisfy desire."[52] Love requires the beloved's *dous regard*, but, as hope replaces desire, the love becomes self-sufficient. The lover creates an Image, an idealized projection of the beloved, and that type supplants the individual as a perfection to be revered and imitated; the love no longer depends on the lady's *merci*, and the lover can thereby achieve a state of perfect contentment. In the *Confessio*, it is true, Amans has formed an image of his lady's perfection, and because "Sche is the pure hed and welle / And Mirour and ensample of goode" (V.2604-05), he can readily express adoration. Until his conversion, however, he does not know contentment. Hope never displaces or sublimates desire; nor is it ever very secure. False and treacherous, it sets "the herte in jeupartie" (III.1173) with wishing and fantasy, and it never allows the lover to be satisfied with his lady's *dous regard*. Amans has given his beloved his whole heart, but she will not pay him back with a

> . . . goodli word . . .
> Wherof min hope mihte arise,
> Mi grete love to compense.
>
> (V.4503-05)

Genius reminds the Lover, however, of an earlier exchange involving the heart:

> Thou seist hou sche for o lokinge
> Thin hole herte fro the tok:
> Sche mai be such, that hire o lok
> Is worth thin herte manyfold.
>
> (V.4540-43)

Driven by desire and obviously not content with "hire o lok," the Lover does not understand that a return of favors is a matter not "Of duete, bot al of grace" (line 555). Even more basically, he refuses to accept the truth he has learned from reason, that in his hope "ther is no feith" (III.1176).

Amans's short-sighted desire underlies Book IV, whose project is to invent and foster hope by encouraging a frantic busyness, wishing, and fantasy. The lover is "so trewly amerous" (line 921) that he has diligently sought advice on how to conduct his suit; despite his enduring curiosity, however, he has "nevere herde . . . man recorde" what might avail to win love without fail. He is thus driven to his primary activity--pursuing his love--

guided only by what is broadly expected of the gentle lover: "to serve is al his besynesse."[53] The activity Amans confesses--"I serve, I bowe, I loke, I loute" (line 1169)--is engagingly silly for its very busyness, but it always reflects an effort to be genteel and courtly. When, to entertain the beloved, he dances and carols, plays at dice, or reads about Troilus, that would seem to be enough to sublimate his love, allowing him, on the model of the ideal *amant* in Machaut, to realize "all his hope in the Image, the sight, and the *bel acueil* of his lady."[54] Throughout, however, he is frustrated by his failed attempts to satisfy his desire, and his "tristesce" is intensified by the knowledge that his entire, ambitious program of love-service is idle:

> Bot thogh my besinesse laste,
> Al is bot ydel ate laste,
> For whan theffect is ydelnesse,
> I not what thing is besinesse.

(lines 1757-60)

This complaint even extends to imagination. When he makes a "collacioun" of his lady, "it doth [him] harm / Of pure ymaginacioun" (lines 1142-43), for he always finds his "besi thoght / Is torned ydel into noght" (lines 1151-52). For him, the lady's *bel acueil* in letting him serve her is insufficient encouragement:

> . . . sche ne wile
> That I have eny causes of hope,
> Noght also mochel as a drope.

(V.4750-52)

Amans, however, is obdurate: a "gentil" and no "vilein," he follows the counsel of will in daring to love, but his tenacity and frustration together threaten to increase his impatience, bitterness, and "tristesce." Genius fittingly advises him to temper his "corage," but Amans already knows in his rational nature "That I myn herte scholde softe" (III.1164). To soften the heart, in this context, is to make it receptive to reason's counsel; it is to become debonaire or--to borrow words from Chaucer's Parson--

"tretable to goodnesse" (Parson's Tale, line 657). And where the Lover cannot effect this end, we might expect the priest to assist him.

What occurs in the confessional sections of Book IV, however, is something quite different: Genius is capable of offering good counsel, but often he merely encourages more wishing and fantasy. In the story of Iphis and Iante, for example, he builds an assurance that Cupid will take pity on a "grete love" (line 489) by making natural whatever in it "stant ayein" Nature's lore. Gower does not yet show us what this might mean to Amans, but the claim is likely to win the regard of a lover whom we shall later see as "olde grisel" (VIII.2407). The priest encourages Amans to believe that a natural fulfillment of love is possible, no matter how remote, implausible, unnatural, or ridiculous that love appears. To the end of nourishing that hope, he also encourages a heightened activity that clearly lacks the ordering of a reasonable intention:

> . . . pull up a besi herte,
> Mi sone, and let nothing asterte
> Of love fro thi besinesse.
>
> (lines 723-25)

Such advice can only increase the frustration Amans feels and succinctly identifies: "I seche that I mai noght finde" (line 289). The failure of the confession to do its work, however, is only partly explained by this kind of counsel. The poet explains more as he develops and arranges the imaginative busyness of the Confessor himself; in that process, he will also generate a range of perspectives on *gentilesse* that will enrich the concept and help to define it most meaningfully.

V

Genius's failure to garner and winnow types of busyness betrays a particular kind of *ingenium*. He is inventive, but not an inventor who consistently uses his "wittes alle." He relies chiefly on imagination, often in its worst form: a running about with vague mind, inspired merely by something seen or done a very short time before.[55] Indeed, in exercising this faculty, Genius most resembles the gentle Ulysses: quick to generate images, he is also quick to forget them, to "flitt his herte aside." Topics fade as new attractions take their place, and in the process "resonable entencion" gets lost. In putting Amans to work in occupations that are sometimes idle, sometimes "leveful," the imaginatively busy priest seems, like the personified Negligence, to set "of no vertu pris / Bot as him liketh for the while" (IV. 908-09).

This is not to say, however, that the poet places no limits on the vagaries of his Confessor's imagination. Genius organizes much of his argument in these middle confessional books around four images of what inspires or nurtures love in the gentle man, and these exemplars set boundaries for his *evagatio mentis*. As certain of his arguments make manifest, all is not bad with Genius. In serving two masters, he is torn between conflicting ideals of *gentilesse*, the one figured in his goddess, the other in "holi bokes wise." Drawing on these conflicting sources, he impresses images on his pupil, but, as Alain de Lille had earlier observed in his own figure of Genius,[56] he forms those images sometimes with the right, sometimes with the left hand, and it is obviously the priest's left-handed efforts that exacerbate Amans's inner strife. In each of his two roles Genius imagines a type and an antitype for the beloved: these images will order the intentions of the "gentil" lover. In Genius's perspective as a priest, the type is Amans's difficult and perplexing mistress; the antitype is Venus. In his perspective as a servant of Venus, the type is Pygmaleon's "lusti wif," originally the statue; the antitype is Araxarathen, a figure introduced in the final tale of Book IV; we shall consider her presently. All of these figures are in one sense or another "gentil," but, as will be readily apparent, only one fully represents the ideal *gentilesse* defined in

Genius's re-creative excursus.

The story of Iphis and Araxarathen is based upon a tale in Ovid's *Metamorphoses*. In the original, Anaxarete--a character Gower renames Araxarathen--spurns the advances of Iphis, and he, in despair, kills himself; Anaxarete is unable to avoid gazing at him on his bier, and while she looks on, as hard-hearted as she has been throughout, the gods turn her physically to stone. Genius transforms this tale significantly, and yet his ultimate exemplary purpose, like Ovid's, is to show the effect of the woman's hard-heartedness not only on another but on herself. Genius makes Araxarathen the antitype of Pygmaleon's "lusti wif," and the difference between these figures is readily apparent in their opposed careers. Whereas the "colde ymage" (line 442) of Pygmaleon's statue literally softens, becoming warm in "fleissh and bon" (line 423), the "fleissh and bon" (line 3679) of Araxarathen turns cold and hardens, literally into the "figure of a Ston" (line 3680). As far as these women are concerned, however, the difference is cosmetic. Neither prospect can be particularly appealing, especially if we recall Genius's major point in the first tale: to the statue, all that being full of life can mean is that Pygmaleon, at last, will have all that he "wolde abedde." The more important difference lies in the male perspective: the statue is "tretable" and therefore good; Araxarathen is not and therefore is wicked. The one is "gentil," the other "vilein."

Nonetheless, Araxarathen's case is more complex than this contrast makes it appear, partly because Genius has so radically altered her character. In the original, Anaxarete is a Teucrian princess, but in character she is, in every respect, the contrary of gentle: *saeva, inmites, dura, ferrea, crudelis, impia, superba, ferox.*[57] In Genius's version, by contrast, Araxarathen is "a Maide of lou astat" (line 3521) who displays true gentility. Iphis also has a new status: though still "soubgit / To love" (lines 3523-24), he is no longer a youth of humble origin but Teucer's own son, "a potestat / Of worldes good" (lines 3522-23). Through these changes, Genius obviously calls attention to the power of goodness and love over "degre," and by changing both figures he draws out an even greater strength in the character of Araxarathen. As Iphis, by the privilege of status, might expect another to yield to the "fantasie" of his love, so Araxarathen, because of her status, might be expected to submit to the wishes of this "potestat." She does not, however, and she rejects him not because she has forgotten her place, or because she is proud or scornful, but because she is wholly devoted to virtue. In this version of the tale, Iphis

> . . . excedeth the mesure
> Of reson, that himself assure
> He can noght.

(IV.3525-27)

By a new pairing of terms--of Iphis's foolish love and Araxarathen's reason--Genius shifts the focus of the original, apparently turning Iphis into the principal negative exemplar:

> He was with love unwys constreigned,
> And sche with resoun was restreigned:
> The lustes of his herte he suieth,
> And sche for drede schame eschuieth,
> And as sche scholde, tok good hiede
> To save and kepe hir wommanhiede.

(lines 3529-34)

Iphis kills himself because the lady "wolt noght do [him] grace" (line 3585), but he has less cause for despair than does Ovid's Iphis because the woman acts not out of malice or cruelty but out of virtue. Araxarathen refuses to yield to the kind of *gentilesse* that would force her to offer the "o word" to heal Iphis, thereby satisfying him with soft speech, proof of a "gentil herte," but also fostering in him a groundless hope and a false impression of her character.

Araxarathen also differs from the Ovidian character in another sense. Whereas Ovid's Anaxarete never really changes-- she is turned to stone "quod fuit in duro iam pridem pectore"

(XIV.758)--Araxarathen "softens" her behavior late in Genius's narrative. A tormented Iphis, just before he kills himself, blames his decision on her "herte hard" (line 3583), and she later confirms his judgment when she "takth upon hirself the gilt" (line 3610) for Iphis's suicide and seeks harsh judgment for what she has done: "For I ne dede no pite / To him, which for mi love is lore" (lines 3628-29).[58] In her remorse, as "Sche wepth, sche crith, sche swouneth ofte" (line 3619), however, she proves that, far from being a "vilein" lacking in sensitivity, she is naturally gentle and perfectly capable of displaying *gentilesse*. Iphis does not give her much chance to reveal this side of her nature: nor is it Genius's wish to imagine it before it serves his exemplary purpose late in the narrative.

We may well ask, however, what that exemplary purpose is. It would seem that, if the priest had wished merely to condemn hard-heartedness, the Ovidian figure would have served his purpose quite nicely. At the very least, Genius's revisions tighten the relationship between the exemplum and Amans's own "tale," for the now gentle Araxarathen displays in her actions the same paradox that Amans imagines in his own mistress, as when he complains, in Book III:

> Ha, who sawh evere such a weie?
> Ha, who sawh evere such destresse?
> Withoute pite gentilesse,
> Withoute mercy wommanhede,
> That wol so quyte a man his mede
> Which evere hath be to love trewe.

(lines 1604-09)

Both Amans and Iphis are bewildered by the lady's cruel response to their "trouthe," and both locate that cruelty in the figure of Daunger. Iphis thus complains that:

> . . . Daunger shal to manye mo
> Ensample be for everemo,
> Whan thei my wofull deth recorde.

(IV.3589-91)

Amans also sees in his beloved a potential for homicide.[59] Should he die because Daunger keeps her from bestowing grace on him, he melodramatically argues, it would be a double pity. If

> . . . I scholde in such a wise
> In rewardinge of my servise
> Be ded, me thenkth it were a rowthe.
>
> (III.1595-97)

And if this happens, the mistress must be blamed, "Whan with o word sche mihte have heled / A man, and soffreth him so deie" (III.1602-03). These words are echoed in the story of Araxarathen: her effigy is presented "in ensample of tho wommen, / That soffren men to deie so" (IV.3676-77).

The parallel between these stories is a curious one, however, for what Genius does with the shared topic of "tristesce." The "askinge of merci," Amans notes, is all that keeps him from despair (IV.3497-99). Coming into the final narrative of Book IV, he has nourished a hope, modeled on the example of Pygmaleon, that repeated pleas for grace will "deserve grace" (IV.616). Very early in this last tale, however, Genius shows the effect of Iphis's pleas on the hard-hearted Araxarathen: "the more he preide, / The lasse love on him sche leide" (lines 3527-28). Amans has made a like point about his own situation a short time before:

> The more that I knele and preie,
> With goode wordes and with softe,
> The more I am refused ofte.
>
> (lines 748-50)

The tale, rather than counteract despair, thereby seems by this precedent to encourage it.

Less superficially, however, the tale provides an exemplum against despair, and how it does so is significant for Gower's larger perception of *gentilesse*. The change in Araxarathen is created to support a certain kind of *gentilesse*: if at the outset of the tale she embodies a *gentilesse* of virtue, at the end, in her self-judgment and conversion, she is made to conform to a *gentilesse* of self-indulgent "kinde." In this metamorphosis she has become the "soubgit" or victim of Genius's own "gentil" imagination, for the priest has her dismiss--indeed, not even consider--her virtue and original "resonable entencion," her justifiable modesty and caution in rejecting a foolish and sensual Iphis. What is worse, in making this flesh-and-blood character choose her status as a cold and lifeless "ymage" Genius effectively has her yield to the desires of such self-indulgent lovers as Iphis and Amans, assigning to herself an image of "vilenie" that they, as well as Genius, project in support of a certain kind of gentle love. Her reductive self-judgment thus legitimizes Genius's criticism of her in the epitaph he invents for the common tomb: "He [i.e., Iphis] was to neysshe and sche to hard" (line 3681). As we shall now observe, this statement, even while it cancels out aspects of Araxarathen's character manifested in the narrative, lends special support to Genius's rhetoric against a particular despair.

Tristesce is wrong chiefly because it represents a breach of decorum--a loss of will or "herte"--in the love of "gentil folk." The fact that Iphis has here been transformed into a "potestat," though it does not technically establish a further parallel with Amans's situation, does call attention to another, shared sense of privilege in these male figures. Both characters, in Genius's lesser vision of *gentilesse*, have right on their side; both enjoy the prerogative of "trewe" love. We have seen it in Amans's complaint in Book III; Iphis also claims it in his final apostrophe, when he complains of the injustice in his dying: "I am ded for love and trouthe" (IV.3587); even Araxarathen evidently comes to recognize this love-prerogative, and that is what her late display of a "gentil herte" may finally signify. In Genius's perspective she is a worthy person who makes a mistake, recognizes it, and regrets it profoundly: in coming to accept the privilege of love, Araxarathen thus "enacts" the lesson

Genius is attempting to teach Amans. Iphis's sin, in Genius's perspective, is not the initial "wrong" of a foolish and sensual love, but effectively the opposite: it lies in being too "neysshe," in forsaking such love and his rights as a lover. As far as Amans is concerned, the special prominence given to Araxarathen at the site of the tomb--her image

> . . . as for miracle
> Was set upon an hyh pinacle,
> That alle men it mihte knowe
>
> (IV.3661-63)

--serves to re-establish the prerogative of love: the focused picture of a female wrong and "vilenie" becomes the antidote for wanhope by consoling, vindicating, hardening the lover, making him even more "soubgit" to his tyrannical will, more inclined to decry the lady's injustice against one who is to "love trewe."

In such a setting of true but unrequited love, Iphis, Genius, and Amans all deal with paradox reductively: they simply fit the gentle woman to images of "vilenie." The "verrai" gentle woman is not so "tretable," of course; she is not, like Pygmaleon's "lusti wif," the mere product of wishing and fantasy; she will not succumb to a lover's desire merely because he claims "trouthe." With characters such as Iphis and Amans that very resistance can obviously cause "tristesce." Genius checks such an inclination to "desesperance" in his charge, however, by inventing a tale that includes the fantasy of a gentle woman admitting her want of pity, a villainy. Ultimately, the story of Araxarathen, like that of Pygmaleon's quickened statue, serves an idolatrous love. The images of women in both stories are the projection of desire; both tales nourish a foolish hope, a hope that "is noght trewe of that he seith" (III.1175).

As Amans moves between "tristesce" and hope, between the stances exemplified by Iphis and Pygmaleon, he refashions his lady accordingly, fitting her variously to the types of gentle woman presented in these two tales: he transforms her sometimes into a character like Araxarathen, the cold "figure of a Ston," stonelike in her "herte hard"; sometimes into a character like Pygmaleon's spouse, the "faire ymage" warm and "full of lif" (IV.423), alive specifically to his "wihssinge."[60] But these are not the only ways in which Amans perceives his mistress. Her image becomes an entirely "good imprint" when he recalls her from contexts other than her relationship to him. On such occasions, she is courteous, friendly, "soft in compaignye," and, as a true "gentil," she is also fittingly restrained. Reason and discretion order her kindness and "kinde," and thus, as Amans himself testifies,

> . . . toward othre, as I mai se,
> Sche takth and yifth in such degre,
> That as be weie of frendlihiede
> Sche can so kepe hir wommanhiede,
> That every man spekth of hir wel.

(V.4753-57)

From what the Lover says about his lady in contexts such as this, Genius forms another exemplar, this one not a single image but a number of partial reflections of the lady's excellence. He uses these principally to explain and justify her seeming hardness--her want of pity--and also to rebuke Amans for lacking grace in implying that his mistress is sometimes less than "gentil." What emerges in the composite of these images is the lady's prudence and "mesure."[61] Following "resonable entencion," she retains a dignity wholly suited to her gentle nature. She is not, like Genius's Araxarathen, too hard; it is rather the case that Amans's suit "to hire honour missit" (V.5213).

Even here Genius does not address complexity of character or the delicate balance the lady achieves between potentially opposed sides of *gentilesse*, as in her "frendlihiede" and "wommanhiede," for example, and yet he forms this image with his right hand. Also with the right hand he forms an antitype in the Venus he serves. From the long excursus in Book V where he

261

explores the "nyce fantasie" of pagan religions, Genius tries but, thanks to Amans, fails to exclude his goddess, and to his shame he must now reveal her character. Whereas Amans in his Iphis state sees his own beloved as too closely guarded by Daunger, Genius now condemns the contrary in a Venus who

> . . . alle danger putte aweie
> Of love, and fond to lust a weie;
> So that of hire in sondri place
> Diverse men felle into grace.

(lines 1389-92)

Unlike Amans's wise mistress, Venus is preoccupied with fleshly comforts and desires. She is incapable of "mesure" or reason, and in her "gentil herte" the soft or "tender" affectus thereby runs too quickly. This "tenterhed or nessched of herte" is obviously not a mark of true gentility; it is, simply, a sloth whereby the goddess "draweþ after þe likynges of [the] body."[62]

Especially in presenting these last two images, Genius reveals a capacity to make distinctions. But he does not seem to use those distinctions profitably; too infrequently does he project the type and antitype of "vertu moral," or the ideal of *gentilesse* he presents in Book IV. As a result, he seems incapable of freeing Amans from images of "gentil love" modelled in the tales of Pygmaleon and Iphis. Neither kind of image--the "lusti wif," the woman of "herte hard"--will make Amans into a "verrai gentil man," of course; nor will either ever allow him to understand true *gentilesse*.

VI

The four exemplars of *gentilesse* we have just considered are not drawn to resolution in a single perspective in the *Confessio*, and the reason lies in the gentle imagination or the *ingenium* of Gower's two major characters. The issue here is a poetics of *gentilesse*: by that I do not mean merely a poetry with *gentilesse* as subject, but *gentilesse* as implying different kinds of imagination out of which poems, loves, and deeds are invented and come to have meaning. If I might follow a metaphoric distinction made by John of Salisbury[63]--and used by Winthrop Wetherbee in a discussion of another Genius[64]--Amans's *ingenium* is the type that creeps or "is mired down to earth, and cannot rise."[65] To the extent that his gaze is fixed on images inspired by a venerian *gentilesse*, he "can make no progress." Genius's *ingenium* is the type that flies: lacking stability, it reaches to both kinds of *gentilesse* but settles in neither. This also, as we have seen, is a form of sloth. At extremes of creeping and flitting about, these two speakers cannot stand and climb or make evident progress to wisdom. What the poem appears to lack in its major characters, then, is a third type of *ingenium*, one "that goes to neither extreme [and walks]"; one that enacts a righteous or truly gentle busyness; one, in short, that follows a "resonable entencion."

Despite the speakers' tendency to get lost in the maze of their own gentle language, however, Gower uses many devices to keep the work advancing steadily toward the wisdom he has promised to his readers. In conclusion, I shall mention three, all of them *recreationes* in some respect detached from the business of the confession and the leisure or state of fulfillment towards which the entire poem moves: all three involve *gentilesse*. One is the re-creative excursus of Book IV, and it requires no further comment. Another is the grace of the lady, whose gift is a gift of resistance, of remaining a "reality" beyond the fiction of the confession, a person who in her complexity remains inaccessible to the fragmenting imagination: she will not conform to the partial images priest and Lover generate. Her complexity, which the speakers can only hint at in their partial reflections, is attributable to her being a truly gentle person: throughout, she is an illusive, yet enduring, reminder of the *gentilesse* that Amans in his own person lacks.

Also at work in moving the argument to wisdom, but paradoxically and on another level entirely, is Genius's own unstable *ingenium*. His divided loyalties and attention destabilize his doctrine of love and *gentilesse*, to be sure; he cannot by example or precept give Amans even a superficial "sikernesse." In that apparent ineptitude, however, he sustains the Lover's attention--the language of Venus is an imperative in this confession--while he also prepares him for the greatest, most consequential profit. Surely Genius cannot be trusted to be wholly committed to arguments he presents on either side of an issue. He is in effect a personified *demande*. In the double perspective of a *demande*, or of this Genius, the excursus on *gentilesse* might be seen as the product either of idle leisure or of "ernest," and the enveloping shrift as the product either of "game" or of just business. Given Genius's centrality to the poem, however, that very doubleness makes the whole of the *Confessio* a "joieuse recreation." The work teaches a fruitful leisure by not allowing us to close the "conversacion," quickly to accept solutions, however right they are, to problems we do not yet fully understand.

The premise underlying this "game" is a doctrine whose import neither Amans nor the priest who utters it can comprehend:

> . . . love moste ben awaited:
> . . . .
> Thou miht noght of thiself ben able
> To winne love or make it stable,
> All thogh thou mihtest love achieve.

(IV.263, 267-69)

The second series of ellipses in this quotation covers another promise of "decerte" for busyness. Genius is always quick to offer such advice because, like Chaucer's "fader of gentilesse," he "loved besinesse, / Ayeinst the vyce of slouthe, in honestee" ("Gentilesse," lines 10-11). Genius is even busier than this exemplar, however, for in him all of Chaucer's terms become protean, variable in content, and that means increased activity, specifically as in word and deed the priest busily combines, mixes, reverses senses of idle and "leveful bisynesse." By that very means, however, Gower builds into this "amoureuse conversacion" a potential of invention or discovery, of a re-created "entencion." Indeed, as busyness, leisure, and idleness change in valence in the course of the work, "gentil" busyness comes to mean "Som newe thing" (Prol. 51*), and Amans is being prepared to discover it with his "wittes alle." That "besinesse" is what he awaits, and ultimately it will come to him in the form of a gift, a love taught in "holy bokes wise" that will make him gentle and give him rest, but a rest far greater than the *otium* that has occasioned his "gentil love" and made him a superficially "gentil man." And so it will be that "Þe verrey nobleie þat a man bigynneþ heere bi grace and vertue is fulfilled in ioie."[66]

NOTES

[1]All quotations from Gower are from the edition of G. C. Macaulay, *The Complete Works of John Gower*, 4 vols. (Oxford, 1899-1902). For other uses of the *topos*, see, e.g., Boethius, *Consolation of Philosophy* 3. par.6, m.6; Jean de Meun, *Le Roman de la Rose*, lines 6549-62, 18577-866, ed. Félix Lecoy, CFMA, 3 vols. (Paris, 1965-70), 2:201, 3:58-67; Dante, *Convivio* 4.3, 10, 14, 15; Boccaccio, *Il Filostrato* 7.94-99; Chaucer, *Gentilesse*; Wife of Bath's Tale 1109-76; Clerk's Tale 155-61; Parson's Tale 460-68; Gower, *Mirour de l'Omme*, lines 12073-96, 17329-412, 23329-436. Pertinent discussions of the *topos* include Lindsay A. Mann, "'Gentilesse' and the Franklin's Tale," *Studies in Philology*, 63 (1966), 10-29; D. S. Brewer, "Class Distinction in Chaucer," *Speculum*, 43 (1968), 290-305; W. O. Evans, "'Cortaysye' in Middle English," *Mediaeval Studies*, 29 (1967), 143-57; Alan T. Gaylord, "*Gentillesse* in Chaucer's *Troilus*," *Studies in Philology*, 61 (1964), 19-34; Donald C. Baker, "Chaucer's Clerk and the Wife of Bath on the Subject of *Gentilesse*," *Studies in Philology*, 59 (1962), 631-40; Jonathan Nicholls, *The Matter of Courtesy: Medieval Courtesy Books and the Gawain-Poet* (Woodbridge, Suffolk, 1985).

[2]See Chaucer, Parson's Tale 460-68, for a definition of *gentilesse* consistent with this sense in the *Confessio.*

[3]On "gentilesse" with a like meaning in various contexts in Chaucer, see: Bernard S. Levy, "The Wife of Bath's *Queynte Fantasye*," *Chaucer Review*, 4 (1969), 106-22; and his "*Gentilesse* in Chaucer's Clerk's and Merchants'

265

Tales," *Chaucer Review*, 11 (1977), 306-18.

⁴Alain de Lille, *The Plaint of Nature*, par. 5, trans. James J. Sheridan (Toronto, 1980), p. 163; *Patrologia latina* 210.459 (hereafter *PL*).

⁵These meanings are taken from Alexander Souter, *A Glossary of Later Latin to 600 A.D.* (Oxford, 1949; rept. 1964), s.v. *otiositas*, p. 281; quoted by Douglas Kelly, *Medieval Imagination: Rhetoric and the Poetry of Courtly Love* (Madison, WI, 1978), p. 278 n. 53.

⁶Sidenote, Macaulay, 2:365.

⁷For like terms, see, for example, Richard de Bury, *Philobiblon*, vol. 9, text and translation of E. C. Thomas, ed. Michael Maclagan (Oxford, 1970), pp. 98-101; on the consequences of shunning the ancients, see John of Salisbury, *Metalogicon* 1.3, ed. Clemens C. I. Webb (Oxford, 1929), pp. 9-12; trans. Daniel D. McGarry (Berkeley, 1962), pp. 13-16.

⁸*Didascalicon* 3.2. Like Hugh, Gower catalogues advances made through study and manual labor: whatever the field of these inventors, however, theirs is an orderly and productive inquiry, providing a lore that endures: it "stant evere alyche greene" (IV.2392). In the Latin verse headnote to this section, the English poet claims a special regard for mental labor and the teacher who transmits knowledge: "Set qui doctrine causa fert mente labores, / Preualet et merita perpetuata parat" (Macaulay, 2:365). On the use of leisure to search for and discover the truth and to impart that knowledge to others, see St. Augustine: "In otio non iners vacatio delectare debet, sed aut inquisitio aut inventio veritatis, ut in ea quisque proficiat et quod invenerit ne alteri invideat" (*De civitate Dei* 19.19, ed. B. Dombart, 2 vols. [Leipzig, 1905-09], 2:387-88).

⁹*Didascalicon* 3.16, trans. Jerome Taylor (New York and London, 1961), p. 99; the Latin is from the edition of Charles Henry Buttimer, *Hugonis de Sancto Victore Didascalicon de studio legendi* (Washington, DC, 1939), p. 67.

¹⁰"Otium sanctum quaerit caritas veritatis," St. Augustine, *De civitate Dei* 19.19 (Dombart, 2:388).

¹¹Ovid, *Remedia amoris* 136, 150, ed. E. J. Kenney (Oxford, 1961), p. 210.

¹²*Remedia amoris* 143 (Kenney, p. 210).

[13]John V. Fleming, *The Roman de la Rose: A Study in Allegory and Iconography* (Princeton, 1969), pp. 72-81. See D. W. Robertson, Jr., *Preface to Chaucer: Studies in Medieval Perspectives* (Princeton, 1963), pp. 92-93. More recently, Douglas Kelly (*Medieval Imagination*, pp. 78-80) sees greater ambiguity in the figure of Oiseuse and raises questions about Fleming's specific interpretation. On the model of *otium-luxuria* in antiquity, see, for example, Jean-Marie André, *L'Otium dans la vie morale et intellectuelle romaine des origines à l'époque augustéenne*, Publications de la Faculté des Lettres et Sciences Humaines de Paris, Série "Recherches," vol. 30 (Paris, 1966), pp. 49-52.

[14]*The Book of Vices and Virtues: A Fourteenth-Century English Translation of the Somme le Roi of Lorens d'Orléans*, ed. W. Nelson Francis, EETS, o.s. 217 (London, 1942; rept. 1968), p. 27.

[15]"Non quia sic se habet veritas, set opinio Amantum" (sidenote, Macaulay, 2:340). Opinion "est acceptio propositionis immediatae et non necessariae" (Vincent of Beauvais, *Speculum naturale* [Douay, 1624; rept. Graz, 1965], col. 1937); it originates in sense-perception: "omnis opinio . . . habet principium a sensu" (Guillaume de Conches, *Glosae super Platonem*, ed. E. Jeauneau [Paris, 1965], p. 109); "the judgments of sensation and imagination are classed as 'opinion'," but "sensation deceives the untutored, and cannot pronounce sure judgment" (John of Salisbury, *Metalogicon* 4.11 [McGarry, pp. 220-21; Webb, p. 177]); "Imagination . . . possesses in itself nothing certain as a source of knowledge" (Hugh of St. Victor, *Didascalicon* 2.5 [Taylor, pp. 66-67; Buttimer, p. 29]). In the *Confessio* the distinction between opinion and truth will fit other perceptions of the self-interested lover, who, as we shall find below, depends on the unreliable judgments of sensation and imagination.

[16]See *Oxford Latin Dictionary*, ed. P. G. W. Glare (Oxford, 1982), s.v. *otium*, pp. 1277-78; Jean-Marie André, *L'Otium*, and, by the same author, *Recherches sur l'otium romain*, Annales Littéraires de l'Université de Besançon, vol. 52 (Paris, 1962); Jean Leclercq, *Otia monastica: Études sur la vocabulaire de la contemplation au moyen âge*, Studia Anselmiana, fasc. 51 (Rome, 1963); Jean Leclercq, *The Love of Learning and the Desire for God: A Study of Monastic Culture*, trans. Catherine Misrahi (New York, 1960), pp. 84-85; Michael O'Laughlin, *The Garlands of Repose: The Literary Celebration of Civic and Retired Leisure* (Chicago, 1978), pp. 164-96. On *acedia* and leisure, see Josef Pieper, *Leisure: The Basis of Culture*, trans. Alexander Dru (New York, 1952), pp. 48-58. On *otium* and *negotium* in relation to courtly leisure and commerce in Chaucer, see Patricia J. Eberle, "Commercial Language and the Commercial Outlook in the *General Prologue*," *Chaucer*

Review, 18 (1983), 161-74.

[17]Glending Olson, *Literature as Recreation in the Later Middle Ages* (Ithaca and London, 1982), pp. 101-02; for terms and distinctions in the present discussion I am especially indebted to Olson, pp. 101-07.

[18]See John Stevens, *Music and Poetry in the Early Tudor Court* (Lincoln, NE, 1961), pp. 154-67; Richard Firth Green, "The *Familia Regis* and the *Familia Cupidinis*," in *English Court Culture in the Later Middle Ages*, ed. V. J. Scattergood and J. W. Sherborne (London, 1983), pp. 87-108.

[19]These and subsequent quotations from Chaucer are from *The Riverside Chaucer*, 3rd ed., general editor Larry D. Benson (Boston, 1987).

[20]I have borrowed these terms from late medieval evidence quoted by Arthur Piaget in "Un Manuscrit de la cour amoureuse de Charles VI," *Romania*, 31 (1902), 601.

[21]*Trésor Amoureux*, lines 3060-3104, in *Oeuvres de Froissart: Poésies*, ed. Auguste Scheler, vol. 3 (Brussels, 1872), pp. 276-78. For a summary of the *Trésor*, see Kelly, pp. 114-20.

[22]See F. S. Shears, *Froissart: Chronicler and Poet* (London, 1930), pp. 15-16.

[23]*Trésor*, *demande* 2 (lines 3070-74):

> Et pour vivre en deduit tousjours,
> Lequel voulríes vous servir
> En vray espoir de desservir
> Sa merite: amours loyaument,
> Ou armes honnourablement?

See also *demande* 1 (lines 3064-69).

[24]It is beyond my present purpose to examine this segment of the excursus in detail, but it should be noted how, in relation to the enveloping shrift, it forms one of the larger *demandes* of the *Confessio*. At the end of Bk. III Genius attacks war both in "worldes" and in "Cristes" cause. He stresses that "After the lawe of charite, / Ther schal no dedly werre be" (III.2261-62). And in responding to Amans's question, "To werre and sle the Sarazin, / Is that the lawe?" (III.2489-90), the priest responds, "To preche and soffre for the feith, / That have I herd the gospell seith" (III.2491-92). There is a sense in which

Genius here voices the poet's own defense of peace (see R. F. Yeager, "*Pax Poetica*: On the Pacifism of Chaucer and Gower," *Studies in the Age of Chaucer*, 9 [1987], 97-121). In the "game" of the excursus in Bk. IV, however, the Priest appears to reverse himself. As he defends the travail of "men of Armes," the Lover, taking the opposed stance, introduces Genius's arguments from Bk. III to buttress his own refusal to travel and fight. Although one might combine Genius's opposed stances in a single, consistent view--"chevalerie" ideally serves the cause of peace--the Confessor does not attempt to reconcile them. Nonetheless, in this section he will indirectly support his earlier statement with a concluding tribute to charity. As I shall note, he reaches that conclusion by means of an argument independently generated in the excursus.

[25]*Demande* 3 (lines 3075-80); 6 (lines 3091-96); 7 (lines 3097-3104).

[26]*Demande* 3 (lines 3075-80):

> Lequel vous seroit mieulz à gré
> Pour vous mettre en haultain degré:
> Ou le fait de bonne science
> Aornee de conscience,
> Ou de bon eür le secours
> A l'aventure en toutes cours?

[27]Contrast Gower's argument when treating *seignours* in the *Mirour de l'Omme*, lines 23329-436; see esp. lines 23355-58:

> Mais les richesces nepourqant
> Ne sont en soy digne a conquerre
> Le meindre que l'en porroit querre
> De les vertus, ne tant ne qant.

[28]*Demande* 4 (lines 3081-86):

> Vous semble il qu'il soit homme né
> En vertu si bien meurginé
> Qu'il puist bien servir tout d'un tans
> Armes et amours, et sentans
> Qu'en tous les deux fesist devoir
> Pour parfaite joie en avoir.

[29]The *topos* is perhaps most succinctly expressed in the opening lines of Guido Guinizelli's *Al cor gentil*: "Love returns always to a noble [*gentil*]

heart / Like a bird to the green in the forest" in *The Poetry of Guido Guinizelli*, ed. and trans. Robert Edwards (New York, 1987), p. 21.

[30]*Demande* 5 (lines 3087-90).

[31]*Book of Vices and Virtues*, p. 85. At this point in the work Genius does not fully expound the concept of charity; nor does he distinguish its elements: love of God, love of one's neighbor. Although traditionally "*amor proximi* is valuable only for God's sake, 'propter Deum'" (R. Freyhan, "The Evolution of the *Caritas* Figure in the Thirteenth and Fourteenth Centuries," *Journal of the Warburg and Courtauld Institutes*, 11 [1948], 68), the emphasis at most points of the confession falls on virtuous behavior in relation to one's neighbor; nevertheless, also evident, and especially at the end of the *Confessio*, is Gower's sense that such behavior must be founded upon, and ordered to, the love of God.

[32]Siegfried Wenzel, *The Sin of Sloth: Acedia in Medieval Thought and Literature* (Chapel Hill, 1967), p. 85.

[33]"Otium, quod [praecipue] industriae et studio maxime contrarium uidetur, praecipue subnecti debet, non quo euanescit uirtus, sed quo recreatur" (Valerius Maximus, *Factorum et dictorum memorabilium libri novem* 8.8, ed. Carolus Kempf [Stuttgart, 1966], pp. 393-94).

[34]Because *gentilesse* is equated with virtue generally, no single virtue or counterposed vice need be accorded necessary, privileged, or exclusive status in housing discussions of it. In the *Mirour de l'Omme*, Gower had used the concept to expound aspects of humility (lines 12073-96) and chastity (lines 17329-412), and that he uses it here to "inform" busyness is unexceptionable; indeed, given the subject of this poem, as I have argued above, his decision is an especially fitting one. What I am also concerned with in the present context is the fact that in treating the concept in relation to sloth Gower is able to place the discussion roughly at the mid-point of the confession.

[35]This and subsequent quotations from the *Purgatorio* are from the translation of Charles S. Singleton, *The Divine Comedy: Purgatorio*, Bollingen Series 80 (Princeton, 1973).

[36]For possible parallels with Oiseuse in the *Roman de la Rose*, see Erich Köhler, "Lea, Matelda und Oiseuse," *Zeitschrift für romanische Philologie*, 78 (1962), 464-69; and Fleming, pp. 77-78.

[37]See Siegfried Wenzel, "Dante's Rationale for the Seven Deadly Sins

('*Purgatorio*' XVII)," *Modern Language Review*, 60 (1965), 529-33.

[38]"Natural Law and John Gower's *Confessio Amantis*," *Medievalia et Humanistica*, n.s., 11 (1982), 229-61.

[39]A list of such virtues appears in Genius's brief tale of Telaphus and Teucer at the end of Bk. III (lines 2639-2717): there, however, "gentilesce" is included as a single virtue in the series, whereas in the excursus the priest says of "vertu" generally, "So mai that wel be gentilesse" (IV.2267).

[40]"Negotium iustum suscipit necessitas caritatis," *De civitate Dei* 19.19 (Dombart, 2:388).

[41]Thomas Aquinas, *Summa Theologiae* 1a2ae, 12.1, ed. and trans. Thomas Gilby, Blackfriars, vol. 17 (London, 1970), p. 113.

[42]For relevant medieval background to Abelard's doctrine, see: *Peter Abelard's Ethics*, ed. D. E. Luscombe (Oxford, 1971), pp. xxxii-xxxv; and Etienne Gilson, *The Spirit of Mediaeval Philosophy*, trans. A. H. C. Downes (New York, 1940), pp. 343-63.

[43]*Ethics* [*Scito te ipsum*], ed. Luscombe, pp. 52-53.

[44]*Ethics* [*Scito te ipsum*], pp. 46-47.

[45]*Ethics* [*Scito te ipsum*], pp. 48-49.

[46]*Ethics* [*Scito te ipsum*], pp. 40-41. Given what Abelard writes, the task of judging the presence of "verrai gentilesse" does not seem humanly possible, since people do not "consider the guilt of a fault so much as the performance of a deed. Indeed God alone . . . truly considers the guilt in our intention." If this is the case in reality, it obviously need not be so in a fiction, should its author choose to invent and reveal intention; in the *Confessio* Gower does so, but he also makes us aware of the difficulty of appraising it.

[47]On the use of this figure by late medieval poets, see J. D. Burnley, *Chaucer's Language and the Philosophers' Tradition*, Chaucer Studies 2 (Cambridge, 1979), pp. 102-04, 106.

[48]*Chaucer's Language and the Philosophers' Tradition*, pp. 151-65.

[49]*Book of Vices and Virtues*, p. 93.

[50]*Heroides* I.58, 80, ed. and trans. Grant Showerman, Loeb Classical Library (Cambridge, MA, 1914; rept. 1963), pp. 14-17.

[51]Kelly, pp. 234, 201.

[52]Kelly, p. 136. For the following discussion of Machaut, I am indebted to Kelly, esp. pp. 130-37, 148-49; and to Kevin Brownlee, *Poetic Identity in Guillaume de Machaut* (Madison, WI, 1984), pp. 115, 125.

[53]Chaucer, "The Complaint of Venus," line 20.

[54]Kelly, p. 136.

[55]For like features, see the description of the bestial as opposed to the rational imagination in Richard of St. Victor, *Benjamin minor* 16 (*PL* 196.11).

[56]*Plaint of Nature*, par. 9 (Sheridan, pp. 216-17; *PL* 210.480).

[57]Ovid, *Metamorphoses* XIV.698-761, ed. Frank Justus Miller, Loeb Classical Library, vol. 2 (New York, 1922), pp. 350-55.

[58]On pity and the "gentil herte," see Burnley, pp. 156-59.

[59]This is, of course, a *topos*: see, for example, Chaucer's Merchant's Tale, where the teller cynically describes the "franchise" of hard-hearted women (lines 1987-94):

> Heere may ye se how excellent franchise
> In wommen is, whan they hem narwe avyse.
> Som tyrant is, as ther be many oon,
> That hath an herte as hard as any stoon,
> Which wolde han lat hym sterven in the place
> Wel rather than han graunted hym hire grace,
> And hem rejoysen in hire crueel pryde,
> And rekke nat to been an homycide.

[60]For an instance of the latter, as well as the "excessive meditation" that produces it, see Amans's confession of sacrilege (V.7108-63); concerning "nimia cogitatione rerum visibilium" and its effects, see: St. Augustine, *De Trinitate* 11.4 (*PL* 42.989); and Andreas Capellanus, *The Art of Courtly Love*, trans. John Jay Parry (New York, 1941), p. 28.

[61]For a useful discussion of "mesure" in late medieval literature, see Burnley, pp. 118-26.

[62]*Book of Vices and Virtues*, pp. 26-27. For a helpful schema of the branches of sloth represented in late medieval popular treatises, see Wenzel, *Sin of Sloth*, pp. 80-82.

[63]*Metalogicon* 1.11 (McGarry, p. 35). "Horum tria sunt genera, sicut Carnotensis senex Bernardus frequenti colloquio suis auditoribus tradere consueuit. Aliud enim aduolans, aliud infimum, aliud mediocre est. Aduolans quidem eadem facilitate, qua percipit, recedit a perceptis, nec in aliqua sede inuenit requiem. Infimum autem sublimari non potest, ideoque profectum nescit; at mediocre, et quia habet in quo sedeat, et quia sublimari potest, nec de profectu desperat, et philosophantis exercitio accommodissimum est" (Webb, p. 29).

[64]Winthrop Wetherbee, "The Theme of Imagination in Medieval Poetry and the Allegorical Figure 'Genius'," *Medievalia et Humanistica*, n.s., 7 (1976), 46-47.

[65]As with many other judgments imported from medieval tradition and applied to Amans, this one may seem too severe. The ambiguity of what Amans's will teaches--that the heart that dares not love is "to vilein"--is that the doctrine is true, provided the love is good. Amans will not judge the "imprint," however, and in yielding to will he commits himself to foolish love. In that regard he resembles another *senex*, the Januarie of Chaucer's Merchant. The Amans who boasts "I am so trewly amerous" (IV.921) is a dreamer caught up in a "slepi hevene" (IV.2916), and after his own fashion he indulges in the "Heigh fantasye and curious bisynesse" (MerT 1577) that so befuddle the foolish Januarie. Of course, even this likeness is a distant one, for the latter figure is coarse, degenerate, and irredeemably sensual, and throughout he is a good deal sillier than Amans ever is: much more seriously than Amans, he is "mired down to earth." Amans, at least on the surface, is gentle. His courtesy and refined behavior, even his presumably "gentil herte," can obviously mask the seriousness of his idleness, but in another sense they reveal a potential for cure. For this lover there is a prospect of becoming truly gentle: what he lacks, but will advance to, is "resonable entencion." Some of the means to ensure his ascent from an earthbound imagination are provided even in the confession itself, as I note below.

[66]*Book of Vices and Virtues*, p. 86.

THE ILLUSTRATIONS
IN NEW COLLEGE MS. 266
FOR GOWER'S CONVERSION TALES

Peter C. Braeger

More than twenty-five of the fifty extant manuscripts of John Gower's *Confessio Amantis* contain, or once contained, some illustrations. These illustrations have been studied in terms of the artistic styles of early fifteenth-century English painting; they have also been analyzed in terms of their relationship to the textual history of the *Confessio*, most recently in the manuscript study by Jeremy Griffiths entitled "The Poem and its Pictures."[1] What follows here is an attempt to consider the series of miniatures in one *Confessio* manuscript, New College MS. 266, from another point of view--that of the interrelationships of the illustrations and the text passages they accompany. While Gower himself may have collaborated with some of the artists who illustrated his manuscripts, New College 266 was produced in the fifteenth century, at least several decades after Gower's death.[2] Consequently the pictures cannot be regarded as necessarily indicating the poet's intention. But one can consider the effectiveness of the illustrations as additions to the text. Placed directly in the columns of writing near the beginning of certain of Gower's narrative exempla, the pictures in New College MS. 266 have a strong potential for influencing the literary responses of the manuscript's readers.

In terms of style the illustrations in this manuscript are undistinguished, perhaps crude. The drapery and features of the figures are linear; the sky and the backgrounds are painted in solid colors with little attempt at three-dimensional depth.[3] In subject matter the pictures in New College MS. 266 differ from those in the earlier manuscript copies discussed by Griffiths. Miniatures in the earliest manuscripts of the *Confessio* illustrate only events of the poem's Prologue and frame. Some of these manuscripts contain a prefatory picture of the statue from Nebuchadnezzar's Dream; some contain a picture of the Lover and the Confessor; some contain both. In New College 266, however, the illustrations depict scenes from Gower's narrative exempla. There are nineteen pictures, one for each of nineteen different exempla; two of these pictures, however, are badly defaced. There are eleven additional spaces in the manuscript where miniatures have been cut out, and one damaged folio (fol. 178) and one folio now missing (originally placed between the present fols. 120 and 121) both probably contained at least one picture each. It would seem, then, that in its original condition New College 266 contained illustrations for at least thirty-two of Gower's narrative tales--just under one-fourth of the total number.[4] The manuscript may have also contained a miniature of the Lover and the Confessor, for the original folio 7, containing the opening of Book I, is also missing; in other *Confessio* manuscripts such an illustration was sometimes placed here.[5] But overall, in the design of New College MS. 266, the emphasis of the iconographic program for the *Confessio* has shifted from the Prologue and the frame of the poem to a selected number of Gower's tales.

In an important recent study of secular book illustration in the late Middle Ages, Lesley Lawton suggests that often a visual emphasis on certain parts of a long work was designed to facilitate the reader's access to key divisions of the manuscript. Lawton finds, for instance, that in the illustrated copies of Lydgate's *Troy Book* the subjects of the narrative illustrations were selected only on the basis of their position in the text. The first episode in each book of the poem was illustrated, regardless of its literary significance, for the pictures were merely designed to function as "visual chapter headings," "a ready reference system to portions of the text."[6] M. B. Parkes and A. I. Doyle have attributed a similar purpose to the Ellesmere pictures of Chaucer's Canterbury pilgrims. Because the beginning of each tale is marked with a portrait of its teller, readers can easily exercise the option offered by Chaucer himself to "turne over the leef and chese another."[7] The series of miniatures in New College MS. 266 for the exempla of the *Confessio Amantis* does not function in quite the same way. Here each miniature is placed immediately before the first line of the tale it illustrates and in this way does signal to manuscript readers where they may find the beginning of a new tale. But the thirty-two exempla selected for illustration are distributed randomly throughout each book of the poem, and often the first exemplum in the book is unillustrated. Consequently, while the pictures help readers of the manuscript find the beginning of some of the tales, these tales do not correspond to the main structural divisions of the *Confessio* as a whole.

Instead of structural position, one factor in New College MS. 266 that seems to have influenced which tales of the *Confessio* received illustration is length. More than eighty of Gower's tales (more than 60% of the total number in the *Confessio*) are less than one hundred lines long; but in New College 266 only four of these many shorter tales are illustrated. Most of the tales accompanied in the manuscript by a picture are longer than two hundred lines. In fact, while only twelve tales in the *Confessio* are longer than three hundred lines, eleven of these twelve were almost certainly featured in the original pictorial program in New College 266. As the pictures have always been placed before the first line of the tales they accompany, they may have been designed in part to guide readers of the manuscript to the beginnings of the longest tales.[8]

Lawton suggests that as visual chapter headings the pictures in the illustrated *Troy Book* "would have aided the process of reading rather than of understanding."[9] However, because they appear at the beginning of tales that lack any obvious structural significance, the pictures in New College 266 can give readers of the manuscript the impression that these tales are of special quality or of special relevance for understanding the poem as a whole. The unusual length of the tales can further that impression. Moreover, many of the tales chosen for illustration in the manuscript are similar in theme, as shown by a summary of the illustrations that accompany Book I of the poem. In New College 266 the first few exempla in the *Confessio* are unillustrated. In these tales, all very short, those who fail to avoid the sins of seeing and hearing are punished and destroyed (I.333-529). Though somewhat longer, the two exempla against hypocrisy are also unillustrated; these are the Tale of Mundus, exiled for his impersonation of a god (I.761-1059), and the Tale of the Trojan Horse (I.1077-1189). Next the Confessor relates the Tale of Florent as a warning against disobedience; in this tale, the protagonist realizes the value of humble obedience and so wins for himself a beautiful and loving wife (I.1407-1861). This tale is accompanied by the first miniature in the manuscript (fol. 14). Next, Genius offers the short example of Capaneus to demonstrate the sin of presumption; for his refusal to pray, God "him to pouldre smot" (I.2003). This tale has no accompanying picture. However, the next tale, also about presumption, has been illustrated (fol. 17ᵛ). In this story, the tale of The Trump of Death, the protagonist, the arrogant brother of the king of Hungary, learns humility when he must confront his mortality (I.2021-2253). Two narratives without illustrations follow: the Tale of Narcissus (I.2275-2358) and the Tale of Albino (Albinus) and Rosemund (I.2459-2547). In each, the protagonists are killed for their pride. In the two final stories in Book I the protagonists, Nebuchadnezzar and King Don Petro, turn from pride to humility. For these two exempla, the artist originally furnished an illustration, as before each of them (fols. 32 and 33ᵛ) a space is left in the manuscript where a miniature has been either cut out or destroyed.

In short, in Book I the reader of New College MS. 266 finds an illustration only for those tales in which Gower's main character moves away from the sin being discussed and takes up instead the corresponding virtue--tales that might be called "conversion" narratives. For the remaining seven books of the poem the pictorial program does not highlight such conversion narratives as exclusively as it does in Book I: a few of the illustrations do feature other kinds of tales in which the protagonist experiences no moral change. For instance, the Tale of Horestes (Orestes) at III.1885-2195 and the Tale of Virgil's Mirror at V. 2031-2224, both long tales of wicked rulers who die without repenting of their crimes, are illustrated in the manuscript. Moreover, the artist does leave unillustrated a few of the shorter conversion narratives. However, for twelve of the perhaps twenty tales in the *Confessio* that feature a protagonist who grows in virtue during the course of the tale, there appears either an illustration or a space where one has been cut away.[10]

The visual emphasis given to these conversion tales by the pictures in the manuscript can have consequences for the reader's interpretation of the text. Since a narrative offers several incidents which can be illustrated, many critics have argued that the choice of incident reflects the artist's response as reader of the literary work. But, as scholars such as Lawton, Derek Pearsall, and others have insisted, medieval artists are likely to have designed their illustrations for secular texts on the basis either of what kinds of pictorial models were available or of what scene in the narrative seemed most arresting visually.[11] Even if the artist's choice to illustrate a narrative incident is based upon such non-literary factors, for the reader of the manuscript the picture still offers a focus for the tale, a way of organizing the narrative material. In the pictures for Gower's conversion tales in New College 266, the artist has employed what Kurt Weitzmann calls the monoscenic method--only one incident from each sequence of events has been selected for illustration.[12] In each case, the moment the picture highlights for the reader is the initial moment of the protagonist's moral insight, the beginning of the conversion. Often this moment features a meeting between the protagonist and some other character who prompts the protagonist to self-evaluation. The emphasis in the pictorial program throughout the manuscript upon such moments of conversion and self-recognition can have a cumulative effect, influencing readers' interpretation not only of individual tales but of the *Confessio Amantis* as a whole. Each tale becomes centered upon a meeting, a moment of self-examination and conversion for its protagonists; in the same way, the confession which encloses the tales provides a kind of meeting and a stimulus to conversion for the Lover--and for Gower's readers.

The miniature for the Tale of the Two Coffers (V.2273-2390) serves as a typical example of the emphasis on moments of conversion in the illustrative program. The Tale of the Two Coffers concerns three courtiers who blame their king for their lack of material success. To teach them that Fortune is responsible instead for their situation, the king presents them with two sealed caskets, identical on the outside, but one full of precious jewels, the other holding only straw and ordinary stones. The courtiers must choose between the caskets; when their selection is opened they find that by chance they have chosen the worthless one:

> "Lo," seith the king, "nou mai ye se
> That ther is no defalte in me;
> Forthi miself I wole aquyte,
> And bereth ye youre oghne wyte
> Of that fortune hath you refused."
>
> (lines 2383-87)

The courtiers concede that luck, not lack of the king's favor, has determined the outcome of the affair; and so they realize the folly of their covetousness and their disparagement of the ruler:

"And thei lefte of here evele speche," Genius says, "And mercy of here king beseche" (lines 2389-90). The illustration for this tale (fol. 102ᵛ) depicts the scene of the courtiers' conversion. The king and the three courtiers stand behind a table; in front of them are the two opened coffers (fig. 1). The moment of the courtiers' moral change here is in a way an ideal one for pictorial illustration, since the written text itself stresses the visual nature of the experience: the courtiers "sihen" the riches that they have not chosen (line 2381) and so "se" (line 2383), as the king says, that they have been wrong in blaming him and not Fortune. The picture thus allows the reader as well to "se" the simple demonstration of the ways of Fortune that the king offers.

Like the courtiers in the Tale of the Two Coffers, the protagonist in the Tale of King Midas (V.141-332) comes to realize that he must put behind him his sin of avarice. This tale is also illustrated, and Genius tells it, he says, to demonstrate that man too often values material wealth over basic needs:

> It is to kinde no plesance
> That man above his sustienance
> Unto the gold schal serve and bowe.

(lines 121-23)

Gower takes the story of Midas from the first part of Ovid's account in *Metamorphoses* XI.85-145, though the two versions differ significantly. As Judith C. G. Moran notes, even after he leaves his avarice Ovid's Midas "remains a foolish man" whose stupidity in preferring Pan's music to Phoebus's wins him a pair of ass's ears. In the *Fall of Princes* Lydgate also brings Midas to an unhappy end: the king becomes a shepherd and in his dire poverty drinks the poisonous blood of a mad bull: "Most bestiali eendid thus his daies" (II.3493).[13] In Gower's version of the story, however, after Midas is cured of the golden touch he "goth him hom the rihte weie" (line 316) and, a wiser ruler than before, instructs his subjects that "mete and cloth sufficeth" (line 320).

The Tale of King Midas is considerably longer than the Tale of the Two Coffers and consequently affords a greater number of possible incidents for an illustrator. The story opens as King Midas treats a priest of Bacchus with great hospitality; next he accepts the god's offer of a gift; he rejoices in his ability to transform such everyday objects as stones and flowers into gold; finally, after he recognizes the folly of avarice, he washes away the golden touch in a stream so that the water and the sediment turn yellow (lines 310-12). But, like the illustration for the Tale of the Two Coffers, the illustration for this tale (fol. 91ʳ) features the moment of the protagonist's initial insight into his sinfulness. The picture shows Midas taking food and drink set before him on a table that is covered with a white cloth (fig. 2). From the text, the reader learns that Midas discovers the dangers of his gift when he is here seated at table: the king realizes that he cannot even attempt to eat or drink without transfoming his food and beverage to gold:

> The cloth was leid, the bord was set,
> And al was forth tofore him fet,
> His disch, his coppe, his drinke, his mete;
> Bot whanne he wolde or drinke or ete,
> Anon as it his mouth cam nyh,
> It was as al gold, and thanne he syh
> Of Avarice the folie.
>
> (lines 283-89)

Significantly, in Gower's version of the story Midas already knows that one should not place more value upon worldly goods than upon the means of sustenance. When he first ponders what gift to take from Bacchus, Midas observes that no one needs to possess more than "o mannes del / . . . Of clothinge and of mete and drinke" (lines 212, 214). To him, however, this is merely intellectualizing, one of the "pointz diverse" in an interior debate (line 218). Eventually he chooses material possessions anyway. Midas is only able to teach his subjects to avoid avarice by the end of the story because, as the text says,

Thus hath this king experience
Hou foles don the reverence
To gold, which of his oghne kinde
Is lasse worth than is the rinde
To sustienance of mannes fode.

(lines 321-25)

That is, Midas's moral change has come about not only through increased knowledge but also through his direct experience of the folly of his vice. Like the courtiers in the Tale of the Two Coffers, he could not understand unless he "syh" (line 288), and the illustration for the tale allows the reader the opportunity to see with Midas by depicting the moment of the moral conversion.

The illustration for the Tale of Rosiphelee (IV.1245-1446) also features the moment of the protagonist's conversion. In this case, the protagonist begins to change when she meets another character who seems to be a version of herself. A beautiful young princess, Rosiphelee, is guilty of idleness in love. But one day in the park she meets, or dreams that she meets, a mysterious parade of beautiful ladies.[14] When she first sees these women Rosiphelee, who realizes that she is not like them, hides herself in the bushes:

For pure abaissht drowh hire adryh
And hield hire clos under the bowh,
And let hem passen stille ynowh;
For as hire thoghte in hire avis,
To hem that were of such a pris
Sche was noght worthi axen there,
Fro when they come or what thei were.

(lines 1330-36)

After the ladies pass, Rosiphelee sees a "wofull" young servant girl following behind them who wears "Aboute hir middel twenty score / Of horses haltres" (lines 1356-57). Rosiphelee asks this servant girl the meaning of the procession, and the girl explains that the noble ladies who have just passed are those who once served Love faithfully and that she serves them because at one time she was idle in love (lines 1388-89). Kurt O. Olsson comments that with the meeting between Rosiphelee and the serving girl in this tale,

> Gower . . . presents . . . an image . . . which strikes the exemplary character with a likeness. . . . Rosiphelee . . . is startled to find that this "wofull womman" who neglected Love is like herself, and her discovery means a conversion.[15]

"Helas!" Rosiphelee exclaims when the serving girl explains her situation, "I am riht in the same cas" (lines 1439-40). The miniature illustrating the story (fol. 77ʳ) shows Rosiphelee's encounter with this girl. Rosiphelee, wearing a tiara and a pink dress, stands behind a bush at the right of the picture; at the left, the serving girl, wearing a plain white wimple, rides a black horse with a red bridle (fig. 3). The horse halters hang from her belt. The picture's emphasis on this moment of the tale seems appropriate. Rosiphelee eventually becomes, like the noble ladies, a servant of Love, but she must begin by confronting that part of herself that is less than they are. This takes place in her conversation with the servant girl, who suddenly "passeth . . . / Al clene out of this ladi sihte" (lines 1436-37) when Rosiphelee resolves to change herself. Fittingly, if Rosiphelee is no longer going to be idle in love, the serving girl no longer exists as a possible future for her. As in the illustration for the Tale of Midas, the monoscenic New College illustration for this tale directs the reader's attention to the one incident that begins the protagonist's moral growth--in this case, an encounter with an alter ego who triggers the protagonist's inner change.

The miniature in New College MS. 266 for the Tale of Constantine and Silvester (II.3187-3496) also features the protagonist in a meeting with others who guide him to the truth about himself. In this tale, taking the advice of his doctors, the emperor Constantine has planned to bathe in the blood of young children to cure his leprosy. In the *Golden Legend* and in the *Speculum historiale* of Vincent de Beauvais, two works which contain analogues for Gower's exemplum, Constantine travels by chariot to the public square where the mothers and children have assembled. Then he announces his decision to spare the children, offering his interest in the dignity of the state as the reason. In the *Golden Legend*, for example, he says:

> Audite me comites et commilitones et omnes populi qui adstatis. . . . Quanta ergo erit crudelitas, ut noc nostius faciamus filiis quod fieri prohibuimus alienis? Quid juvat barbaros superasse si a crudelitate vincamur?[16]

> (Hear me, friends and knights and all you people who stand nearby! . . . How much, therefore, is our cruelty, that we do to our children what we do not allow to be done by others? Why delight to have conquered barbarians, if we by cruelty are conquered?)

Instead of having Constantine make this kind of public announcement, the *Confessio Amantis* shows him deciding to spare the children as the result of personal reflection in his palace. When he hears the weeping of the mothers and children, Gower's Constantine ponders the basic equality of all men in a private prayer to Divine Providence. Realizing that every man, even the "povere child," has the same capacity for virtue, the emperor evaluates himself from a new perspective:

> And thus this worthi lord as tho
> Sette in balance his oghne astat
> And with himself stod in debat.

> (lines 3280-82)

Constantine notes that a ruler must "ben of good condicioun" (disposition) towards his subjects, for they "ben of his semblance" (lines 3271, 3273). Hence he determines that he must not kill the children, even if it means his own death. As Judith Shaw notes, this decision results directly from Constantine's "sense of kinship with these unfortunates"; for, through his experience, the emperor learns that each person must be ready to regard others as potential versions of himself.[17]

The miniature is appropriate for Gower's version of the tale, then, for it shows Constantine meeting the mothers and children inside a blue architectural frame apparently meant to provide an interior view of the palace. The arrangement of the figures in the picture highlights the forces mentioned in the poem in Constantine's "debat" with himself. At the center of the picture is seated Constantine, wearing a crown and a kingly robe; he and a naked infant, held up by its mother, gaze intently at each other. The confrontation in this picture thus anticipates the confrontation in lines 3246-47, 3258-59 in Constantine's reflections: "The povere is bore as is the riche / And deieth in the same wise," "The povere child is bore als able / To vertu as the kinges Sone." The courtiers on the right and the mothers on the left further suggest to the reader the emperor's opposing impulses.[18] Actually, the scene depicted in the illustration is only one way the events of the text might be envisioned. Gower mentions that the mothers and babies have been brought into the palace, but it is not clear from the text whether they have been taken before the emperor or whether Constantine pities them when he hears their weeping from another room:

> The yonge babes criden alle:
> This noyse aros, the lord it herde,
> And loked out, and how it ferde
> He sih. . . .

(lines 3238-41)

From the text alone it is not clear if Constantine ever calls the mothers and children into his presence; after his change of heart, when he wishes to give the mothers gifts, he does not distribute them in person but orders his treasurers to do so. Given the imprecision of the text on this point, the New College illustration is especially likely to influence a reader's impression of how the events of the story took place. Moreover, by depicting a face-to-face meeting between Constantine and the child, the illustration places the tale clearly among those exempla in the poem in which the protagonist undergoes a moral conversion as a result of his visual experience. Like the courtiers opening the coffers and King Midas at table, when he confronts the children Constantine at last "sih" (line 3241). The Tale of Constantine and Sylvester, like the other conversion exempla, contains other dramatic moments suitable for illustration--for instance, the emperor's baptism by Silvester; nevertheless, the picture for the tale, like the illustration for the Tale of Rosiphelee, directs the reader's attention to the moment in Gower's narrative when, through a meeting with someone else, the protagonist realizes something important about himself.

The New College illustration for the tale of The Trump of Death (I.2010-2253) also highlights the episode from the narrative in which the protagonist begins to understand himself and so changes. Critics have read Gower's version of this story as a comment on kingship; Elizabeth Porter, for instance, interprets the tale as advice for Richard II: "The story . . . has as its central character a king who, recognising his own mortality, practices the royal virtue of humility."[19] But Gower places as much emphasis upon the king's brother, an emphasis shared by the illustration in New College MS. 266 (fig. 5). This character, the brother of the king of Hungary, rebukes the king for showing kindness to some haggard pilgrims. Later that night the brother hears the trump of death blowing outside his home, which in the laws of the realm signifies that the king has designated him for execution in the morning. The moment in which the brother hears the trumpet is not described in detail in other versions of the story. In the analogue found in the *Vita Barlaam et Josaphat*, for example, the protagonist's consternation at hearing the trumpet blast is mentioned only briefly: "Ut igitur ille hanc tubam audivit, desperata salute per totam noctem domesticis rebus consuluit" (and therefore when he heard this trumpet, having despaired of safety, throughout the night he attended to his affairs). In the verson in the *Gesta Romanorum* the reaction of the king's brother is mentioned only in passing: "Audiens frater regis de mane tubas ante domum suam, sunt commota omnia viscera ejus" (The brother of the king hearing the trumpet before his house in the morning, all his innards were troubled).[20] Gower, however, makes the brother's response to the trump of death a focal point in the narrative. First, when he realizes that under the law he will now be killed, the king's brother feels confused and helpless: "he wot no red," the poet says (line 2146). So he sends at once for his friends, whose questions draw out even further his sorrow and perplexity:

> [He] sende for hise frendes alle
> And tolde hem how it is befalle.
> And thei him axe cause why;
> Bot he the sothe noght forthi
> Ne wiste, and ther was sorwe tho.
>
> (lines 2147-51)

In the illustration on folio 17ᵛ of New College MS. 266 the king's brother peers over the wall of his castle while, at the left, the king's messenger sounds the dire blast. Again, the scene in the illustration represents only one way the meeting described by the text might be envisioned. The picture, as an eye-oriented medium, makes the meeting between the protagonist and the trumpeter a visual encounter: not only does the king's brother hear the trumpet which symbolizes his death, he also sees it. Furthermore, in the poem the wife and children of the king's brother are not mentioned until after the trumpet has been sounded; the king's brother only turns to them after his friends suggest that he take his whole family to court the next day to appeal to the king's mercy (lines 2168-74). But in the illustration, as the king's brother hears the trumpet outside, his wife and "children five" (line 2163) huddle behind him, also listening. The protagonist's wife and children play a role in his new self-perception. Before, his companions were "lordes" and "grete nobleie" (line 2032); now with his family he goes dressed in shabby clothes to plead humbly for mercy from his brother. Once again, the illustration in the manuscript highlights an exemplary narrative with a protagonist who turns away from sin; once again, despite numerous other episodes in the tale, the illustration directs the reader's attention to the one moment in the story when the protagonist first begins self-examination and moral conversion.

One final example, the illustration for the Tale of Florent (I.1403-1861), shows the knight Florent riding in the woods and meeting the loathly lady who will teach him the meaning of obedience and fidelity to his promises (fol. 14; fig. 6). According to Maria Wickert, it is this first meeting between Florent and the lady that marks the knight's movement "from *typus* to *individuum*." At the beginning of the story, Wickert notes, Florent is "a model knight without individual characteristics." He is not unaccustomed to questing, for the text explains that generally "Strange aventures forto seche / He rod the Marches al aboute" (lines 1416-17). His quest in the tale, to find what women most desire, is an especially unusual one, and so when Florent sets out from court he soon finds himself uncertain of how to proceed:

> And thus he wente forth his weie
> Alone as knyht aventurous,
> And in his thoght was curious
> To wite what was best to do:
> And as he rod al one so,
> And cam nyh ther he wolde be,
> In a forest under a tre
> He syh wher sat a creature,
> A lothly wommannysch figure,
> That forto speke of fleisch and bon
> So foul yet syh he nevere non.

(lines 1522-32)

According to Wickert, the repetitive wordplay upon "al one / alone" here emphasizes the knight's uncertainty and isolation.[21]

Precisely at this moment, then--as he comes "nyh ther he wolde be"--Florent meets the mysterious woman who will lead him to a deeper understanding of obedience. Eventually, in marriage, she even becomes "on" (one) with him (line 1793). The miniature for the tale thus represents the same kind of meeting between the protagonist and an instructive character as is found in the illustrations for the Tale of Rosiphelee and the Tale of Constantine and Sylvester, a meeting which signals the beginning of the protagonist's moral growth.

In a number of tales illustrated in New College MS. 66 the protagonist does not experience a moral conversion. Nevertheless, the illustrations for these often feature moments of self-examination and insight similar to those in the conversion narratives. Like the illustrations for the tales of Rosiphelee and Constantine and Sylvester, the miniature for the tale of Alexander and the Pirate on folio 68^r of the manuscript (fig. 7) depicts a meeting between the protagonist and a second self. In this tale (III.2363-2417), a pirate is taken prisoner and brought before Alexander the Great, who reproves him for his life of plunder and murder. In response, the pirate points out that the only difference between such murdering outlaws as himself and mighty conquerors like Alexander is the number of supporters they have. Thus the conversation between the two men, the event depicted in the illustration, teaches Alexander something about himself. Unlike Rosiphelee's encounter with the serving girl or Alexander's meeting with the pirate, Alceone in the Tale of Ceix and Alceone (IV.2927-3123) does not meet a second self; however, the phantasms from the Cave of Sleep, Morpheus, Panthasas, and Ithecus, do lead Alceone to self-knowledge, revealing to her the fate of her husband and her marriage (fol. 85^v; fig. 8). Other miniatures which, while they do not depict a protagonist who changes morally during the tale, nevertheless call attention to a moment of self-examination which leads to moral change include: the illustration for the Tale of Calistona (V.6225-6337) which depicts the moment when the nymph

Calistona's pregnancy is discovered and she is forced to leave her companions (fol. 124); the illustration for the Tale of Theseus and Ariadne (V.5231-5495) which depicts Ariadne's tormented self-examination as she is deserted by Theseus (fol. 119); and the illustration for the Tale of Ulysses and Telegonus (VI.1391-1767) which depicts the meeting between Ulixes and his illegitimate son (fol. 140ᵛ).

For some of the conversion narratives in the *Confessio* that were originally illustrated in New College MS. 266, the miniatures have been cut from the manuscript and lost. One cannot know which episodes from these narratives were originally chosen for illustration, but it is not impossible that in these missing pictures, as in the ones surviving, the protagonists' moments of self-recognition were depicted. There is, for example, a space in the manuscript on folio 23 where an illustration, apparently of Nebuchadnezzar, has been cut away. This tale, based on the events in Daniel 4, is told as a warning against vainglory: Nebuchadnezzar is so proud of his power that he considers himself a god, and so as to punish him God transforms him into a beast and requires him to wander in madness for seven years. After that time the king repents and is restored to his position as ruler. The Vulgate does not explore the motive behind the king's repentance: in Daniel 4:31 the king explains only that "igitur post finem dierum ego Nabuchodonosor oculos meos ad caelum levavi et sensus meus redditus est mihi" (Now at the end of the days, I Nebuchadnezzar lifted up my eyes to heaven, and my sense was restored to me).[22] In Gower's version of the story, however, Nebuchadnezzar changes when he looks at himself closely and assesses his true nature:

> Upon himself tho gan he loke;
> In stede of mete gras and stres,
> In stede of handes longe cles,
> In stede of man a bestes lyke
> He syh. . . .

(lines 2992-96)

291

The missing illustration for the tale might have depicted this moment of self-examination and conversion; it is, at least, the kind of narrative incident highlighted in so many of the illustrations that remain in the manuscript. Other conversion narratives for which a miniature has been cut from the manuscript include the Tale of the Three Questions (I.3067-3425; space on fol. 24), the Tale of Nauplus and Ulysses (IV.1815-91; space on fol. 71), the Tale of the Beggars and the Pasties (V.2391-2430; space on fol. 95), and the Tale of the King and His Steward's Wife (V. 2643-2825; space on fol. 95). In each of these tales--as in the tales of Midas, Constantine, and The Trump of Death--the protagonists grow in virtue; like Rosiphelee or Constantine, they often are led to change and self-awareness through a confrontation with some other character. In the Three Questions, for instance, the king of Spain learns humility when he meets a young maiden who can answer his challenging questions with amazing wisdom. In the Tale of Nauplus and Ulysses, Ulixes, by plowing with a team of wolves, feigns madness to avoid joining the Greeks en route to Troy; but he repents of his sloth when Nauplus, one of the Greek kings, sets Ulixes's own infant son in the path of the plow. These tales, then, contain the same kinds of eipsodes featured in the manuscript's remaining "conversion" illustrations. Their inclusion in the original program of illustration in New College MS. 266 may well have supported the same kind of response to Gower's poem.

The pictorial emphasis throughout the manuscript on individual conversion tales and the moments of encounter and self-recognition within them can help direct a reader of the manuscript to one kind of interpretation of the *Confessio*'s narrative frame. The relationship between the Lover and Genius in the frame is too complex to explore in great detail here, but its general similarity to the conversion episodes in the exempla illustrated in New College 266 should be noted. The confession can be understood as a meeting between the Lover, narrator of the poem, and the confessor, Genius, who directs the Lover through detailed self-examination. Just as the emperor Constantine "with himself stod in debat" after his meeting with the children (II.3282), so, too, does Amans discover himself in, and through, his dialogue with Genius. Russell Peck has suggested that in the *Confessio*

> We should understand Amans' confession as a reappraisal of his personal orientation, . . . both a turning outside himself to discover objectively man's use and misuse of his creative energies throughout history and a turning within himself to rediscover his own creative ability.

Peck later suggests that by the end of the poem, when the Lover forsakes love at the end of the confession, he has become more like Genius. "Genius," he writes, "has been reincorporated into his proper dwelling place, Amans' contemplative mind."[23] In addition, as he recounts his experience for readers of the poem, telling the stories he claims Genius told him, the man who was once the Lover has become, like Genius, a moral teacher. In at least these ways the figure met by the Lover at the beginning of the confession can be considered an aspect of the Lover's own character that has not yet developed for him. It is interesting that, while New College MS. 266 does not include a picture of the statue from Nebuchadnezzar's Dream, it does appear to have had a confession miniature on the original folio 7, now missing. Such a picture seems an appropriate introduction for the rest of the series of miniatures; for, like the illustrations that feature characters from the exempla in meetings with their alter egos, a picture of the Lover confessing to Genius shows the moment in which the Lover meets, and begins to become, his future self.

The Lover also meets potential versions of himself in the protagonists of these exempla, as Genius several times invites him to compare himself with the characters he hears about.[24] Even after the eight books of exempla, however, the Lover is still not ready to follow the law of Reason which the Confessor advocates. He and Genius begin to debate, a scene recounted, as

Peck notes, as though it were Amans's own interior conflict:[25]

> Tho was betwen mi Prest and me
> Debat and gret perplexete:
> Mi resoun understod him wel,
> And knew it was soth everydel
> That he hath seid, bot noght forthi
> Mi will hath nothing set therby.
>
> (VIII.2189-94)

The distinction here between knowledge and desire recalls a point suggested in some of the conversion narratives: the Lover knows intellectually that it is now time for him to put courtly love aside but needs the challenge of experience to move him. In so many of the narrative exempla the protagonists' insights and changes develop from a direct, often visual, encounter with truth. The courtiers need the visual demonstration of the two coffers, Midas needs to see the folly of his avarice, Alceone needs a vision of her drowned husband. The Lover's experience is perhaps most like the young maiden Rosiphelee's: like her, he sees a strange procession in a garden which reveals to him his true self. For after the confession, in a vision sent from Venus, the Lover sees a parade of young lovers, many of whom are characters he has already met in the verbal narratives of Genius's exempla. This group is followed by a procession of older men, including moral philosophers and poets of ancient times such as Aristotle, Virgil, and Ovid (VIII.2450-2807). For a second time, then, the Lover encounters characters from the Confessor's narratives to compare to himself. But this time, instead of simply hearing about the characters' actions, he sees them; as Pecks notes, as he recounts the names of those in the company he repeats "I sih" over and over again.[26] The last of these potential versions of himself that the Lover sees in the poem is, appropriately, his own image in the mirror of Venus (VIII.2821-57). Just as Nebuchadnezzar changes from his proud, bestial state when he "upon himself . . . gan to loke," (I.2992), the Lover, when he sees his reflection in the mirror, withdraws from

294

the self-deceit of love and takes up the honesty of prayer:

> . . . In mi self y gan to smyle
> Thenkende uppon the bedis blake,
>
> . . . .
> And in this wise, sothe to seyn,
> Homward a softe pas y wente
> Wher that with al myn hol entente
>
> . . . .
> I thenke bidde whil y live.
>
> (VIII.2958-70)

There is a self-fulfillment in this conversion to prayer: the Lover turns to it, he says, "in mi self" with a "hol entente." So through all these encounters with potential second selves the Lover learns who he really is, and, through that recognition, he begins to take up virtue. In the exempla illustrated in New College 266 the characters who change through their encounters with versions of themselves thus anticipate the progress of the Lover in the conversion narrative described in the *Confessio*'s frame.

The conversion narratives and episodes emphasized in the pictorial program also offer a model for the manuscript reader's own moral behavior; for, just as the Lover confronts characters who are versions of himself in the narratives he hears, readers confront potential versions of themselves in their experience of the Lover and the exemplary characters. The story of the Lover's conversion in the frame of the *Confessio* can be considered, as Olsson puts it, as one large exemplum in which the various parts demonstrate on a smaller scale how the audience should respond to the whole.[27] The conversion illustrations in New College MS. 266 highlight this kind of reading of Gower's poem. In them, the exemplary characters such as Rosiphelee, Constantine, and the brother of the king of Hungary need to "see" others to understand themselves. So too the Lover in the frame does not change simply as a result of the Confessor's verbal narratives; he needs the "avision" of Book VIII to recognize himself and to prompt his movement from courtly love to prayer. For the reader of New College MS. 266, the illustrations supplement the verbal text's account of the moral conversions with a visual dimension. In this way, the combination of text and pictures in the manuscript invites readers to an experience similar to that of the Lover and many of the exemplary characters, an opportunity for moral conversion by hearing about, and seeing, potential versions of themselves in others.

Generally medievalists have urged caution when discussing the relationship of manuscript pictures and the texts they accompany. In the course of her analysis, for instance, Lesley Lawton remarks that "the claims made must be severely limited" because we cannot always be sure that artists and manuscript producers matched their images to the text carefully. One must grant that the similarity of the illustrations and the exempla chosen to be illustrated in New College 266 may reflect only the skills and the available models of the artist: the workshop had on hand patterns for such pictures as "a meeting in the woods" or "the emperor greeting subjects," and this made the depiction of certain kinds of narrative incidents more convenient than others.[28] But, even if the program of illustrations was constructed from models in this way and not from a careful consideration of the text, each illustration in the manuscript can still contribute to a reader's interpretation of the tale it accompanies in the manuscript. For by emphasizing one moment from the tale in particular the picture presents the reader with a focus for the sequence of events in the story. In this sense claims about the interrelationships between the literary text and the illustrations need not be severely limited until close attention has been given to the meaning of both. The illustrations for Gower's exempla in New College MS. 266 offer the readers of the manuscript visual analogues for certain scenes in the tales. Moreover, many of the illustrations depict the same kind of scene, moments of moral conversion and insight. The repeated emphasis in the manuscript on these scenes can reinforce an interpretation of the *Confessio Amantis* as a "conversion" narrative in which the Lover, and the reader, find similar models for self-recognition and moral growth in the characters of the exempla. In this way, the pictures for Gower's *Confessio* in New College MS. 266 work with the text, guiding readers of the manuscript in the process of understanding individual exempla and Gower's poem as a whole.

NOTES

[1]On the relationship of some *Confessio* illustrations to the styles of Herman Scheerre and John Siferwas, two important English painters of the early fifteenth century, see Gereth M. Spriggs, "Unnoticed Bodleian Manuscripts Illuminated by Herman Scheerre and His School," *Bodleian Library Record*, 7 (1964), 193-203. Kathleen M. Scott, in "Lydgate's 'Lives of Saints Edmund and Fremund': A Newly-Discovered Manuscript in Arundel Castle," *Viator*, 14 (1982), 337-38 n. 8, and Michael Seymour, in "Manuscript Portraits of Chaucer and Hoccleve," *Burlington Magazine*, 102 (1982), 622, also make comments on the artistic hands in *Confessio* manuscripts. On the production and transmission of prefatory illustrations of the Lover's Confession and Nebuchadnezzar's Dream in Gower manuscripts, see Jeremy Griffiths, "'Confessio Amantis': The Poem and its Pictures," in *Gower's "Confessio Amantis": Responses and Reassessments*, ed. A. J. Minnis (Cambridge, 1983), pp. 163-78. This essay concludes with an indispensable chart listing the positions in each manuscript of prefatory illustrations or spaces for them.

[2]Derek Pearsall, John Fisher, and Russell Peck have all speculated that Gower had some role in the design of the prefatory illustrations for the *Confessio Amantis*. See Derek Pearsall, "The Gower Tradition," in *Gower's "Confessio Amantis,"* p. 183; John Fisher, *John Gower: Moral Philosopher and Friend of Chaucer* (New York, 1964), p. 354 n. 2; Russell Peck, *Kingship and Common Profit in John Gower's "Confessio Amantis"* (Carbondale and Edwardsville, IL, 1978), p. 193.

[3]J. J. G. Alexander, in "William Abell 'lymnour' and 15th-Century English Illumination," in *Kunsthistorische Forschungen Otto Pacht zu seinem 70 Geburstag*, ed. Artur Rosenauer and Gerold Weber (Salzburg, 1972), p. 168, tentatively lists the manuscript among the works of the school of William Abel, known by its use of stylized and abstract forms that contrasts sharply with the more representational styles of mid-fifteenth-century English illumination made popular by Flemish and other continental influences. In style and in subject matter the pictures in New College MS. 266 contrast sharply with those of the other heavily-illustrated *Confessio* manuscript, Mor-

gan M. 126, which has 106 miniatures for the Prologue, the frame, the exempla, and Genius's lecture on astronomy executed in an Anglo-Flemish style.

[4]My comments concerning the miniatures in New College MS. 266 are based upon observation of a microfilm copy of the manuscript and black-and-white photographs and color slides of the miniatures; citation of the text is, however, to *The Complete Works of John Gower*, ed. G. C. Macaulay, 4 vols. (Oxford, 1899-1902). A full bibliographic discussion of the manuscript will appear in the catalogue of Gower manuscripts currently being prepared by Derek Pearsall, Jeremy Griffiths, Kate Harris, and Jeremy Smith, forthcoming from Garland Press. In his description of the manuscript (pp. clx-clxi), Macaulay provides a list of the miniatures and the spaces; he suspects that there may have been three pictures for the Tale of Apollonius of Tyre on the missing portion of fol. 171. The original fol. 113 probably contained a miniature for the Tale of Tereus and Procne: while a complete folio of text holds about 180 lines, only 157 lines are missing, including the beginning of the tale.

[5]The original fol. 7, including the end of the Prologue and the beginning of Bk. I, is also missing from New College MS. 266. Given that fewer lines of the poem are missing than are contained in a complete folio of text, it seems not impossible that fol. 7 once contained a miniature of the Lover and the Confessor. Griffiths's chart ("*'Confessio Amantis'*: The Poem and its Pictures," p. 177) lists several manuscripts in which this picture is placed at the beginning of Bk. I, including Bodley MS. Fairfax 3, the manuscript from which Macaulay (p. clx) holds New College 266 to be derived.

[6]Lesley Lawton, "The Illustration of Late Medieval Secular Texts, with Special Reference to Lydgate's 'Troy Book'," in *Manuscripts and Readers in 15th-Century England: The Literary Implications of Manuscript Study*, ed. Derek Pearsall (Cambridge, 1983), pp. 63-65.

[7]Malcolm Parkes and A. I. Doyle, "The Production of Copies of the *Canterbury Tales* and the *Confessio Amantis* in the Early Fifteenth Century," in *Medieval Scribes, Manuscripts, and Libraries*, ed. M. B. Parkes and Andrew G. Watson (London, 1978), pp. 177-80. A similar argument is advanced by Martin Stevens, "The Ellesmere Miniatures as Illustrations of Chaucer's *Canterbury Tales*," *Studies in Iconography*, 7-8 (1981-82), 113-34. Stevens's essay is particularly interesting because he also considers some of the interpretive, literary, problems the illustrations present to Chaucer's readers. Other manuscripts that seem to use pictures as visual chapter headings in this fashion include: the Rosenbach manuscript of Lydgate's *Fall of*

Princes (with seven miniatures, one placed at the beginning of each book of the poem); the Auchinleck manuscript (National Library of Scotland's Advocates MS. 19.2.1), an anthology of romances and other texts in which a single picture was once placed at the head of each separate item; and manuscripts of the *Dicts and Sayings of the Philosophers*, in which portraits of the philosophers are often placed in the manuscript at the point where the summary of each man's ideas begins in the text.

[8]Included among the twelve longest tales in the poem (all three hundred lines or longer) are the Tales of Tereus and Procne and of Apollonius of Tyre. See n. 4 above for the argument that these tales were once included in the original program of illustrations even though there is no illustration or picture space for them remaining. At 395 lines, the Tale of Paris and Helen (V.7195-7590) was apparently the only long tale in the manuscript not illustrated. The tale comes near the end of Bk. V, however, in which twelve tales have already been illustrated by line 7195. The designers of the illustrative program for the manuscript may have felt that they had already done justice to this long book of the *Confessio*.

[9]Lawton, p. 51.

[10]Only in a small number of exempla in the *Confessio* do the characters experience moral growth; more prevalent are exempla in which sinful protagonists are destroyed. Hence the attention to conversion tales in the illustrative program is especially noteworthy. The conversion narratives not originally illustrated in New College MS. 266 are all short tales less than one hundred lines long; they include the Tale of Athemas and Demophon (III. 1757-1856); the Tale of Telaphus and Theucer (III.2639-2717); the Tale of Ulixes (Ulysses) and Penolope (Penelope) (IV.147-233); the Tale of Julius and the Poor Knight (VII.2061-2114); and the Tale of King Lucius and the Fool (called The Courtiers and the Fool in Macaulay's side note) (VII.3945-4010).

[11]Jennifer Lee's essay on the illustrations in Cotton Nero A.X. presents the typical argument that manuscript illustrations represent the literary interpretation of the medieval artist. Claiming that the artist was the first critic of the four poems in the manuscript, she comments: "He had to make certain critical and artistic judgments based upon his interpretation of the text." See her "The Illuminating Critic: The Illustrator of Cotton Nero A.X.," *Studies in Iconography*, 3 (1977), esp. 17-19.

Lesley Lawton provides a convenient summary of scholarly articles that employ this notion (pp. 45-52); she is generally skeptical of it. "Medieval artists tended to copy or follow instructions," she remarks, "rather than to invent for themselves on the basis of the text" (p. 45). It seems reasonable that even medieval artists who designed illustrative programs from their own experience of the text had non-literary concerns, often reading, as Derek Pearsall and Elizabeth Salter note, "with an eye only for the illustratable scene, not for the scene that is particularly significant in narrative terms." See their essay "Pictorial Illustration of Late Medieval Poetic Texts: The Role of the Frontispiece or Prefatory Picture," in *Medieval Iconography and Narrative: A Symposium*, ed. Flemming G. Andersen et al. (Odense, 1980), pp. 100-03.

[12]Kurt Weitzmann, *Illustrations in Roll and Codex: A Study of the Origin and Method of Text Illustration* (Princeton, 1947; second printing with addenda, 1970), pp. 18-25. Weitzmann contrasts the monoscenic method with the multiscenic (or simultaneous) method, in which two or more incidents are fused in a single picture, and with the cyclic method, in which a narrative is illustrated one incident at a time over a series of pictures. Sixten Ringbom also discusses these options for illustrating the scenes of a narrative (in the essay "Some Pictorial Conventions for the Recounting of Thoughts and Experiences in Late Medieval Art," in *Medieval Iconography and Narrative*, pp. 38-41).

[13]Judith D. Moran, "The Tale of Midas," in *John Gower's Literary Transformations in the "Confessio Amantis,"* ed. Peter G. Beidler (Washington, DC, 1981), p. 55. Citations to the *Fall of Princes* are to *The Fall of Princes*, ed. Henry Bergen, EETS, e.s. 121-24 (London, 1918-19).

[14]In his *Tradition and Poetic Structure* (Denver, 1960), pp. 65-66, J. V. Cunningham cites Rosiphelee's experience when he discusses the *Confessio Amantis* as a dream vision.

[15]Kurt O. Olsson, "Rhetoric, John Gower, and the Late Medieval Exemplum," *Medievalia et Humanistica*, n.s., 9 (1977), 194.

[16]Jacobus de Voraigne, *Legenda Aurea*, ed. Th. Grasse (Osnabrück, 1965), pp. 71-72. The account of Constantine's conversion in the *Speculum historiale* is quite similar; see Vincent de Beauvais, *Speculum quadruplex*, vol. 3 (Douai, 1624; rept. Graz, 1964-65), col. 521. The version of the story in Lydgate's *Fall of Princes* more resembles Gower's version in its general outlines; as in Gower's version, Constantine's mercy for the children is the result of private reflections. Lydgate does not show Constantine comparing the children to himself, however; he only mentions the "roial compassioun" and the magnificence of a ruler who "wolde nat suffre innocentis bleede, / Preferrying pitee & merci more than riht" (VIII.1212-17).

[17]Judith Davis Shaw, "The *Confessio Amantis*: Gower's Art in Transforming His Sources into Exempla of the Seven Deadly Sins" (Ph.D. diss., University of Pennsylvania, 1977), 146. Or, as Derek Pearsall puts it in his essay "Gower's Narrative Art," *PMLA*, 81 (1966), the Emperor's prayer "embodies the very substance of charity and pity" (p. 478).

[18]The courtiers in the New College miniature for the Tale of Constantine might be described as "complementary" figures, which Kurt Weitzmann defines (p. 165) as figures or objects in an illustration that are not specifically required to illustrate a given moment in the text but have been added to balance or fill in the picture. The courtiers are not essential for depicting the scene described in the poem, but they can contribute to the reader's sense of how the meeting between the emperor and the children took place, and they can suggest to the reader the role Constantine's advisors and "tresorers" play at other points in the story.

[19]Elizabeth Porter, "Gower's Ethical Microcosm and Political Macrocosm," in *Gower's "Confessio Amantis,"* p. 147. Masayoshi Ito finds that the story, like many in the *Confessio*, serves mainly to emphasize "the wisdom or virtuousness of a king by a prefixed description of his subjects' imprudent behaviors." See his essay, "Gower's Use of *Vita Barlaam et Josaphat* in *Confessio Amantis*," *Studies in English Literature*, 9 (English no., 1979).

[20]Prunaeus, trans., *Vita Barlaam et Josaphat, Patrologia latina* 73.463; *Gesta Romanorum*, ed. H. V. Oesterly (Hildesheim, 1963), p. 499. Ito traces the history of The Trump of Death story and then discusses its role in the *Confessio*; however, he does not point out that, more than its analogues, Gower's version of the story places emphasis upon the perplexity and confusion of the king's brother. Shaw claims that Gower's source for The Trump of Death was the version of the story in the *Speculum historiale*, Bk. XV, cap. 10; here, too, the brother is not so much of a character as Gower makes him, for he is described only as "de salute desperas" (col. 581).

[21]Maria Wickert, *Studies in John Gower*, trans. Robert Meindl (Washington, DC, 1981), pp. 227-29. Wickert compares the tale in some detail to its analogue in Chaucer's Wife of Bath's Tale.

[22]*Biblia Sacra: Iuxta Vulgatam Versionem* (Stuttgart, 1975); transl. from *The Bible: Douai-Rheims Translation* (New York, 1914).

[23]Peck, pp. 34-35; see also his analysis of Bk. VIII, esp. pp. 172-84. In her *Laughter and the Courts of Love: Comedy in Allegory from Chaucer to Spenser* (Norman, OK, 1981), pp. 69-70, Frances McNeely Leonard also

holds that Genius is "the 'second self' of Amans." I do not mean to imply that the contrasts between the Gower personae in the *Confessio* (the Lover, Genius, the moral voice of the Prologue and conclusion) can all be erased, only that Gower suggests complex interrelationships linking these three distinct voices. Additional treatment of the Lover at the end of the confession and his relationship to other aspects of Gower's personae can be found in Porter, in *Gower's "Confessio Amantis,"* pp. 144-46; J. A. Burrow, "The Portrayal of Amans in *Confessio Amantis,"* in *Gower's "Confessio Amantis,"* pp. 5-24; Donald G. Schueler, "The Age of the Lover in Gower's *Confessio Amantis,"* *Medium Aevum*, 36 (1967), 52-59; and Paul Strohm, "A Note on Gower's Persona," in *Acts of Interpretation: The Text in Its Contexts* (Norman, OK, 1982), pp. 293-98.

[24]For instance, at the beginning of the Tale of Rosiphelee, Genius tells the Lover: "Thou miht so per cas / Ben ydel, as somtime was / A kinges dowhter unavised" (IV.1239-41); or, at the end of the Tale of Nebuchadnezzar: "Forthi, my Sone, tak good hiede / So forto lede thi manhiede / That thou ne be noght lich a beste" (I.3043-45).

[25]Peck, p. 174. Gower, he says, "stages the scene as that of a man in confrontation with his own nature." See also Leonard, pp. 69-70.

[26]Peck, p. 178; see, for example, VIII.2452, 2462, 2472, 2487, 2504, etc.

[27]Olsson, p. 196.

[28]Lawton, p. 69. She suggests that the pictures in BL MS. Harley 1766 for the *Fall of Princes* offer "a good example of the construction of an extensive picture cycle from a few frequently repeated figure-types" (pp. 55-56 n. 26).

Figure 1 (fol. 102ᵛ): The Two Coffers Opened

Figure 2 (fol. 91^r): King Midas at his Table

Figure 3 (fol. 77^r): Rosiphelee and the Maiden

Figure 4 (fol. 53ʳ): Constantine and the Children

Figure 5 (fol. 17ᵛ): The Trump of Death

Figure 6 (fol. 14): Florent and the Loathly Lady

Figure 7 (fol. 68ʳ): Alexander and the Pirate

Figure 8 (fol. 85ᵛ): Alceone Dreams of Ceix

MINIATURES AS EVIDENCE OF READING IN A MANUSCRIPT OF THE *CONFESSIO AMANTIS* (PIERPONT MORGAN MS. M. 126)

Patricia Eberle

At the end of the description of manuscripts in his edition of the *Confessio Amantis*, G. C. Macaulay added an account of "nine good miniatures" in a private collection belonging to A. H. Frere. Although he could not identify the subjects of all the miniatures with confidence, Macaulay was able to furnish some information about their provenance, stating with some circumspection that they were "supposed to have belonged to Sir John Fenn, editor of the Paston letters" and that they were all cut from the same manuscript, which "seems to have been of the middle of the fifteenth cent."[1] Macaulay gave no indication of the basis for these conjectures, but he must have had some confidence in his source, since he makes indirect use of the same source again in his account of New College, Oxford, MS. 266. Although the series of miniatures illustrating the tales in New College MS. 266 was, he said, "unique" in his experience of the *Confessio* manuscripts, he nevertheless asserted confidently that "other copies similarly illustrated must once have existed" (1:clxi).

In 1902, two years after his edition appeared, a manuscript of the *Confessio* that Macaulay had not described was sold at a Sotheby's auction to the bookseller Bernard Quaritch for £1550.

The manuscript and the price it commanded were considered remarkable enough to warrant notice in *The Athenaeum*, the *Archiv für das Studium der Neueren Sprachen und Literaturen*, and the *Zentralblatt für Bibliothekswesen*.[2] Quaritch listed the manuscript in their catalogue at the still more remarkable price of £8000, and it was bought the following year by J. Pierpont Morgan. Morgan was in the process of forming the important collection of manuscripts that later became the nucleus of the Pierpont Morgan Library in New York, and he evidently recognized the manuscript for what it was, one of the most lavishly illustrated English secular manuscripts of the fifteenth century, in excellent condition and lacking only one leaf of text and eleven of the 110 miniatures it had originally contained. Its value was increased still further in December 1926, when the Morgan Library bought at auction the "nine good miniatures" described by Macaulay and replaced them in the manuscript now designated Morgan M. 126.[3]

Earlier in 1926, a letter from A. H. Frere appeared in *Notes and Queries* which sheds some light on how the miniatures came into the possession of the Morgan Library. Frere, who was apparently planning to sell his miniatures, inquired after "the present whereabouts of the large MS of Gower which was sold in the Fountaine sale in Sotheby's in 1902 for 1500 guineas and subsequently featured in Quaritch's catalogue at £8000."[4] This letter also offers some explanation for the curious combination of circumspection and precision in the account of the provenance of the miniatures in Macaulay's edition. Macaulay must have suspected that Frere knew the manuscript from which his miniatures had been taken, that the source of Frere's information was his great-uncle Sir John Fenn, and that Fenn himself had been a party to the mutilation of the manuscript. The recent research of A. N. L. Munby confirms these suspicions. Fenn had a collection of miniatures cut from other manuscripts, and at the time when he acquired the *Confessio* miniatures the manuscript to which they belonged was in the possession of one "Thomas

Worth, a chemist of Diss in Norfolk" from whom Fenn had bought the manuscripts he used in producing his edition of the Paston letters.[5] One can only imagine Macaulay's frustration at having excellent grounds for believing in the existence of a manuscript of the *Confessio* with a full program of miniatures and being unable to see it.

What may be most remarkable in this story of the recovery and restoration of an important illuminated manuscript of the *Confessio Amantis* is the subsequent lack of attention the manuscript has received from those interested in Gower or in the illumination of English secular manuscripts of the fifteenth century. A formal description of the manuscript has never been published, and we must now await the appearance of the catalogue of Gower manuscripts in preparation by Jeremy Griffiths, Kate Harris, and Derek Pearsall, with an analysis of the language by Jeremy Smith.[6] Of the 110 miniatures, only one, to my knowledge, has been reproduced for publication, the miniature on folio 32^v illustrating the Tale of Constance, which V. A. Kolve includes in his discussion of the visual imagery he associates with Chaucer's Man of Law's Tale.[7] And, apart from Jeremy Griffiths's account of the miniatures illustrating Nebuchadnezzar's dream of a statue (fol. 4^v) and the Lover's confession (fol. 9), both of which are found in a number of other *Confessio* manuscripts as well, there has been no discussion of the miniatures and their relation to the text in M. 126.[8] The fullest account of the miniatures remains the information in the Morgan Library catalogue, where the manuscript is said to be "written and illuminated in England by an Anglo-Flemish artist in the second half of the XVth century."

I

The purpose of this essay is to encourage further work on the manuscript by suggesting something of the value of the miniatures as evidence for the response of at least some of Gower's fifteenth-century readers. Recent work on English secular manuscripts of the fifteenth century, particularly those of Chaucer and Lydgate as well as Gower, has aroused interest in the study of what might be called "the archeology of reading" (to borrow a term from Lee Patterson), the study of what can be discovered about the ways medieval texts were read by their medieval audiences.[9] Elizabeth Salter, Derek Pearsall, Lesley Lawton, and Sandra Hindman, approaching the subject from different perspectives, have all recommended the use of miniatures as evidence that may prove valuable for this purpose.[10] At the same time, there is widespread recognition of the problems involved in making what Pearsall calls a "proper evaluation"[11] of this evidence.

Some of these problems have been summarized in what is still the most ambitious attempt to make use of the evidence of miniatures in interpreting a medieval text, John Fleming's study of the iconographic tradition of the *Roman de la Rose*. What Fleming says about his sources is true for English illuminated manuscripts of the fifteenth century as well:

> . . . we know too little about the actual ways in which copies of the *Roman* were commissioned and executed; the degree to which illustrators followed formal instructions, existing exemplars, and iconographic clichés from sources outside the *Roman* rather than simply their own reading of the text; and, in many cases, the kinds of people for whom illustrated copies were made.[12]

Ideally, then, any attempt to use miniatures as evidence in the "archeology of reading" should be grounded in a detailed and thorough study of the program of illumination in each manuscript as a whole, its interrelations with the programs of other manuscripts, and the conditions under which it was produced, the combination of studies involved in the approach to codicology which J. D. Farquhar calls the "archeology of the manuscript" in his account of some of its basic principles.[13]

A recent study of mid-fifteenth-century French manuscript

illumination by Eberhard König exemplifies this approach to codicology admirably.[14] By meticulous detective work, drawing on evidence gathered by an eye that seems to miss nothing, König is able to provide systematic criteria for analyzing the elements that make up an illuminated manuscript and for distinguishing among the various artists involved in the illumination of a manuscript in a given workshop. His method allows him to specify, at times with unprecedented precision, the point at which the hand of one artist left off and another took up the task. There is much that the student of English manuscripts can learn from this approach, which is designed to educate the eye to see with clarity and precision and to discipline the mind to organize the observed data in a systematic manner.

In one fundamental way, however, König's method may be difficult to apply to English manuscripts, especially to secular manuscripts produced during the fifteenth century. What we know of the conditions of manuscript production, from the work of A. I. Doyle and M. B. Parkes, K. L. Scott, Graham Pollard, and C. Paul Christianson on interrelated problems, shows that there is little evidence in fifteenth-century London for the kind of organization of the activities of scribes and illuminators in one workshop which König finds in Paris and even on a smaller scale in Nantes.[15] All the English evidence seems to point to a different arrangement: an independent entrepreneur who might or might not be a craftsman in the book trade, or alternatively a "stationer," who might have other types of business as well, accepted commissions for manuscripts, then farmed out the work to various scribes, illuminators, and illustrators, many of whom might also have worked on manuscripts from other stationers. The work on a given manuscript did not take place under one roof. Textwriters (as contrasted with writers of court-letter) and limners became part of the same London guild in 1403, but they continued to work as independent craftsmen. The manuscripts of Gower studied by Doyle and Parkes and the illuminated manuscripts studied by Scott both appear to be the result of ad hoc collaboration of independent scribes, illuminators, and limners, coordinated by an entrepreneur who might or might not do any of the work on the manuscript himself.[16]

Under such working conditions, it might seem that a coherent and consistent program of illumination would be difficult to achieve, because individual quires of the manuscript might be parcelled out to scribes and artists working in different locations. If those working on the illustrations were not well acquainted with the text, the absence of the scribes who copied the text could create problems. Lawton has found telling examples of errors in labelling in a manuscript of Lydgate's *Troy Book*, where a miniature illustrating a dispute between Ajax and Ulysses is furnished with the inappropriate labels "Daniell" and "Exechiell" because the labeller apparently was not familiar with the text being illustrated and simply copied names he found in a passage of text near the picture.[17] Under these conditions, the tendency of illustrators to use stereotyped images would be expected to increase; where an innovation on the stereotype did occur, the most likely explanation would be an error or idiosyncrasy on the part of the painter rather than an original interpretation of value as evidence for a reading of the text. A busy shop painter would be unlikely to have time to do more than glance at the text, as the labeller of the *Troy Book* did. If more than one painter were working on the miniatures, the situation which Doyle and Parkes, as well as Jeremy Smith, have found in the text of a Gower manuscript (MS. Trinity College, Cambridge, R.3.2) written by five hands might well be expected to have its counterpart in the program of illustration: an attempt to conserve the distinctive features of Gower's language is repeatedly frustrated by the linguistic propensities of five different scribes.[18]

In this context, Morgan M. 126 offers some surprising evidence of a coherent and consistent program of illumination despite indications provided by the borders that a number of different artists were involved. In many instances, moreover, the miniatures display a degree of faithfulness to the tales they illus-

316

trate which could only have been achieved on the basis of a reading of the text, either by the painter or, more likely, by someone who devised the program of miniatures as a whole.[19] Both in the program as a whole and in individual miniatures there are many signs of an attempt to make visible what were viewed as distinctive and important features of Gower's poem. At the same time, however, there is also the evidence one would expect to find of difficulties in coordinating and carrying out this program, evidence which reflects the decentralized conditions of manuscript production. In addition, there are signs, common enough in any enterprise, of what is most likely to be simple human error (the most likely explanation, for example, of the sole place in the manuscript where a three-line initial beginning the text beneath a miniature is not provided with an attached border [fol. 171]). The remainder of this study will look at both kinds of positive evidence for a coherent general plan and, in selected miniatures, for faithfulness to the plan and to Gower's text, while allowing for the existence of difficulties and mistakes in realizing these goals. Much more work on the manuscript is necessary, but this pilot study should suggest some of the rewards that this work is likely to offer to those who are interested in fifteenth-century reading of the *Confessio Amantis*.

II

An examination of what can be discerned of the plan for the manuscript as a whole is necessary before the role of the miniatures in the plan, and the relation between individual miniatures and the text, can be fully understood. The nature of the general plan has a direct effect on the degree of freedom allowed to the program of miniatures, affecting such matters as the number of illustrations allotted to each tale and sometimes even the kinds of episodes that are likely to be illustrated. In a manuscript like the most elaborately illustrated copy of Lydgate's *Fall of Princes*, Harley 1766, where the illustrations appear in the margin (which has been made wide for this purpose) the work of the scribe still leaves ample room for discretion in the design of a program of miniatures since the number, size, and placement of images is not predetermined by the layout of the text.[20] In Morgan M. 126, by contrast, the program of illustration is so integral a part of the plan of the manuscript as a whole, including layout of the text and decoration of the margins, that it must have been planned at the same time.

One of the most remarkable features of the plan as a whole is that, despite the departure from tradition represented by the inclusion of 110 miniatures instead of the customary maximum of two, Morgan M. 126 follows the same layout of text found in fifteen of the manuscripts examined by Doyle and Parkes: two columns of forty-six lines each.[21] Again, like a number of other *Confessio* manuscripts, Latin prose summaries of the tales (as well as other comments in Latin prose) appear as part of the column of English text. In M. 126 this Latin commentary is written in red, as are the Latin verse epigraphs that stand at the head of the sections into which each book of the poem is subdivided. Modern scholars do not all agree that the Latin prose was written by Gower, or had his approval; in the case of the prose summary of the Tale of Narcissus there are significant departures from the version in English verse.[22] For fifteenth-century readers of this manuscript, however, these passages of Latin prose would appear to have the same authority as the Latin verse epigraphs and to supplement their function by indicating and summarizing the main subsections of the text.

The miniatures illustrating the tales are arranged so as to articulate these subdivisions of the text still more clearly and to call attention to certain subsections as especially worthy of notice. The miniatures illustrating the tales are uniform in size and placement, always appearing just below the Latin prose summary of the tale and filling a space one column wide and twelve lines long (7.62 x 8.65 cm.). The frame is uniformly plain, as in the examples reproduced here, and is usually a simple rectangle in shape. Variations on this shape are dependent on the place of the miniature in the page layout. Miniatures which appear at the top of a column of text have an arched form that extends into the upper margin somewhat higher than the text in the adjoining column.[23] Miniatures like figures 2, 4, and 5, which come below a line of text that does not extend the full width of the column, often (but not always) break the upper part of the frame so that the upper right corner of the picture becomes a sort of line filler for the text. In three cases (fols. 21^v, 68, 168^v), the miniature falls at the bottom of a column of text and must be made a line or two shorter than the usual size (see fig. 3). This kind of compression testifies to the rigor of the rules governing the text layout, which evidently have a higher priority than the rules governing the choice of tales to be illustrated.

At the same time, the evidence provided by the three smaller-size miniatures suggests that there may have been certain tales like these three (Narcissus, Dido, and Carmidotrius) which were believed to require illustration; if there were no such requirement, then the simplest solution to the problem presented by the layout on these pages would have been to omit the miniature where the layout did not permit the inclusion of one of standard size. The design of M. 126 must have presented a challenging problem in the logistics of layout. Even if the exemplar included the Latin prose commentary within the column of verse, the addition of miniatures within the column as well would mean that the quires of this copy would differ from those of the exemplar. Given their cost, the number of miniatures (and perhaps at least some of the tales to be illuminated) was likely specified by the one who ordered the manuscript. Fitting the miniatures into the layout took some careful advance planning; traces of this planning remain in some places (as in fig. 6, very difficult to see in reproduced form) where the guidelines for the miniature have not been entirely covered by the frame of the picture.

Under these circumstances, the decision of which tales to illustrate may well have been determined in part by the demands of the layout. The conclusion to be drawn for the study of the manuscript as evidence for reading is clear: although we can say with confidence that, in the finished work, the miniatures appear to call special attention to the tales they illustrate, we cannot have the same confidence in claiming that, in each case, the interest or merit of the tale was the only factor in the decision about whether to provide the tale with a miniature.

In additon to the miniatures illustrating the tales, another kind of miniature appears in Book VII, illustrating the discussion of astronomy. The change in the program of illustration coincides with a change in the announced plan of the poem at just this point. Books I through VI follow the plan as described by the confessor Genius, to describe "the vices" (I.255), that is, the Seven Deadly Sins, relating them to the Lover's condition, allotting one book to each sin. At Book VII, just where the plan calls for an account of the last, and most relevant, sin of *luxuria*, the Lover requests a discussion of "al that to a king belongeth" (VI.1413). Genius obligingly furnishes him with a discussion of the "wisdom" befitting a ruler, which he claims to base on a book of instruction written for Alexander the Great by his teacher Aristotle.

The instruction of "Aristotle"[24] in Book VII is divided into two main parts, theoretical and practical knowledge. Theory, in turn, is subdivided into theology, physics, and mathematics (with a brief digression on the four elements, the humors, and the parts of the world). In this scheme the discussion of astronomy and astrology (for Gower the two are closely connected) is the last of four branches of mathematics, the other three being arithmetic, geometry, and music. In the course of this discussion there are three twelve-line miniatures marking its principal divisions, together with twelve smaller miniatures illustrating the signs of the zodiac, and fifteen, smaller still, illustrating the fifteen stars. The total of thirty miniatures in the fourth subsection

under mathematics is thus more than the twenty-seven miniatures illustrating the tales told as exempla of the five basic moral
principles in the second half of Book VII, on practical knowledge.

The inclusion of so many miniatures in the discussion of astronomy appears to contradict a basic principle evident in the
plan for the rest of the manuscript, by which the miniatures are
to be allotted according to the relative number of tales in each
book of the poem. Thus, according to this principle, Book VI is
allotted only three miniatures, while Book V, with the largest
number of tales, has thirteen. The inclusion of only one miniature in Book VIII may be explained by the fact that the tale illustrated, that of Apollonius, is the only tale of any length in the
book. But the addition of miniatures illustrating astronomy, plus
the decision to illustrate even brief tales in Book VII, un-
balances this system, resulting in fifty-four miniatures allotted
to Book VII.

The program of miniatures in Morgan M. 126 thus represents
an important exception to the usual tendency in secular manuscript illustration noted by Salter and Pearsall, the tendency to
concentrate the illustrations in the earlier part of the manuscript.
This tendency is evident in *Roman de la Rose* manuscripts described by Alfred Kuhn, and it is also evident in the twenty-six
manuscripts of the *Confessio* which have at most one miniature in
the Prologue and one at the start of Book I.[25] Morgan M. 126 not
only attempts to distribute the miniatures according to the distribution of tales in the work as a whole but, in the one departure
from this rule, concentrates the largest number of miniatures by
far in the penultimate book of the text. In devising this program
of illustration, an important consideration seems to have been a
response to the nature of Gower's text.

Some understanding of the relation between the program of
miniatures and the text in M. 126 can be gained from a closer
examination of what Gower says about the special character of
Book VII. As Genius states at the end of Book VI (line 2421),
and restates at the beginning of Book VII, the matter of this

book is entirely devoted to "wisdom":

> For wisdom is at every throwe
> Above alle other thing to knowe
> In loves cause and elleswhere.

(lines 15-17)

The Latin epigraph and the Latin prose summary written beneath it restate the same point: *sapiens doctrina*, *doctrina bona*, confers *salutem* (salvation) on mankind. In the Prologue Gower describes the *Confessio* as a whole as a combination of "wisdom" and "pley" (lines 84*-85*), but it is clear from these lines in Book VII that he regarded wisdom as much the more important, and Book VII, being entirely devoted to wisdom, as the most important book of his poem. So, in concentrating by far the largest proportion of miniatures in Book VII, the program of Morgan M. 126 is faithful to Gower's own estimation of its special importance.

In light of the importance Gower attributed to *bona doctrina*, it is not difficult to understand the heavy concentration of miniatures illustrating the five moral principles that make up the discussion of practical knowledge in the second part of Book VII. What is less readily comprehensible is the emphasis placed by the miniatures on the discussion of astronomy, especially when Gower himself seems to emphasize the first branch of theoretical knowledge, theology, which stands, he says, "above alle othre" (VII.66). One is tempted to invoke a principle common enough in manuscript illustration, that "the availability of appropriate compositional models is an important consideration for the professional illuminator."[26] The wealth of material described by Fritz Saxl and his collaborators in their catalogues of astrological manuscripts makes clear just how available the models were for such miniatures as those in M. 126 illustrating the signs of the zodiac and the fifteen stars.[27] A second possible explanation might be the special interest of the one who commissioned the illustrations, an interest common among those

322

who ordered books of hours with calendars illustrated with the signs of the zodiac.[28]

A third kind of explanation, and a likely one in light of the attention paid by the program of illustration to the proportions and relative importance of the various books in the *Confessio*, is the degree of importance placed on astronomy in the text, as signalled by the number of lines devoted to the subject. Despite Gower's declaration of the supreme value of theology, he only allots a relatively modest number of lines (seventy-four) to describing this first branch of theoretical knowledge, more than the fourteen lines allotted to the second branch, physics, but far less than the 946 lines allotted to mathematics, the third. By introducing the discussion of mathematics with a standard twelve-line miniature showing a scholar contemplating a large astronomical clock in his study (fol. 150^v), the program of illustration agrees with Gower's text in placing special emphasis on this third branch, and within mathematics, on astronomy as the most important subdivision; of the lines allotted to mathematics (873) an entire subsection (iv) of Book VII is allotted to astronomy.

The content of these lines, as well as their number, gives an indication of the reasons for this special emphasis. For Gower, the influence of the heavenly bodies on the sublunary world manifests an important principle inherent in all hierarchical order, the principle that the higher should govern the lower: a planet as "thing above" has power over the earth "benethe" (VII. 633-36). Moreover, the operation of the influence of the heavens on earth is part of the "lawe original" which God has established for his creatures (line 559); all creatures are subject to this law, and only man, by virtue of his immortal soul, can transcend its effects, if he has both wisdom and the grace of God: "Vir mediante deo sapiens dominabitur astris," as the Latin epigraph at the beginning of the section puts the notion in proverbial form. The study of astronomy, and astrology as its practical application (lines 67-680), show that the world is not governed by "fortune" (line 640) as the lover Amans maintains throughout his confession, but by the operation of divine law working from the higher to the lower in the created world. The importance to Gower of the rule of law has been demonstrated in convincing detail by Russell Peck and John Fisher;[29] the emphasis he places on astronomy, as he interprets it in Book VII, is further evidence of the importance of the law that rules from "above" to him.

The illustrations in section iv call attention to the special importance of this section and make clear its division into three main subsections: a discussion of the seven planets introduced by a miniature of a scholar seated in his study and gesturing towards an astronomical clock (fol. 153ᵛ); a discussion of the signs of the zodiac, introduced with a miniature of a scholar seated in his study and gesturing towards his books (fol. 155ᵛ); and a discussion of fifteen stars, each with the herb and stone in which the characteristic power of the star is concentrated, introduced by a miniature of the magician Nectanabus instructing Alexander (fol. 158). In the placement of these three twelve-line miniatures to demarcate the three main subdivisions of the section on astronomy, one can see an intelligent adaptation of the principle that uses miniatures to demarcate tales as subdivisions within the discussions of the branches of the sins.

At this point, two further levels of hierarchy are introduced into the subdivision of section iv, and they are signalled by miniatures of smaller size. The twelve signs of the zodiac are each provided with a miniature, but the miniatures are consistently only eight lines long, so as to show that the divisions they mark are not of the usual level of importance. Apparently the discussions of the stars, which are not as long as the discussions of the signs of the zodiac, were judged to represent a still lower level in the hierarchy, since they are allotted only six lines. Thus, although the section on astronomy represents a departure from the general rule of the program, that miniatures are to be used to illustrate tales, it nevertheless gives expression to a more fundamental principle, that miniatures signal important subsections of the work. We can also see that the consistent size of the miniatures illustrating the tales is not merely for convenience in planning the layout but represents a recognition that in the hierarchy of organization of the work the tales are on the same level, and beneath that level discussion of particulars should be allotted miniatures of smaller size according to the relative importance accorded to them by the length of the text.

At this point, it is necessary to pause in this analysis of the systematic habit of mind evident in this program to admit that the program does not fully reflect the hierarchical design of Gower's poem in all respects. The two miniatures which illustrate the story of Amans, his meeting with Cupid and Venus (fol. 8ᵛ) and his confession to Genius (fol. 9), are both assigned the standard size of twelve lines. Their size does not give due recognition of the fact that the story the miniatures depict is not one of the exemplary tales illustrating the various sins but the story that serves as frame narrative for the work as a whole, provides the work with its title, *Confessio Amantis*, and embodies what the Latin colophon at the end calls the *materia* of the work, "love and the infatuated passions of lovers." To represent the function of the story of Amans and its place in the design of the work, the illustration should follow the example of many *Roman de la Rose* manuscripts and serve as a larger frontispiece for the work as a whole, or perhaps for Book I.

Here, too, the departure of the plan from what might be expected is revealing. The failure to assign a larger size to an illustration of the story of Amans might, of course, be attributable to reasons of cost, but in view of the very large number of miniatures commissioned this seems an unlikely consideration. A more likely explanation is that the story of Amans was viewed as part of the "pleye" of the work and hence not worthy of great emphasis. The text itself suggests that this story is not to be taken seriously; a Latin note points out that Gower is only pretending (*fingens* se . . . *Amantem*, note to I.60), or playing at being Amans, and his story is thus a fiction. Given this preference for "wisdom," it would have been appropriate to omit all illustration of the story of Amans entirely, as does the program of illustrating the tales in New College MS. 266. Apparently, however, the one who planned the program was as conservative and traditional in his inclusion of a miniature illustrating the confession as he was in other respects. The other traditional miniature, of Nebuchadnezzar's dream of the statue, is also included in Morgan M. 126 but is omitted from New College 266, which represents in this respect a more radical innovation in illustrating Gower's text. Although there was no precedent in Gower manuscripts for the miniature showing Amans confronting Venus and Cupid, the example of *Roman de la Rose* manuscripts may have played a part in recommending this episode as suitable for illustration. It is worth noting, however, that this miniature does not simply copy a traditional motif; it follows Gower's text (see I.144-45 and the Latin side-note to section ii) in arming Cupid not with the traditional bow and arrow but with a "dart" or *iaculum*. One final influence in the decision to treat the story of Amans as a tale is the wording of the Latin prose summary in the version of M. 126; in the versions used by Macaulay for his edition, the summary begins "Hic declarat . . ." while M. 126 reads "Hic narrat . . . ," the same formula used for the majority of the exemplary tales.

Whatever the explanation, these two miniatures are the only exceptions to the otherwise remarkably coherent and consistent program of miniatures, a program exceptional in its attention to the order and hierarchy of parts in the text illustrated. One further piece of evidence for these characteristics of the plan is furnished by the use of borders attached by tendrils to three-line initials, which reinforce the role of miniatures in marking off the tales as subsections. Despite the variety in appearance of these borders, which were evidently done by more than one hand, they all serve the same function; like the miniatures, these borders are not merely decorative but "functional," as Farquhar and König use this term.[30] In the program of this manuscript they have an important function to fill, for at those places in the text where it was decided not to provide a miniature they signal and set off the unillustrated tale as nevertheless an important subsection in the structure of the work.

Taken altogether, the evidence of page layout, distribution of miniatures throughout the manuscript, and the relationship between miniatures and functional borders argues for the importance of the requirements of the program as a whole, especially the requirement that the program faithfully articulate Gower's *ordinatio*, the division of the text into a hierarchical arrangement of parts. In this respect Morgan M. 126 shares the concern for decorative hierarchy which Lawton found in manuscripts of Lydgate's *Troy Book*, a concern not different in kind, though involving a less complicated hierarchical scheme, than many of the French manuscripts described by König.[31] Despite the difficulties created by conditions of production in fifteenth-century London, the devisor of the program of illumination for Morgan M. 126 had as keen a respect for order and the principle of decorative hierarchy as those working on the Continent. Respect for traditional standards went well beyond the forty-six-line column of text; as Doyle and Parkes have shown, in the case of Gower texts it seems to have extended to an effort to retain the traditional spellings as well. Jeremy Smith suggests that this kind of traditionalism was associated with Gower's texts because he was viewed as "a respected monument" among English poets; Alastair Minnis reinforces this suggestion from another point of view by arguing that Gower considered himself, and wished to be viewed by others, as not merely a versifier but as "*sapiens*" or as an "*auctor*" in the traditional sense.[32] In devising a systematic program of illumination, then, the one who planned Morgan M. 126 was paying Gower the supreme compliment of understanding and responding to his own design for his work.

Beginning in the twelfth century, manuscripts of those regarded as *auctores* show increasing signs of an interest in various kinds of apparatus[33] designed to facilitate reading by making clear the structure of the work; signs of that same interest appear in Gower's own plan for the text of the *Confessio* as well as in Morgan M. 126 as one realization of that plan. The *Confessio* is remarkable among English medieval texts in making clear its own *ordinatio* in terms of books, sections, and subsections, all clearly numbered and set off by Latin verse or prose. The kind of arrangement producers of manuscripts often added to the works of Augustine or Gregory the Great, Gower provided for himself.

The concern for *ordinatio* is not merely a matter of the physical arrangement of the text on the page; it is discussed within the text of the *Confessio* itself. As author, Gower announces in the Prologue both the *forma tractatus* and the *forma tractandi* of the work to follow, in language which Minnis has shown to be an echo of the academic prologues commonly added to a variety of *auctores* including Ovid as well as Augustine.[34] In addition, at many points in the course of the work Genius, the priest of Venus who tells the tales and acts as commentator on them, takes over the role of commentator on the formal structure of the work as well. When he describes his plan to relate a discussion of the vices to the "matiere" of love by means of examples (I.233-87), his description identifies the *forma tractandi* as "exemplorum suppositivus."[35] Genius is equally articulate about the *forma tractatus*, announcing by number each branch of each sin as he discusses it and explaining when the number of branches is greater or fewer than might be expected.[36] The *forma tractatus* includes digressions as well, such as the whole of Book VII, which is announced as "noght to the matiere / Of love" (VII.7-8). Even these digressions are carefully structured, unlike the rambling discourses familiar from the *Roman de la Rose*.

Book VII is so carefully structured, following a hierarchical plan that begins with Theory and the "things above" and continues with Practice and the "things below," that it creates the illusion that Genius is indeed doing what he claims, repeating the contents of a book he has read (VI.2435). As Book VII shows, Gower had very definite ideas about what made up a well-ordered book, and the *ordinatio* of the *Confessio* is intended to be not only well-designed but readily apparent. The devisor of the program for Morgan M. 126 was able to construct a systematic plan in large part, I would suggest, because Gower himself had taken such pains to make that plan and to make it apparent.

In one unusual feature, however, Morgan M. 126 shows signs of an interest in reading Gower's text in a manner different from the one prescribed by the *ordinatio* designed by the author and reinforced by the program of illumination. The last twelve pages of the manuscript are a *tabula* in the form of an alphabetical index to the *Confessio* which was apparently produced at the same time as the rest of the manuscript. Although both indices, topical and alphabetical, are found in later Latin works from the thirteenth century onwards, alphabetical indices for vernacular texts were a much later and a much less common development. An index would not have been made for the *Confessio* without the specific request of the one who commissioned the manuscript; that he did request one suggests that he took seriously Gower's request to be regarded as an *auctor*. But he did not necessarily understand or want to follow Gower's *ordinatio* in reading the text. One use of an index, as Richard and Mary Rouse have pointed out,[37] was to enable the user of a manuscript to read the text in an order and for a purpose other than that originally designed by the author. The patron who commissioned M. 126, on the evidence supplied by his request for an index, was probably a reader of this sort, who wanted to be able to find and return to passages that interested him without having to understand and remember their place in Gower's design.

Unfortunately for this patron, the infrequency with which such indexes were requested for vernacular works seems to have resulted in a lack of knowledge about how to prepare one. Those who prepared the index for Morgan M. 126 were very unsystem-

atic, sometimes using a substantive as a reference word, sometimes listing under "O" references beginning "Of . . ." or under
"H" references beginning "How. . . ." Almost half of the letter
"A" is filled with references to the story of Apollonius, for example, while towards the end of the index the references seem to
have been based very often on the Latin prose summaries. At
several points the preparer of the index stopped translating and
unthinkingly copied passages of Latin into the text. What is
more puzzling, the references in the index are to the *capitula*
numbers, but the only numbers in the text are *capitula* numbers
on folios 1-50 and folio numbers on folios 51-54, all written in
later hands. Whatever may have been desired by the one who
commissioned the text, the index he received would have been
of much less help in finding a passage than the program of illumination and the miniatures were.[38] Indeed, the miniatures,
which were for the devisor an integral part of the program he
designed, may have served the commissioner of the manuscript
in lieu of the index as an aid in finding only a part without
working through the whole text.

The evidence of reading provided by the program of illumination in the manuscript as a whole, then, is of two related
but different kinds: the reading done by the devisor in planning
the program; and the reading of the one who commissioned the
manuscript. In his reading, the devisor needed to understand the
ordinatio of Gower's work in order to articulate it faithfully in
the program of illumination he designed. His management of the
section on astronomy in Book VII shows that he understood the
ordinatio so well that he could adapt its hierarchical principles
where necessary to smaller units of text than usual. The devisor
evidently took the request to produce a manuscript with a large
number of miniatures as a request not just to decorate a text but
to reproduce the *ordinatio* of the text in a systematic program in
which the miniatures would play a duly ordered function.

The one who commissioned the manuscript did not have to
come to grips with Gower's *ordinatio* in the same way or to the

same extent. The decorative hierarchy, the miniatures, and the index (if it had realized its purpose) were all designed to help him find a given part without having to remember the order of Gower's design. He could read selectively if he chose, because the devisor of the program had already done the work of reading more systematically so as to comprehend and make visible the underlying structure of the text as a whole. At the same time, it does look as though the patron knew in advance what he was looking for; in commissioning a manuscript of the *Confessio* with such a large number of miniatures, in specifying in at least some cases (such as the three smaller miniatures of Narcissus, Dido, and Carmidotrius) some of the tales to be illustrated, as well as illustration of the discussion of astronomy, and in introducing the further novelty of an index into his commission, he showed that he knew Gower's work and valued it as a repository of "wisdom" in the sense in which Gower himself understood the term.

III

Thus far, however, there is no clear indication that the one who devised the plan behind the format of the manuscript, arranging for the size, placement, and distribution of the miniatures so intelligently, needed to have the kind of knowledge of the content of the poem which the commission of the manuscript suggests. Gower's own attention to the *ordinatio* meant that, insofar as the hierarchy of decoration was concerned, one need only follow systematically the clear indications provided by the author in his division of the work into books, sections, and subsections, with tales as exempla. Once the decision had been made to use the miniatures as supplements to the Latin prose summaries in marking off the subsections of the text, the main problem remaining was one of logistics, allowing enough space for the standard twelve-line picture.

Nevertheless, there is some evidence that the plan takes into account the content of the stories, in those instances where two miniatures are arranged on a page in such a way as to suggest a connection of similarity or contrast between them. The most obvious example of this arrangement occurs on folio 179, where the tales first of the corruption of the people of Lydia by "flesshly lust," second of the similar corruption of the Hebrews by a group of fair women sent (by Balaam's counsel) to attract their "lustes" and render them weak in battle, are illustrated with very similar miniatures on the same page. Two Lydians are shown holding hands and gazing intently into the eyes of two women, while another plays the harp. The Hebrews are pictured in the same style of clothing with what appear to be the same women; the principal difference from the first picture is that matters have proceeded somewhat further. One couple is depicted engaged in animated conversation, another shows the man fondling a complaisant woman, while a third couple is shown in a full embrace.

The arrangement of miniatures on other folios suggests other kinds of parallels. On folio 171, for example, there are two miniatures illustrating *pietas* in a king. This page seems designed to set the viewer a sort of puzzle, for although they are supposed to illustrate the same virtue the pictures appear to be in systematic contrast with one another. In the first, a king is shown standing, holding a sword, and unsuccessfully attempting to defend his life against an enemy; in the second, a king is shown seated on his throne, holding his scepter,[39] and pardoning the enemy who kneels before him. The text helps to solve the puzzle: the first is the story of Codrus, who willingly gave his life in single combat to save his people; the second is the story of Pompey, who set aside his pride in victory to restore the crown to the defeated king. Both are illustrations of complementary aspects of *pietas* as described in the opening lines of the section (VII.3102-62), the self-sacrifice and willingness to show mercy for which the actions of Christ, our Heavenly King, set an example to kings of this world.

In the third instance of two miniatures on the same page, the contrast between the images is designed to serve a different purpose, to make clear the contrast between the sin of pride and its *remedium*, humility. On folio 20, to the left of the miniature illustrating the tale Macaulay calls The Trump of Death but the Latin summary calls the story of the humility of the King of Hungary (I.2021-2257), shown here as figure 2, is a miniature illustrating the pride of Capaneus. Capaneus, according to Gower's version of the story, took it upon himself to assault the city of Thebes single-handed and was struck down by the hand of God "in alle mennes sihte there" (I.1995). The image shows a fallen knight, and to the left a group of knights looking down at him. Capaneus, whose "surquidrie" caused him to set himself above others, was struck down by violence; in contrast, the King of Hungary, whose humility causes him to descend from his horse to embrace a poor old man, is shown standing upright. As in the Capaneus miniature, there is a group of onlookers, this time on the right, observing and discussing what they see. In the tale these onlookers play an important role, because it is their presence that angers the king's brother (shown here in a tall hat, astride a white horse), who reproaches the king for lowering himself in this way, "that every man it myhte se" (I.2064). In representing the implied contrast in these two stories between pride brought low by violence and humility voluntarily lowering itself, the painter of the miniatures arranged the composition so that the two groups of onlookers, one on the left, the other on the right, reinforce the point about the significance of "mennes sihte."[40]

The arrangement of three pages is not conclusive evidence, of course, that the devisor of the format of the whole took into account the content of the tales when he arranged for the placement of the miniatures. Even if one adds the evidence of facing pages which show signs of the same interest in parallelism,[41] the possibility remains, given the length of the text, the number of miniatures, and the rules governing their placement, that these are matters of chance rather than foresight; given, in addition, Gower's own interest in tales that are "like" one another in some way, two such tales might well end up on the same page in this convenient way. What is strongly suggested, however, by the choice of episodes to represent and the arrangement of the composition in these three pairs, is that whoever gave the instructions for the miniatures did read the text and, noting the opportunity presented by the layout, chose images and arrangements that would reinforce Gower's own suggestions about the likenesses between the tales. The choice of these particular episodes was not inevitable; New College 266, in illustrating the tale of the King of Hungary, chooses an entirely different episode from the end of the story.

These three sets of parallels give some indication, then, that even though the one who provided instructions for the content and arrangement of the images in the miniatures may not have been the same person as the one who devised the format, he does show the same kind of interest in reproducing important features of the design of Gower's text. It would be helpful to know to what degree larger patterns may be discovered in the choice of episodes for illustration in the miniatures taken as a group, but that must be the subject of a larger study.[42] In this essay, it is possible to examine only the few miniatures reproduced here, in order to see the kinds of evidence they can provide of reading of the text either by the painter or by someone who gave the painter instructions.

Before we look at individual miniatures, the possibility must be considered that they do not represent a direct response to the text but were simply copied from another manuscript of the same text. New College 266 is so heavily mutilated, with only about two-thirds of its original program of miniatures remaining, and with a much shorter program (approximately only one-third the length of Morgan M. 126), that its value for this purpose is much reduced. Of the still "other manuscripts similarly illustrated" which Macaulay proposed, no more have been found. Despite its limitations, however, a comparison between the two programs is enlightening.

Although the Morgan and the New College manuscripts are based on different recensions of the text, it is interesting to note that they share some basic features of layout, notably the page of two forty-six-line columns of text, with the miniatures included as part of the column. The similarity of layout would seem to argue a common tradition of illustration, but surprisingly enough the miniatures in the two manuscripts have little in common. Since the Morgan manuscript has a much longer program, one would expect to find some of the same tales illustrated in the New College manuscript; indeed only a small proportion of the longer tales in Gower's text are not illustrated in M. 126. But three of these longer tales, not illustrated in M. 126, *are* illustrated in New College 266: Florent, Nebuchadnezzar's Punishment, and Midas. Of the tales that are illustrated in both manuscripts, eight are illustrated either with different episodes, as in the case of the tale of the King of Hungary already discussed, or with the same episode presented in different ways. In New College 266 (fol. 68), for example, the miniature illustrating the tale of Dido's suicide shows Aeneas riding away on his horse, while Morgan M. 126 (fol. 68) shows him leaving by ship.[43] The interesting conclusion one is encouraged to adopt on the basis of this evidence is that New College 266 and Morgan M. 126 reflect the same tradition of layout and placement of miniatures, but that the content of the miniatures attests to different responses to the text. The degree of similarity which Kuhn found in the illuminated manuscripts of the *Roman de la Rose* (despite the large number, longer timespan, and differences in origin involved) is greater than in these two fifteenth-century English manuscripts of the *Confessio*. The shared nucleus of images in *Roman* manuscripts is not visible in this case; New College 266 does not even include the miniatures found in many other *Confessio* manuscripts which have only the illustration of Nebuchadnezzar's Dream and the Lover's confession.

What evidence there is, then, suggests that the miniatures in Morgan M. 126 were based on a reading of Gower's text; the degree to which they represent an accurate reading is the next question. A good way of testing the degree of accuracy in a manuscript like this one which uses realistic rather than abstract backgrounds is to see to what extent the background represents the setting of the story. Without specific instructions based on a reading of the text, backgrounds can often be filled with decorative filler in ways that create discrepancies with the text. Weitzmann notes an example of a miniature in which a painter has used trees in this way as filler despite the fact that the text requires the image of a desert.[44]

In order to avoid problems of this kind, instructions about the background treatment had to be explicit. In one of the few surviving full sets of instructions for the illustration of a manuscript, written by Jean Lebègue (1368-1457) for a manuscript of Sallust, the description of an ambush shows how much detail could be specified:

> Let there be made a high mountain on which there will be large trees and in the middle on the downward slope there will be small trees in a sort of thicket in which will be hidden Jugurtha and his people and some elephants, but the trees will not be so high that one cannot see clearly what is lying in ambush in these woods.[45]

In the wealth of detail here, one can see signs of what must have been an ongoing point of tension between painters and those who gave them instructions: the demands of the text contesting with problems of representation and the desire to create a pleasing composition.

The background treatments in the Morgan M. 126 miniatures reproduced here must have been based either on a reading by the painter or on instructions like these. Settings are often of symbolic importance in Gower's tales and, in these miniatures, evident care has been taken to represent the setting specified in the text, or, if one was not specified, to choose one that is appropriate.

In the six which represent a specified setting, the background of the miniatures reflects the setting faithfully. The dining halls in figures 4 and 6 are depicted so as to give prominence to the large table which plays an important part in the tale. In figure 4, it represents the scene of the feast where Albinus displays the bride he won by conquest, inviting her to drink from a cup which, she now sees, is made from her father's skull. The feast, which is intended to celebrate the return of peace and an alliance between the warring peoples, in this scene becomes the cause of renewed hostility in his wife and leads to the death of Albinus, pictured at the right. In figure 6 the table, which should be a scene of social harmony, bears witness instead to Dives's gluttony, which Gower emphasizes in his version, as well as to his lack of charity for the poor leper whom he waves away with one hand as he reaches for his knife with the other.

The two outdoor scenes in figures 5 and 6 are both meant to represent a coastal region, as specified in the texts for different reasons. In figure 6, the miniature illustrating the tale of Alexander and the Pirate shows the "Marche" (III.2367) where Gower places the tale as a logical meeting place because it represents the boundary between the pirate's domain and the domain of a king who controls so much territory on land. The painter of this miniature has also used this background as an opportunity to depict a large ship, not mentioned in the story but serving to identify the barefoot man as the pirate described in the story. The significance of this background, as of the backgrounds for all of the miniatures, emerges fully only when the miniature is seen in connection with Gower's text. When Macaulay encountered this miniature separately, as one of the nine in Frere's collection, he was unable even to identify its subject, guessing that it might represent an episode from the story of Apollonius, in which a king's voyages by ship figure so largely.[46]

The coastal scene in figure 5 shows signs of a painter trying to follow rather detailed and complicated instructions derived from Gower's text; what he is trying to show, without complete success, is the scene where Polyphemus (shown standing on the right) confronts the young knight Acis with his lady Galatea, "under a banke nyh / The grete See" (II.144-45) and hurls part of the bank down on Acis, killing him. In the picture the "banke" is shown as a small outcropping of rock, a piece of which Polyphemus has pushed down on Acis's chest. The details are all there, but the picture does not convey the drama of the occasion: the anger of Polyphemus cannot be seen in his face, nor can one tell that Acis is near death. This miniature is not inaccurate but it is inadequate as a representation of the tale, as might be expected if a painter were working from instructions rather than from firsthand knowledge of the text.

In the two miniatures representing a countryside setting specified by the tale, figures 2 and 3, we can see additional signs of an attempt to represent the main features of the tale combined with a neglect or misrepresentation of some details. In figure 3, the trees and the deer reflect the mention of "the forest" (I.2292) where Narcissus went to hunt "the grete hert" (I.2299), but on the whole the miniature departs markedly from the account of the setting in the text, which is as explicit as the instructions written by Lebègue:

> . . . under a linde
> Beside a roche, as I thee telle,
> He syh wher sprong a lusty welle.

> (I.2304-06)

When he saw the well, Gower says,

> He teide his Hors unto a braunche,
> And leide him lowe forto stuanche
> His thurst. . . .

> (I.2311-13)

It is hard to believe that any painter who read these lines would have produced the image we see in figure 3. What is more likely is that the painter or the instructions he followed were based on the Latin prose summary, which makes no mention of the horse but says instead that Narcissus was hunting "with his dogs" (*cum suis canibus*), one of which we can see in the background. The Latin text also explains the crown on Narcissus's head, because it calls him *Principis filius*, and the substitution for the "well" of a formal raised fountain (*compulsus ad bibendum de quodam fonte pronus se inclinauit*). It looks as if the Latin prose summary were the basis for the miniature, rather than the English text; but neither explains the presence of the unicorn or the fence which turns the area around the fountain into what may be intended as a *hortus conclusus*. The discrepancies between Gower's English text and the miniature here suggest something more than a painter's failure to understand instructions. The instructions for this picture seem to have been based on an interpretation of the tale as well as a reading of the Latin summary. The meaning of that interpretation is not clear, but it may have involved the traditional association of the unicorn with virtuous chastity, as contrasted with the perverse chastity based on self-love represented by Narcissus.[47]

A similar impulse to add interpretive detail appears in the two miniatures reproduced which illustrate tales for which a setting is not explicitly described in the text. Under these circumstances one might expect merely a generalized indoor or outdoor setting, as seemed most appropriate. In figure 1, which illustrates Arion, that seems at first the explanation for the surrounding grass with patches of flowers. A comparison with figure 3, however, suggests that the background in figure 1 is intended as a representation of a similar setting. The tale shown in figure 3 describes the setting as a country scene "in the Monthe of Maii" (I.2026), with the "freisshe floures" (line 2084) and the "grene leves" (line 2085) harmonizing with the age of the young King of Hungary and contrasting with the old man he embraces, whose beard is white "as a bussh which is besnewed" (line 2044). This spring setting is appropriate for the Arion tale as well, although nothing in the text, either the Latin or the English, indicates the season or the setting. The scene depicted does faithfully represent the details that are specified: Arion with his harp, bringing about by the "mesure" (line 1056) of his music a "good accord" among all creatures, represented here by the examples in the tale, the hind at peace with the lion, the wolf with the sheep, the hare with the hound, as well as "the lord with the comun."[48] This scene seems to be interpreted in the miniature as a return of the Golden Age, which is so often represented in manuscript illustrations, especially those of the *Roman de la Rose*, with a setting suggesting a lasting spring.[49]

The setting in figure 8, another example of a setting not specified by the text, makes a good contrast with figure 1 and suggests another instance of interpretation on the part of the one giving instructions for illustration. The scene depicted is the moment at which Apollonius guesses the meaning of the riddle he must answer if he is to win the hand of the daughter of Antiochus, shown here with her back to Apollonius, facing her father. The severed heads at her feet belong to her previous unsuccessful suitors, a reminder of the fate that awaits Apollonius if he guesses incorrectly. From the dismay registered visibly in Apollonius's expression as he observes the exchanged glances between father and daughter, one can see that he realizes that the answer turns on the illicit "privite" (VIII.425), as Gower puts it, between the father and daughter. Neither the Latin summary nor the English text describes the setting in any detail, the English saying only that Apollonius approaches "the Kinges Court and his presence" (VIII.389), which may be a reference to his chamber or merely to his entourage, although it is so perfunctory that it looks suspiciously like a periphrasis for "king" chosen only to fill up the line.

The setting in the miniature in figure 8 is remarkably detailed, given the absence of clear instructions in Gower's text.

In the foreground are low hills, with sparse vegetation, in the middle distance more fertile land with trees, and in the distance the castle of the king. The puzzling feature is the barren land in the foreground. It cannot be viewed as conventional filler, like the ornamental trees inappropriately inserted as filler in a wasteland, as noted by Weitzmann.[50] Unlike trees, barren land is something unexpected which is not likely to be the result of an unthinking rendering of a pictorial convention. Like the other backgrounds in the miniatures reproduced here, it seems to be designed to set the episode against a background that helps to convey its meaning. The barren ground suggests what Gower calls the "unkinde" (VIII.312), that is, unnatural, quality of Antiochus's relationship with his daughter; while his faraway castle may suggest that in becoming "a wylde fader" who "devoureth his oghne fleissh" he has departed from his proper role as king. The proper role of a king, as another tale, Athemas and Demephon (III.1757-1856) makes clear, is precisely to prevent his kingdom from becoming a wasteland by protecting and succoring his people, rather than putting them to death.

This interpretation of the barren ground in figure 8, on which the unnatural father and daughter confront each other amid the bodies of those who have been put to death, helps to reinforce the interpretation of the flourishing spring setting of figure 1 as a symbol of the ideal kind of love, which Gower calls "accord" or *concordia* (Prol. 1065). There is a pleasing symmetry, which Gower would no doubt have appreciated, in the contrast between the two images: the one of an ideal love which is based on *mesure* (meaning an order based on the principle of number or *regula*) and which results in harmony, even among natural opposites; the other of a corrupt love which flouts all principle of rule or moderation, perverting and destroying proper harmony even between members of the same family. The one, represented by the Tale of Arion, leads to life, represented by fertile ground and blooming flowers; the other, represented by the episode of Antiochus in the story of Apollonius, leads to death, symbolized by barren ground and severed heads. The Tale of Apollonius is the longest in the *Confessio*, and it has an almost bewildering number of episodes--so many that, as we have seen, G. C. Macaulay, who had an editor's knowledge of the *Confessio*, guessed wrongly that one of Frere's nine miniatures was taken from the story. In choosing just this episode to illustrate, and in providing it with a background designed to convey something of its significance as well as its contrast with the image of ideal love provided by the miniature of Arion, the plan evident in the painting of these miniatures reflects an intelligent reading of Gower's text.

Convincing evidence of the existence of an intelligent reading behind all of the miniatures in Morgan M. 126 is beyond the means of this study. Much more work is needed on the manuscript itself and on the conditions under which it was produced.[51] From the evidence presented here, however, it seems a workable hypothesis. Even where a miniature does not adequately represent Gower's text, it can be shown to be based on an inadequate attempt to render instructions given by someone who evidently had read the text, as in the illustration to the Tale of Acis and Galatea (fig. 5), or a faithful rendering of instructions from someone who preferred the Latin prose summary to the English version and who had, in addition, his own ideas about the meaning of the story, as in the illustration to the Tale of Narcissus (fig. 3). The interest in parallelism and contrast, which can be seen from a comparison of the settings of figure 1 and figure 8, from those pages where two miniatures are set side by side, as well as from repeated use in different miniatures of similar figures, all suggest that something of the evident love of system and respect for Gower's *ordinatio* carried over into the decisions about what was to be represented in individual miniatures.

Even from the limited selection reproduced here, some basic features of the program of miniatures as a whole emerge. The guiding principle behind the miniatures seems to have been similar to Gower's own announced purpose in telling the tales:

to provide exempla of the virtues and vices. The two criteria of economy of means and subordination of ornament to function, visible in the images, complement some of the qualities Pearsall and others have found in Gower's own narrative style.[52] Details that are not judged necessary to convey the moral point are often omitted in the miniatures; thus figure 3 shows only one old man instead of the two in the tale and omits the king's sedan chair as unnecessary. Details not in the tale that appear in the miniatures can often be shown to make a moral point which relates the tale to the general discussion of the vice it illustrates; thus, in figure 6 the presence of the female companion of Dives (not mentioned in the tale) serves as a reminder of the point made in the discussion of "delicacy" (*delicie*), that devotion to the sensual pleasures of the table is closely connected with "love-delicacy," devotion to other pleasures of the flesh as well.

In all of these miniatures there is evidence of the same interest in the moral "wisdom" of Gower's poem in preference to the "pleye" represented by the story of the Lover's confession, which characterizes the plan of the manuscript as a whole. It is worth recalling that a wealth of stock images illustrating episodes from a lover's life was available, not only from illuminated manuscripts of romances but from marginalia in sacred texts, as well as from tapestries, ivories, and indeed all of the ornamental arts. The charming passage in Book IV (lines 1122-1223), for example, describing how the Lover whiles away the time musing on his lady's "fyngres long and smal" as she sits embroidering or playing with her "litel hound," "Now on the bed, now on the ground," could easily have been illustrated with images drawn from these sources. The program of illustration in Morgan M. 126, however, reflects a reading in which these images of "pleye" are consistently neglected in favor of the images of moral wisdom provided by the exemplary tales.

The reading promoted by this program of illustration thus does not fully represent Gower's own design for the *Confessio* as a combination of "pleye" and "wisdom," but it does fairly

343

represent one kind of partial reading which Gower himself envisioned for his poem. At the conclusion of the description of the "maner" of his poem (its *forma tractandi*) in the version of the Prologue used in this manuscript, Gower says that his poem may be read in two ways, as "wisdom to the wise" or as "pley to hem that lust to pleye" (83*-84*). The one who commissioned Morgan M. 126, as well as those who carried out the commission, seem to have taken the first of these two alternatives.

IV

In reviewing the value of the evidence provided by the miniatures in Morgan M. 126 it is worth paying attention to one of the most radical criticisms that has been made of the use of miniatures as a way of understanding the meaning of a text. In his study of fifteenth-century books and manuscripts, Curt Bühler admits that a picture may at times function as a "visual aid" by depicting clearly what words can describe only vaguely or with difficulty; the illustrations of the zodiac would be an instance of this use of miniatures. Bühler denies, however, that illustrations can contribute to an understanding of the meaning of the text in any other way:

> For example, a Vergil or Dante can have illustrations, but the message of the verse is not rendered any clearer thereby. Indeed, there may be some doubts, philosophically, as to the propriety of such illustrations. How would the author have felt about it?[53]

Bühler's question makes the important point that no illustration, in book or manuscript, can be taken as a direct expression of the author's meaning, unless of course the author supervised the production, as Christine de Pisan is known to have done for some of her manuscripts. Leaving aside the philosophical question of whether the meaning of words can ever be the same as the meaning of visual images,[54] Bühler's objection rests on the obvious fact that those who illustrated a manuscript were always at some remove, at times a very considerable one, from the author. The title of this paper reflects my agreement with Bühler's view that miniatures should not be used as evidence for the meaning of the text, if "meaning" is taken to be the "message" intended by the author; miniatures can, however, be used as evidence of reading, of the way that message was received and interpreted by one or more people, including the one who commissioned the manuscript, those involved in the design of the format and the program of miniatures, and those involved in actual writing and painting on paper or vellum.

The value of miniatures for reading is, as Lawton and others have pointed out, something that varies from one manuscript to another. There are manuscripts, such as those of the medieval French *Lancelot* discussed by M. A. Stones,[55] which have little value as evidence for reading because they are merely based on stock motifs rather randomly inserted. There are others, like the French manuscript *Livre de Merveilles* (Paris, BN fonds fr. 2810)[56] which do show evidence of a consistent reading of the text, but a reading that can be shown to be in conflict with the interpretation in the text of the events reported. What makes Morgan M. 126 of such potential importance for those who are interested in fifteenth-century reading of Gower is that even this first attempt at an examination of the program of illustration shows a good deal of evidence of a response to features of the text which can be shown to be of importance to Gower himself: his interest in *ordinatio*, his view of the tales as playing an important role in conveying the "wisdom" of his poem, his interest in suggesting parallels and contrasts among the stories, and perhaps above all his desire to be taken seriously as an *auctor*. The evidence reviewed so far does suggest that those involved in the manuscript's commission and production took a view of the text that gave rather less emphasis to the Lover's confession than that implied by the title of the poem, but any reading of a work is likely to emphasize some aspects of its meaning at the expense of others.

In order to understand the conditions under which this reading was made, as well as the relationships among the patron, scribes, and artists involved in the production of the manuscript, a study of Morgan M. 126 comparable to the important studies of other fifteenth-century English illuminated manuscripts by K. L. Scott and G. M. Spriggs would be needed. A study of the miniatures and their relation to the text cannot pretend to answer any of the questions that a specialist in the "archeology of manuscripts" would ask. Even in the absence of answers to these important questions, however, the miniatures of M. 126 have much evidence of value for the "archeology of reading."

NOTES

[1]*The English Works of John Gower*, 2 vols., EETS, e.s. 81-82 (Oxford, 1900-01; rept. London, 1957), 1:clxvi-clxvii. This standard edition is used for all citations from the text. Macaulay's titles for the tales, which do not appear in any of the MSS, are retained here for convenience.

[2]*Athenaeum*, 1 (1902), 784; *Archiv*, 110 (1903), 103; *Zentralblatt*, 19 (1902), 362.

[3]This account draws on information from the catalogue of the Morgan Library. Two miniatures are still missing, one on fol. 48ᵛ illustrating the Tale of Constantine and Sylvester (II.3187-3496) and another on 171ᵛ illustrating the Cruelty of Leontius (VII.3267-94). The gap between fol. 72 and fol. 73 represents 151 lines of English verse, IV.841-992, as well as a four-line Latin epigraph at the start of sect. iv and two Latin prose summaries, one before line 888 and the other before line 978. The layout adopted in the manuscript, at ninety-two lines per page and a minimum of ten lines per miniature, would not have permitted a miniature illustrating the Tale of Phaeton, which begins in the section omitted. I am grateful to the librarians of the Morgan Library for assistance with research on the manuscript and for permission to reproduce the eight miniatures included here.

[4]*Notes and Queries*, 150 (1926), 389. This letter suggests that Frere knew his miniatures had been cut from this manuscript. The notice of the sale of A. H. Frere in Sotheby's catalogue 14 December 1926 mentions that "the MS.

from which these miniatures were taken is now in the Morgan."

[5]*Connoisseurs and Medieval Miniatures 1750-1850* (Oxford, 1972), pp. 31-32. In fairness to Fenn, it is worth noting that the practice of vandalizing manuscripts in this way was common at the time. John Ruskin, who did much to promote the study of illuminated manuscripts by art students and who assembled a good collection of them himself, was in the habit of cutting up even some of his prize pieces; and, on one occasion, used twenty miniatures and some cuttings from borders to make a collage on pasteboard; see James S. Dearden, "John Ruskin, the Collector, With a Catalogue of the Illuminated and Other Manuscripts formerly in his Collection," *The Library*, ser. 5, 21 (1866), 124-54. The collage is reproduced as plate IX.

[6]To be published by Garland Press, New York. Morgan M. 126 is included in the descriptive list of Gower manuscripts in John Fisher, *John Gower: Moral Philosopher and Friend of Chaucer* (New York, 1964), p. 304; and in the list of manuscripts in the section "John Gower," by Fisher, R. Wayne Hamm, Peter G. Beidler, and Robert F. Yeager in *A Manual of the Writings in Middle English, 1050-1500*, general editor Albert E. Hartung, vol. 7 (New Haven, 1986), p. 2409.

[7]*Chaucer and the Imagery of Narrative: The First Five Canterbury Tales* (Stanford, 1984), p. 307. My attention was first drawn to Morgan M. 126 by a note in Kolve's article, "Chaucer and the Visual Arts," in *Geoffrey Chaucer*, ed. Derek Brewer, Writers and their Background ser. (Athens, OH, 1975), p. 295, n. 1.

[8]"'Confessio Amantis': The Poem and its Pictures," in *Gower's "Confessio Amantis": Responses and Reassessments*, ed. A. J. Minnis (Cambridge, 1983), pp. 163-78. In an essay on "The Gower Tradition" in the same volume, Derek Pearsall suggests that these two miniatures may well have been part of Gower's own plan for the illumination of the *Confessio* (p. 183).

[9]In "Ambiguity and Interpretation: A Fifteenth-Century Reading of *Troilus and Criseyde*," *Speculum*, 54 (1979), 299, Patterson coins the term "archeologist of reading"; Kate Harris adopts the term and demonstrates its usefulness in her work on manuscript anthologies that include selections from the *Confessio*, "John Gower's *Confessio Amantis*: The Virtues of Bad Texts," in *Manuscripts and Readers in Fifteenth-Century England: The Literary Implications of Manuscript Study*, ed. Derek Pearsall (Cambridge and Totowa, NJ, 1983), pp. 28-40. Other contributions to this volume valuable for the study of late medieval reading are: Julia Boffey, "The Manuscripts of English Courtly Love Lyrics in the Fifteenth Century" (pp. 3-14); A. S. G. Edwards,

"Lydgate Manuscripts: Some Directions for Future Research" (pp. 15-26); and Lesley Lawton, "The Illustration of Late Medieval Secular Texts, with Special Reference to Lydgate's *Troy Book*" (pp. 41-69). Pearsall contributes an introduction discussing the interdependence of manuscript studies and the study of literary texts.

[10]Salter and Pearsall, "Pictorial Illustration of Late Medieval Poetic Texts: The Role of the Frontispiece or Prefatory Picture," in *Medieval Iconography and Narrative: A Symposium*, ed. Flemming G. Andersen et al. (Odense, 1980), pp. 100-23; Lawton, in *Manuscripts and Readers*, ed. Pearsall, pp. 41-52; Hindman, "Authors, Artists, and Audiences," in *Pen to Press: Illustrated Manuscripts and Printed Books in the First Century of Printing*, by Hindman and James Douglas Farquhar (College Park, MD, 1977), pp. 157-212.

[11]"Texts, Textual Criticism, and Fifteenth-Century Manuscript Production," in *Fifteenth-Century Studies: Recent Essays*, ed. Robert F. Yeager (Hamden, CT, 1984), p. 131. See also Kathleen Scott, "*Caveat Lector*: Ownership and Standardization in the Illustration of Fifteenth-Century English Manuscripts," in *English Manuscript Studies 1100-1700*, ed. Peter Beal and Jeremy Griffiths (Oxford, 1989), pp. 19-63.

[12]*The 'Roman de la Rose': A Study in Allegory and Iconography* (Princeton, 1969), p. ix. Criticism of this important study has not always taken into proper account this acknowledgement of its own limits.

[13]"The Manuscript as a Book," in Hindman and Farquhar, *Pen to Press*, pp. 11-100. A description of this approach to codicology, as represented by the work of L. M. J. Delaissé, by Farquhar and Eberhard König, is in preparation.

[14]*Französische Buchmalerei um 1450: Der Jouvenel-Maler, der Maler des Genfer Boccaccio und die Anfänge Jean Fouquets* (Berlin, 1982).

[15]Doyle and Parkes, "The Production of Copies of the *Canterbury Tales* and the *Confessio Amantis* in the Early Fifteenth Century," in *Medieval Scribes, Manuscripts and Libraries: Essays Presented to N. R. Ker*, ed. Malcolm Parkes and Andrew G. Watson (London, 1978), pp. 163-210; Scott, "A Mid-Fifteenth-Century English Illuminating Shop and Its Customers," *Journal of the Warburg and Courtauld Institutes*, 31 (1968), 170-96; Pollard, "The Company of Stationers before 1557," *The Library*, 18 (1937), 1-38; Christianson, *Memorials of the Book Trade in Medieval London: The Archives of Old London Bridge* (Cambridge, 1967); König, "Un atelier d'enluminure à Nantes et l'art du temps de Fouquet," *Revue de l'Art*, 35 (1977), 64-75. In her introduction to *The Mirroure of the World* (London, 1980) Scott amends her hypo-

thesis of an illuminating shop in which more than one artist worked, to accept the view of Doyle and Parkes that the arrangement was unlikely. The "Caxton master," for example, "was his own 'shop' and could go where the commission took him" (p. 50).

[16]Pollard, *The Library*, 18 (1937), 9; Scott, *Journal of the Warburg and Courtauld Institutes*, 31 (1968), 194-95. Scott studies six manuscripts decorated by two artists, no two of which "contain the same text, have an identical format, or are illustrated by the same major artist. Only two of them may have been written by the same scribe" (p. 170).

[17]Lawton, in *Manuscripts and Readers*, ed. Pearsall, p. 60.

[18]Doyle and Parkes, see n. 15 above; Smith, "Linguistic Features of Some Fifteenth-Century Middle English Manuscripts," in *Manuscripts and Readers*, ed. Pearsall, pp. 104-12.

[19]For a discussion of the work of Jean Lebègue, a devisor whose instructions to painters have survived, together with the manuscript produced in accordance with them, see the introduction by Jean Porcher to Lebègue, *Les Histoires que l'on peut raisonnablement faire sur les livres de Salluste* (Paris, 1962), pp. 9-16; reproductions of the miniatures are included. For a discussion of evidence in illustrated manuscripts of the work of "un concepteur, qui travaille en étroite collaboration avec le peintre," see Beat Brenk, "Le Texte et l'image dans la Vie des Saints au Moyen Age: rôle du concepteur et rôle du peintre," in *Texte et Image: Actes du Colloque International de Chantilly (13 au 15 octobre 1982)*, Centre de Recherche de l'Université de Paris (Paris, 1984), pp. 31-40.

[20]Some of the questions raised by this unusual manuscript are discussed by A. S. G. Edwards, "Lydgate Manuscripts: Some Directions for Future Research," in *Manuscripts and Readers*, ed. Pearsall, pp. 15-26; a description of the 157 miniatures in the manuscript appears in Lydgate, *Fall of Princes*, ed. Henry Bergen, pt. 4 (Washington, DC, 1927), pp. 30-51.

[21]In *Medieval Scribes*, ed. Parkes and Watson, p. 165.

[22]The Latin verse epigraphs are usually accepted as written by Gower or, at least, produced with his authorization; the authority of the Latin prose summaries and commentary is still a matter of some dispute. A. J. Minnis, *Medieval Literary Theory of Authorship: Scholastic Literary Attitudes in the Later Middle Ages* (London, 1984), pp. 274-75, n. 45, and pp. 181-82, 188-90, discusses the similarity of the prose summaries in the *Confessio* and similar sum-

maries in the *Vox Clamantis*, both as reflections of the *intentiones* often found prefixed to chapters in manuscripts of *auctores*. Peter Nicholson has a study in preparation on the discrepancies between the Latin prose and the English verse in the *Confessio*; Robert Yeager, in "English, Latin, and the Text as 'Other': The Page as Sign in the Work of John Gower," *Text: Transactions of the Society for Textual Scholarship*, ed. D. C. Greetham and W. Speed Hill, vol. 3 (New York, 1987), pp. 251-67, emphasizes their general accuracy and their close connection with the English text.

[23]Fol. 118 represents the single exception to this rule; it looks very much as if, in this case, the artist started to draw the usual rectangle, then remembered the rule and began to draw an arch after a centimeter or so of straight line.

[24]Gower's two main sources for Bk. VII both claimed to derive from Aristotle's works, but there is no evidence that Gower had direct knowledge of Aristotle. The main source for the first part of Bk. VII, Brunetto Latini's *Tresor*, does adapt passages from Aristotle (via translation) at a number of points; see the edition by Francis J. Carmody, Univ. of California Publications in Modern Philology XXII (Berkeley and Los Angeles, 1948). Brunetto is also the main source for the discussion of rhetoric in sect. ii, but Gower reduces Brunetto's account to 136 lines, so that rhetoric is not equal in importance to the two main divisions of knowledge, theory and practice. The discussion of practical knowledge is based on the *Secretum Secretorum*, a pseudo-Aristotelian work widely believed to be an authentic letter from Aristotle to Alexander the Great; see G. L. Hamilton, "Some Sources of the Seventh Book of Gower's *Confessio Amantis*," *Modern Philology*, 10 (1912), 323-44.

[25]Salter and Pearsall, in *Medieval Iconography*, ed. Anderson, p. 104; Kuhn, "Die Illustration des *Rosenromans*," *Jahrbuch des allerhöchsten Kaiserhauses* 31 (Vienna/Leipzig, 1913-14), pp. 1-66. The pattern does not characterize many manuscripts of Lydgate, however, such as Harley 1766, discussed above, where the program calls for the uniform distribution of miniatures; nor does it seem to fit manuscripts of Boccaccio's *De casibus* tales in the French translation of de Premierfait, as described in C. Bozzolo, *Manuscrits des Traductions françaises d'oeuvres de Boccacce* (Padua, 1973). The proportional distribution of miniatures in the majority of the books of the *Confessio* is an indication that it was treated, in Morgan M. 126, as a similar collection of moralized tales.

[26]Salter and Pearsall, cited in n. 25.

[27]Fritz Saxl, Hans Meier, and Patrick McGurk, *Verzeichnis astrologischer und mythologischer illustrierter Handschriften des lateinischen Mittelalters*, 4 vols. (Heidelberg and London, 1915-66).

[28]A fine example of this use of the zodiac is the calendar in *The Très Riches Heures of Jean, Duke of Berry*, intro. Jean Longnon and Raymond Cazelles, with preface by Millard Meiss (New York, 1969).

[29]Fisher, *Gower*, pp. 135-204; Peck, *Kingship and Common Profit in Gower's "Confessio Amantis"* (Carbondale and Edwardsville, IL, 1978), passim, esp. pp. 141-49, 156-58.

[30]See Farquhar in *Pen to Press*, ed. Hindman and Farquhar, pp. 75-76, drawing on a distinction between "functional" and "decorative" borders he attributes to König, p. 95, n. 108.

[31]Lawton, in *Manuscripts and Readers*, ed. Pearsall, p. 61; see the discussion of the schematic analysis of the systems of decoration in König, *Französische Malerei*, pp. 149-52, and the analysis of the decoration in the catalogue of manuscripts, pp. 153-249.

[32]Doyle and Parkes, in *Medieval Scribes*, ed. Parkes and Watson, pp. 163-210 passim; Smith in *Manuscripts and Readers*, ed. Pearsall, pp. 104-12; Minnis, "John Gower, *Sapiens* in Ethics and Politics," *Medium Aevum*, 49 (1980), 207-29, rept. in part in his *Medieval Theory of Authorship*, pp. 177-90.

[33]The best overview of this subject is Minnis, *Medieval Theory of Authorship*; two studies of special aspects of the apparatus which developed, of special relevance here, are M. B. Parkes, "The Influence of the Concepts of *Ordinatio* and *Compilatio* on the Development of the Book," in *Medieval Learning and Literature: Essays Presented to Richard William Hunt*, ed. J. J. G. Alexander and M. T. Gibson (Oxford, 1976), pp. 115-40, and Richard H. Rouse and Mary A. Rouse, "*Statim invenire*: Schools, Preachers, and New Attitudes to the Page," in *Renaissance and Renewal in the Twelfth Century*, ed. Robert L. Benson and Giles Constable with Carol D. Lanham (Cambridge, MA, 1983), pp. 201-25.

[34]"The Influence of Academic Prologues on the Prologues and Literary Attitudes of Late-Medieval English Writers," *Mediaeval Studies*, 43 (1981), 342-83, and *Medieval Theory of Authorship*, pp. 177-90.

[35]Doyle, in *Medieval Learning*, ed. Alexander and Gibson, p. 120, cites

351

this as one of the common *formae* from a commentary by Jordan of Saxony on Priscian.

[36]Compare Genius's account of his procedure in Bk. V, the longest book in the poem:

> And tak good hiede also therfore
> Upon what forme, of Avarice
> Mor than of eny other vice,
> I have divided in parties
> The branches. . . .

(lines 7610-14)

and his account of his procedure in Bk. VI, the shortest book:

> This vice, which so out of rule
> Hath sette ous alle, is cleped Gule;
> Of which the branches ben so grete,
> That of hem alle I wol noght trete,
> Bot only as touchende of tuo
> I thenke speke and of no mo;
> Wherof the ferste is Dronkeschipe. . . .

(lines 9-15)

Genius often claims to be repeating what he has learned "in the bokes as I finde" (VI.8), and this self-conscious attention to *forma tractatus* creates the illusion that he is indeed reciting from memory the contents of a book and that he is aware of the *forma tractatus* of the book in which he appears as a character. In inscribing the *ordinatio* of his text in the speech of one of its fictional characters, Gower may have been inspired by the description of the broad outlines of the poem which Jean de Meun puts into the mouth of the God of Love in the *Roman de la Rose* (lines 10495-654, Langlois ed.), but the *Confessio Amantis* takes this device to unprecedented lengths.

[37]In *Renaissance and Renewal*, ed. Benson and Constable, pp. 206, 212. In providing for alternative ways of using a text, the index thus exploits a potential inherent in any written, as opposed to oral, text: the option of reading in an order which does not follow the order of the author's presentation. On this and other habits characteristic of readers, as opposed to listeners, of texts, see Franz H. Bäuml, "Varieties and Consequences of Medieval Literacy and Illiteracy," *Speculum*, 55 (1980), 237-65.

[38]A lack of knowledge of the text appears in the index in various other

ways as well, perhaps the most remarkable being an entry under the letter H: "How the poete had two pipes wyn in his seler the on was Doucete and the other bitter," which must be due to a misreading of the Latin summary of the story of Jupiter's Two Tuns (VI.325-90). The Latin summary, "Hic narrat secundum Poetam, qualiter in suo celario Iupiter duo dolea habet, quorum primum liquoris dulcissimi, secundum amarissimi. . . ." This entry in the index reveals a good deal about the carelessness with which it was prepared.

[39]On fols. 168[v] and 172 appear two seated kings which are evidently based on the same stock image as the seated king in fol. 171 (2), with the difference that these face right while Pompey faces left. Other images of seated kings, representing somewhat different realizations of the image, may be found on fols. 26[v], 162, 166[v], and 176. For discussion of the early history of this very old image, see Kurt Weitzmann, *Illustrations in Roll and Codex: A Study of the Origin and Method of Text Illustration* (Princeton, 1947; second printing with addenda, 1970), p. 156. These stock images function here to encourage the habit of comparing good kings with bad, which is one of the moral purposes of the tales in the text.

[40]A very large number of the miniatures in M. 126 show what I would like to call "functional" observers, to contrast them with the bystanders who serve as traditional filler in a decorative way in miniatures in other manuscripts. Discussion of the role of these observers in the manuscript, and their relation to the emphasis in Gower's text on seeing and being seen, appears in my study of these themes in the *Confessio* as a whole, *Vision and Design in Gower's "Confessio Amantis,"* to be published by the Medieval Academy of America, in the Speculum Anniversary Monographs series.

[41]Facing pages juxtapose the following scenes: the meeting between Amans and Cupid and Venus (fol. 8[v]) and Amans's confession to Genius, priest of Venus (fol. 9); a king directing the opening of two coffers, one filled with treasure, the other with refuse (fol. 102[v]) and the emperor Frederick directing the opening of two pasties, one full of money, the other of chicken (fol. 103); Carmidotrius about to kill himself with the sword brought before him, because he unthinkingly violated his own law in wearing it to the council chamber (fol. 168[v]) and Ligurgius about to leave his people to be governed by the good laws he has made for them (fol.169); the story of the cruelty of the tyrant Leoncius, who cut off the nose and lips of Justinian (fol. 171[v], cut out) and the story of the cruelty of the tyrant Siculus, who tortured Berillus by burning him to death in the brass bull he had made (fol. 172).

[42]A complex pattern of cross-references seems to be created in the program by the use of very similar figures to illustrate characters in different

stories. One example of this practice appears in figs. 2 and 3, where the figure used to represent Narcissus is very similar in dress and facial characteristics to the figure used to represent the King of Hungary. I am presently pursuing a fuller study of cross-references and parallels in the manuscript as a whole.

[43]The seven other miniatures which differ markedly from one another are: The Trump of Death, a scene from the first part of the tale (M. 126, fol. 20, fig. 2 here), a scene from the second part (New College 266, fol. 18); Orestes, a scene showing Clytemnestra murdering Agamemnon (M. 126, fol. 62), a scene showing her being drawn by horses (New College 266, fol. 65^v); Alexander and the Pirate, a scene by the shore (M. 126, fol. 65, fig. 5 here), a scene in the king's court (New College 266, fol. 59); Ceix and Alcyone, a scene where she bends over the body of Ceix in the water (M. 126, fol. 84^v), a scene where she lies dreaming in bed (New College 266, fol. 77); both Virgil's Mirror and Crassus, closely associated in the text, a scene with Crassus supervising the undermining of the tower with its mirror (M. 126, fol. 101), a scene showing gold being poured down Crassus's throat (New College 266, fol. 93); Calistona, Calistona as a bear being shot by her son (M. 126, fol. 126), a scene of Calistona pregnant, bathing with other nymphs (New College 266, fol. 117); Ulysses and Telegonus, a scene of Ulysses in bed with Circe, as well as a scene of his murder by Telegonus (M. 126, fol. 143^v), a scene of the murder only (New College 266, fol. 133). The folio numbers for New College 266 are based on my examination of the text, and they differ from the numbers listed in Macaulay's edition.

[44]*Illustrations in Roll and Codex*, pp. 164-65.

[45]"Soit faite une montaigne haulte sur laquelle aura grans arbres et ou milieu en descendant seront faiz petiz arbres comme boscage dedens lesquelx seront mussez Jugurta et ses gens et plusiurs loifans, mais ne seront pas les arbres si hauls que l'en ne veist bien que en ces bois eust embusche" *(Les Histoires*, instruction to the text, "*Erat in ea parte Numidie* [48,3]," not paginated). This represents only one-third of the instructions for one miniature. Although the miniature is faithful to the instructions, Lebègue was evidently not satisfied; a note in the margin adds, "Et soit encores un capitaine fait en la tente." For full reference, see n. 19 above.

[46]"King on a quay with bales and gold vessels, apparently landed from a ship near, perhaps Apollonius landing near Tarsis," *English Works of Gower* 1:clxvi.

[47]On the unicorn, see Gertrud Schiller, *Iconography of Christian Art*, trans. Janet Seligman, vol. 1 (trans. from 2nd German ed. of *Ikonographie der*

christlichen Kunst, 1969; Greenwich, CT, 1971), pp. 52-55.

[48]For a discussion of the iconography of the joined hands as a bond, and its frequent use as a bond of marriage, see Jan Baptist Bédaux, "The Reality of Symbols: The Question of Disguised Symbolism in Jan van Eyck's *Arnolfini Portrait*," *Simiolus*, 16 (1986), 5-28. The miniature in M. 126 does not make a clear distinction, however, between "lord" and "comun."

[49]A good example is the illustration on fol. 58[v] in the copy of the *Roman de la Rose* in Valencia, Biblioteca de la Universidad, MS. 387 (ca. 1420). I am grateful to Professor Eberhard König for calling this manuscript to my attention.

[50]See n. 44 above.

[51]Malcolm Parkes, who read and commented on an earlier version of this essay and examined selected reproduced pages from M. 126, suggests that the scribe may well be Ricardus Franciscus and the painter of the miniatures may be William Abell. On Franciscus, see Richard Hamer, "Spellings of the Fifteenth-Century Scribe Ricardus Franciscus," in *Five Hundred Years of Words and Sounds: A Festschrift for Eric Dobson*, ed. E. G. Stanley and Douglas Gray (Cambridge, 1983), pp. 63-73. On Abell, see Jonathan Alexander, "William Abell 'lymnour' and 15th Century English Illumination," in *Kunsthistorische Forschungen Otto Pächt zu seinem 70. Geburtstag*, ed. Artur Rosenauer and Gerold Weber (Salzburg, 1974), pp. 166-73. Christianson, *Memorials*, p. 51, finds in the records of the London Bridge a reference to a "William Abell, Limner, Stationer (f. 1447-74)" who paid rent for one to three shops in Paternoster Row during the period 1469-74; it seems likely that this is the same limner studied by Alexander. Morgan M. 126 has not previously been mentioned in studies of Franciscus or Abell, but Alexander suggests the possibility that Abell may have painted the miniatures in Oxford, New College MS. 266, the only other extant manuscript of the *Confessio* with an ambitious program of miniatures. Further work on the manuscripts ascribed to Franciscus and to Abell in comparison with Morgan M. 126 may reveal more evidence about the conditions under which the manuscript was prepared.

I would like to thank Malcolm Parkes for these suggestions and for other comments that helped to clarify and correct this essay in several places. Full discussion of the work of Franciscus and Abell in connection with this manuscript must be the subject of another study, where I hope to be able to address some of the other questions he raised as well.

[52]Pearsall, "Gower's Narrative Art," *PMLA*, 81 (1966), 475-84; see also

Anne Middleton, "The Idea of Public Poetry in the Reign of Richard II," *Speculum*, 53 (1978), 94-115, which emphasizes Gower's clarity and economy of expression. For a detailed assessment of the style of Gower's exemplary tales in the context of medieval theories of the exemplum, see Charles Runacres, "Art and Ethics in the 'Exempla' of 'Confessio Amantis'," in *Gower's "Confessio Amantis,"* pp. 106-34.

[53]*The Fifteenth-Century Book: The Scribes, the Painters, the Decorators* (Philadelphia, 1960), pp. 70-71.

[54]The issue is indeed a very old one; it was already old when it was discussed in the influential treatise by Lessing, *Laökoon* (1766). A treatment of the question of special relevance to the issues raised by illustrated manuscripts is Meyer Schapiro, *Words and Pictures: On the Literal and the Symbolic in the Illustration of a Text*, ed. Thomas A. Sebeok, Approaches to Semiotics 11 (The Hague/Paris, 1973).

[55]"Secular Manuscript Illumination in France," *Medieval Manuscripts and Textual Criticism* (1976), 83-102; the implications of this manuscript are discussed by Salter and Pearsall in *Medieval Iconography*, ed. Andersen, p. 103.

[56]See the discussion of the implications of work done on this manuscript by Lawton in *Manuscripts and Readers*, ed. Pearsall, pp. 47-50.

Figure 1 (fol. 7ᵛ, enlarged detail): Arion

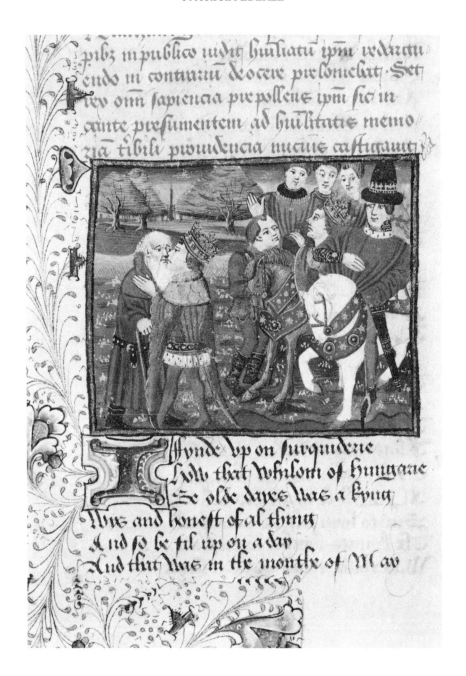

Figure 2 (fol. 20, detail): The Trump of Death

Figure 3 (fol. 21ᵛ, enlarged detail): Narcissus

Figure 4 (fol. 23, detail): Albinus and Rosemund

Figure 5 (fol. 29ᵛ, enlarged detail): Acis and Galatea

Figure 6 (fol. 65, detail): Alexander and the Pirate

Figure 7 (fol. 141, detail): Dives and Lazarus

Figure 8 (fol. 187ᵛ, detail): Apollonius

CONTRIBUTORS

DAVID G. ALLEN is Associate Professor of English at The Citadel in Charleston, South Carolina.

PETER C. BRAEGER was Assistant Professor of English at Loyola College in Baltimore, Maryland.

LINDA BARNEY BURKE is Assistant Professor of English at Elmhurst College in Elmhurst, Illinois.

ROBERT M. CORREALE is Associate Professor of English at Wright State University in Dayton, Ohio.

JAMES DEAN is Associate Professor of English at the University of Delaware in Newark, Delaware.

PATRICIA EBERLE holds a joint appointment as Senior Lecturer at Victoria College and at the Centre for Medieval Studies, University of Toronto, Ontario, Canada.

MICHAEL P. KUCZYNSKI is Assistant Professor of English at Tulane University in New Orleans, Louisiana.

KURT OLSSON is Professor of English at the University of Idaho in Moscow, Idaho.

RUSSELL A. PECK is Professor of English at the University of Rochester in Rochester, New York.

GÖTZ SCHMITZ is Professor of Early English at the University of Bonn in West Germany.

WINTHROP WETHERBEE is Professor of English at Cornell University in Ithaca, New York.

HUGH WHITE is a Lecturer in the Department of English, University College, London, England.

R. F. YEAGER is Professor of Literature at the University of North Carolina in Asheville, North Carolina.

DATE DUE